THE STRENGTH OF HER WITNESS

THE STRENGTH OF HER WITNESS

JESUS CHRIST IN THE GLOBAL VOICES OF WOMEN

Edited by Elizabeth A. Johnson

ORBIS BOOKS
Maryknoll, New York 10545

Third Printing, April 2022

Founded in 1970, Orbis Books endeavors to publish works that enlighten the mind, nourish the spirit, and challenge the conscience. The publishing arm of the Maryknoll Fathers and Brothers, Orbis seeks to explore the global dimensions of the Christian faith and mission, to invite dialogue with diverse cultures and religious traditions, and to serve the cause of reconciliation and peace. The books published reflect the views of their authors and do not represent the official position of the Maryknoll Society. To learn more about Maryknoll and Orbis Books, please visit our website at www.maryknollsociety.org.

Manufactured in the United States of America

Library of Congress Cataloging-in-Publication

Names: Johnson, Elizabeth A., 1941- editor.
Title: The strength of her witness : Jesus Christ in the global voices of
   women / Elizabeth A. Johnson, editor.
Description: Maryknoll : Orbis Books, 2016. | Includes bibliographical
   references and index.
Identifiers: LCCN 2015047817 | ISBN 9781626981720 (pbk.)
Subjects: LCSH: Women in Christianity.
Classification: LCC BV639.W7 S68 2016 | DDC 230.082—dc23 LC record available at
   http://lccn.loc.gov/2015047817

CONTENTS

Introduction

Elizabeth A. Johnson (USA)

The day was hot and Jesus was tired and thirsty. Arriving at Jacob's well in Samaria, he asked a woman who was drawing water with her jar if she would give him a drink. As John's gospel tells the story, she responded with a question of her own, wondering why he had asked this favor given that Jews did not use the drinking vessels of Samaritans. Then they were off and running on one of the most profound theological exchanges in the gospels. Their genuine dialogue, including critical repartee and mutual sharing of knowledge about themselves, produced startling insights. At one point the woman "perceived" that this traveler was a prophet. Their conversation deepened to the point where Jesus revealed his identity as the Messiah: "I am he, the one who is speaking with you."

The scene is interrupted when the men disciples, who had gone to get food, returned. They "were amazed that he was talking with a woman." For her part, she had heard and experienced and figured out enough. In an act of discipleship parallel to that of the Galilean fishermen who left their boats and nets, "the woman left her water jar." Heading into town, she announced her discovery to the people. Many came to believe in Jesus "through the word of the woman bearing witness." They persuaded him to stay two more days, and they came to see for themselves that "this is truly the savior of the world" (John 4:4–42).

Contemporary biblical scholarship finds in this narrative the post-resurrection memory of a very successful early Christian missionary to her own people, the Samaritans. Laden with symbolism, the story follows the pattern of other scenes in John's gospel where people are brought to Jesus by a disciple and come to full faith in him on the basis of his own word. In this sense, "there are no second-generation disciples in John,"[1] all having been introduced to Jesus by the word of another but then coming to believe in him definitively through their own personal encounter. Like too many other significant women in the

Bible, this Samaritan disciple and apostle is unnamed in the text. The Eastern Church has a long tradition of calling her Photine, from the Greek word for light.

Photine's story gives the title to this book, a collection of writings about Jesus Christ from the pens and computers of women around the world. In no way are these writings meant for women only. Like the word of Photine, they are addressed to the whole town. Each author has perceived something important, and the strength of her witness aims to affect understanding of the faith of the whole church, even to the point of conversion.

Note that this book and others like it signal the coming of a new historical season. One of the vital tasks of theology has always been to seek understanding of Jesus Christ in view of new patterns of thought and questions that arise as culture changes. The history of theology is replete with these efforts, from Irenaeus to Athanasius to Gregory of Nyssa, from Augustine to Anselm to Aquinas, from Luther to Barth to Cone, from Schillebeeckx to Rahner to von Balthasar, from Gutiérrez to Boff to Sobrino, to name but a few. But where are the women? Of course, women have always been there, nourishing the church with prayer and service. In rare instances they wrote treatises on Christ that affected the wider community. Hildegard of Bingen (German), Catherine of Siena (Italian), Julian of Norwich (English), Teresa of Avila (Spanish), and Thérèse of Lisieux (French) are major examples.

Several factors, however, mark the current era, dating roughly from the mid-twentieth century, as a different time under the sun: the sheer increase in the number of women theologians; their geographic spread on every continent; their connection with each other in circles, consultations, and associations, either free-standing or within professional societies; their education to the highest level in university programs; and their functioning as teaching and writing professionals in academic settings. Diverse and even contradictory though their insights be, the majority of women theologians, and certainly the authors gathered here, are also characterized by a conscious awareness of the history of oppression of women in society and church.

What difference do women's voices make in interpreting the meaning of Jesus Christ? One might argue that the Bible along with the ongoing traditions of doctrine, liturgy, and ethics are the common heritage of all in the church, so the result will be the same whether the interpretation comes from a man or a woman. But this universalizing view woefully overlooks the vital importance of context in shaping every theologian's angle of vision. The social location of scholars by gender, race, class, sexual orientation, disability, ethnic heritage, and other factors forms their identity, influences their personal experience, affects what they suffer and hope for as individuals and in community, and thus forges their method and insight. The claim that women's voices make a difference in christology stems not from gender essentialism but from multifaceted female experience.

The articles gathered here from every continent on the planet do not exhaust the work women are doing on this subject; indeed, the bibliography is growing to mammoth length. Each in its own way, however, shows a path being taken. Some are intensely relational in tone, setting up an empowering way of connecting to Jesus. Some use new metaphors taken from local religions or from experiences unique to women, such as maternity. When liberation motifs are employed, they spotlight women's specific situations of suffering and oppression, which can be lost in generic references to the poor. Salvation is seen as distinctly affecting persons and structures in this world in terms of healing and justice. There is little direct wrestling with the dogmatic tradition except with regard to its practical effects. Along with many men of this era, women call for new Niceas and Chalcedons to do for our age what the early councils did for their own, namely, to express the meaning, challenge, and love of Jesus Christ in the idiom of our day.

Running through many of these articles is also a thread of critique. Of all the doctrines of the church, christology is the one most used to oppress women. The difficulty resides in the fact that as a historical human being Jesus is located toward the male end of the spectrum of sexuality, rather than the female. In itself, this should not pose a problem. But theology has long worked with a philosophy of hierarchical dualism, adopted when early Christianity encountered the Hellenistic world. This worldview sees the man as the normative sex of the human species, representing the fullness of human potential, whereas the woman by nature is either defective physically, morally, and mentally, or "other" because of her presumed feminine genius. When interpreted within this framework, the incarnation of the Logos of God in a male human being is taken to endorse the superiority of men over women. Subliminally it even points to the maleness of God, in forgetfulness of divine incomprehensible mystery. Women, of course, can be Christ-like in service and suffering; they can be the heart. But they cannot be the head, assuming active leadership. Jesus Christ becomes the male son of a male God whose official representatives can only be male.

Such a theology that relegates woman to inferior status in both creation and redemption was long taken for granted as revealed truth, rather than being itself a projection of elite thinkers of a patriarchal so-cial order—an elite form of contextual theology, one might say. The pressing need now, as women articulate the meaning of Jesus Christ, is to redeem christology from its male-centered blinders and give it fresh meaning that is liberating for all persons. Rosemary Radford Ruether's bold, poignant question lays out the agenda in unmistakable terms: "Can a male Savior save women?"[2] Not all women theologians find this a pressing question. In situations of intense suffering and struggle, it is more important to find Jesus as friend, comforter, and companion, as one who brings hope; if the compassionate Jesus is Lord, then other male authorities such as father, brother, and husband are not lords and their power over women is relativized. The issue of how to interpret the maleness of Jesus with its practical effects, however, remains a burning issue with which many of the following essays wrestle.

This book is divided into four sections. The first explores the mean-ing of the encounter between Jesus and Mary Magdalene at the tomb on Easter morning, a pivotal narrative of a liberating relationship that high-lights women's call to leadership and sets the tone for what follows. The second section presents overviews of women's work in christology in the last decades, including strong criticism from a Jewish feminist per-spective. Drawing from the work of women across the continents, the third section sets out a wealth of particular constructive understandings of Jesus from different cultural contexts. The final section explores what it means for women to belong to the body of Christ in all fullness, an identity whose implications have yet to be realized.

The hope in gathering these essays together is to provide a re-source for all manner of folk: for theologians who work on christology; for teachers, preachers, and those who minister in the church; for grad-uate and undergraduate students; and for adults who want to reflect further on the critical meaning of Jesus Christ in today's world. The theological insights generated by the work of women, whose long si-lenced voices are now thrillingly speaking out, make a rich contempo-rary contribution to the vital task of faith seeking understanding. The strength of their witness is an accumulating treasure.

A heartfelt, appreciative word of thanks goes to James Robinson, my graduate assistant, whose research abilities and dogged, skillful pursuit of permissions helped this book come to fruition. Robert Ells-berg, editor and publisher of Orbis Books, willingly agreed to this pro-ject, and I am grateful for his lively support. All royalties that accrue from this book will be given to Fonkoze, an indigenous organization that builds a ladder out of poverty for rural women in Haiti, the poor-est country in the western hemisphere.

Notes

1. Sandra Schneiders, *Written That You May Believe: Encountering Jesus in the Fourth Gospel* (New York: Crossroad, 1999): 143.

2. Rosemary Radford Ruether, *To Change the World: Christology and Cultural Criticism* (New York: Crossroad, 1981): 45–56. For sustained analysis of the patriarchal nature of traditional christology, see Elisabeth Schüssler Fiorenza, *Jesus and the Politics of Interpretation* (New York: Continuum, 2000).

I

THE EASTER EXPERIENCE

According to all four gospels, Mary Magdalene is the primary witness for the fundamental data of the early Christian faith: she witnessed the life and death of Jesus, his burial and resurrection. She was sent to the disciples to proclaim the Easter kerygma. Therefore Bernard of Clairvaux correctly calls her "apostle to the apostles." Christian faith is based upon the witness and proclamation of women. As Mary Magdalene was sent to the disciples to proclaim the basic events of Christian faith, so women today may rediscover by contemplating her image the important function and role which they have for the Christian faith and community.

Elisabeth Schüssler Fiorenza, "Feminist Theology as a Critical Theology of Liberation," *Theological Studies*, 1975.

1

ENCOUNTERING AND PROCLAIMING
THE RISEN JESUS

Sandra Schneiders (USA)

MARY MAGDALENE
(JOHN 19:25; 20:1–2, 11–18)

Like the Beloved Disciple, Mary Magdalene does not appear in the Fourth Gospel until the hour of Jesus' glorification has come. Her role is that of witness to the paschal events. She is at the foot of the cross at Jesus' death (19:25), discovers the empty tomb on Easter morning (20:1–2), and receives the first Easter Christophany including the apostolic commission to announce the exaltation of Jesus and its salvific effects to the disciples (20:11–18). Mary Magdalene is, without any doubt, the disciple whose place in the paschal mystery is most certainly attested by all four gospels. She holds a place in the tradition about Jesus' women disciples analogous to that of Peter among the male disciples, and for the same reason, namely, the tradition that she received the first appearance of the glorified Jesus and the foundational apostolic commission.[1] Consequently, we will concentrate on these two aspects of the Mary Magdalene material.[2]

The question of who first saw the risen Jesus is theologically significant because the early church regarded the protophany [foundational first appearance] as the manifestation of the primacy of apostolic witness which is the foundation of the church's faith.[3] According to Paul (1 Cor. 15:3–8) and Luke (24:34), Jesus appeared first to Simon Peter. According to John (20:14–17), Matthew (28:1, 9–10), and the Markan appendix (16:9–11), he appeared first to Mary Magdalene, who, in Matthew, is accompanied by another woman. There are no scholarly grounds for questioning the authenticity of the tradition that the first Christophany was to Mary Magdalene. In fact, since this tradition

3

clearly challenged the Petrine tradition, there would have been strong motivation for suppressing it if the evidence for it were at all weak. The fact that it has survived in two independent witnesses, John and Matthew (the Markan appendage is a collage that cannot be considered independent), is excellent evidence that it was a primitive and authentic tradition, different from the Petrine tradition, carefully preserved by some churches.

In the history of exegesis (in contrast to the liturgy, which celebrates Mary Magdalene as "apostle to the apostles"),[4] the Christophany to Mary Magdalene has been consistently trivialized as a "private," that is, unofficial event without ecclesial significance. The only grounds for such a position, which is clearly contrary to the evidence of the text, is the longstanding and unjustified assumption that all of the early Christian communities shared the Jewish proscription of testimony given by women.[5] As we saw in regard to the Samaritan woman passage, John regarded the apostolic testimony of women as valid, effective, and approved by Jesus.

The only conclusion that an unbiased interpretation of the Mary Magdalene episode in John 20 can yield is that, according to the Fourth Gospel, Jesus did appear to Mary Magdalene on Easter morning, and that appearance was the first Christophany. He assigns no individual Christophany at all to Peter. That the theological significance of this protophany to Mary Magdalene is the same as that intended by Paul and Luke in assigning the protophany to Peter, namely, that it identifies the "apostle to the apostles" in the respective traditions, will be clearer once we have examined Jesus' commission to Mary.

The commission that Jesus gives to Mary is, "Go to my brothers and sisters and say to them: I ascend to my Father and [who is now] your Father, to my God and [who is now] your God" (20:17).[6] It is not necessary to enter into all the detail that a complete exegesis of this text would require in order to make the point that this message is the Johannine version of the Easter kerygma.

First, it is addressed to Jesus' "brothers and sisters," whom Mary understands to mean the "disciples" (20:18). This is the first time in the Fourth Gospel that Jesus refers to his disciples as sisters and brothers, because it is only by his exaltation that he accomplishes the purpose of the incarnation, namely, to give the power to become children of God to those who believe in his name (see 1:12). The message entrusted to Mary is precisely that Jesus' Father is now truly Father of the disciples and thus that they are now truly the sisters and brothers of Jesus.

The second part of the message is equally vital: that Jesus' God is now the God of the disciples. This is an expression of the new covenant mediated by Jesus, the new Moses, through whom comes the grace and truth (*hesed* and *'emet*) foreshadowed by the Sinai covenant (see 1:17).[7] Until his glorification Jesus alone possessed the Spirit of the new covenant (see 7:37–39), but the very meaning of his return to the Father is that the Spirit is now handed over to his disciples (cf. 16:7; 19:30). In short, the message Jesus entrusts to Mary Magdalene is that all is indeed accomplished and that by his exaltation Jesus has become the source of the Spirit of filiation and of the new covenant for those who are doubly his brothers and sisters, children of the same Father and members of the same covenant. There can be no question of regarding this message as anything but the good news of salvation in its characteristically Johannine formulation.

Mary Magdalene, unlike the women in Mark (16:8), hastens to fulfill the commission by announcing the gospel to her co-disciples. The formula with which she opens her proclamation is the Fourth Gospel's technical credential statement of revelation as the basis of one's witness: "I have seen the Lord" (cf. 20:18 with 20:25, in which the disciples announce the Easter message to Thomas; also 3:11; 19:35). The disciples in John, unlike those in Matthew (28:17), the Markan appendix (16:11), and Luke (24:10–11), give no indication of not accepting Mary's testimony. Indeed, when Jesus appears to them later that day, they are not astonished or unbelieving but rather filled with joy (see 20:20).

The Mary Magdalene material in the Fourth Gospel is perhaps the most important indication we have of the Gospel perspective on the role of women in the Christian community. It shows us quite clearly that, in at least one of the first Christian communities, a woman was regarded as the primary witness to the paschal mystery, the guarantee of the apostolic tradition. Her claim to apostleship is equal in every respect to both Peter's and Paul's, and we know more about her exercise of her vocation than we do about most of the members of the Twelve. Unlike Peter, she was not unfaithful to Jesus during the passion, and, unlike Paul, she never persecuted Christ in his members. But, like both, she saw the risen Lord, received directly from him the commission to preach the Gospel, and carried out that commission faithfully and effectively.

THE STRUCTURE OF JOHN 20:11–18 AND ITS POSITION IN THE TRADITION

Two preliminary considerations that are important for the interpretation of the Mary Magdalene scene concern the literary structure of the pericope and the place of the Johannine account in the theological tradition history of the resurrection appearances.

Structurally, the episode can be divided into three sections, each governed by a thematic participle. The first section, verses 11–15, stands under the sign of *klaiousa*, weeping, which occurs at the very beginning of that section. Mary stands outside the tomb, weeping.[8] The second section, v. 16, is governed by *strapheisa*, "turning," which occurs exactly in the middle of the verse as the pivot between Jesus' address to Mary and her response to him. This turning, as we will see, is not a physical action but a conversion of the pre-Easter disciple away from the "things that lie behind" and toward the glorified Jesus, the only true Teacher. The third section, verses 17–18, culminates in *angelousa*, "announcing," which occurs at the end of the scene when Mary goes to the community to proclaim that she has seen the Lord and to deliver the Easter kerygma that he has entrusted to her. We will take up each of these sections in more detail shortly.

But first it is necessary to situate this pericope theologically and ecclesiologically. Until quite recently postpatristic commentators have, virtually to a man (and I use the word designedly), treated the appearance to Mary Magdalene as a minor, private, personal, or unofficial encounter between Jesus and his (hysterical?) female follower, in which he kindly consoles her before making his official and public Easter appearances to male witnesses and commissioning them to carry on his mission in the world.[9] More recently, commentators under the influence of feminist scholarship have tended to recognize the raw sexism of this traditional interpretation, which ignores the plain content and intent of the Johannine text because patriarchal bias and the ecclesiastical power agenda blinded the interpreters to the apostolic identity of a woman witness and its potential repercussions on contemporary church order.[10]

Although I cannot mount the entire argument in this chapter, it should suffice to point out that the tradition that the first appearance of the risen Jesus was to Mary Magdalene, either alone or with women companions, is attested in Matthew 28:9–10, in the Markan appendix 16:9–10, as well as in John. It is most likely that John and Matthew, at least, represent literarily independent traditions, while Mark conflates a variety of traditions. In conjunction with the agreement of all four gospels that women were the primary and/or exclusive witnesses of the death, burial, and empty tomb,[11] the multiply attested tradition that the first resurrection appearance was to Mary Magdalene must be judged as probably authentically historical.[12] This is especially because the Mary Magdalene tradition rivaled the Lukan and Pauline tradition that the Easter protophany...was to Peter and would surely have been suppressed if that had been possible. The rivalry between Peter and Mary Magdalene is vividly detailed in the extracanonical literature of the first Christian centuries such as the *Gospel of Peter*, the *Secret Gospel of Mark*, the Coptic *Gospel of Thomas*, the *Gospel of Mary*, the *Wisdom of Jesus Christ*, and others, which François Bovon reviewed in a 1984 article in *New Testament Studies*.[13] Bovon suggests that this literature was declared heterodox less because of its doctrinal content than because of the embarrassing priority among the disciples, and especially in relation to Peter, that it assigns to Mary Magdalene. In any case, it is clear from the text itself that the Fourth Gospel intends to present Mary Magdalene as the recipient of the first Easter Christophany upon which the paschal faith of the Johannine community was based, just as Luke's community's faith rested on the appearance to Peter, the gentile churches on that to Paul, and the Jerusalem community's on the appearances to James and the eleven. According to John, it is Mary Magdalene to whom the glorified Jesus entrusted the paschal kerygma in its characteristically Johannine form, whom he sent to announce that Easter message to the community of disciples, and who fulfilled successfully that apostolic commission so that the disciples in John, unlike those in Luke who dismissed the testimony of the women returning from the empty tomb (see Luke 24:11), were fully prepared to recognize and accept Jesus' appearance in their midst that evening (see John 20:20). From every point of view and according to every criterion developed in the New Testament, Mary Magdalene is, in John's gospel, the apostolic witness upon whom the paschal faith of the community was founded.

Section One: Hopeless Suffering and Spiritual Blindness
Let us turn now to section one of the Mary Magdalene episode. This is a highly symbolic scene. It is still dark. The pre-dawn obscurity noted in verse 1 seems still to preside at least over Mary's inner landscape if not over the garden itself.[14] Only the Fourth Evangelist places the tomb of Jesus in a garden and describes Mary's ironic mistaking of Jesus for the gardener. His address to her as "woman" and her action of "peering" through her tears into the tomb expressed by *parekypsen*, a word that occurs rarely in the New Testament[15] and, strikingly, in the Septuagint of the Canticle of Canticles 2:9 in describing the search for the beloved, alert the reader to the fact that this garden setting is intended to evoke both the creation account in Genesis, where God walks and talks with the first couple in the garden (see Gen 2:15–17; 3:8) and promises salvation through a woman (see Gen 3:15), and the Canticle

of Canticles, which, by the time this gospel was written, was under-stood to be the hymn of the covenant between Israel and Yahweh. In this garden of new creation and new covenant, Jesus, who is both the promised liberator of the new creation and the spouse of the new Is-rael, encounters the woman, who is, symbolically, the Johannine com-munity, the church, the new people of God.

But Mary is distraught, overcome with hopeless sorrow. She is so fixated on the loss of the body of Jesus, which she obviously exhaus-tively identifies with Jesus himself, that she does not even register sur-prise at being addressed by angelic messengers. Like the cherubim in Exodus 25:22 and 38:7–8, who sit, one on either end of the mercy seat of the ark of the covenant, these angels in white sit "one at the head and one at the feet where the body of Jesus had lain" (v. 12). Mary is seek-ing Jesus, a quintessentially positive enterprise in John's gospel, but her grief has spiritually blinded her, rendered her incapable of revelation even when Jesus himself stands before her and speaks to her. She does not recognize him. The evangelist indulges in delicious irony in having Mary identify Jesus as precisely who he is, the gardener, while com-pletely missing the symbolic point of her own materially correct identi-fication. Jesus challenges her weeping, trying to refocus her distraught attention from his physical body to his person with the question, "Whom [not what] do you seek?" (v. 15). But Mary remains fixated in her obsession, again interchanging "him" who is missing with the "body" which is missing as she had interchanged "the Lord" and "the stone" in reporting the body missing in verse 2. In this first section of the pericope, under the sign of *klaiousa*, that is, blinding spiritual sad-ness and hopelessness, the evangelist dramatically prepares the reader to accept a new mode of Jesus' presence. To do this one must surrender the obsessional fixation on the physical presence of the earthly Jesus and prepare to cross the threshold from the economy of history into that of the resurrection.

Section Two: Conversion
Section two of the pericope is made up of a single verse, one of the most moving in the New Testament. The utter simplicity and symme-try of verse 16 makes the point with lapidary eloquence. "Jesus said to her, 'Mary!' Turning [*strapheisa*] she said to him, in Hebrew, 'Rab-bouni.'" The turning, as has been said, is obviously not physical. Al-ready in verse 14, after Mary responded to the angels with a repetition of her lament that "they have taken away my Lord," we are told, "And saying this she turned back (*estraphē eis ta opisō*) and saw Jesus stand-

ing." Two things are to be noted. First, the phrase usually translated "around" or "back" (*eis ta opisō*) means literally "toward the things that lie behind" or "backwards." Second, as she turns away from the angels, she faces Jesus and speaks with him. Consequently, when Jesus speaks her name she is already face to face with him. Her "turning" in verse 16 in response to his address, now not qualified as "backwards" or "around" but simply as turning, is the second member of the "turning and turning again," the "turning away" and "turning back," the apostasy and conversion, which the word *šûb* in the book of Jeremiah captures so well.[16]

What Mary does spiritually, by insisting that the absence of Jesus' dead body constitutes the absence of the living person of Jesus, is to turn back, or to turn toward what lies behind, namely, the historical dispensation, which came to a close with the glorification of Jesus on the cross. In the historical context of the Johannine community, it is probably also to turn back toward the synagogue, toward religious experience governed by the coordinates of Judaism, toward Moses as teacher of the way. When Jesus speaks her name, as most commentators have recognized, he is calling his own by name (see 10:3). Mary did not, as some have suggested, recognize Jesus by the sound of his voice in the ordinary sense of the word, for she had already spoken with him, heard his physical voice, without recognizing him (see v. 15). It is being called by name that effects the conversion. Jesus knows his own as the Father knows him and he knows the Father (see 10:14–15). He calls his own sheep by name, and they know his voice and they follow him (see 10:3–5). Consequently, the evangelist makes certain that the reader does not miss the significance of Mary's response, "Rabbouni." He tells us that she spoke in Hebrew and that the word means, "Teacher." Throughout the Fourth Gospel, beginning with the Prologue, in which the reader is told proleptically that the law came through Moses but that grace and truth came through Jesus Christ (see 1:17), major questions are: Who is the true teacher of the way of salvation? Of whom are you (the reader) a disciple? Do you look to Moses or to Jesus? A choice must be made, as was dramatically presented in the story of the man born blind, who asks his Jewish questioners, "Do you also want to become his [Jesus'] disciples?" and they emphatically choose Moses while the healed man chooses Jesus (see 9:27–34) and his parents try to remain neutral (9:20–21). Here Mary, symbolic representative of the new Israel, the Johannine community and the readers, makes the salvific choice. Jesus, and Jesus alone, is the Teacher, even, according to the Fourth Gospel, for the Jews.[17]

Section Three: The Easter Apostle
The third section of the Mary Magdalene pericope contains the notoriously difficult verse 17, which begins with Jesus' prohibition, *mē mou haptou*, which is translated most often as "Do not hold on to me" (cf. NRSV and NIV) or "Do not cling to me," followed by the even more difficult reference to Jesus' ascension to the Father. If one puts aside, as I think we must, the temptation to interpret this text in John in the light of Matthew 28:9, in which the women clasp the feet of the risen Jesus and worship him, and stick to what the text actually says rather than imagining Mary's psychological responses, we should read, "Do not continue to touch me," or even more literally, "Not me (emphatic) continue to touch" but "Go to my brothers and sisters." The emphatic placement of the "me" at the beginning of the command and closest to the negative, which thus seems to govern the pronoun "me" rather than the verb "touch," suggests that what Jesus is forbidding is not so much the touching itself but Mary's selection of the object to touch, namely, the Jesus who stands before her as an individual. What Mary is told not to do is try to continue to touch Jesus, that is, to encounter him as if he were the earthly Jesus resuscitated. The time for that kind of relationship is over. The negative present imperative of "touch" does not really mean "cling" or "hold," for which there is a perfectly good Greek word, *krateō*, which John uses in 20:23 and Matthew in 28:9. Furthermore, "to touch" often means not simply or even primarily the physical gesture of laying one's hands on a person but rather interpersonal relating such as being deeply touched by a person's kindness or touched by the Evil One as in 1 John 5:18, which is the only other place the word occurs in the Johannine corpus. In other words, I would suggest that what Jesus is really doing is redirecting Mary's desire for union with himself from his physical or earthly body (which in any case no longer exists because it is the glorified Lord who stands before her in an appearance which is temporary) to the new locus of his presence in the world, that is, the community of his brothers and sisters, the disciples.

What then are we to make of the reason Jesus seems to offer, "I am not yet ascended to my Father"? If anything, this seems less a reason for not touching him than a contradiction. If Jesus is not yet ascended, that is, if he is still present in the earthly sphere, it would seem that Mary, like the pre-ascension disciples in Luke 24:29, could be invited to touch him and verify his bodily reality. But, as most commentators have pointed out, the entire mystery of Jesus' glorification takes place in the Fourth Gospel when he is lifted up on the cross. It is virtually impossible, theologically, to understand Jesus in this scene as being somewhere in between (whether ontologically, spatially, or temporally) his resurrection and his ascension. The Jesus Mary encounters in the garden is clearly the glorified Jesus. Although it would take us too far afield to develop the thesis here, I would propose to translate this part of Jesus' address to Mary not as a declarative sentence, "I am not yet ascended to my Father," as if this supplied some reason why she should not or could not touch him, but as a rhetorical question expecting a negative reply, that is, "Am I as yet (or still) not ascended?" The proper answer to the question is, "No, you are indeed ascended, that is, glorified." The grammar and syntax of the sentence allow its translation as a question,[18] and, in my opinion, that makes much better sense of the passage because Jesus' ascension to the Father, that is, his glorification, is precisely the reason Mary will now encounter him in the community of the church rather than in his physical or earthly body, which may appear to be resuscitated but is not. In brief, a paraphrastic translation of verse 17 would be the following: "It is no longer in and through my physical or earthly historical individuality that you can continue to relate to me. After all, am I still unascended to my Father? Rather, go to the community, the new locus of my earthly presence."

Jesus continues by commissioning Mary Magdalene to announce to the disciples what is clearly the Johannine version of the Easter kerygma. The message is not, "I have risen" or "I go before you into Galilee." The message is that all has been accomplished. The work of the Word made flesh is complete, and its fruits are available to his disciples. In the Prologue the reader was told that the Word became flesh to give the power to become children of God to those who believed in him (see 1:12–14). Now that the work of Jesus is completed by his glorification, those who believe in him have become children of God. They are Jesus' brothers and sisters; his Father to whom he ascends is now their Father. It is important to note that 20:17 is the first time in John's gospel that the disciples of Jesus are called *adelphoi*, that is, siblings. Since it is abundantly clear in this gospel that the circle of the disciples is not limited to males and Mary is sent not to the apostles (a term not used for Jesus' disciples in John) or to "the Twelve" (which is a term the evangelist does use, e.g., in 6:70 and 20:24) but precisely to the disciples, the plural of "brother" in this verse is evidently a collective noun in masculine form, inclusive of male and female siblings, as our English masculine collective "brethren" once was considered inclusive. We can regret the masculine form in the text, which reflects the androcentric character of the Greek language and the culture of the times, but in reading and translating it we should honor its obviously inclusive meaning.[19]

The message Jesus sends to his disciples is hauntingly reminiscent of the Old Testament. My ascension, he says, "is to my Father and your Father, my God and your God." It recalls the words by which the foreigner, the Moabite Ruth, entered into the covenant people of her mother-in-law, Naomi: "Your people will be my people and your God will be my God" (Ruth 1:16). It echoes also the prophetic promise that in the time of the new creation God will make a new covenant with a renewed people, to whom God promises, "I will be your God and you will be my people" (cf. Jer 31:31–34). The conclusion of this scene, which takes place in a garden reminiscent of both Genesis and the Canticle of Canticles and in which Jesus, the true Gardener and the true Beloved, encounters the one who is searching for him, is the announcement that the work of Jesus is now complete. He ascends to the God he calls by right his Father. For his disciples this means that they are the first to participate in the salvation of the new creation, the first to be born not of blood, nor of the will of the flesh, nor of the desire of a man but of God (see 1:13). They are now truly his sisters and brothers, members of the new Israel, with whom God, through Jesus, the new Moses, has sealed a new covenant. The gift of God in Jesus, according to John, is divine filiation, eternal life in the Spirit springing up from within the believer (see 4:10–11) and flowing forth for the life of the world (see 7:37–39 and 19:34–37).

In verse 18 Mary Magdalene, now again given her full name as in verse 1, goes to fulfill her apostolic mission. She comes "announcing" (*angelousa*). This is the third thematic participle. Mary who began this episode in the depths of spiritual darkness and sorrow, *weeping*, has been converted by *turning* away from the dispensation that lies behind to the new life offered to her in the glorified Jesus, who lives now with God and in the temple of his body (see 2:21–22) which is the community, and she now goes joyfully *announcing* that which has been revealed to her.

There is an evident redactional seam visible in this verse, which the evangelist could scarcely not have noticed and must have left for a reason. The verse says literally, "Mary Magdalene went and announced to the disciples, 'I have seen the Lord' and he said these things to her." In other words, the sentence goes from first person direct discourse to third person indirect discourse without transition or explanation. Apparently the source verse with which the evangelist was working was, "Mary Magdalene went and announced to the disciples that he had said these things to her." The evangelist has opened up the sentence and inserted, in direct address, "I have seen the Lord." This is precisely the witness of the disciples to Thomas in verse 25, "We have seen the Lord," a testimony that Thomas evidently was expected to accept as the Easter kerygma. In John's gospel, bearing witness is always based on what one has seen and heard. Jesus bore witness to what he had seen and heard with God (see 3:11). The Beloved Disciple bore witness to what was seen on Calvary (see 19:35). In other words, to claim to have seen and/or heard is to claim to be an authentic and authenticated witness. It is, quite simply, a credential formula. In the early church it seems to have been particularly the credential statement for resurrection witnesses. Paul's ultimate self-vindication as an apostle is, "Have I not seen Jesus our Lord?" (1 Cor 9:1), which is not a reference to the earthly Jesus, whom Paul had never met, but to his experience of the risen Jesus on the road to Damascus. In other words, Mary Magdalene, contrary to what generations of condescending male commentators would have us believe, is by all accounts an official apostolic witness of the resurrection. She is the one who, in the Johannine community, takes Peter's role of confirming the brothers and sisters once she herself has been converted (cf. Luke 22:31–32). She is the only person in this gospel to receive an individual Easter appearance and a personal and individual commission from Jesus. The meaning and particular Johannine formulation of the Easter message are given only to her, and she communicates it to the church. Jesus does not repeat it when he appears to the disciples on Easter evening (20:19–23). He presumes it, and on the basis of Mary's confirming of the disciples he commissions them to live out what he has accomplished in and for them by extending to all his work of taking away of the sin of the world (cf. 1:29 and 20:23).

CONCLUSION

I have tried to establish two points in my interpretation of the encounter between the glorified Jesus and Mary Magdalene. First, Mary Magdalene is presented by the Fourth Evangelist as the official Easter witness in and to the Johannine community. She is symbolically presented, by means of Old Testament allusions, as the beloved of the lover in the Canticle of Canticles, the spouse of the new covenant mediated by Jesus in his glorification, the representative figure of the new Israel, which emerges from the new creation. Symbolically, she is both the Johannine community encountering its glorified Savior and the official witness to that community of what God has done for it in the glorification of Jesus.

Second, the answer to the question, Where is the Lord? is that Jesus is with God, face unveiled, in the glory that he had with God before the world was made, and he is intimately present within and among his own of the first and all later generations to whom he has returned as he promised to fill them with a joy no one can take from them. By the time the first Easter ends in the Fourth Gospel, the promise made in the last discourse(s) by the departing Jesus has been fulfilled: "I will not leave you orphaned; I am coming to you. In a little while the world will no longer see me, but you will see me; because I live, you also will live. On that day you will know that I am in my Father, and you in me, and I in you" (14:18–20). And this saving revelation comes to us, as it did to the first disciples, through the word of a woman bearing witness.

Notes

1. Hengel, "Maria Magdalena," 256.

2. Other features of this important pericope will be taken up in the chapter devoted to Mary Magdalene.

3. Félix Gils, "Pierre et la foi au Christ ressuscité," *Ephemerides Theologicae Lovanienses* 38 (1962): 5–43. For a summary of the tradition of interpretation and an excellent marshaling of the data for reinterpretation, see Gerald O'Collins and Daniel Kendall, "Mary Magdalene as Major Witness to Jesus' Resurrection," *TS* 48 (1987): 631–46.

4. See Brown, "Roles of Women," 190 n. 336.

5. Robert G. Maccini, *Her Testimony Is True: Women as Witnesses According to John*, JSNTSup 125 (Sheffield: Sheffield Academic Press, 1996), on the validity of female testimony in Judaism and particularly in John's gospel.

6. I am translating this text differently from the way it appears in the New Revised Standard Version. *Adelphoi*, the plural *of adelphos* (brother) is, in Greek, an inclusive collective noun including siblings of both genders if applied to a group including both. Obviously, the community to which Mary Magdalene is sent includes both women and men, since Mary herself is clearly a part of it, and one would certainly assume that it includes the mother of Jesus as well. Hence, my translation of *adelphous mou* as "to my brothers and sisters" (which was the sense of the older English translation, "brethren," a once inclusive English term). The word usually translated "I am ascending" in a future sense, *anabainō*, is present tense, "I ascend." I believe it would be clearer in English to translate it paraphrastically as "my ascension is to my Father who

is now your Father, my God who is now your God." The ascension in John takes place on the cross (thus it is accomplished by the time Jesus encounters Mary Magdalene in the garden), and the emphasis is not on the ascension but on the disciples' sharing in Jesus' relation to God, which is effected by this ascending.

7. Cf. John 1:16–18; see Xavier Léon-Dufour, *Resurrection and the Message of Easter*, trans. R. N. Wilson (New York: Holt, Rinehart & Winston, 1975), 180–81.

8. "Wept" or "weeping" occurs four times in the five verses of this section, in v. 11 twice, in v. 13, and in v. 15.

9. E.g., Raymond E. Brown, *The Virginal Conception and Bodily Resurrection of Jesus* (London: Geoffrey Chapman, 1973), 101 n. 170; Xavier Léon-Dufour, *Resurrection and the Message of Easter*, trans. R. N. Wilson (New York: Holt; Rinehart & Winston, 1975); Augustin George, "Les récits d'apparitions aux onze à partir de Luc 24, 26–53," in *La Résurrection du Christ et l'exégèse moderne*, Lectio Divina (Paris: Cerf, 1969), 76.

10. For a summary of the tradition of interpretation and an excellent marshaling of the data for reinterpretation, see Gerald O'Collins and Daniel Kendall, "Mary Magdalene as Major Witness to Jesus' Resurrection," *TS* 48 (1987): 631–46.

11. Matthew 27:55–56, 61; 28:1–8; Mark 15:40–41, 47; 16:1–8; Luke 23:49, 55–56; 24:1–10; John 19:25–30; 20:1–2. Interestingly enough, John's is the only gospel that does not explicitly state that the burial was witnessed by the woman/women, although this is clearly implied by the fact that Mary Magdalene knows the location of the tomb on Easter morning.

12. Raymond E. Brown, even in his early and already cited work *Virginal Conception* (p. 101 n. 170), suggests that the tradition of the appearance to Mary Magdalene, although "minor" and not the basis of apostolic witness, was very possibly historical.

13. François Bovon, "Le privilège pascal de Marie-Madeleine," *NTS* 30 (1984): 50–62.

14. See Corina Combet-Galland, "L'Aube encore obscure: approche sémiotique de Jean 20," *Foi et vie* (September 1987): 17–25.

15. Actually, it occurs only here and in 20:5, where it describes the Beloved Disciple looking into the tomb before the arrival of Simon Peter, and in Luke 24:12, which is a "western non-interpolation" very possibly dependent on John or on a common source.

16. The standard exploration of this theme is the monograph of William L. Holladay, *The Root ŠÛBH in the Old Testament, with Particular Reference to Its Usages in Covenantal Contexts* (Leiden: E. J. Brill, 1958). Donatian Mollat explored the relevance of this to John's gospel ("La conversion chez saint Jean," in *L'espérance du royaume*, Parole de Vie [Tours: Mame, 1966], 55–78).

17. The other two papers delivered at the 1993 SBL Johannine Section, by Werner Kelber and R. Alan Culpepper, deal with the problem this Johannine perspective creates for the contemporary reader because of its anti-Jewish and potentially anti-Semitic cast.

18. I am applying to this verse the theory Albeit Vanhoye developed in "Interrogation johannique et exégèse de Cana (Jn 2,4)," *Biblica* 55 (1974): 157–67. Vanhoye proposed that John uses double-meaning or ironical questions whose answer is both positive and negative to lead the reader into theological reflection. In this case, Jesus *appears* to be not yet ascended because he is interacting with Mary, but what she (and the reader) must realize is that *in reality* he is now in a very different state, that is, glorified.

19. It is unfortunate that the NRSV and the NIV both retain the translation "brothers."

2

THE SIGNIFICANCE TODAY
OF JESUS' COMMISSION TO MARY MAGDALENE

Teresa Okure (Nigeria)

The appearance of the risen Jesus to Mary Magdalene in John 20:11–18 constitutes his first recorded appearance in John's gospel. It would seem that Jesus interrupted his journey of ascent to the Father (cf. 20:17a) in order to make this appearance before her. On this proto resurrection appearance, Jesus gave Mary a special commission: "Go and tell my brethren: I am ascending to my Father and your Father, to my God and your God" (v. 17b).

Unfortunately, when this appearance is recalled, what comes readily to mind is not this commission but Jesus' preamble to the commission: "Do not cling to me for I have not yet ascended to my Father" (v. 17a). This scene has been immortalized in the famous medieval painting entitled *Noli me tangere* (Do not touch me). In the painting Mary is shown in a kneeling position stretching out toward Jesus to touch him, while Jesus, standing withdrawn, prohibits her with a majestic gesture of the hand from coming near him. The impression created by this depiction of the scene, and later influenced by a puritanical culture, is that if Mary were to touch Jesus she would contaminate him with her human, specifically female, hands, and that Jesus now belongs to a new and divine sphere, different from that of Mary's. To touch him would be to commit a serious act of defilement, not only as a human being, but also as a woman; so interpreted since Jesus later invited Thomas to touch and feel him (20:27).[1]

But is this interpretation true to the evidence of the gospel itself? Was this the main point of Jesus' appearance to Mary Magdalene? What of the commission that he gave her in verse 17b? This study undertakes to re-examine the significance of this commission in its Johannine and New Testament contexts and to draw out its implications for us today in the work of evangelization. It will do this against the back-drop of modern understanding of mission generally and by John's gospel in particular.

Generally mission is said to entail a sender, one sent, a commission (or the message), and in some cases, a reporting back to the sender of the task accomplished. But the Johannine approach to mission, as I have indicated elsewhere, requires that great emphasis be laid on the role and response of the audience for whose sake the mission is undertaken in the first place.[2] Second, John's gospel knows only of one mission, that of Jesus. All other missions are derivative of his and in function of it.[3] The purpose of his mission is to give life in all its fullness (John 10:10) or to empower those who believe to become the children of God (John 1:12–13).

One enters into this mission not primarily by being commissioned but by opening oneself to it, to receive its fruit, to be or to harvest from its fruit (John 4:34–38).[4] The discovery and experience of the new life in Jesus and in God then fills one with joy and moves one to share this joy with others. The author of 1 John states this very vividly, using three of the five senses:

> That which was from the beginning, which we have heard; which we have seen with our own eyes and looked upon, and touched with our hands, the word who is life, this we declare to you...that you may share in our common life, that life which we share with the Father and with his Son Jesus Christ ...that our common joy may be complete. (1 John 1:1–4)

Entry into the mission of Jesus is rightly described as a witnessing to him, a confessing of him and the God who sent him, and an abiding in him. This constitutes the primary mode of participation in Jesus' mission. Without this primary participation, one cannot be commissioned or given a special mission.

Yet, ironically, over the years the understanding of mission has been restricted to its secondary sense, the commissioning. As a result, undue emphasis has been laid on the criteria for determining who was and who was not given a commission by Jesus. Arguments that hold that Jesus did not send women are based on this erroneous or one-sided conception of mission. The case of Mary Magdalene is no exception, even though long ago Augustine called her an "apostle of the apostles," based on the commission given her by Jesus (see John 20:17–18). In the church, the commissioning has been tied to apostleship. This has been seen as the sole prerogative of men, since it is argued that Jesus did not choose women among his twelve apostles. Apostleship itself has been defined primarily in terms of governing, ruling, and teaching. Women have been excluded from these activities, and divine intention has been cited to justify the practice (cf. 1 Tim 2:11–12; 1 Cor 14:33–36).

Finally, there has been a tendency in the past to equate mission with outreach to "pagans" in the third world. This has resulted in a complacency on the part of first-world Christians, a complacency that has led in many cases to the loss of faith itself among Christians in this first world. Though the picture is slowly changing, the effects of this past formation endure and will take a long time to eradicate. It is our hope that a re-examination of the commission to Mary Magdalene, of its importance in the life of the early Christian community, and of Mary's personal response to the mission of Jesus prior to her commissioning will help to resolve some of these errors and move us to a more authentic understanding and practice of mission in the third millennium.

THE COMMISSION TO MARY MAGDALENE

On the first day of the week after the passion, death, and burial of Jesus, Mary Magdalene went to the tomb "while it was still dark." This is Mary's second appearance in John's gospel. She is first mentioned among the women who stood at the foot of the cross (19:25). On neither occasion is she introduced, as are other characters in the gospel (cf. 11:1–2; 19:38–39). One may conclude that she is so well known in the Johannine community or in the tradition generally that she needs no introduction. The story of Jesus' passion began with the key role of a woman—Mary of Bethany, who anointed him (John 12:1–8; cf. Matt. 26:6–13; Mark 14:3–9). That of his resurrection also begins with the unique role of a woman—Mary Magdalene. In the Synoptics, Mary visits the tomb in the company of other women to anoint the body of Jesus (cf. Matt 28:1; Mark 16:1; Luke 24:10). Here in John she is portrayed alone even though the allusion to "we" in verse 2 implies that she was in the company of other women. Scholars see in this portrayal a fidelity to the oldest tradition, which made her the first witness of the empty tomb.

Finding the stone removed from the tomb, she ran to Peter and to the other disciple whom Jesus loved and reported in her grief: "They have taken away the Lord and we do not know where they have put him" (v. 2). Peter and the beloved disciple then set out to see for themselves. The beloved disciple outran Peter and reached the tomb first. When Peter arrived and entered the tomb to verify the evidence, the other disciple also went in: "He saw and believed" (v. 8). Both disciples then returned home, forgetting Mary completely and leaving her to her own devices. It is as though she did not exist. Yet in the framework of the narrative, were it not for her, they would not have known in the first place that Jesus had risen from the dead (v. 9) nor would the beloved disciple have believed.

Mary's mission to the disciples thus started even before she encountered the risen Jesus himself. This mission arose out of her love for him. By it she surrendered her life entirely to him and became oblivious of everything else. This love drove her to visit the tomb in the dark hours of the morning at great risk to her own life while the men disciples were behind locked doors for fear of the Jews (20:19, 29; cf. 19:38). It kept her to the spot while the men returned home: "While the men returned, the weaker sex was fastened to the place by a stronger affection."[5]

As Mary continued to stand by the tomb weeping disconsolately, she too stooped down as the beloved disciple had done and peered into the tomb. This time she saw, not the linen cloths lying there as Peter and the other disciple had seen, but two angels in white, one at the head and the other at the feet where Jesus' body had lain. Their position, like that of the linen cloths in verse 7, is seen as indicating that the body had not been taken away. In the Synoptics, angels also appear to the women at the tomb, and they are frightened (Matt 28:2–8; cf. Mark 16:5–8). Mary was too engrossed in her love and grief to be moved or alarmed by the sight of the angels. To their question, "Woman, why are you weeping?" she reiterated the cause of her grief, but this time on a more personal note: "They have taken *my* Lord away and *I* do not know where they have put him" (v. 13). Previously she had spoken of "the Lord" and "we," now it is "my Lord" and "I"; she is now on her own in her quest for Jesus.

Then, probably as the angels look over her shoulders or at the sound of Jesus' footsteps, she too turns round and sees Jesus standing there without recognizing him. Jesus in turn repeats the question of the angels: "Woman, why are you weeping?" adding, "Who are you looking for?" The Greek verb *zetein* (to seek, look, or search for intensely) used here by Jesus has an evangelistic sense in the gospel. It is used, for instance, of the two disciples who follow Jesus as a result of the witness of John the Baptist that Jesus is the Lamb of God (John 1:38). The same word is used also to speak of God's seeking for true worshipers who will worship him in spirit and in truth (4:23–24). Mary's quest for Jesus is intense and from the heart. Her answer to Jesus' question is as bold and courageous as it is possible for her to undertake: "Sir, if you have removed him, tell me where you have laid him and I will carry him away" (v. 15).

Strikingly, throughout all this narrative Mary never refers to the Lord's "body," as is done in other parts of the gospel (cf. 19:38, 40; 20:12), but always to "the Lord" and "him." It is as though for her Jesus never really died in the first place. This explains why she could weep and search passionately for what was no more than a corpse. In the Synoptics, the women go to anoint the body of Jesus, since this was not possible on the burial day because of the Passover. But, according to John's gospel, the body had been properly anointed by Joseph of Arimathea and Nicodemus (19:38–42). Mary's concern, therefore, was not to prevent Jesus' body from being desecrated, especially as he had died a criminal's death; her love was too strong to accept that he could be dead and gone forever: "Love is strong as death" (Cant 8:6).

Marveling at such a love, Jesus then calls Mary by name, perhaps with a shake of the head at her unabashed love. She in turn recognizes him, turns completely round to him, and calls him "my master/ teacher" (*hrabbouni*). In her joy she holds on to him for dear life, hardly believing that he is alive. The entire scene recalls John 10:3–4. Jesus the Good Shepherd calls each sheep by name and they recognize and follow him. Mary is one of those sheep for whom Jesus laid down his life to take it up again, to the great delight of the Father (10:11, 17–18). In this regard, she is in every sense of the word the first fruit of Jesus' accomplished mission.

Mary called Jesus "my teacher." Some scholars hold that this title lacks the loftiness of the Easter faith, which refers to Jesus as Lord and God (cf. 20:28). From this it is concluded that Mary did not see in Jesus anything more than she did before his death, hence hers was not yet an Easter faith.[6] This is an interesting conjecture. "My teacher" here is a term of endearment. When she reports on the encounter she calls him "the Lord" (v. 18), using the technical Easter formula: "I have seen the Lord." The question is: What did he teach her on this occasion?

First, he taught her that she was important enough for him to interrupt his journey to the Father in order to let her know that he was still alive. This is shown by the particle "for" (*gar*) and the adverb "not yet" (*oupō*) in the statement: "Do not hold on to me thus, for I have not yet ascended [*anabebēka*] to my Father." The Johannine schema on the ascension is different from that of Luke, which allows a forty-day interval between the resurrection and the ascension.[7] Second, he taught her that he saw and valued her love and concern for him, and that he accepted this love and was moved by it.

The statement, *mē mou haptou* (v. 17a), popularly translated as "do not touch me," or worse still, "stop clinging to me,"[8] actually means "do not hold on to me" (for I have not yet ascended to my Father). The whole context makes this evident. Mary had believed all along that somebody had taken away the Lord. This concern is repeated three times (vv. 2, 12 and 15). Now that she had seen him, she was not going to take any chance of letting him go (cf. Cant 3:4).[9] She obviously then held on to him in such a way that he would not be wrenched from her grasp. Mary's action is a very natural one in the circumstances. It is done out of astonishment and delight. (The situation recalls that [as reported by Arrian]...Alexander received severe wounds in the chest from an arrow. His soldiers could not believe that he was alive. When he appeared among them recovered from the wounds, they took hold [*haptomenoi*] of his hands, knees, and clothing in delight and astonishment.)[10] If this is the situation, and the context supports this interpretation, then Jesus is not in any way rebuffing Mary. Quite the contrary; he gives her a message both for herself and the brethren to assure her that from now on both she and he and the other disciples are inseparable. This message constitutes the peak of his teaching on this occasion. What was this message? And how important was it to the early Christians?

The Message

Jesus sent Mary with a message to his disciples, while he, it is understood, would complete his ascent to the Father: "But go to my brethren and tell them: I am now ascending to my Father and your Father, to my God and your God" (John 17b). We are so accustomed to the formality whereby Christians address one another as "dear brothers and sisters in Christ," especially in liturgical settings, that we miss the impact of this message and its newness at the time it was uttered. Scholars have remarked on the solemn tone of this commission.

This is registered by the repetition "my," "your" in the expression "my Father and your Father," "my God and your God." This solemnity underscores the importance of the commission. The rhythm of the statement: "my Father and your Father," "my God and your God," recalls that of Ruth to Noami (Ruth 1:16), where the former, the Moabitess, tells her Jewish mother-in-law that, despite the differences of race between them, their lot is now so woven together that they cannot be separated: "Your people shall be my people and your God my God." As a result of this pact, which not even death or the grave could separate, Ruth became an ancestress of Jesus, listed in the Matthean genealogy (Matt 1:5–6).

Prior to the resurrection, God's "fatherhood" (or parenthood) in John's gospel was restricted to Jesus. At the last supper, Jesus gave the disciples the status of friends as opposed to slaves (John 15:15). On the cross, he further gave his mother to the Beloved Disciple to be his mother and the disciple to her to be her son (John 19:26–27). But now, for the first time, the disciples are given to understand, through the message entrusted to Mary Magdalene, that they and Jesus now share the same parent or ground of being in God. They are in truth brothers and sisters of Jesus in God in much the same way as children relate who share the same father and mother. In other words, the message declares and proclaims the new status of the disciples after the resurrection: only now does Jesus make his Father and God in the full sense the Father and God of his disciples. This declaration appears in this form only here in the whole New Testament tradition. It expands and fulfills the statement of Jesus in 14:6, that he is the only way to the Father.[11] Thus, while the repetition of "my/your" underscores the identity in the relationship between Jesus and the disciples in relation to God, it also pinpoints his uniqueness in this regard as the agent by which this relationship becomes possible.

Equally important, the statement declares that in Jesus believers now have a new relationship to one another. The "your" in the statement is plural (*hymon*). They relate to one another in Jesus as blood brothers and sisters relate to one another. Hence Jesus' relationship with his Father and with them now becomes the norm of their relationship with one another (cf. 13:1, 34–35; 15:9–14).

This interpretation finds a solid contextual backing in John's gospel and epistles, and in the rest of the New Testament. The prologue to the gospel declares that to all who believe in him Jesus gave the enabling power (*exousia*) to become the children of God; these were born not "of any human blood or by the will of any human being or father, but of God himself" (John 1:12–13). The Greek word *teknon* (child) used here in the plural "children" denotes the child in relation to its parents or grandparents. It differs from the other word for child (*pais*), which denotes other types of relationship of one human being to another, or emphasizes the age of the person concerned (cf. Mark 9:37; Luke 18:17; Matt 18:3–4; John 4:49).[12] It also differs from "son" (*hyios*), which can also denote other types of relationship, though in John's gospel it designates Jesus' unique and untransferable relationship with the Father.[13]

In John 1:12–13 the status of believers as children of God is reinforced by the statement that they are born of God (*ek theou egennēthēsan*). This birth is brought about by Jesus' passion, death, and resurrection. Jesus gave birth to believers on the cross (cf. 12:20; 16:21), through his pierced side whence blood and water gushed out as happens to a woman's womb when she gives birth to a child. The fathers of the church systematically saw in the piercing of Jesus' side and the outflow of water and blood the birth of the church. Water and blood signify the sacraments of baptism and the Eucharist.[14] But the church is the gathering of the children of God, branches of the vine that is Jesus himself (15:1–8), the multifarious fish caught in his net (John 21:1–17). Hence the church cannot be born of Jesus unless individuals who make up the church are first born of him. Placed in the prologue, the statement in John 1:12–13 about the divine birth of believers stems from the message entrusted to Mary Magdalene by Jesus. It is written from this post-Easter perspective, and serves as evidence of the community's acceptance of her commission.

The importance of this message is reinforced in the dialogue with Nicodemus (John 3:1–21). One must be (*dei*) born of God if one is to have eternal life. This birth from God, Jesus explains, happens through his passion, death, and resurrection (his *hypsēthēnai/doxasthēnai*, 3:14). Nicodemus's persistent misunderstanding of the nature of this birth and his insistence on its impossibility for a grown-up person only serve to underscore its reality. This birth is effected by the Spirit (3:5) whose coming depends on Christ's glorification (cf. 7:39; 14:16; 19:34; 20:22). As in John 1:12–13, this insight in the dialogue is influenced by the Easter message entrusted to Mary Magdalene. The Johannine community understood this birth to be real, not metaphorical. Hence the author of 1 John exclaims with a great sense of wonder:

> How great is the love that the Father has shown to us! We are called God's children, not only called, we really are... we are God's children, what we shall be has not yet been disclosed but we know that when he appears, we shall be like him. (1 John 3:1–2)

The author then draws upon this relationship to exhort the believers to demonstrate their sonship and daughtership of God by loving one another as God and Jesus love them. It is only in this way that they can claim in truth to be children of God who is love (1 John 3:16; 4:16).

Indeed, not only the Johannine corpus but the entire New Testament bears witness that after the resurrection the followers of Jesus regarded one another as brothers and sisters. [Examples that give evidence of this are] too numerous to be cited. There is hardly any book of the New Testament that does not corroborate this evidence (cf. Rom 15:14; 1 Cor 1:10, 11, 26; Gal 1:2, 11; Eph 6:21; Phil 1:12; Col 1:2; 1 Thess 1:4; Heb 2:11; Jas 1:2; 2 Pet 1:10; 1 John 2:9; Rev 1:9; 22:9). But we may note in particular Romans 8:15–17, where Paul is thrilled that believers can now call God "Abba! Father!" based on the testimony of the Spirit that "we are children of God." In the Acts of the Apostles, believers consistently designate one another as brothers and sisters (cf. Acts 1:15; 6:3; 9:17, 30; 10:23; 12:17; 15:1, etc.). The striking point here is that this designation cuts across ethnic barriers and applies equally to persons of non-Jewish origin, whereas previously the term "brethren" (*adelphoi, andres adelphoi*) was reserved only for fellow Jews (cf. Acts 2:29, 39; 3:17, 22), that is, people of the same race and blood.

The instance in Revelations 22:9 is even more significant; the angel revealer is described as a "fellow servant" of the prophet in contradistinction to the rest of the believers who are designated as his "brothers and sisters." So pervasive is the New Testament evidence that one is led to conclude that the designation of believers as children of God or brothers and sisters of Jesus *before* the resurrection has been influenced by this post-Easter message entrusted to Mary Magdalene (cf. Matt 23:8; 25:40). The point of this whole survey is to underscore that the New Testament understanding that believers are in the fullest sense children of God as are children of human parents is rooted in and derives from the Easter message entrusted to Mary Magdalene. Interestingly, in Matthew 28:10, it is to the women at the tomb that Jesus gave the commission to inform his "brethren" that he was going before them to Galilee. The message given to Mary in John 20:17 is here given to other women in a different form in the Synoptic tradition. This is the primary and foundational Easter message. Mary is, therefore, not simply an apostle of apostles; she was commissioned by the risen Jesus himself to bear and proclaim the message of messages to the disciples. This message, which concerns the significance of Jesus' resurrection for believers, their common parenthood in and brotherhood/sisterhood in Christ, sums up the entire purpose of Jesus' mission and God's work of salvation.

Mary Magdalene was not, therefore, primarily or even secondarily commissioned to tell the disciples that Jesus had risen from the dead. That was self-evident. She had seen him and would naturally have reported on that as did the disciples on the way to Emmaus and the other disciples (Luke 24:33–35). Rather, her commission lay in the charge to proclaim the good news, which we have examined at length. In other words, Mary was not only the first to see the risen Lord; she was also the first to be commissioned by him to proclaim the Easter message concerning the new status of believers, that they are children of God and brothers and sisters to one another. All subsequent proclamation has this goal in view, to bring new members into this sonship and daughtership of God with its accompanying rights and duties (cf. 1 John 1:1–4; 2 Cor 5:18–20).

Mary's own report to the disciples corroborates this interpretation of the significance of her commission. She reported that she had seen the Lord and that "he had said these things to her" (John 20:18). Seeing the Lord was an important motif in the New Testament. But of itself it was not enough, except for catechetical and apologetic purposes (cf. 1 Cor 15:1–9). The emphasis on seeing the Lord lay in the authority it gave one to proclaim the good news and to be an apostle. So Paul declares in 1 Corinthians 9:1; 15:8–9. Some, like the disciples on the way to Emmaus, saw the Lord but were not specifically commissioned, yet in their joy they ran to share the news with others. Mary had both. She saw the Lord and was commissioned by him to bear the foundational message of the resurrection to the community. Here was a proclamation in every sense of the word (*aggelousa*), not a mere storytelling.[15] This is all the more striking in an age and in a culture where the witness of women was regarded as null and void.

On the cross, Jesus entrusted his mother to the disciple whom he loved. From that day on the disciple took her into his own home, that is, he accepted her as his own mother. Following his example, the church has done so ever since. After his resurrection, Jesus, through the commission given to Mary Magdalene, also entrusted all believers into one another's keeping as his brothers and sisters in God. The New Testament evidence shows that the early Christians took this message seriously to heart and transformed it into a program of action; they designated one another as brothers and sisters and forged a communitarian way of life to enable them to live out this new relationship. Thus they ensured that none of their brothers or sisters were ever in want (cf. Acts 2:43–46; 4:32–37). The Johannine community and Paul in particular emphasized the wonder of this new identity and urged their members to show that they were indeed children of God by loving one another as God loved them.

The insight that as Christians we are children of God, born to him/her through baptism and the Holy Spirit and through the blood of Christ shed on the cross, is not new to us (1 Cor 12:13). We have no difficulty in believing that God is our Father and Mother. But to what extent have we grasped the corresponding truth that in Christ we are in truth, not metaphorically, related to one another as are blood brothers and sisters? What challenges does this awareness hold for us today as people entrusted with this same Easter message for the third millennium? Let us attempt to answer these questions in the last part of this study.

THE SIGNIFICANCE OF MARY'S COMMISSION FOR TODAY

There is concern today to identify new emphases in mission as we move into the third millennium. In my view, this concern calls us first to re-examine our understanding of our common identity as Christians and to evaluate how we have lived this identity in the second millennium. In the light of the foundational Easter message entrusted to Mary Magdalene, we need to ask whether it is possible for us Christians to see ourselves as brothers and sisters in the way Jesus intended and as the early Christians understood and endeavored to live it out.

To Africans, it is not an impossibility for Christians of different races to regard one another as brothers and sisters, children of God. The love of one's family, extended family, clan and ethnic group constitutes a natural, cultural background for imparting and assimilating this message. It is a common saying in Africa that "blood is thicker than water." By this is meant that any relationship by blood takes precedence over all other types of relationship. This applies no matter how far down the line the blood may be. Indeed, it is the blood of the ancestors and ancestresses who are always alive and who exercise a protective and watchful role within the community that unites peoples of the same family or ethnic group.

If this is true of human blood, should it not be more so of the blood of Christ, which has given birth and life to us all as children of God, and which continues to nourish us daily through the Eucharist? But unfortunately the Christianity that the Africans inherited was riddled with divisions caused by the political quarrels of Europe. These divisions and their accompanying discriminations have deeply entrenched themselves into the psyche of most African Christians. In some parts of Nigeria, Christians of one denomination would rather side with Moslems in certain socio-political undertakings than with Christians of another denomination. Ecumenism remains for the most part no more than an academic exercise.

Second, in the African culture, it is possible for persons who are not in any way related by blood to forge a lasting bond of friendship that can be as thick as blood. Such friendships are sealed in some cultures by the letting out and mingling of the blood of the parties concerned.[16] Through this "covenant of blood" the parties see themselves not only as brothers or sisters, but as their other self. These practices and beliefs can be used as a solid cultural, hence natural, background for transmitting the message of the resurrection given in the commission to Mary Magdalene.

The recognition of our common parentage in God carries with it an obligation to love all God's children as Jesus did, even to the point of breaking the bread of his life so that we may live. In the New Testament evidence, this is the only authentic way by which one can claim to know and represent God in the community and in the world. John 13:35 is the Christian identity card. To do otherwise is to demonstrate one's ignorance of God (1 John 3:16; 4:20–21).

Fidelity to our relationship to one another as brothers and sisters in Christ demands that we eschew all activities that smack of superiority and inferiority complexes. It also rules out all types of discrimination based on race, class, and sex, since it recognizes that we are all one person in Christ (Gal 3:28). It leads us to "speak the truth in love" if a brother or sister errs, rather than deny them their fundamental human rights, deprive them of the freedom of theological speech, or treat them as inferiors in their own parents' house (cf. Heb 23:22–24).

In the socio-economic and political spheres, the challenge of Mary Magdalene's commission will move the so-called Christian countries of the West to care for their less fortunate sisters and brothers in the two-thirds world. This will be done out of a sense of duty, not of benevolence, the same duty that one has toward one's blood brothers and sisters, at least in the African context, to enhance their overall growth. The belittling relationship that often exists between donors and receivers should give place to a genuine sharing not only of goods but of technology and skills. The Christian culture is essentially one of sharing. It stands out against the modern one, which is based on accumulation rather than distribution of wealth. This also demands that a stop be put to all the covert and overt ways of exploiting the peoples of this two-thirds world.

More especially, the recognition that we are all brothers and sisters in Christ will help toward according to women their rightful place in church and society. In Africa nobody jokes with his sister or mother, women to whom one is related by blood. The wife and widow may be a different matter, because she is not related to the husband and the husband's family by blood. But whether wife or widow, as Christians we are all related to one another through the blood of Christ. In particular this will demand that the church listen to the witness of women to Christ today, that it take seriously the commission that they alone can declare to be what they have received from Christ for the good of the community. Instead of citing arguments based on what "Jesus did not do" with regard to women, the church should listen with open ears and learn from what Jesus actually did when he sent a woman like Mary Magdalene to carry and proclaim the crucial or most significant message of his accomplished mission to the Christian community. The charge given to all the disciples in John 20:22–23 has been interpreted as admitting new members into this new relationship. It rests on and presupposes the commission to Mary Magdalene. Hers was the foundational commission.

This commission has to do essentially with life and relationships. The new approach to mission in the third millennium will need to focus its attention on ways of promoting genuine life and relationships between peoples and between them and God. It will not succeed in this undertaking if it continues to ignore the significant contributions of women who are by nature endowed by God to be covenanted with life, bearers and fosterers of life (cf. Gen 3:20).[17]

CONCLUSION

This study has attempted to highlight that the risen Jesus entrusted to Mary Magdalene, a woman, the foundational message of the resurrection for the entire group of believers, namely, that they are now children of God and hence brothers and sisters to him and to one another. The early Christians took this message seriously and evolved concrete ways of putting it into practice. They did this even though in their culture women's witness did not count. In the course of history the significance of this message was lost sight of or at best reduced to a mere formality of greeting in liturgical settings.

We noted, too, that Mary's involvement in the mission of Jesus lay first in her personal love and commitment to him. This love, which was stronger than death, made her a fitting bearer of this key Easter message, which is about love and lasting relationship between Christ and all his followers.

This analysis of the commission to Mary Magdalene challenges us today to re-examine our whole understanding of the concept of mission, our attitude toward and our relationship with one another as children of God, south–north, and east–west. It also challenges the church to take seriously the contributions of women in the missionary undertaking if it is to remain faithful to its mission in the third millennium. Today Jesus commissions all believers as he commissioned Mary Magdalene: "Go and tell the brethren: I am ascending to my Father and your Father, to my God and your God." Fidelity to him requires that we make this commission the heart and nerve center of the work of evangelism in the third millennium.

Notes

1. See the discussion on this issue in R. E. Brown, *The Gospel According to John XIII–XXI*, AB 29A (New York: Doubleday, 1970), 1012–14; Pheme Perkins, "The Gospel According to John," in *New Jerome Biblical Commentary* (London: Geoffrey Chapman, 1989), 983; Saint Augustine, "Tractate CXXI, 1," *in Nicene and Post-Nicene Fathers*, first series, vol. 7 (Edinburgh: T. & T. Clark, 1986), 437.

2. Cf. T. Okure, *The Johannine Approach to Mission: A Contextual Study of John 4:1–42*, WUNT 31/2 (Tübingen: Mohr/Siebeck, 1988), esp. 1–6, 39–49, 192–225.

3. Ibid., esp. 140–45.

4. Ibid. 145–64.

5. Augustine, "Tractate cxx, 1," 436.

6. Cf. R. Schnackenburg, *The Gospel According to St John*, vol. 3 (New York: Crossroad, 1982), 317; Brown, *The Gospel According to John*, 1010; Perkins, *The Gospel According to John*, 1983.

7. For a lengthy discussion on "ascension" in John, see, e.g., Brown, *The Gospel According to John*, 1012–14; and Schnackenberg, *The Gospel According to John*, 318–20.

8. Thus M. Zerwick and M. Grosvenor, *A Grammatical Analysis of the Greek New Testament* (Rome: Pontifical Biblical Institute, 1981), 345.

9. "I found him whom my soul loves. I held him and would not let him go until I had brought him into my mother's house" (Cant. 3:4). The entire episode is in many ways evocative of this canticle.

10. Arrian, *Anab.*, 1.13.3; cited in Bauer, Arndt, and Gingrich, *Lexicon*, 7.

11. Cf. G. Shrenk, "Pater," in *Theological Dictionary of the New Testament*, v. 958, 996.

12. Cf. Colin Brown (ed.), *The New International Dictionary of New Testament Theology*, vol. 1 (Exeter: Paternoster Press, 1978), 285–86.

13. Cf. Okure, *Johannine Approach*, 240, 249.

14. See, e.g., John Chrysostom, "Baptismal Instructions, 16–19," in *Ancient Christian Writers* (London: Longmans, Green, 1963), 61–62.

15. From the verb *aggello* (here aor. ptc. fem.) used for Mary's proclamation are derived the nouns *aggelos* (angel) and *aggelia* (good news, message). It is used in John 1:15 of the gospel itself and in 1 John 3:11 of the command to love the brethren. BAG (p. 7) applies it to the Easter message proclaimed by Mary. The noun *euaggelion* (gospel) comes from the same root.

16. Thus P. K. Sarpong observes: "This is done, for example, in the northern part of Ghana. When such pacts of blood have been made, nothing can break the bond of fidelity between the two friends." In a talk on "Inculturation" given to the members of the Indigenous West African Religious Union (IWARU) at St. Louis, Kumasi, 3 Jan. 1987; mimeographed, 7.

17. Cf. T. Okure, "Biblical Perspectives on Women: Eve, the Mother of All the Living, Gen. 3:20," in *Voices from the Third World* (Philippine Edition 8/2, 1985), 17–24, esp. 23; "Women in the Bible," in *With Passion and Compassion: Third World Women Doing Theology,* ed. V. Fabella and. M. A. Oduyoye (Maryknoll, NY: Orbis, 1988), 51, 56–57.

3

RISING WITH MARY: RE-VISIONING A FEMINIST THEOLOGY OF THE CROSS AND RESURRECTION

Joy Ann McDougall (USA)

Pioneers are those persons who not only blaze a new path, but also leave signposts for those that follow to pick up their trail and travel farther along their way. Feminist theologian Elisabeth Moltmann-Wendel certainly fits this description. She helped to ignite the feminist theological debate in Germany in the 1970s when she brought insights from the American feminist liberationist movement back to her home context. Moltmann-Wendel did not simply import the American feminist movement; she inculturated it. She helped form a grassroots women's movement among the Protestant churches in Germany and fostered academic dialogue through lectures and workshops at the annual national church gathering, *Kirchentag*, and by co-founding the European Society for Women in Theological Research, a unique forum in which women across Europe could gather to share their research. In her own numerous books Moltmann-Wendel has pursued a wide-ranging theological agenda, uncovering Good News in the various New Testament traditions about the women around Jesus, drawing attention to the body as central to a holistic and ecologically sensitive theological anthropology, and more recently claiming redemptive possibilities in the various patterns of women's friendships. While Moltmann-Wendel opened new frontiers in feminist theology, she also did not hesitate to challenge this fledging movement, even when she found herself paddling upstream.

This essay focuses on one of these critical challenges, one which has not often featured in the foreground of Moltmann-Wendel's research, but in which she identified a mounting danger in feminist theology and sounded a warning bell. In the late 1980s, Moltmann-Wendel published a brief essay with the provocative title, "Is There a Feminist Theology of the Cross?" In her essay Moltmann-Wendel surveyed the landscape of feminist liberationist theology in the USA and Germany at the time, particularly the works of American theologians Carter Heyward, Rita Nakashima Brock, and that of the European theologians, Elga Sorge and Regula Strobel, and drew attention to their outright rejection of a theology of the cross. As Moltmann-Wendel quickly acknowledged, there are certainly more than enough grounds for their feminist critique. As she remarked in her typical matter-of-fact manner, "the cross as it is often preached has often had fatal consequences for women."[1]

And yet, this feminist consensus against the theology of the cross did not sit well with this Reformed theologian. In particular, she challenged three feminist objections to the cross. First, feminist theologians often interpret the cross event as sadomasochistic, emphasizing the Father's violent murdering of his own Son as the means through which to redeem humanity. Moltmann-Wendel points out that while Paul does present God as the agent of the crucifixion, in the gospel accounts it is the human being Judas who hands Jesus over to his death. What one has to grapple with in the gospels, she argues, is that enigmatic *paradidonai*, the surrendering of the Son as the critical moment in the passion story. It appears, concludes Moltmann-Wendel, that "the giving and enduring of pain" by the Godhead must somehow belong to the enigma of the cross-event.[2]

Second, feminist theologians often respond to the violence of the cross by re-mythologizing the story with the help of goddess myths. For example, she recalls one such story of the goddess Inana journeying into the underworld and, by means of a birth-like death, redeeming the world from death. Moltmann-Wendel does not mince words in criticizing such efforts to re-mythologize the gospel. For her, they amount to a dangerous de-politicization of the crucifixion; what disappears is the "violence of the death of Jesus as an act of the brutal power of the state."[3] Here, too, she warns that the feminist account of redemption risks skipping over a crucial moment of the New Testament account: "the dereliction of Jesus expressed in the cry: why have you forsaken me?"[4]

Third and finally, feminists argue that the bloody sacrifice of the cross establishes a dangerous paradigm for women's discipleship, "an ethic of obedience and subjection," which often propels women to accept exploitation and oppression.[5] Rather than focusing on Jesus' obedience unto death, feminists turn instead to his life and action, to his healing ministry and his relations of mutuality as the key to redemption.

While Moltmann-Wendel agrees wholeheartedly with feminist efforts to anchor in Jesus' ministry an "ethics of reciprocity," she questions whether an exclusive focus on Jesus' life ends up reducing redemption to human beings' moral action.[6] Are we being asked, she wonders skeptically, "to place our hope in the hands of human beings themselves?"[7]

Moltmann-Wendel's three criticisms all underscore the same point: feminist theology's rejection of the theology of the cross appears not fully consistent with the depth and complexity of the biblical witness and limits the most painful realities and hopes of human existence. Moreover, she poses a disquieting question to her feminist sisters: "The women's concept of an absolutely non-violent religion must ask itself whether it is overlooking reality in its dream and taking refuge in a life-of-Jesus without perceiving the death of Jesus."[8] "May there no longer be any despair in feminist theology?"[9] In other words, is feminist theology destined to become a theology without the cross?

Fortunately these were not her final words in her essay. Moltmann-Wendel offers three brief constructive proposals for how feminist theologians might shift away from a narrow focus on atoning sacrifice and the forgiveness of sins toward a life-giving theology of the cross—one that could do better justice to the biblical witness and to women's experiences. First, she encourages feminists to pay closer attention to the witness of the women gathered at the cross, and how they reflect the compassionate solidarity of women throughout history with the suffering ones.[10] Second, Moltmann-Wendel recalls the overwhelming positive response from women to the Christa sculpture, a depiction of Christ in female form that had also spawned considerable controversy. The Christa sculpture gives iconic form to the manifold sufferings of women in history, many in which Christianity has been sadly complicit. Here, too, Moltmann-Wendel encourages her feminist colleagues to do the constructive work of tending to women's dangerous memories of their own sufferings, and to find ways to heighten their visibility. Third, and most provocatively, she insists that feminist theology attend to the paradoxical way in which the gospels speak at once of the fear and the Godforsakenness of the cross, and of the startling experience of the women who meet the resurrected one on Easter morning. Perhaps feminists can rediscover in the dialectic of the cross and resurrection "a sign of salvation that we *can* erect out of death and nothingness and transplant into new spheres."[11]

On my reading of her essay, Moltmann-Wendel invites feminist theologians to develop a more inclusive representation of humanity in the cross-event, one in which the androcentrism of the tradition is "exposed" and "reformed" through careful biblical exegesis and deepened existential reflection on the life-experiences of women. In so doing, her work embodies two key tenets of the Reformation: to go back to the biblical sources (*ad fontes*) and to attend more fully to the testimony of the priesthood of all believers—in this case the witness of women to untold sufferings and to their courage to stand their ground at the suffering cross. Indeed, Moltmann-Wendel's brief proposals have turned out to be quite prescient. If one looks at developments in feminist, womanist, mujerista, and Latina christologies over the past twenty years, [one finds that] an enormous amount of theological attention has been devoted to reflecting on how women's diverse sorrows as well as the sacrifice of their bodies and of their spirits can be mirrored in the cross-event. We might think of Elizabeth Johnson's sorrowful witness at the end of her work, *She Who Is*, in which she rehearses a litany of remembrance written for the midwives, healers, mothers, and young girls all suspected of witchcraft and murdered brutally during the Inquisition.[12] Serene Jones's more recent work, *Trauma and Grace*, offers a moving account of women survivors of violence finding solace and strength in a mysterious exchange between themselves and Christ in the ritual of a passion play.[13]

This essay builds on the one of Moltmann-Wendel's three proposals that has received the least attention thus far in feminist theology: what might we discover afresh about the meaning of redemption by attending to the witness of the women on Easter morning following the desolation of the cross-experience? How might feminist theology attend to women's particular experiences of Godforsakenness—what is sometimes described as women's "dark night of the soul"—without being imprisoned by it? In particular, can the startling shock of the empty tomb on Easter morning provide a clue to the rising into new life of freedom and flourishing that women fervently seek?

In what follows, I begin my theological work by stepping back and looking first at the problem of sin in contemporary feminist theology. Only when we grapple with specific forms of alienation, cycles of exploitation, and broken relationships from which women yearn for redemption, does the feminist quest to revision a theology of the cross and resurrection life gain existential urgency.

The Bondage of the Eye/I: Re-visioning the Condition of Sin

Arguably, no doctrine has been more central to feminist theology than that of sin. In the North American context, it was the issue of sin that sparked the second wave of feminist theology as Valerie Saiving, Judith

Plaskow, Rosemary Radford Ruether, among others, challenged the androcentric notion of sin as pride that had become the status quo in modern theology. How could sin depicted as boastful arrogance or self-aggrandizing ego describe the dilemmas of women who more often struggle with exaggerated humility, permeable or diffuse ego boundaries, and, in some cases, the failure to become a self altogether?[14] Not only does this picture of pride "miss the mark," but it compounds the problem of sin for women; it conjures up false guilt and self-blame that imprisons women further into unhealthy patterns of self-sacrifice and self-abnegation. If the theological tradition needs reform, there is no more critical place to begin than with the troubled doctrine of sin.

The doctrine of sin is indispensable to feminist theology, however, for quite a different reason. As Rebecca Chopp points out, feminist theology relies on "an implicit doctrine of sin." Feminist theology is predicated on the assumption that something is drastically wrong. More specifically, sin is identified with patriarchy.[15] Behind this theological critique of patriarchy lies a classical Protestant understanding of sin as idolatry—the placing of one's trust in a self-created false god instead of in a gracious God. The idols of patriarchy are the dominant patterns of gender hierarchy—male over female, spirit over matter, history over nature—all of which falsely claim our allegiance instead of belief in a God who is life-affirming and beneficent to all human beings, and as such subverts such false dichotomies. As a pernicious and all-encompassing idolatry, patriarchy demands a high price from women and men—it exploits their life-energies, diminishes their creative potential, and can ultimately rob them of emotional and physical well-being. As Serene Jones describes it, there are multiple faces to women's experiences of oppression—exploitation of women's labor, marginalization of their status, gendered power dynamics in institutions, and violence. While women may not suffer acutely and all the time from these different forms of oppression, they are familiar faces to most women, for they greet them regularly in the workplace, in their churches, and in the intimacy of their families.

A key current running through contemporary feminist theology is the recognition that the evils of patriarchy are more than unjust social structures [for] which one needs institutional remedy. They are also evils that deeply distort the depth structures of women's psyches, their language-worlds, and very patterns of thought. Again as Serene Jones puts it, gendered forms of oppression have a "total hold" on our existence; they go "all the way down."[16]

Given the depth and interdependence of these distortions, feminist theology would do well, in my view, to recover the notion of "original sin"—not in the sense of a "first sin" of our progenitors transmitted through sexual relations, but "original" in the sense of a radical and universal distortion that infects the whole human condition. Sexism is a continuous corrupting force that reaches down to the depths of our personal identity formation, captivating our minds, siphoning our emotional energies, and impeding the pursuit of our callings. When we appeal to the idea of original sin, feminist theologians affirm that women are born into a world with distorted gender roles, expectations, and demands not of our making, but which we nevertheless embody and pass on. In other words, we become complicit in this distorted gendered economy without conscious choice. We are always and everywhere subject to, and the subjects of, forces of sexism—its victims and its perpetrators.

Note that affirming this universal solidarity in sin does not do away with personal responsibility or afford us an excuse not to take ethical action against sexist institutions and rituals. Rather, solidarity in sin recognizes the insidious character of such distortions and their ability to reproduce from generation to generation and from one culture to another. From this perspective of gender, oppression is more than a passing cultural phenomenon; it is a perduring idolatry that cuts to the heart of the broken and unjust relationships in which men and women forge their daily existence.

Finally, I want to appeal to the notion of original sin not only to underscore the gravity and undertow of patriarchy, but also to insist that patriarchy is a theological issue. Patriarchy represents a profound distortion and idolatrous refusal of God's beneficent will for all creatures; it is a diminution and contradiction of our true self—a fall away from the goodness and flourishing that God intends for all of God's creatures. In other words, with the language of original sin and fall, I contest a purely immanent analysis of sexism that focuses attention solely on the harmful gender realities within the social order. Such an immanent analysis risks overconfidence in humankind's ability to remedy this distortion through our own redemptive work—a moral utopianism against which Moltmann-Wendel rightfully cautioned her feminist friends.

While a feminist re-definition of original sin is productive, I contend that the classic Western description of the condition of sin as "the bondage of the will" is less helpful. Of course, the will is always engaged in distorting patterns of existence; as human agents we enact or commit actual concrete sins, including gender oppression, through our actions or failure to act. And yet, the kind of distortions and injustices that feminists seek to expose are not well described in terms of the will, that is, as the result of either an agonistic overactive will or a passive compliant one. The gendered spirals of violence and violation that mar human relations and institutions elude such titrations of the will. Appeals to the will do not explain many structural sins, which resist assigning individual responsibility and therefore culpability. Moreover, describing the human condition in terms of the "bondage of the will" creates a double bind: women are either blamed for their own victimization or deprived of the personal agency necessary to resist patriarchy's force.

Instead, the gendered condition of sin can better be described as a dual "bondage of the eye/I." Here, I am building on an insight drawn from Protestant theologian Kathryn Tanner, namely that sin can be quite helpfully understood as a blockage or blindness to the reality of God's overflowing good gifts to oneself or others.[17] In sin, human beings blind themselves (or are blinded) to the boundless possibilities of receiving God's gifts, including seeing themselves as a "good gift," and to the human vocation of distributing these good gifts to others. Extending Tanner's notion, I propose that feminist theology describe the complex personal and structural forms of gender oppression in terms of the double-edged metaphor of "bondage of the eye/I." The "bondage of the eye" describes how personal agency, gender constructions, and social structures collude to block women's clear vision of their own grace-filled identities. The "bondage of the eye" signifies women's inability to see through the inherited oppressive gender roles, which deceive women because they appear as natural realities rather than as social fabrications. I call this "bondage" because the problem is far more than a fleeting mistake or temporary moment of ignorance; it is a profound distortion of the gender economy that should govern a good creation. At the same time, the "bondage of the eye" also describes the condition of those who perpetuate and exploit gendered hierarchies (for example a man whose androcentrism distorts his perceptions of women's nature, their desires, and capacities). Finally, "bondage of the eye" applies equally well to numerous institutions that turn a blind eye to patriarchal structures, for example the significant wage disparities that exist between women and men in most professions.

The other side of this double-edged metaphor, "bondage of the I," describes the fallout from gender oppression: the captivity of one's self to the desires, the expectations, and the needs of others. Women often experience themselves as imprisoned in gender roles that undermine the possibility of flourishing in life-vocations. This imprisonment takes the form of both psychological and social bondage. For example, women are held hostage by the deep lack of self-worth cultivated by unsafe domestic situations or else by the "tyranny of slenderness" promulgated by the media. More visibly, social forms of bondage, such as limited access to education, food, or, in the worst scenarios, the violation of women's bodies, remain the tragic lot of women worldwide.

Why should contemporary feminist theology retain the language of "bondage to sin" at all? Why retain an aspect of the doctrine of sin that seems to undermine women's agency and their ability to resist gendered oppression? One urgent reason is that this language of "bondage" underscores the imprisoning nature of gender troubles. The image of captivity illumines the insidious hold that gender constructions, that is, gender expectations, stereotypes, and power relations, have on women's and men's bodies, minds, and souls. Here, I return to an insight of Moltmann-Wendel's. The twofold metaphor of the "bondage of the eye/I" testifies to the real despair and Godforsakenness that often accompany women's concrete sufferings—sufferings that refuse moral or social remedy. Many women experience profound abjection in their lack of self-development, the loss of family, and the lack of realistic hope for their flourishing, an abjection that demands an outcry against God: How can you have turned me over to such a cruel fate?

RISING WITH MARY: RELEASE FROM THE BONDAGE OF THE EYE/I

With this notion of the "bondage of the Eye/I" in hand, I turn back now to the question of a feminist theology of redemption. Is there a feminist account of the cross and resurrection that can help disclose this "bondage of the Eye/I" and spring us free from its captivity? What might risen life look like as redemption from this gendered bondage to sin?

The first clue Moltmann-Wendel offers in her essay is not to rush too quickly to a feminist theology of empowerment, bypassing over in silence the despair and Godforsakenness witnessed at the cross. The cross opens up a unique holding-space for women's painful testimony to the ills of patriarchy, to women's cries of disbelief and lamentations over violence endured, their precious life-energies squandered, and to relationships torn apart by the gendered bondage of sin. Dwelling at the foot of the cross neither romanticizes nor valorizes such suffering; rather, it offers bold testimony that women's deepest wounds are not hidden from God's sight. Moreover, by joining women's tears of despair to Jesus' cry of abandonment on the cross, women do more than mourn and protest. They inscribe their unique life-stories onto the body of Christ and stake their claim to his inclusive representation, his taking up of their particular sufferings—their fear, betrayal, and separation from God into the life of God.

This cannot be the whole of the story of redemption, however. To remain frozen at the cross signifies nothing other than ongoing bondage to that suffering. The present moment of grief, lament, and mourning holds us fast without the possibility of a different present or a genuine future. Here, too, Moltmann-Wendel's insights are helpful. She directs us to the women at the empty tomb: what might women discover here about their passage out of despair into new life, and about the life-long task of living into that resurrected life?

As I pondered her suggestion, I discovered some much-needed help in Rowan Williams's extraordinary reading of Mary Magdalene's encounter with Jesus at the empty tomb in John 20. Mary wakes early on Sunday morning to go to the tomb. We know that she walks there with the heavy footfall of inconsolable grief. She has stood and watched with the other women at the cross. She has seen and smelled the signs of Jesus' death and knows what now to expect—a tomb holding her beloved teacher's body and the piercing pain of her loss. At the tomb her despair is sharpened. Even the body is gone. It, too, has been cruelly taken away with no hope of return. And what do we discover here? As Williams astutely remarks, John confronts us not only with Jesus' death, but with Mary's own. In that moment, Mary's past, her present life, and her imagined future are all swept away: "Here we are in the world of dead souls . . . The grave of self is what is before us, the death of a sense of being valued, being loved, being given a place; to the dead Christ comes the robbed self."[18]

And then occurs that curious series of Mary's "turnings around" in John's gospel. First, Mary turns away from the tomb to run back and proclaim her horrible news to her fellow disciples: "The Lord's body is gone; now our despair, our forsakenness is complete." But then she turns back again, returning to the tomb, this time weeping openly in her grief. Now she moves even closer to the resurrection, peering into the tomb, but seemingly blind to what stands before her, the two angels marking the site of God's grace. They speak directly to her heart: "Why are you weeping? What are you looking for?" And she cries out with an even more personal confession: "*my* Lord is gone and I know not where he is to be found." Mary turns again, this time to be met by the very truth that she seeks. Here we realize that her blindness is complete, for she mistakes her beloved Lord for an utter stranger, the gardener who has carried his body away. We empathically listen as Mary's pleas for the return of "what once was" grow more insistent: "If you have done this, let me know where he is, and *I* will take him away."

We then arrive at the final turning around in the story. With an unusual economy of words, the stranger, who seems to have taken everything away, gives her everything back and more—he calls out her very name: "Mary." In that moment she comes to her senses. Mary's vision clears and at once she recognizes him: "Rabboni," a word of endearment, spills forth from her lips. She rushes toward him only to be stopped mid-track and turned around once again: "do not hold onto me, because I have not yet ascended to the Father." It is as if he says, "my story and yours are not complete; instead, you go forth, run quickly and tell the good news—that I am ascending to my father, your father, and my God is your God."

The redemption that Mary experiences in her encounter with the risen Jesus is difficult to put into words. Certainly there is a release from the bondage of her past, but it is clearly not from the chains of guilt, but seemingly from her shattered hopes and the narrow confines of her expectations. In the presence of the risen one, Mary rises up out of her blocked vision about her world, herself, and her God into a genuinely new life. This new life is one held utterly secure by the extravagant love of a God who recognizes her as a precious child—my father, your father. What returns to Mary here is the gift of her own identity, not as it once was, but a transformed identity crafted out of real hope, a hope that gives strength and clarity of vision. As Williams writes, "What Mary finds is that her name, her protest, her dissatisfaction with dissatisfaction are decisively vindicated. Mary is not dead because Jesus is not dead."[19] Even more, Mary rises up into a genuinely new future; she receives not only her past back, but also a commissioning that propels her into a future to proclaim and to embody that risen life to others.

Much more can be said, but let me close by suggesting that Mary's encounter with the resurrected Jesus holds profound insights about the workings of grace in women's lives and about what it means to break free from the imprisoning effects of patriarchy and the "bondage of the eye/I." First, there is the basic insight that coming to one's self occurs in the presence of God and as a gift of God, in which we see ourselves held fast as the precious children of God, as recipients of an inexhaustible and faithful love in the midst of the deepest deceptions and disappointments of human life. This is a deeply edifying truth because it grants to women a clear vision of one's goodness and inviolable worth in the midst of a myriad of gender distortions and destructive forces. At the same time, Mary's encounter with the risen stranger reminds us that grace is equally a disruptive and demanding presence in our midst, turning us around and confronting us with the diminished hopes that we bear about ourselves, our families, and the communities in which we continue to forge our identities. Rising with Mary means a letting go of well-worn and quite comfortable expectations of ourselves and others. This is a letting go that demands self-examination, forgiveness, and courage.

Finally, there is the critical insight that grace not only transforms the past, it reconfigures our present and engenders a new future—one with genuinely prophetic and creative power. Mary's encounter with the risen one is a deeply empowering vision, one that sends her forth with a tremendous vocation to be both an edifying and disruptive sign of grace to others. To borrow a familiar feminist phrase from Rebecca Chopp, rising with Mary means gaining "the power to speak": to speak a Word on behalf of life, a word of protest against the squandering of women's gifts, a word of affirmation for challenges met, and a word of visionary hope that counters the familiar faces of gender oppression. I am not suggesting that standing in solidarity with the risen Mary is a panacea for broken gender relations or a safe passageway around women's crosses, but it is an unquenchable source of hope for a world in which women and men are not condemned to an economy of domination and loss, but rather are granted delight, plenitude, and perfect freedom.

Notes

1. Elisabeth Moltmann-Wendel, "Is There a Feminist Theology of the Cross?" *God: His and Hers,* in Elisabeth Moltmann-Wendel and Jürgen Moltmann (New York: Crossroad, 1991), 77.

2. Ibid., 81.

3. Ibid., 83.

4. Ibid.

5. Ibid., 84.

6. Ibid.

7. Ibid., 85.

8. Ibid., 85–86.

9. Ibid., 83.

10. Ibid., 87.

11. Ibid., 91.

12. Elizabeth Johnson, *She Who Is: The Mystery of God in Feminist Theological Discourse* (New York: Crossroad, 1992), 262.

13. Serene Jones, *Trauma and Grace: Theology in a Ruptured World* (Louisville: Westminster John Knox, 2009), 75–83.

14. Mary Grey, "Falling into Freedom: Searching for a New Interpretation of Sin in Secular Society," *Scottish Journal of Theology* 47, no. 2 (1994): 234.

15. Rebecca Chopp, "Feminism and the Theology of Sin," *The Ecumenist* (1993): 12.

16. Serene Jones, *Feminist Theory and Christian Theology: Cartographies of Grace* (Minneapolis: Fortress, 2000), 104–5.

17. Kathryn Tanner, *Jesus, Humanity and the Trinity: A Brief Systematic Theology* (Minneapolis: Fortress, 2001), 46.

18. Rowan Williams, *Resurrection: Interpreting the Easter Gospel* (Cleveland: Pilgrim, 1982), 40.

19. Ibid.

II
SWEEPING OVERVIEWS

If one can say Christ comes to the oppressed and the oppressed especially hear him, then it is women within these marginal groups who are often seen both as the oppressed of the oppressed and also as those particularly receptive to the gospel. The dialogue at the well takes place not just with a Samaritan, but with a Samaritan woman. Not just a Syro-Phoenician, but a Syro-Phoenician woman is the prophetic seeker who forces Jesus to concede redemption to the non-Jews. Among the poor it is widows who are the exemplars of the most destitute; among the moral outcasts it is the prostitutes who represent the bottom of the list. This is not accidental...

Jesus as liberator calls for a renunciation and dissolution of the web of status relations by which societies have defined privilege and unprivilege. He speaks especially to outcast women, not as representatives of the "feminine," but because they are at the bottom of the network of oppression. His ability to be liberator does not reside in his maleness, but on the contrary, in the fact that he has renounced this system of domination and seeks to embody in his person the new humanity of service and empowerment.

Rosemary Radford Ruether, "Christology and Feminism: Can a Male Savior Save Women?" *To Change the World: Christology and Cultural Criticism*, 1981.

4

WOMEN AND CHRIST:
TOWARD INCLUSIVE CHRISTOLOGIES

Ellen Leonard (Canada)

Christology claims a universal significance for Christ. Contemporary
Christologies struggle with the implications of this claim, raising questions about the inclusivity of Christology from many perspectives, including questions arising from Jewish-Christian dialogue, dialogue
with other religions, and most recently ecological concerns. My focus is
on the inclusion of women in our understanding of Christology, and on
the impact of images of Christ on women's well-being.

   The image of Christ is ambiguous for many contemporary women,
serving as both a source of life and the legitimation of oppression.
Women have found and continue to find comfort, strength, and
courage through their faith in Christ, while at the same time the image
of Christ can be interpreted as a symbol of male dominance and female
submission. As women become aware of the patriarchal and androcentric bias of Christianity, the fact that the central symbol in Christianity
is a male Savior raises basic questions about the nature of humanity
and divinity. What is the significance of the maleness of Jesus? Does it
support the view of the male as normative humanity? Does it reveal
God as male? How has the symbol been used in the praxis of the community? Is it possible to develop a Christology that is non-androcen-
tric, a Christology that is truly inclusive of women and men?

   The history of Christian theology is not reassuring on this point.
Christ has generally been presented throughout the ages as the male revealer of a male God whose divine authority supports the patriarchal
structures of church and society. Nor does the present praxis of the
Christian churches encourage Christian feminists who hope to retrieve
the Christ symbol. Fundamentalist groups continue to preach the headship of Christ over the church in order to uphold male headship in the

family as well as in the church. The Orthodox and Roman Catholic Churches use the maleness of Jesus as a reason for not recognizing the leadership gifts of women. Ordained women in other churches suffer from the patriarchal patterns that endure not only within society but also in their churches.

A visit to the art gallery, where we are able to see how succeeding ages have imaged Christ, reinforces the view of the male as dominant, the female as supportive. The young mother is portrayed on her knees before her infant son while the sorrowful mother stands with other women at the foot of the cross. The message from all sides is that women's role is one of support for men. History, contemporary church praxis, and art all present images of Christ that legitimate the subordination of women. It is not surprising that for some contemporary women there is no place for Christ. Naomi Goldenberg expresses the conviction of these women: "Jesus Christ cannot symbolize the liberation of women. A culture that maintains a masculine image for its highest divinity cannot allow its women to experience themselves as the equals of its men. In order to develop a theology of women's liberation, feminists have to leave Christ and the Bible behind."[1]

Can women who have experienced Christ as a source of life, and who continue to find strength and courage in their own struggles for justice in the image of Christ, abandon the symbol that has shaped their religious response to life? What would Christology be like if it were truly inclusive? Perhaps even more important, how might popular devotion image Christ in ways that do not contribute to male domination? Can the central image of Christianity support the full personhood of women?

I speak as a middle class, white, anglophone Canadian. I cannot presume to speak for all women, but I have listened to some women's voices as they confront images of Christ and either reject or transform those images. These voices are not only North American, including Canadian voices of francophone, native, immigrant, and poor women, but are also Asian, African, and Latin American. This paper reflects on a portion of what I have heard. Part one will consider specific problems that the Christ symbol poses if one takes the experience of these women seriously. Constructive attempts to transform the image of Christ are presented in part two. Part three explores characteristics that must be found in any Christology if it is to be truly inclusive.

I. Feminist Critique of Christology

Studies of women's lives show that women's experience is pluralistic and deeply influenced not only by gender but also by race, class, and culture. Across all differences women's ways of being in the world, often ignored, denied, or subsumed under male experience, are becoming a resource for new understandings of human life and new insights into the Christian tradition. They raise central questions about the way that Christology has functioned and point to ways that it must be rethought.

Take, for example, the experience of being embodied. Within the Christian tradition female embodiment has been viewed in a largely negative way. Western theology has been based on a dualistic worldview that placed history over nature, soul over body, male over female. This polarized view identified women with bodiliness, closer to change and death, while connecting men ontologically with spirit, closer to rationality and the light of the divine. Female bodies were even viewed by some so-called church "fathers" as "the gateway to hell." Today a growing awareness of the sacredness of the female body leads to a rejection of both this philosophy and of the way it has framed christological doctrine. Rita Nakashima Brock articulates the problem with acuity: "The doctrine that only a perfect male form can incarnate God fully and be salvific makes our individual lives in female bodies a prison against God and denies our actual, sensual, changing selves as the locus of divine activity."[2]

One of the strongest reactions to the androcentric image of Christ is that of Mary Daly who in her 1973 book, *Beyond God the Father,* was already calling women to move "beyond Christolatry" to a world without models. She wrote: "As a uniquely masculine image and language for divinity loses credibility, so also the idea of a single divine incarnation in a human being of the male sex may give way in the religious consciousness to an increased awareness of the power of Being in all persons."[3] In response to those who admit that the Christ symbol has indeed been used in oppressive ways but that it need not be so used, Daly replied: "If the symbol can be used that way and in fact has a long history of being used that way, isn't this an indication of some inherent deficiency in the symbol itself?"[4] It is not just that the symbol is male, with the result that "If God is male, then the male is God."[5] The problem also lies in the way that the image of Jesus as sacrificial victim is destructive for women. The qualities that Christianity preaches as pertaining especially to women are those of a victim: sacrificial love, passive acceptance of suffering, humility, meekness, and so forth. Women are neither able to measure up to this impossible model nor, in the Catholic Church, to identify ritually with Christ's sacrifice as priests. "Thus doomed to failure even in emulating the Victim, women are plunged more deeply into victimization."[6]

The doctrine of the atonement raises special problems. Acutely aware of issues of domestic violence, Brock argues that the language of the Father handing over his Son to death sets up pattern of child abuse on a divinely-approved, cosmic scale. If the "father allows, or even inflicts, the death of his only perfect son,"[7] where can humans look for strength to resist such violence? It is all too easy for Christology to glorify suffering and to discourage the acceptance of personal responsibility for one's own life and that of others who are vulnerable. As women become autonomous subjects of history, the myths that have encouraged women to be passive victims within families and society are being shattered. Is Christology such a myth, or can it offer women the energy, courage, and hope to work for change and, if necessary, to move out of oppressive situations?

In light of these concerns, I will consider some efforts to rethink the central image of Christianity, addressing three questions in each case: Does this approach to Christology affirm female embodiment? Does it reject victimization based on patterns of domination and submission? Does it enable women to move from past oppression into a more hopeful present and future?

II. Transforming Images of Christ

To re-image Christ requires courage and creativity. [Like] the early Christian communities who remembered Jesus in many different ways according to their own situation and community needs, women today have embarked on new interpretations of Christ. In the early decades of the church no one image was adequate, and thus we find many different images and Christologies within the New Testament itself. This pluralism has continued throughout the tradition as succeeding ages transformed images of Christ according to their needs. In our day, as women reflect on Christ in the light of their gendered experience, new insights into the meaning of Jesus the Christ for the lives of twentieth-century women and men are emerging. Along with scholarly reflection, women's prayers, poems, songs, and stories also contribute to changing images of Christ and provide a resource for further insight. We turn now to five constructive attempts to work out an inclusive Christology.

Woman Christ

Images of the Christa, Christ imaged as female, and particularly as a crucified woman, provide strong visual evidence of the female imagination at work. Such an image carries a certain shocking power. This became evident in both New York and Toronto when sculptures of a crucified woman were presented to congregations.[8] The Christa invites the viewer to see Christ in a female body and to recognize that God suffers in the suffering of women. Women who have drawn strength from this image turn to Christ as one who was despised, who died as a criminal, and who willingly associated with the marginalized, including women. They see themselves not only as standing by the cross, but also as on the cross. Some query whether a Christology flowing from this image can help women to address structures of domination and submission. Perhaps it contributes to the victimization of women? To the contrary, some argue, identifying suffering women with Christ on the cross opens up a source of empowerment.

Other womanly images of Christ have a long history in the Christian tradition. There are references to Christ as mother in the writings of Clement, Origin, Irenaeus, John Chrysostom, Ambrose, Augustine, Bernard, Anselm, and numerous other traditional theologians. Christ as woman was particularly popular during the Middle Ages as a way of emphasizing the humanity of Christ. The prevailing dualistic worldview associated divinity with maleness, humanity with femaleness. Lacking a human father, Christ took his flesh from Mary, a fact that led a number of mystics to refer to the flesh that Christ put on as in some sense female. In her study of medieval writers Caroline Walker Bynum shows that both men and women saw the female body as fleshly and connected with food. Both men and women described Christ's body in its suffering as a mother giving birth and feeding her children from her own body.[9]

The fourteenth-century theologian Julian of Norwich developed the image of Jesus as Mother in unparalled fashion:

> But our true Mother Jesus, he alone bears us for joy and for endless life, blessed may he be. So he carries us within him in love and travail, until the full time when he wanted to suffer the sharpest thorns and cruel pains that ever were or will be, and at the last he died. And when he had finished, and he had borne us so for bliss, still all this could not satisfy his wonderful love.[10]

Our medieval sisters and brothers saw human mothering as a sacrament of divine love. Their view was based on a stereotype of the female or mother as generative and sacrificial, bringing forth her child in pain, and as loving, tender, and nurturing, feeding her child from her own body. They were able to express the mysteries of the Word made flesh, of Christ's sacrificial death, and of the Eucharist through the lens of human mothering. In doing so they gave meaning to their own lives, especially to the reality of suffering and of service.

The image of Christ as woman offers one avenue for taking women's embodiment seriously. Powerful symbols of Jesus' nurturing love for humanity, his saving work on Calvary, and his gift of nourishing grace in the Eucharist arise from women's experience of bodily giving life to others. In third-world countries where women often bear the total responsibility for children and family, the work of finding food and the water and fuel with which to cook it are exhausting activities. Jesus as mother expresses a strong sense of relatedness to these women in their struggle for survival, perhaps one of the reasons that our medieval sisters and brothers as well as our third-world sisters have found it a helpful image for Christ.

Note that for the most part this first pattern attributes a conventionally female function to Christ while he remains basically a male human being. In the search for an inclusive Christology, I turn now from an idea that includes the female in the still predominant male humanity of Jesus to a Christology that draws Christ's male humanity into a female image of divinity.

Christ as Incarnate Wisdom
A number of scholars have noted the biblical use of the female image Sophia as an image for Jesus. Elizabeth Johnson provides a careful study of the wisdom tradition where this attribution can be found.[11] She shows how the Jewish tradition used personified wisdom or Sophia to describe God's creative and saving involvement with the world. Johnson traces the relationship of Sophia to goddess material and demonstrates how the biblical writers were able to use this material while maintaining their monotheistic faith.

The communities of Jewish Christians drew on this Sophia tradition as a way to describe their experience of Jesus of Nazareth. Beginning with Paul and the early christological hymns, they identified Jesus with divine Sophia. Whereas the earlier Q material interpreted Jesus as the child of Sophia, Matthew saw Jesus' actions embodying Sophia's ways, the deeds of the Christ being equated with Wisdom's deeds. Starting with the Prologue, John's gospel continues this identification of Jesus with Sophia. Although the Prologue replaces the female term Sophia with the male term Logos, its descriptions find precedent verse for verse in the pre-Christian wisdom traditions. Rather than portraying incarnation as the act by which an invisible and all-powerful male person becomes visible in the world, the Sophia tradition "reflects the depths of the mystery of God who has approached us in Jesus Christ and points the way to an inclusive interpretation of the humanity of Jesus in genuine solidarity with the whole human race, women as well as men."[12]

Wisdom Christology offers a bracing alternative to a male-centered view of Jesus. Besides categories of Father and Son, the New Testament presents Jesus in wisdom categories of divine Sophia and her child who is Sophia incarnate. While recognizing the maleness of Jesus as part of his historical specificity, the distorted theological use of the maleness of Jesus is challenged by the blend of female and male imagery in Jesus/Sophia. All who are disciples of Jesus/Sophia can do the works of Sophia.

Johnson takes seriously women's experiences of embodiment, oppression, and interrelatedness. In particular she sees the need to develop ways of relating to one another that are non-hierarchical and inclusive, and she recognizes the power of images in addressing structures of dominance and submission. Consequently, she develops a resource from within the tradition for thinking about Jesus and God in ways that are inclusive. Wisdom Christology can be a contribution to "the redesign of Christology in the face of enormous cultural changes in the position of women."[13]

We have seen how Woman Christ introduces female characteristics into the male image of Christ, while Christ as incarnate Wisdom includes Jesus' male humanity in the female image of the divine. Both are attempts at inclusivity. However, in societies where maleness is the norm the results are not inclusive. I turn now to a different approach. Instead of attempting to resolve the male-female dilemma, it will consider how Jesus actually functions within the tradition.

Jesus as Prototype
Elisabeth Schüssler Fiorenza claims that Jesus and the praxis of the earliest church should function as prototype rather than as archetype for contemporary life. Thus they become a possible *resource* for women's struggle for liberation rather than an authoritative source. Schüssler Fiorenza uncovers this resource through her reconstruction of Christian origins using feminist critical hermeneutics. The hermeneutical center of her feminist biblical interpretation is women-church, which she describes as the movement of self-identified women and women-identified men in

biblical religion. The experience of contemporary women struggling for liberation and wholeness is the hermeneutical principle for critically evaluating biblical texts.[14]

Schüssler Fiorenza presents the Jesus movement as a renewal movement within Judaism. She asks what was it like for a woman in Palestine to be involved with Jesus and his movement. Jesus' vision of the *basileia* was one of inclusive wholeness that found expression particularly in his table community with the poor, with sinners, with tax collectors and prostitutes. Jesus is Sophia's prophet who, through his teaching and his healing miracles, calls forth a discipleship of equals. At the heart of his proclamation of the *basileia* of God is liberation from patriarchal structures. Schüssler Fiorenza argues that Jesus' use of father as a name for God does not legitimate patriarchal structures but is a critical subversion of domination. The *basileia* vision of Jesus is a feminist vision that "calls all women to wholeness and selfhood, as well as to solidarity with those women who are the impoverished, the maimed, and the outcasts of society and church."[15] In this feminist historical reconstruction, Jesus is "the woman-identified man" who called forth a community of the discipleship of equals.

Unfortunately, the church did not live up to the vision of Jesus. Patriarchal structures were soon imposed on the followers of Jesus, even within the period covered by New Testament writing. While Schüssler Fiorenza traces the growing patriarchy of the church and its ministry, she also focuses on women as paradigms of true discipleship in the gospels of Mark and John, seeing in these gospels indications of the apostolic leadership of women.

Schüssler Fiorenza has reclaimed the gospels for women by showing that women were at the center of the movement around Jesus and of the early Christian communities. She argues that the discipleship of equals was submerged and often oppressed by ecclesiastical patriarchy, but that it has never ceased to exist. It challenges contemporary patterns of male domination and female submission.

Jesus as Iconoclastic Prophet

The fact remains that Jesus the Christ was historically a male human being. Rosemary Radford Ruether asks the important soteriological question: "Can a male saviour save women?"[16] Her own answer to this question is focused on the Jesus of the Synoptic gospels, whom she sees as an iconoclastic prophet speaking on behalf of the marginalized and despised groups of society and challenging the social and religious hierarchical structures of his day. Women in the gospels often represented the lowly, the last who will be first in the reign of God. One thinks of the Samaritan woman, the Syro-Phoenician woman, the widows and prostitutes. Jesus brought a message of liberation to such persons.

For Ruether, while Jesus' maleness has no ultimate theological significance, it does have a symbolic significance within societies of patriarchal privilege. In the way he privileged non-persons and especially in his self-emptying death on the cross, he subverted the masculine ideal of power. "In this sense Jesus as the Christ, the representative of liberated humanity and the liberating Word of God, manifests the *kenosis of patriarchy*, the announcement of the new humanity through a lifestyle that discards hierarchical caste privilege and speaks on behalf of the lowly."[17]

According to Ruether and other liberation theologians, what is most significant about Jesus is his message of good news to the poor. It is this message which needs to be carried on by his followers, for Christ as redemptive person and Word of God is not confined to the historical Jesus. Jesus is seen as paradigm for liberating personhood, but Christ includes all of redemptive humanity. Ruether insists that the image of Christ must take on ever new forms, forms as woman, as black and brown woman, as impoverished and despised woman of those peoples who are the underside of Christian imperialism.

Both Schüssler Fiorenza and Ruether have found in the Jesus of the Synoptics a figure sympathetic toward women. His life and teachings challenged, and continue to challenge, all structures of dominance and submission. It was a challenge that led ultimately to his death. However, the fact remains that this saving figure is a male figure in the past. By presenting Jesus of Nazareth either as prototype or as anticipatory of redeemed humanity, Schüssler Fiorenza and Ruether leave room for future revelations of the divine in our sisters as well as our brothers.

Christa/Community
Rita Nakashima Brock criticizes Ruether's iconoclastic Christ as a unilateral hero and liberator who finds his strength in a private relationship with his Abba. Seeing the need for mutuality in relationships, she looks for a Jesus who draws on the community and together "they cocreate liberation and healing from brokenheartedness."[18] She relocates Christ in the community of which Jesus is one historical part. The community as a whole generates the erotic power that heals and thus becomes the locus for redemption. She chooses the term "Christa/ Community" to describe this reality. For Brock, Christa/ Community is not limited to the historical Jesus even during his lifetime, but always includes the whole community.

Brock rejects understandings of Jesus' death as necessary and divinely willed, claiming that such beliefs mute our ability to be angry about unnecessary suffering. With liberation theologians, she understands Jesus' death as a political act that was the result of the way Jesus chose to live for himself and the people he loved. The disciples did not allow Jesus' death to be the end of their community but rather they remembered his presence and affirmed divine power amidst themselves. In Brock's words: "The Christa/ Community incarnated and reincarnates the power which restores heart."[19]

Rita Nakashima Brock speaks out of her own experience of embodiment as an Asian American woman of color who has experienced oppression by both race and gender. Her project is to salvage and transform Christianity as a faith that has nurtured as well as wounded her. A strong sense of interrelationship underlies her christological enterprise, which locates healing in the erotic power of love flowing between persons.

III. Toward Inclusive Christologies

The approaches we have considered are not complete Christologies, but rather attempts to re-image Jesus who is the Christ in ways that take women's experience seriously. Woman Christ and Christ as Incarnate Wisdom try to make room for the female within the male image. The other attempts consider how Jesus functions in the tradition. Some authors, such as Ruether, emphasize the historical Jesus, distinguishing him from later christological developments. Schüssler Fiorenza and Nakashima Brock de-emphasize the historical Jesus and stress instead the community of his disciples, particularly his women disciples. Jesus is seen as part of a community rather than as an isolated individual, an approach supported by contemporary scripture studies, which insist that it is impossible to separate Jesus from the communities of faith who remembered him and whose witness is expressed in the writings of the New Testament.

Whether the primary focus is the historical Jesus and his teaching or the community of faith that gathered around him during his life and continued to live by his Spirit after his death and resurrection, the hermeneutical principle of interpretation is the same: the reality of contemporary women moving from a position of inferiority to full personhood. Both the praxis of Jesus and that of the early communities of disciples can support this movement of liberation.

From the work that has been done, is it possible to suggest criteria for inclusive Christologies? I believe that all contemporary Christologies need to take seriously the half of humanity which has often been silenced and made invisible in theological reflection. No Christology stands alone. It is built upon an anthropology and forms the basis for an ecclesiology. To be inclusive, Christology must be built upon an inclusive anthropology and be reflected in an inclusive ecclesiology.

Christology influences how we understand humanness, how we cope with suffering, and how we live with one another and with nature in our world. In considering criteria for inclusive Christologies I turn to women's experiences of embodiment, oppression, and interrelatedness that have been woven throughout this essay. In relation to female embodiment, I see the need for an inclusive anthropology that accords full humanity to the female person as embodied spirit and as revelatory of the divine. The experience of female oppression must recognize and name women's suffering and evoke an active response that offers hope and energy for change. The experience of interrelatedness raises issues concerning ecclesiology, the nature and mission of the church, and our relationship to one another and to our world. Patterns of submission and domination must be recognized and new ways of relating discovered.

The maleness of Jesus need not be an insurmountable problem. The fact that the historical Jesus was male should be seen as one particularity along with the fact that he lived in the first century and was Jewish. Diane Tennis expresses the experience of many women when she refers to Jesus as "the one utterly reliable man in the lives of many women." For her, Jesus' maleness has a positive dimension. "It delivers a judgment on patriarchy through the model of self-giving for men, and transcends patriarchy by legitimatizing experimental authority for women."[20] An inclusive Christology recognizes the maleness of the historical Jesus but does not equate maleness with humanity.

An inclusive Christology will be based on interdependence and mutuality. It will not support an ecclesiology that assigns responsibility to one class of men who can represent Christ, while all other persons are expected to be silent and submissive. Rather, an inclusive Christology will empower all persons to be responsible for one another and for our world. While recognizing the significance of the past, it will not be locked into the past but open to new ways of responding to this new moment in human history. An inclusive Christology that is empowering for all women and men will also be reflected in the praxis of inclusive Christian communities. Only then will Christ and Christianity be experienced as "good news" for women.

Notes

1. Naomi Goldenberg, *The Changing of the Gods: Feminism and the End of Traditional Religions* (Boston: Beacon Press, 1979), 22.

2. Rita Nakashima Brock, "The Feminist Redemption of God," in *Christian Feminism: Visions of a New Humanity*, ed. Judith Weidman (San Francisco: Harper & Row, 1984), 68.

3. Mary Daly, *Beyond God the Father: Toward a Philosophy of Women's Liberation* (Boston: Beacon Press, 1985), 71.

4. Ibid., 72.

5. Ibid., 19.

6. Ibid., 77.

7. Rita Nakashima Brock, *Journeys by Heart: A Christology of Erotic Power* (New York: Crossroad, 1988), 56.

8. The "Crucified Woman" by Almuth Lutkenhaus was hung in Bloor Street United Church in Toronto in 1979. In 1986 it was presented to Emmanuel College, Toronto, and placed on the grounds. The *Christa* by Edwina Sandys was shown in the Episcopal Cathedral of St. John the Divine in New York in 1984. For details concerning these sculptures and reactions to them see Doris Dyke, "Crucified Woman: Art and the Experience of Faith," *Toronto Journal of Theology* 5 (Fall 1989): 161–69; and Edwina Hunter, "Reflections on the Christa," *Journal of Women and Religion* 4 (1985): 22–32.

9. Caroline Walker Bynum, *Holy Feast and Holy Fast* (Berkeley: University of California Press, 1987), 260–76.

10. Julian of Norwich, *Showings*, ed. Edmund Colledge and James Walsh (New York: Paulist Press, 1978), 297–98.

11. Elizabeth A. Johnson, "Jesus the Wisdom of God," *Ephemerides Theologiae Lovanienses* 61 (1985): 261–94.

12. Ibid., 284.

13. Ibid., 294.

14. Elisabeth Schüssler Fiorenza, *In Memory of Her: A Feminist Theological Reconstruction of Christian Origins* (New York: Crossroad, 1983), 3–95 and 343–51.

15. Ibid., 153.

16. Rosemary Radford Ruether, *Sexism and God-Talk: Toward a Feminist Theology* (Boston: Beacon Press, 1983), 116–38.

17. Ibid., 137.

18. Brock, *Journeys by Heart*, 67.

19. Ibid., xv.

20. Diane Tennis, "Reflections on the Maleness of Jesus," *Cross Currents* 28 (1978): 137–40.

5

"BUT WHO DO YOU SAY THAT I AM?": AN AUSTRALIAN FEMINIST RESPONSE

Elaine Wainwright (Australia)

The opening question—"Who do you say that I am?"—has echoed from the gospel text (Matt 16:15/Mark 8:29/Luke 9:20) across the history of Christian theologizing and has received myriads of answers depending on the social location of the various respondents and the way each has interpreted either the question and/or the gospel text in which it is embedded. That these responses have been exceedingly varied even when focusing on the same gospel story already alerts us to the partial, the fragmentary nature of any attempt to answer the question, not only because of the complexity and even "mystery" involved in the very question, but also because of the nature of the interpretive process, a point which has often been ignored.[1]

In this essay, which takes its place in an issue of *Pacifica* which explores feminism/s and theology in Australia and looks toward the next stage in that theologizing, I have chosen to focus on this question which has received little attention in Australian feminist theology to date, but which will, I believe, require the fruits of feminist theological imagination as Australian Christian communities take the next steps into the future. The essay will first lay out a necessarily limited overview of some of the key issues which the question has raised within feminist theology generally; it will situate the scant attention given to the question within Australian feminist theological studies in the context of this broader framework, and will conclude with some brief pointers as to how the question of this paper might be answered within an Australian feminist context.

59

A. THE CRISIS OF HISTORICAL NARRATIVE: ISSUES IN FEMINIST CHRISTOLOGY

Life experiences and critical analyses of these experiences by women around the globe have led to the recognition of the constructed nature of textual interpretation and meaning generally.[2] No longer, therefore, can the Christian scriptures or the christological discourses that have characterized Christian tradition be considered universal and value neutral but they are being seen as socio-rhetorical practices of particular readers in particular social locations. Below, I can only outline aspects of some of these productions or practices, especially those that have been and need to be problematized within the framework of a feminist re-reading of Jesus.

Within such an analysis, it is important not to universalize women's experience. The work of Jacquelyn Grant, Kwok Pui Lan, Virginia Fabella, Chung Hyun Kyung, Anne Pattel-Gray[3] and many other women of colour from a vast number of nations challenges any articulation of women's experience that is simply white, middle-class, and particular to a limited and somewhat privileged group of women. Listening to the voices, the experiences of women from different races, classes, ethnic and economic backgrounds will ensure that the analysis of these experiences is not undertaken simply on the basis of gender but rather on the basis of patriarchy or more particularly kyriarchy as a multi-dimensional form of oppression.[4]

1. "Ecce Homo!" — Behold the Man
The most resounding critique of traditional Christology is the centrality given to the maleness of Jesus, an issue which is at the heart of the feminist critique in Europe, Asia, the Americas and the Pacific. This in no way suggests that the actual Jesus of Galilee was not biologically male.[5] Indeed his biological maleness was a constitutive element of his identity, part of the "perfection and limitation of his historical contingency" as Elizabeth Johnson notes.[6] She goes on to say that "it is as intrinsic to his historical person as his familial, ethnic, religious, linguistic, and cultural particularity, his Galilean village roots and so forth." Elisabeth Schüssler Fiorenza has pointed out, however, that to make this claim immediately implicates both writer and reader in the socio-cultural construction of the sex/gender system within Western first-century and twentieth-century thought.[7] The problem is exacerbated when the maleness of Jesus is theologized in a way that diminishes or renders invisible women and the female, constructing a theological universe that

is androcentric and that supports ecclesial and socio-cultural practices which are exclusionary.

This is demonstrated in the opening paragraph of the 1987 Conference of Asian Women Doing Theology which clearly states that

> ...the classical ecclesiastic view is of God as male and of the Christ as the male image of God. In this traditional view, Jesus is a triumphal king and an authoritative High Priest. This traditional Christology has served to support a patriarchal religious consciousness in the Church and in theology. Traditional theology has justified and guaranteed male dominance over women and the subordinate status of the female.[8]

Significantly, within this statement, there is a critique of the hierarchical/kyriarchical images of "triumphal king" and "high priest" not just as male images underpinning patriarchy but [as] images which support the understanding of power as domination in a way which has led to class and race hierarchies within the patriarchal system.

A significant nuance to this critique is the possibility given us within the gospel narratives of imagining divine incarnation in the concrete particularities in history—in humanness, in relationships, in a seeking after what is of God, as well as a wide range of human qualities. Ironically, however, it is Jesus' maleness which is given universal significance while other particularities of his life are ignored or dismissed as particularities. As Monica Melanchthon says:

> neither the Jewishness of Jesus nor his physical presence in the first century community is particularized. His maleness is understood to be his humanity. His maleness is therefore particularised [sic] and emphasized to keep women away from ordination and meaningful participation in the life of the Church and community.[9]

Her insight sounds a warning note that in giving attention to gen-- der in a feminist reading of the Jesus character of the gospel story, care be taken that such a reading not separate the maleness of Jesus from his Jewishness and the many other aspects of his first-century context in a way that would continue the focus on that maleness. Judith Butler in her discussion of gender likewise draws attention to the danger of giving "ontological integrity" to gender terminology while ignoring its cultural and political construction.[10] It is, however, Donna Haraway's description of the figure of Jesus as "complex and ambiguous from the start, enmeshed in translation, staging, miming, disguises, and eva-sions"[11] which shifts attention from the generic figure. Gender, there-fore, cannot be simply accepted as one cultural given among others, but must be problematized with other cultural constructs within a fem-inist reading of the characterization of Jesus within the gospels and of traditional Christology.[12]

2. Lord! To Whom Shall We Go? Images, Symbols, Metaphors and Language
For many women within Western traditions, Asia, and elsewhere, there is a growing awareness that many of the titles and images that devel-oped in the proclamation of the Jesus story were embedded within pa-triarchal familial or imperial structures of the first century. As such, they function to create an entire symbolic universe which is not only kyriarchal but also completely foreign to the lives of women and men at the end of the twentieth century. Kyrios or "Lord" carries with it what Elizabeth Johnson calls the "assumed contours of the male head of household or the imperial ruler."[13] Rita Nakashima Brock empha-sizes even more strongly the problems and the abuse which have en-sued, not only for women but also for children, as a result of the as-sumption within early Christianity of the patriarchal familial structure as the source of foundational metaphors and images, not only for Jesus, but also for the believing community. This structure was not only hier-archal but also gave ultimate power which could be used as domina-tion to the male heads of the household. She concludes one such critical analysis with the statement: "Hence, I believe such christological doc-trines reflect views of divine power that sanction child abuse on a cos-mic scale and sustain benign paternalism."[14]

While some would wish to argue that the "lordship" of Jesus, for instance as depicted in the gospel story and as experienced by some women, was not that of the dominant patriarchal ruler,[15] the radical cri-tique that has been made of the functioning of this and other related images within the history of Christianity provides a very timely and se-rious warning. As long as an image has the potential to function op-pressively within patriarchy and it has been demonstrated that it has so functioned structurally over generations and centuries, there is a dan-ger in reclaiming such an image too readily while still seeking to move beyond patriarchy.

On the other hand, in relation to the title "Lord," Susan Brooks Thistlethwaite has drawn attention to the fact that for many African-American Christian women this title is central to their experience of

Jesus and their spirituality.[16] Jacquelyn Grant, who, on the one hand, recognizes this and similar trends among her black sisters ("Black women have been able to transcend some of the oppressive tendencies of White male...articulated theologies"), also proposes, on the other hand, that "womanists must investigate the relationship between the oppression of women and theological symbolism."[17]

It can be seen above that images are rarely one-dimensional in their rhetorical function. The image of the suffering servant is claimed by many women who suffer profoundly in order to give meaning to their suffering;[18] and it is the image which is central for those who stand in solidarity with people who suffer under the weight of extraordinary oppression. Chung, however, identifies the danger inherent in this image: "making meaning out of suffering is a dangerous business. It can be both a seed of liberation and an opium for the oppression of Asian women."[19]

One of the most systematic critiques offered by women in relation to the image of suffering central to Christianity is that it has been used to render women subservient to various modes of domination and to keep them in that position.

Closely associated with this image is the metaphoric language of redemption, and more particularly atonement, central to some forms of traditional Christology. One of the most radical critiques of this aspect of Christology comes from Joanne Carlson Brown and Rebecca Parker,[20] who point out that their critique is not unique but is shared by "many theologians of the modern and post-modern period."[21] Given the embeddedness of redemption and atonement in Christianity's historical narrative, however, it is little surprise that there are many who consider these theological categories essential to Christianity and, therefore, able to be reinterpreted or rightly understood.[22] Perhaps Luce Irigaray leaves us with the most challenging question: "Must the individual be immolated if unity with God is to be achieved once more?"[23]

The images of the suffering servant and redemptive atonement must, therefore, be treated with extreme caution. They draw attention to the polyvalent nature of images and metaphors which the feminist critique has raised and this, in turn, points to the need to establish a theoretical basis for dealing with metaphor and its rhetorical effect within a hermeneutical framework for reading the story of Jesus. In this regard, it is necessary to theorize the heterogeneous nature of meaning making and metaphor within the meaning-making process in a context that acknowledges the agency of women even while they are embedded in pervasive patriarchal structures and ideology.[24]

Other images, metaphors, and titles such as "Son of Man," "Son of God," "King," and even "Shepherd" function with those already examined in more detail both within the gospel text and ongoing Christian tradition to construct a symbolic universe which is gendered almost exclusively male and which functions to exclude female metaphors and images from this universe. The rhetorical effect over centuries has been devastating in terms of female subjectivity within a constructed male universe. As Mary Gerhart points out, many of our Christian metaphors have been "assimilated into the network of everyday meanings which support the cognitive status quo."[25] As a result, in many instances they have lost their metaphoric and symbolic qualities and hence could be described as "dead metaphors" in that they fail to evoke new meaning in relation to the mystery of Jesus; but within a gendered culture, they still function to maintain that system.

Feminist critical theologians have, therefore, sought those images from the tradition which resound powerfully in women's experience as they seek liberation from patriarchy. The one that has emerged most consistently is that of Jesus as liberator. It is the fundamental image for Nelly Ritchie speaking from the context of Latin America.[26] For Chung, it is the first of the new emerging images among Korean women and she links it with the images of "revolutionary" and "political martyr."[27] It is also the image proposed by Rosemary Radford Ruether.[28] This arena of the evoking of metaphors in relation to Jesus that are both ancient and new is one which can engage Australian feminists in the context of multicultural Australia with its unique history, geographic location, and socio-cultural situation.

3. And the Eyes of All Were Fixed on Him: Isolated Focus on Jesus

As women have sought to "re-member" Jesus, and to "re-member" their foresisters and themselves at the center of the "reign of God" movement, they have, in various ways, critiqued those aspects of traditional Christologies which make universal claims for Jesus as the Christ, which separate him from his revelatory work of proclaiming the liberating "reign of God," and which separate him and his work from the "reign of God" community. The most radical of these critiques and perhaps the earliest came from Mary Daly, who claimed that those christological formulas which isolate Jesus from humanity "reflect and encourage idolatry in relation to the person of Jesus."[29] She goes on to state:

It will, I think, become increasingly evident that exclusively masculine symbols for the ideal of "incarnation" or for the ideal of the human search for fulfillment will not do. As a uniquely masculine image and language for divinity loses credibility, so also the idea of a single divine incarnation in a human being of the male sex may give way in the religious consciousness to an increased awareness of the power of Being in all persons.[30]

Rita Nakashima Brock and Carter Heyward both see the limitations of the historical particularities of both Jesus in his earthly life and the early theological claims about Jesus as challenges to absolute or universal claims. Heyward states that "Christological truth is neither unchanging nor universally applicable. It is created in the social, historical, personal praxis of right relation, which is always normative, or central, in christology."[31] Brock, on the other hand, locates the problem in the absolutizing of christological formulations within a dualistic world view, a world view which she claims is one of the most dangerous legacies of patriarchy:

Of the life of Jesus we are only allowed shadowy glimpses, veiled in New Testament theological claims full of early church social-political agendas, agendas including the patriarchal demand to make absolute either/or choices on the basis of the "ideal" divine incarnation.[32]

Rosemary Radford Ruether bases her critique of the once and for all claims regarding Jesus on their lack of a fundamental basis in the life of Jesus. She says that "Jesus does not think of himself as the 'last word of God' but points beyond himself to 'One who will come.'"[33] It could be added that the gospel stories likewise point beyond, especially the close of the Matthean gospel (Matt 28:18–20). At the same time, however, it would seem that the seeds of the universalizing tendencies are already there within that same text. This alerts us once again to the socio-rhetorical effects of particular texts, as well as of particular theological and christological formulations, and to the need to examine the effects of these formulations not only in their communities of origin but in today's believing communities. While a text may have functioned in a particular way in one socio-cultural context, it may function very differently in another separated from the first in space and time and in world view.

As women in Christian communities are becoming aware of the ways in which christological formulations have been used to support a patriarchal worldview that has been sacralized because of its link to Christianity, so too feminist philosophers and critical theorists, especially in the Western traditions, have recognized that many of the "universal theories" that have governed the Western way of knowing and way of being have likewise supported and maintained patriarchy.[34] Rosi Braidotti, like Brock, has highlighted the inherent dualism within this "universalistic stance" of Western patriarchy and, in response, she explores the metaphor of "nomadism" to characterize the journey toward female subjectivity and away from patriarchy.[35] The question that faces feminist theologians is whether new or newly appropriated understandings of Jesus can contribute to such a journey.

While many women have not entered into this theological and philosophical discussion at the theoretical level, they have begun to articulate their own understanding of Jesus, re-membering Jesus in a way that renders their lives and their experience central to their shaping of new understandings of Jesus. Chung raises the voices of two Korean women. Park Soon Kyung names Jesus as the "woman Messiah," as liberator of women's oppression, while Choi Man Ja identifies "Korean women's historical struggle for liberation with 'the praxis of messiahship.'"[36] For Korean women, Jesus is also a priest of *han*, an image which carries more female than male symbolism. Elizabeth Amoah and Mercy Oduyoye likewise point out that Christ is being perceived in a variety of contemporary images emerging from African women's experience of being woman and being African.[37] For these women, their experience not only shapes their imaging of Jesus but inhabits it. Such re-imaging highlights the extent to which male experience has inhabited traditional images of Jesus. The re-imagining considered here breaks the hold of the link between the uniqueness of Jesus and maleness in the lives of many women. These new metaphors, however, also need to be considered within a critical evaluation of patriarchy so as not to leave in place the gender binary oppositions which support such patriarchy.[38]

The re-imaging of Jesus in the words of women has been accompanied by an even more dramatic re-imaging in the visual arts. The figure of "The Crucified Woman" which hung in the Bloor Street United Church in Toronto and now stands in the garden of Emmanual College has called forth celebration and controversy as has "The Christa" in the Church of St. John the Divine in New York.[39] Less controversial but equally evocative of new understandings of Jesus beyond traditional iconography is Arthur Boyd's "Crucifixion, Shoalhaven."[40] Maybe one of the most expressive depictions of Jesus' embeddedness within the human context is "The Pregnant Mary," a sculpture in wood and ochre by Australian Aboriginal George Mung, in which an adult Jesus is visible in the open womb of Mary.[41]

Other women are looking toward the embeddedness of Jesus and the Jesus story within a community context as it is refracted in the biblical text. Mary Rose D'Angelo and Elisabeth Schüssler Fiorenza, both scholars of the Christian scriptures, explicitly focus their interpretations in this way. For D'Angelo, "the first shift to be made in imagining the context of Jesus' life is from the person of Jesus to the movement in which he acted."[42] Schüssler Fiorenza questions whether "the historical man Jesus of Nazareth can be a role model for contemporary women,"[43] and she directs attention more specifically to the Jesus movement with its focus on the proclamation of the *basileia* of God as a renewal movement within Judaism.[44] Rosemary Radford Ruether, a historical theologian, sees the mission of Christ continued in the Christian community;[45] and Elisabeth Moltmann-Wendel examines "Beziehung" or "inter-connectedness" as the forgotten dimension of Christology.[46]

Theologians Elizabeth Johnson and Rita Nakashima Brock likewise shift the focus from the individual Christ to the community. Johnson takes up the image of "the body of Christ" to demonstrate that "the beloved community shares in this Christhood, participates in the living and dying and rising of Christ."[47] Brock uses a similar image but names it "Christa/Community" and characterizes it by erotic power within connectedness. This Christa community is linked to Jesus in his lifetime so that he is not considered apart from it, but it is not limited to that period of time. It continues on as "an ocean which is the whole and compassionate being, including ourselves."[48] The voices of women from across the globe are joining with these voices reclaiming Jesus within the liberating process in which they are participants.[49]

In all this, women have, out of their own experience of claiming agency within the theological process that characterizes their lives as members of believing and praxis-oriented Christian communities, demonstrated that christological formulations are not universal truths of "once and for all" validity but are partial truths carrying with them the historical context and ideological particularities of those who constructed them. In this they share in what has been articulated theoretically by Donna Haraway who has coined the phrase "situated knowledges" to argue for "politics and epistemologies of location, positioning, and situating, where partiality and not universality is the condition of being heard to make rational knowledge claims."[50] These "situated knowledges" are, she claims, "about communities, not about isolated individuals. The only way to find a larger vision is to be somewhere in particular."[51]

It is from this particularity of women's experience, refracted through the lens of feminist critical analysis, that new images, new interpretations, new reclamation of the person and work of Jesus are emerging.

The question arises in relation to this paper—is there an Australian contribution to these new voices?

B. In An Australian Feminist Key

In 1986, Majella Franzmann and Wrex Woolnough jointly authored an article in *Compass* entitled "Interpreting Christ in an Australian Context."[52] Within that article, both authors raised issues similar to those noted above—the cultural particularity of both New Testament theologians as well as contemporary ones; the necessity to analyze critically both cultural contexts; the limitations inherent in both gospel and Australian imaging of Jesus; and the heterogeneity and open-endedness of the exploration.[53] While it was recognized that there would not be a single image that would emerge from an exploration of an Australian Christ, the heterogeneity was not articulated in any detail in this short article. As a result, there was no indication that the perspective of women and their differences from men and the differences among women in the Australian context would need to be included. The article did, however, raise significant issues for the contextualization of theology in an Australian context and its import in relation to the remembering or re-imaging of Jesus in which Australian feminist christologies would take their place. Failure to give attention to our sociocultural location in future theologizing will further fuel the tendency for Australian theologians to participate in a global theologizing which may not touch the specifics of the Australian locale and this may have a particular impact in relation to women whose attentiveness to experience has become more acute.

It is perhaps this tendency which has characterized the more specific attention to feminist Christology within Australian publications in recent years. Both Robert Simons and Denis Edwards have recognized the significance of feminist Christology in addressing the ecological or cosmological claims on theologizing at the end of the twentieth century.[54] Simons examines the contribution of Rosemary Haughton, Rosemary Radford Ruether, and Sallie McFague while Edwards is informed by the exploration of Wisdom as source for not only christological but also trinitarian re-imaging undertaken by Elizabeth Johnson and the import of this for ecological theology.[55]

Patricia Fox also draws attention to the retrieval of Wisdom in Johnson's work, especially its trinitarian implications, but within that she gives brief attention to Johnson's exploration of "Jesus-Sophia." According to Fox, Johnson "sets out to put in place some foundations for a genuinely liberating wisdom Christology."[56] It is this same symbol, Wisdom or Sophia, which I explored for its potential for a feminist reading of Jesus in the gospel of Matthew in my contribution to *Claiming Our Rites.*[57] Most recently, Marie Louise Uhr has brought into dialogue both the international authors and the Australian theologians noted above in her essay "Jesus Christ, the Sophia of God: A Symbol for Our Salvation."[58] Certainly within feminist Christology generally, and it would seem among at least some women and men in Australia in particular, the image and the myth of Sophia/Wisdom is providing one source toward a re-imaging of Jesus.[59] One particular and significant effect of this image/myth is that it breaks the gender binary nexus and hence can function metaphorically to tease the mind into new images in relation to Jesus beyond the sex/gender system. Wisdom is also cross-cultural and can be explored in many different ways in different contexts.

C. Toward the Future

It is only in coming to the final section of this essay that I have realized the impossibility of the task I set myself at the outset—to offer an Australian feminist response to the question who is the Jesus in whom Christians believe. It is a response that will need to be constructed over time and in dialogue between many different female and male voices from the myriads of social locations that constitute Australia. It has already begun in a variety of ways and locations both indicated in and beyond the references in this article. It will, however, need to broaden its scope as it continues.

What I have chosen to offer in this final section, therefore, is a brief reading of one small segment of Matthew's gospel in the light of some of the critical principles that have emerged in Section A above as a contribution to the developing of a feminist response to the question of Jesus appropriate in an Australian context at the end of the twentieth century. I will not have the scope here to develop the different ways in which this text may have been read/received by different sectors of the Matthean community, a study which opens up possibilities for contemporary feminist readings.[60] I will simply offer a reading, from a contemporary feminist perspective, of Matthew 11:2–19, a biblical text which is one among many of the sources both old and new on which the Christian community draws for its ongoing response to the question—"Who do you say that I am?"[61]

In the context of the narrative unfolding of the character of Jesus, Matthew 11 holds in tension two aspects of characterization which subsequent theology has separated, namely the identity or naming of Jesus—the symbols and metaphors pointing to the answer to the "who" question of Jesus—and the deeds of Jesus.[62] In the opening verse of this section,[63] it is the hearing of the deeds of the Christ (the *erga tou Christou*) which prompts John to ask whether Jesus is the Coming One. The reply of Jesus turns attention not to titles but back to what is seen and heard, the deeds or *erga*—the blind receive their sight and the lame walk, lepers are cleansed and the deaf hear, the dead are raised up and the poor have good news preached to them (Matt 11:5). This is God's dream for humanity, the "reign of God" imagined and preached by the prophets. It is this which the Matthean story links intimately with Jesus. It is not titles, names, symbols, metaphors that will finally answer John's question but it is what is seen and heard, the deeds. And this "reign of God" with which Jesus is so intimately connected is not exclusive. It has drawn in both women and men, boys and girls, ethnic "outsiders" and "insiders," clean and unclean (Matt 8–9). It is a *basileia* quite unlike that of Rome, which was grounded in the patriarchal and hierarchal family or *oikos*[64] and structured according to status.[65]

The next section (11:7–19) spins out the threads of the opening verses and draws readers both ancient and contemporary into an intricate web of traditions linking John, Jesus, the *basileia,* and the crowds. Jesus, identified as prophetic messenger of God's *basileia,* directs attention away from himself and toward John and the *basileia.* John is proclaimed as "prophet" and even more than prophet, the one who makes way for God's inclusive *basileia.* Both John and Jesus participate in the long line of Israel's prophets who do not close off Israel's traditions but open them out to the full realization of God's dream for humanity.[66] The enigmatic verse 12, together with the lament of verses 16–19a–c, evokes the tradition of the persecution and even death of the prophet of the *basileia* vision.

For at least some of the first-century readers, these verses together with verse 19d would have recalled not only Israel's prophetic tradition but also another stream of tradition. The righteous one deemed to suffer for God's vision for humanity, for God's righteousness, is not only a figure within Israel's prophetic tradition but also in the Wisdom tradition. The Wisdom of Solomon 2:12–20 portrays the righteous one, the one who is child of Wisdom/child of God, as one who will be insulted, tortured, and even put to death by the "ungodly." Indeed, it is quite possible that this text together with Wisdom 3:1–9 may well have provided the paradigm among some early reign-of-God communities for interpreting, for making meaning of the death and resurrection of Jesus.[67] Also, it is generally agreed among scholars that, in the early stages of the tradition of the reign-of-God and Jesus story, both Jesus and John the Baptist were considered prophets of Sophia/Wisdom. Indeed, an earlier layer of verses 16–19, proclaiming the works of both John and Jesus, may well have concluded with the Q saying: Wisdom is justified by her children.[68]

In Matthew 11:19d, however, Wisdom/Sophia is justified not by her children, but by her deeds. For the reader, this calls attention back to verse 2, the deeds of the Christos, and forms a frame around the closely interwoven fabric linking Jesus, John, and God's inclusive *basileia* to which all in the marketplace are invited. Images of Christos and Sophia interpret one another. Jesus Christos is also Jesus Sophia but not in isolation from the vision and works of the *basileia*, or from John the prophet who goes before, or from the prophets of the marketplace who will follow.

This short section of the Matthean gospel invites Australian feminist theologians from their different social locations to continue the meaning-making process begun by those women and men who shaped the Matthean gospel, taking up and giving new meaning to first-century images and metaphors but also reading the story in ways that enable new meanings to emerge. The very text itself is symbolic and can be read today to give contemporary symbolic meaning to the person and the work of Jesus.

In the passage we have considered, Jesus is image-maker, herald of an inclusive vision, for humanity and doer of *basileia* deeds, emissary of the God of the prophets and of Sophia God of the wisdom tradition. The parable of the "children in the marketplace" invites those who continue the reign-of-God movement which found expression in those two traditions and in the life and story of Jesus of Nazareth to take up the doing of deeds and the image making in response to the call of our own Australian feminist context, imaged in the "pipe" and the "wail" of the parable. Jesus is named metonymically both Christos and Sophia, a naming that breaks the genderizing of the proclaimed Jesus and invites our continued participation in this naming. Finally, Jesus does not stand alone but within both the prophetic and wisdom traditions shared by John and the new *basileia* movement. So too today, Jesus will be found, will be imaged, will be proclaimed, and the *basileia* vision lived from within and among the variety of traditions which constitute Christian Australia and from within the varieties that constitute those traditions shaped by concerns that are ecological, ethnic, feminist, and many others. Many different voices will be raised in response to the "who do you say I am" question in Australian feminist keys.

Notes

1. It has only been in recent decades with the emergence of liberation theologies that the social location of the interpreter has begun to receive significant attention in the interpretive process. See Jon Sobrino, *Christology at the Crossroads* (Maryknoll, NY: Orbis, 1978); Mary Rose D'Angelo, "Re-membering Jesus: Women, Prophecy, and Resistance in the Memory of the Early Churches," *Horizons* 19 (1992): 205; and Carter Heyward in Ellen C. Davis, eds., *Speaking of Christ: A Lesbian Feminist Voice* (New York: Pilgrim Press, 1989), 21. More generally, this issue has received significant attention in the two volumes edited by Fernando Segovia and Mary Ann Tolbert, *Reading from This Place*, vol. 1, *Social Location and Biblical Interpretation in the United States* and *Reading from This Place*, vol. 2, *Social Location and Biblical Interpretation in Global Perspective* (Minneapolis: Fortress, 1995).

2. Fernando F. Segovia, "Cultural Studies and Contemporary Biblical Criticism: Ideological Criticism as Mode of Discourse," in Segovia and Tolbert, *Reading from This Place*, 1:1–17, details how the emergence of cultural studies and the recognition of differences among interpreters not only on the basis of gender but also socio-political and cultural, ethnic, racial, and religious differences have led to this awareness of the constructed nature of meaning.

3. Jacquelyn Grant, *White Women's Christ and Black Women's Jesus: Feminist Christology and Womanist Response*, AARAS 64 (Atlanta: Scholars, 1989); Kwok Pui Lan, "Racism and Ethnocentrism in Feminist Biblical Interpretation," in *Searching the Scriptures*, vol. 1, *A Feminist Introduction*, ed. Elisabeth Schüssler Fiorenza (New York: Crossroad, 1993), 101–16; Virginia Fabella, "A Common Methodology for Diverse Christologies," in *With Passion and Compassion: Third World Women Doing Theology — Reflections from the Women's Commission of the Ecumenical Association of Third World Theologians*, ed. Virginia Fabella and Mercy Oduyoyeeds (Maryknoll, NY: Orbis, 1988), 108–17; Chung Hyun Kyung, *Struggle to Be Sun Again: Introducing Asian Women's Theology* (Maryknoll, NY: Orbis, 1991); and Anne Pattel-Gray, "Not yet Tiddas: An Aboriginal Womanist Critique of Australian Church Feminism," in *Freedom and Entrapment: Women Thinking Theology*, ed. Maryanne Confoy, Dorothy A. Lee, and Joan Nowotny (Melbourne: Dove, 1995), 165–91.

4. Elisabeth Schüssler Fiorenza continually emphasizes the necessity of this form of analysis. See, especially in relation to Christology, *Jesus, Miriam's Child, Sophia's Prophet: Critical Issues in Feminist Christology* (New York: Continuum, 1994), 34–49; and it is explicated by Jacquelyn Grant in the final analytical chapter of her book, *White Women's Christ, Black Women's Jesus*, 195–230.

5. For a very clear discussion of the distinctions between the "actual" Jesus, the "historical" Jesus, and the "proclaimed" Jesus, see Sandra Schneiders, *The Revelatory Text: Interpreting the New Testament as Sacred Scripture* (San Francisco: HarperCollins, 1991), 100–2.

6. Elizabeth A. Johnson, *She Who Is: The Mystery of God in Feminist Theological Discourse* (New York: Crossroad, 1992), 152.

7. Schüssler Fiorenza, *Jesus*, 34–43, analyses the sex/gender system as "discursive frame of meaning" in relation to Christology.

8. Dulcie Abraham et al., eds., *Asian Women Doing Theology: Report from Singapore Conference, November 20–29, 1987* (Kowloon, Hong Kong: Asian Women's Resource Centre for Culture and Theology, 1989), 165.

9. Monica Melanchthon, "Christology and Women," in *Asian Women Doing Theology*, 183.

10. Judith Butler, "Variations on Sex and Gender: Beauvoir, Wittig and Foucault," in *Feminism as Critique*, ed. Seyla Benhabib and Drucilla Cornell (Minneapolis: University of Minnesota Press, 1987), 128–42; and Judith Butler, "Gender Trouble, Feminist Theory, and Psychoanalytic Discourse," in *Feminism/Postmodernism*, ed. Linda J. Nicholson (New York/London: Routledge, 1990), 324–40. See also Rosi Braidotti, *Patterns of Dissonance: A Study of Women in Contemporary Philosophy* (Cambridge: Polity Press, 1991), especially 128–31.

11. Donna Haraway, *"Ecce homo,* Ain't (Ar'n't) I a Woman, and Inappropriate/d Others: The Human in a Post-humanist Landscape," in *Feminists Theorize the Political*, ed. Judith Butler and Joan W. Scott (New York/London: Routledge, 1992), 90.

12. In this regard, see also Schüssler Fiorenza, *Miriam's Child*, 34–43.

13. Johnson, *She Who Is*, 151. Johnson points out in her discussion of the "imperial Christ" that this aspect of Christology is also radically critiqued by Latin American liberation theologians.

14. Rita Nakashima Brock, "And a Little Child Will Lead Us: Christology and Child Abuse," in *Christianity, Patriarchy, and Abuse: A Feminist Critique*, ed. Joanne Carlson Brown and Carole R. Bohn (New York: Pilgrim Press, 1989), 43. Her critique, however, is not limited to the image of Lord or Suffering Servant (which we will consider below) but is directed to the Christian understanding of redemption needing to be wrought by the death of Jesus. This is developed in her *Journeys by Heart: A Christology of Erotic Power* (New York: Crossroad, 1988), 1–9. Elisabeth Schüssler Fiorenza, "Zur Methodenproblematik einer feministischen Christologie des Neuen Testaments," in *Vom Verlangen nach Heilwerden: Christologie in feministisch-theologischer Sicht*, ed. Doris Strahm and Regula Strobel (Fribourg/Luzern: Edition Exodus, 1991), 121–22, identifies redemption through the cross as the second critical issue for feminist Christology along with the maleness of Jesus.

15. Choi Man Ja, "Feminist Christology," 176. Chung Hung Kyung, *Struggle to Be Sun*, 58–59 also demonstrates how some Asian women have reclaimed this image. In the same text, she has previously laid out the ways in which it has functioned oppressively in many Asian women's lives.

16. Susan Brooks Thistlethwaite, *Sex, Race, and God: Christian Feminism in Black and White* (New York: Crossroad, 1989), 116–17.

17. Grant, *White Women's Christ, Black Women's Jesus*, 219.

18. Chung, *Struggle to Be Sun*, 53–54, 56–57, recognizes aspects of Korean women's experience within this perspective. See also Johnson, *She Who Is*, 161.

19. Chung, *Struggle to Be Sun*, 54.

20. Joanne Carlson Brown and Rebecca Parker, "For God so Loved the World?" in Brown and Bohn, *Patriarchy and Abuse*, 1–30.

21. Brown and Parker, "For God so Loved the World?" 13.

22. Margo G. Houts, "Atonement and Abuse: An Alternative View," *Daughters of Sarah* 18, no. 3 (1992): 29–32. See also Carter Heyward, "Suffering, Redemption, and Christ: Shifting the Grounds of Feminist Christology," *Christianity and Crisis* 49 (1989): 381–86, for a more critical feminist reclamation.

23. Luce Irigaray, *Marine Lover of Friedrich Nietzsche* (New York: Columbia University Press, 1991), 164. For a study of the theme of the immolation of the beloved son within Judaism and early Christianity, see Jon D. Levenson, *The Death and Resurrection of the Beloved Son: The Transformation of Child Sacrifice in Judaism and Christianity* (New Haven/London: Yale University Press, 1993).

24. Here I have been influenced by Rita Felski, *Beyond Feminist Aesthetics: Feminist Literary and Social Change* (Cambridge: Harvard University Press, 1989), 66, who argues that a "theoretical model which is able to situate language in relation to social life by foregrounding its semantic and pragmatic functions allows a more differentiated analysis of women's communicative practices by moving away from the abstract dichotomy of 'masculine' versus 'feminine' speech."

25. Mary Gerhart, "Imaging Christ in Art, Politics, Spirituality: An Overview," in *Imaging Christ: Politics, Art, Spirituality*, ed. Francis A. Eigo (Villanova: Villanova University Press, 1991), 4.

26. Nelly Ritchie, "Women and Christology," in *Through Her Eyes: Women's Theology from Latin America*, ed. Elsa Tamez (Maryknoll, NY: Orbis, 1989), 81–95.

27. Chung, *Struggle to Be Sun*, 62.

28. Rosemary Radford Ruether, *Sexism and God-talk: Toward a Feminist Theology* (Boston: Beacon, 1983), 137–38.

29. Mary Daly, *Beyond God the Father: Toward a Philosophy of Women's Liberation* (Boston: Beacon, 1973), 69. Irigaray, *Marine Lover*, 190, speaks too of "the universe already made flesh or capable of becoming flesh, and remaining in excess to the existing world."

30. Daly, *Beyond God the Father*, 71. For a similar radical critique but from the perspective of feminist critical theory and psychoanalysis, see Luce Irigaray, "Equal to whom?" *Differences* 1 (1989): 62.

31. Heyward, *Speaking of Christ*, 22.

32. Rita Nakashima Brock, "The Feminist Redemption of Christ," in *Christian Feminism: Visions of a New Humanity*, ed. Judith Weidman (San Francisco: Harper and Row, 1984), 57.

33. Ruether, *Sexism and God-talk*, 121.

34. By way of example see many of the essays in Michèle Barrett and Anne Phillips, eds., *Destabilizing Theory: Contemporary Feminist Debates* (Stanford: Stanford University Press, 1992), and similarly Nicholson, *Feminism/Postmodernism*.

35. Rosi Braidotti, *Nomadic Subjects: Embodiment and Sexual Difference in Contemporary Feminist Theory* (New York: Columbia University Press, 1994), in which she explores the metaphor extensively.

36. Chung, *Struggle to Be Sun*, 66.

37. Elizabeth Amoah and Mercy Amba Oduyoye, "The Christ for African Women," in Fabella and Oduyoye, *With Passion and Compassion*, 44. See also Teresia M. Hinga, "Jesus Christ and the Liberation of Women in Africa," in *The Will to Arise: Women, Tradition and the Church in Africa*, ed. Mercy Amba Oduyoye and Musimbi R. A. Kanyoro (Maryknoll, NY: Orbis, 1992), 183–94.

38. Miriam Peskowitz in her contribution to "Roundtable Discussion: What's in a Name? Exploring the Dimensions of What 'Feminist Studies in Religion' Means," *Journal of Feminist Studies in Religion* 11, no. 1 (1995) 111–15, offers a significant warning to feminists in their claiming of new images, to be attentive to the vestiges of patriarchy within most images. She examines in particular the image of "weaving" and "weaver," popular within feminist theology, and its link to the classical story of Penelope and also the exploitation of many women as weavers even today, noting the need to re-evaluate such feminist metaphors and tropes for the possibility of their re-enacting elements of their history within patriarchy.

39. See Doris Jean Dyke, *Crucified Woman* (Toronto: The United Church Publishing House, 1991).

40. A reproduction of this painting by Arthur Boyd depicting a female crucified figure against the backdrop of the Australian landscape can be found in Rosemary Crumlin, *Religious Images in Australian Art* (Kensington: Bay Books, 1988), 158–59.

41. This piece was discovered by Rosemary Crumlin during her curation of an exhibition of the religious art of traditional Australian Aboriginal artists during the bicentenary of European settlement in Australia, and a very beautiful photograph can be seen in Rosemary Crumlin and Anthony Knight, eds., *Aboriginal Art and Spirituality* (Melbourne: CollinsDove, 1991), 38.

42. D'Angelo, "Re-membering Jesus," 206.

43. Elisabeth Schüssler Fiorenza, "Toward a Feminist Biblical Hermeneutics: Biblical Interpretation and Liberation Theology," in *The Challenge of Liberation Theology*, ed. Brian Maher and L. Dale Riches (Maryknoll, NY: Orbis, 1981), 107.

44. Elisabeth Schüssler Fiorenza, *In Memory of Her: A Feminist Theological Reconstruction of Christian Origins* (New York: Crossroad, 1983), 105–159. For her much more extensive treatment of these issues, see her *Miriam's Child*.

45. Ruether, *Sexism and God-talk*, 138.

46. Elisabeth Moltmann-Wendel, "Beziehung—die vergessene Dimension der Christologie: Neutestamentliche Ansatzpunkte feministischer Christologie," in Strahm and Strobel, *Vom Verlangen nach Heilwerden*, 100–11.

47. Johnson, *She Who Is*, 72.

48. Brock, *Journeys by Heart*, 66–70, 105–108.

49. In addition to the many voices already cited, see also Nelly Ritchie, "Women and Christology," 82, who links Jesus to the active call to people to participate in their own liberation.

50. Donna Haraway, "Situated Knowledges: The Science Question in Feminism and the Privilege of Partial Perspective," *Feminist Studies* 14 (1988): 575–99.

51. Haraway, "Situated Knowledges," 590.

52. Majella Franzmann and Wrex Woolnough, "Interpreting Christ in an Australian Context," *Compass* 20, no. 1 (1986): 2–7.

53. The above is my own summation of the issues raised in the article using the language of this article more than the language of the authors.

54. Robert G. Simons, "The Impact of the Feminist Critique on Christology: Towards an Enhanced Cosmological Soteriology," *Compass* 33, no. 4 (1989): 36–44; and Denis Edwards, "Jesus—the Wisdom of God," *Australasian Catholic Record* 70 (1993): 342–53.

55. More recently Edwards has published a full-length work, *Jesus the Wisdom of God: An Ecological Theology* (Maryknoll, NY: Orbis, 1995); see especially chapters 1–3 in relation to Jesus and Wisdom.

56. Patricia Fox, "The Trinity as Transforming Symbol: Exploring the Trinitarian Theology of Two Roman Catholic Feminist Theologians," *Pacifica* 7 (1994): 713–94.

57. Elaine Wainwright, "Wisdom Is Justified by Her Deeds: Claiming the Jesus-Myth," in *Claiming Our Rites: Studies in Religion by Australian Women Scholars*, ed. Morny Joy and Penelope Magee (Adelaide: The Australian Association for the Study of Religions, 1994), 57–78.

58. Marie Louise Uhr, "Jesus Christ, the Sophia of God: A Symbol for Our Salvation." *Women-Church* 19 (1996): 15–21.

59. There is significant difference among scholars as to the most explicit terminology to use in relation to Wisdom. Elisabeth Schüssler Fiorenza, "Wisdom Mythology and the Christological Hymns of the New Testament," in *Aspects of Wisdom in Judaism and Early Christianity*, ed. Robert L. Wilken (Notre Dame: University of Notre Dame Press, 1975), 26–33, notes the distinction between "living myth," as the myth of Wisdom behind both Jewish and gnostic speculations about wisdom, and "reflective mythology" as a form of theology "appropriating mythical language, material, and patterns from different myths." Celia Deutsch, "Wisdom in Matthew: Transforming of a Symbol," *Novum Testamentum* 32, no. 1 (1990): 13–47, refers to Lady Wisdom as "metaphor" (p. 21), but after analysis of the Wisdom texts in the Hebrew scriptures speaks of the early Christian use of "the Wisdom myth."

60. This is an aspect that I am exploring in my current research, *Shall We Look for Another? Engendering Reading and the Matthean Jesus*, to be published by Orbis, 1997.

61. Hugh Anderson, "Christology: Unfinished Business," in *Earthing Christologies: From Jesus' Parables to Jesus the Parable: Faith and Scholarship Colloquies*, ed. Walter P. Weaver and James H. Charlesworth (Valley Forge: Trinity Press International, 1995), 81–85, points to the necessity of ongoing exploration of how we understand Jesus as well as the significance of the Christian scriptures in that exploration.

62. This very tension raises critical questions with regard to the isolating of the question in the title of this paper.

63. Verse 1 could be considered the close of the previous section since it is

one of five formula verses which close the five discourses in the Matthean gospel—"When Jesus had finished . . ."—7:28; 11:1; 13:53; 19:1; 26:1.

64. Michael Crosby, *House of Disciples: Church, Economics, and Justice in Matthew* (Maryknoll, NY: Orbis, 1988).

65. Stephenson Humphries-Brooks, "Indicators of Social Organization and Status in Matthew's Gospel," in *SBL Seminary Papers* 30, ed. Eugene H. Lovering (Atlanta: Scholars, 1991), 31–49.

66. Schüssler Fiorenza, *Miriam's Child*, 142.

67. It is becoming more commonplace among contemporary scholars to recognize the significance of the Wisdom literature and Wisdom tradition in the earliest stages of Christian meaning-making in relation to the life and work of Jesus of Nazareth. See Schüssler Fiorenza, *Miriam's Child*, 139–54, for a comprehensive analysis of this. See also Silvia Schroer, "Jesus Sophia: Erträge der feministischen Forschung zu einer frühchristlichen Deutung der Praxis und des Schicksals Jesu von Nazaret," in Strahm and Strobel, *Vom Verlangen nach Heilwerden*, 112–28.

68. Antoinette Clark Wire, "The God of Jesus in the Gospel Sayings Source," in Segovia and Tolbert, *Reading from This Place*, 1:279, notes not only in relation to this saying but to the Sayings Source (Q) generally: "The first third of the Sayings Source appears to be about John the Baptist and Jesus, beginning with John speaking of Jesus as the coming one, and ending with Jesus speaking of John as the greatest of the prophets. But a sharper look shows that neither one is focusing on the other but on what God is announcing through them both."

6
DICTIONARY OF FEMINIST THEOLOGIES

Kelly Brown Douglas (USA)
Carter Heyward (USA)
Francine Cardman (USA)

KELLY BROWN DOUGLAS:
CHRIST JESUS

Christian communities of every generation have to discern the significance of Jesus Christ for their own lives, because their affirmations of Jesus Christ are contextual. They must answer for themselves what it means for Jesus, the first-century Jew from Nazareth, to be Christ (i.e., the Messiah, the bearer of God's salvation). Moreover, the community's historical, cultural, social, and political contexts inevitably shape their christological answers. It is essential, therefore, to identify the context out of which any Christology or theological definition of Jesus Christ emerges.

The following definition derives from a womanist context. It reflects the meaning of Jesus Christ for African-American women as they struggle for life and wholeness for themselves and their community/family. This definition also reflects the faith of the wider African-American community, male and female, given the life situation of resistance to oppression that African-American women share with African-American men. From a womanist perspective, *Jesus Christ means that God is real*. Christ brings God down to earth. Christ is God's actual presence in the daily lives of African-American women. Christ is a living being with whom African-American women have an intimate relationship. The relationship has several dimensions that clarify the womanist meaning of Jesus Christ.

First, *Christ is a friend and confidant*. African-American women are certain that Christ knows intrinsically the complex reality associated

78

with being black and female in a society that is hostile to both blackness and femaleness. Christ is one to whom African-American women can cry, talk, and share their pains and sorrows. Refrains such as "Jesus is my bosom friend" and "A little talk with Jesus makes it right" echo through their songs. African-American women's confidence in Christ as a friend and confidant is based on their knowledge of Jesus' relationship to the poor and oppressed in his own time. Luke's birth narrative provides them with the needed evidence that Jesus experienced from the moment of his birth what it meant to be on the margins of society. African-American women testify in song: "Poor little Jesus boy / Made him to be born in a manger / World treats him so mean / Treats me mean too."

Second, *Christ is a co-sufferer*. African-American women believe that Christ is one with them in their peculiar suffering. Sojourner Truth, in her speech at the 1851 Women's Rights Convention, captured this aspect of Christ's meaning for African-American women when she testified, "I have borne thirteen children, and seen them most all sold off into slavery, and when I cried out with my mother's grief, none but Jesus heard me!"...Jesus' crucifixion is the event that most clearly demonstrates to African-American women Christ's solidarity with them in their suffering. The pain of the cross poignantly confirms that Christ existentially knows their painful struggles to make it through each day.

Third, *Christ is a healer and provider*. African-American women are sure that Christ will help them take care of their needs. They call to Christ in song: "Feed me, Jesus, feed me," or "Clothe me, Jesus, clothe me." Again, this assurance that Christ will respond to their needs is based on their knowledge of Jesus' ministry. They reason that if Jesus helped the oppressed of his own time, he will surely do the same for them. They have sung, "Jesus make de dumb to speak. / Jesus make de cripple to walk. / Jesus give de blind his sight. / Jesus do most anything."

Fourth, *Christ is a liberator*. African-American women believe that Christ is working through, for, and with them to liberate the African-American community from its complex oppression. They believe Christ is stridently against all that is hostile to the life and wholeness of African-American women and men. They also believe that Christ will help them to defeat that which oppresses. The resurrection provides the foundation of this belief. It reveals that oppression and death are not the last word; wholeness and life are.

Essentially, the life, ministry, and actions of Jesus provide the vital keys to a womanist definition of what it means for Jesus to be Christ. A womanist meaning of Jesus Christ is revealed, therefore, in who Christ is and through what Christ does in the life of the African-American community. The meaning of Christ is found in the relationship that Christ shares with African-American women and men. This rich relationship primarily shows that Jesus Christ means life, freedom, and wholeness.

CARTER HEYWARD:
CHRISTA

Christa is the name of a sculpture by English artist Edwina Sandys. On April 19, 1984, this four-foot-tall bronze of a crucified woman was put on exhibit in the Cathedral Church of St. John the Divine in New York City. Eleven days later, it was removed in a storm of controversy. The term *Christa* subsequently emerged as a christological image among some Christian feminists, where it also has been controversial.

Some theologians have used Christa to represent the creative, liberating Spirit of God/dess. Attempting in their christologies to differentiate many women's experiences of salvation from the church's traditional teachings about Jesus Christ, Rita Nakashima Brock and Carter Heyward employ the term *Christa* for the Spirit that is sacred, vulnerable, deeply embedded in women's lives, and erotic (source of creative power and sexual pleasure: cf. eros).

Emphasizing [its] collective and erotic character, Brock describes "Christa/Community" as "a revelatory and redemptive witness of God/dess's work in history...the church's imaginative witness to its experiences of brokenness and [the] sacredness of erotic power in human existence"...Citing Christa as the "eternal resource of nourishment on the sacred journey toward justice," Heyward writes: "There is no greater delight than to celebrate and share the body of Christa," which she locates "in the power between us, in our relation, as well as in the persons we are and are becoming"...

By contrast, other women have criticized Christa as an icon that too readily can be used to glorify women's suffering. They contend that feminists who wish to celebrate either women's vulnerability or the erotic power in women's lives risk colluding with the massive social, political, and economic systems that violate women. Using Christa to signify redemptive power requires distinguishing the christological significance of the Jesus story from the man himself. In this way, Christa can be an iconoclastic image that shatters the maleness of Christ.

FRANCINE CARDMAN:
CHRISTOLOGY

Classical Christology

The person and work of Jesus Christ, particularly as defined by the ecumenical councils of the early church, has traditionally been the subject
matter of Christology. Jesus Christ was understood as the "only begot-
ten Son of God" who "for us [humans] and for our salvation became
human" (Creed of Nicaea, 325 CE); he was truly God, truly human"
(Definition of Chalcedon, 451 CE). God the Son or Word (Logos) was incarnate in Jesus of Nazareth; having taken on human nature, he saved
humankind from sin, death, and the consequences of the Fall by his
death and resurrection, through which he was also made known to be
the Christ (God's anointed One, the Messiah). Classical Christology's
concentration on the metaphysics of divine-human relation in Jesus
(one person, two natures) tended to obscure the underlying concerns
about salvation that motivated these early debates. The weight of christological thought came to rest on the divine nature of Jesus Christ,
overshadowing the significance of his humanity.

Doctrinal decision making through councils, intended to define or
delimit the faith of all Christians, became possible only after the emperor
Constantine took an interest in the Christian God and the affairs of the
church (311 CE and afterward) and put imperial resources toward the res-
olution of theological controversies that were socially as well as ecclesias-
tically disruptive. In addition to changing the way in which doctrinal authority was exercised, the trinitarian and christological controversies tied
the interests of church and empire more closely together; in both theology and art, the portrait of Jesus often took on imperial outlines.

Contemporary Developments

Since the Enlightenment, biblical scholars and systematic theologians
have undertaken various "quests" for the historical Jesus, seeking the
man behind the christological doctrines and even behind the gospels
themselves. Social-political or theological agendas (often unacknowl-
edged) have inevitably accompanied these quests and their resultant
portraits of Jesus. With the emergence of black theology in the United
States in the 1960s and Latin American and other liberation theologies

in the 1970s, classical Christology increasingly came to be regarded as either irrelevant metaphysically or dangerous politically, as a legitimation of dominating power relations. Instead, these new theologies focused on the historical Jesus as liberator and source of empowerment for those struggling against injustice and oppression.

Black and liberation theologies and Christologies emphasized the social-political context of faith and the centrality of liberating praxis for Christian life. But their analyses of race and class oppression often failed to attend to the presence and experience of women. Feminist theology, with its explicit commitment to the full humanity and well-being of women, offered a corrective to this myopia but suffered from short-sightedness of its own: the assumption that the experience of the relatively privileged white women who predominated in feminist movements was an adequate description of all women's experience and the basis for doing theology.

Confronted by the realities of difference and the increasingly strong voices of womanist, *mujerista*, and Asian, African, and Latin American women theologians, white feminists have come to recognize the limitations of their own experience, the particularity of women's lives, and the complexity of analyzing the interconnection of oppressions within which sexism is a multivalent factor. A multiplicity of feminist theologies has developed in the past decade, sharing some common foundations and goals but specified in the context of concrete communities of struggle and accountability. When these theologies turn their attention to the subject of Christology, they do so in relation to the historical issues of classical Christology; the developments of black, liberation, and other contemporary theologies; and the particularities of women's experiences of oppression and resistance. There are a variety of approaches to feminist-womanist Christologies.

Decentering the Classical Tradition

The Maleness of Jesus
Mary Daly's (1973) naming of "christolatry" and denial of women's need for a savior and Rosemary Radford Ruether's (1981) pointed posing of the question "Can a male savior help women?" were early defining moments in the feminist discussion of Christology. Daly rejected classical Christology as damaging to women, and she found no value in attempting to reconstruct the male symbol of Jesus. Ruether (1983) refocused the issues of classical Christology and redirected attention to the

historical Jesus, understood as a messianic prophet who critiqued structures of oppression, including patriarchy, and whose praxis was liberating and socially transformative. She regarded Jesus' maleness as nonnormative, but did not resolve the methodological issue of how to construct a nonsexist Christology, suggesting androgynous or spirit Christologies as alternative possibilities. Jesus is the Christ, but he is not the exclusive or final revelation of redeemed and redeeming humanity.

Jesus-Sophia

Elisabeth Schüssler Fiorenza offered a feminist theological reconstruction of Christian origins (hence of christological beginnings) in *In Memory of Her* (1983). Jesus was Sophia's prophet, proclaiming a vision of the *basileia* (kingdom/reign) of God that engendered a discipleship of equals; the community's praxis of inclusive wholeness subverted patriarchal relations of domination in empire and household. Despite the subsequent repatriarchalization of Christianity, Schüssler Fiorenza sees Jesus and the movement gathered around him as a possible prototype for women struggling for liberation today. In *Jesus: Miriam's Child, Sophia's Prophet* (1994), she further develops the issues and implications of Sophia Christology for a feminist critical practice of transformation.

Wisdom/Sophia traditions are also a source for Elizabeth Johnson's reconceptualizing of the triune God in *She Who Is*. Jesus-Sophia is Wisdom made flesh, the compassionate presence of God in the words and deeds of Jesus as he teaches, heals, and calls women and men into inclusive table community. After his death and resurrection, he is known to be the Christ and the community continues his redeeming and liberating work. Returning to Sophia as the interpretive symbol of Jesus the Christ overcomes sexist Christology, Johnson claims, by shattering the connection between maleness and divinity in the mystery of God, the humanity of Jesus, and the reality of Christ.

Contextualizing Women's Experience of Jesus

Black Women's Experience

While acknowledging the feminist critique of classical Christology, Jacquelyn Grant took feminist theology and Christology to task in *White Women's Christ and Black Women's Jesus* (1989) for being white and racist, inadequate for black women. Instead she proposed a womanist Christology beginning from a tridimensional analysis of black women's experience of race, sex, and class oppression and the meaning of Jesus in their lives. In the womanist tradition, Jesus is divine co-sufferer who identifies with the sufferings of black women; Jesus is God, hence white people are not; Jesus Christ is black, and as "least among the least" Christ is a black woman.

Kelly Brown Douglas further develops womanist Christology in *The Black Christ* (1994). Her multidimensional analysis of black people's experience includes sexual orientation; her bifocal vision considers the effects of oppressions on the black community and the ways in which the community nurtures oppressions within itself. Both affirming and challenging, the black Christ is found wherever the community is engaged in the struggle for wholeness and is seen particularly in the faces of the poorest black women. His maleness is not essential; he is Christ because of what he did, not because of who he was.

Third-world women from Africa, Asia, and Latin America approach Christology from the dual context of their particular community's history and struggle for liberation and from their experience as women in that community. Although there are differences among them, most of the theologians whose writings are available in the English-speaking world (e.g., in Fabella/Oduyoye) tend to focus on the historical Jesus as liberating in his ministry, egalitarian in his relationships with women, and suffering in solidarity with the people in each situation of oppression. They emphasize what Jesus does and where Jesus is, not who he is. Western (i.e., white North American/European) feminist critiques of Christology are acknowledged, but neither the questions nor the answers are taken for granted as applicable to non-Western contexts.

Relocating Christology: Christic Community

Any notion of Jesus as savior or hero (including liberator) is rejected by Rita Nakashima Brock in *Journeys by Heart: A Christology of Erotic Power* (1988). Neither does she consider Jesus to be the Christ. Rather, Christology is centered in community and relationship. Jesus is but one participant in the revelation or embodiment of redemptive community that Brock terms *Christa/Community*. There is no exclusive locus to this redemptive community; wherever the erotic power of "heart" flows in mutual relation, there Christa/Community engenders wholeness, the healing of brokenheartedness that is salvation.

Shifting the understanding of Jesus' historical context by locating him in the Spirit-driven reign-of-God movement, Mary Rose D'Angelo

views Jesus as a prophet in a community of shared prophecy that resists imperial rule and expects the establishment of justice for the impoverished and marginalized of Israel.

In addition to the issues and approaches noted here, two concerns
are of particular importance for the ongoing work of feminist, womanist, and liberation Christologies: Christian anti-Judaism's classical
christological roots and its feminist manifestations, and religious pluralism and christological exclusivism.

7

FEMINIST ANTI-JUDAISM
AND THE CHRISTIAN GOD

Judith Plaskow (USA)

It is with much ambivalence that I stand here this morning to speak with
you about feminist anti-Judaism. First of all, I am a firm nonbeliever in
Jewish-Christian dialogue. To be sure, as a Jewish woman in the field of
feminist theology, I have always worked with Christian and post-Christian women. We formulated a critique of patriarchal religion together; we
argued about the depths of patriarchy in Judaism and Christianity; we
discussed together what it means to recover and make visible women's
history, and we struggled together with integrating women's experience
into our respective traditions. But these are substantive questions that we
have in common, and talking about substance is very different from talking about talking with each other. Dialogue for its own sake, I find, too
often breeds dishonesty, defensiveness, guilt, or breast-beating, none of
which is particularly useful for dealing with anti-Judaism.

Secondly, I am ambivalent about being here because to speak English in a German context makes me feel like an ugly American. There is
a part of me that would rather remain silent. Yet, I am aware, third of
all, that there are specific reasons why I cannot speak German. I was
brought up in a house where I was taught to hate and fear Germans and
Germany. When it came time for me to pick a foreign language in
school, my mother forbade me to put German on my list of choices.
When I signed up for a course in theological German as part of my
graduate studies, she began to cry and shout, "How do you say 'Fry the

---

This paper originally concluded with a long discussion of Jewish feminist efforts to reconstruct Jewish images of God. That discussion has been eliminated
for the purpose of this symposium.

Jews' in German?" I report this not to evoke guilt—for I myself struggled with and against these feelings for many years—but simply to elucidate the context out of which I address the topic of anti-Judaism.

Yet while these various sources of ambivalence might have led me to refuse your invitation to speak, instead they came together as reasons that I *had* to speak. Here of all places, it is necessary to discuss feminist anti-Judaism if there are feminists who wish to discuss it. Let me then begin.

For me, the issue of Christian feminist anti-Judaism—while personally painful—is just one piece of a larger question of how we as feminists, and as members of various religious, national, and international communities, can learn to see diversity not as a threat but as a source of enrichment and even a cause for celebration. The dream we had in the heady, early days of the feminist movement, that the bonds of sisterhood would annul or eradicate traditional divisions of religion, race, and class, and that we could formulate an analysis of women's situation and a program for action that would embrace all women, was based not on engagement with the particularities of women's experience but on a wave of a magic wand that made differences invisible. Racial/ethnic feminists have increasingly made clear that feminist theory and priorities often have ignored the multiple communities that shape women's lives.[1] Assuming that male/female difference is the oldest and only important social difference, white middle-class—often heterosexual, often Christian—feminists have constructed accounts of women's experience that falsely universalize a particular cultural, religious, and class perspective. This bias is illustrated by the persistence of anti-Semitic stereotypes in feminist literature; the additive analyses of sex, race, and class that ignore their interpenetration in women's lives; and the exclusionary phrases "women and blacks" or "women and minorities" that appear and reappear in feminist writing. The message such work communicates to women rooted in dominated communities is that if we want to be part of the "women's movement," we should bring ourselves as women in the abstract (which is to say women of the dominant group), leaving aside the particular women we happen to be.

Confronting feminist anti-Judaism, as well as all other types of oppression, is part of a process through which we face the fact that *there is no reason* why becoming feminists should suddenly free us from the other forms of hatred that mark our world or the groups to which we belong; that without continual self-examination and vigilance we are as likely to use feminism to perpetuate other forms of domination as to overcome them; and that feminism at best commits us to struggle against traditional forms of dominance; it does not guarantee that we will be successful.

In the case of the relationship between Jewish and Christian feminists, there are profound asymmetries that make it difficult for us to respect, and on the Christian side, even to perceive, the differences between us. On the one hand, there is the long history of Christian anti-Judaism, firmly rooted in the New Testament, and expressing itself historically in social, economic, political, and religious sanctions against Judaism and Jews. Christians have had the power to forbid Jews to practice Judaism, to herd Jews into ghettoes, to restrict Jews to certain professions, and to kill Jews. And in a continuing way, they have had the more subtle power of any dominant group to impose their own world view without the slightest idea that they are doing so. Not surprisingly, this history makes it very difficult for Jews to take seriously Christian claims—traditional or feminist—that Christianity is a religion of love, liberation, or right relation.

On the other hand, feeding anti-Judaism in a different way is the religious and psychological reality that Christians need Jews in a way that Jews do not need Christians. Wondering what Jews think about Jesus or why Jews reject Jesus as the Messiah, Christians seem to find it almost impossible to hear that Jews *don't* think about Jesus—except when Christian questions and a Christian culture force them to do so—and that they do not reject Jesus, they are simply not interested in him. The fundamental irrelevance on a religious level of Christianity to Judaism means that Christians taking Judaism seriously as an independent, living tradition must rethink the self in a way that is not true for Jews in relation to Christianity. What does it mean to affirm Christian identity without defining it over against Judaism? This is a question that the Christian tradition has never found a way to answer. And in large measure, it still has not been resolved by Christian feminists, who have simply turned feminism into a new way of yet again defining Christian identity at the expense of Judaism.

While there are a number of areas of feminist discourse I could turn to to illustrate this point, the conference topic, images of God, in many ways brings us to the center of Christian feminist anti-Judaism. I would like to discuss, therefore, three places where anti-Judaism asserts itself in relation to the subject of God: the contrast between the supposedly wrathful God of the "Old Testament" and the New Testament God of love, blaming Jews for the death of the Goddess, and the "Jesus was a feminist" theme as an aspect of the broader—and to my mind most difficult—subject of the specialness of Jesus. I will make no attempt to be exhaustive, but will simply cite some typical examples of feminist use of traditional anti-Jewish themes in order to open up some of the questions they raise.

The idea that the God of the "Old Testament" is a jealous, wrathful, and essentially tribal deity in contrast to the New Testament God of universal love is a well-established stereotype that long predates feminism. (I place the term "Old Testament" in quotation marks, for obviously it is not a Jewish term, and the contrast "Old Testament"/"New Testament" itself implies a supercession that can be applied to any of a host of issues: law/gospel, people of the flesh/people of the promise, God of wrath/God of love, and so on). The idea of two contrasting natures of God has been seized by feminist mythmakers who, perhaps in an effort to free themselves from some of the more problematic aspects of God's nature, have depicted an internal development in the nature of God that amounts to a virtual dualism. Sheila Collins, for example, began her early feminist theology, *A Different Heaven and Earth*, with a story about the son of the great Queen of Heaven who one day inexplicably arrogates kingship to himself, turning against the Goddess who bore and nurtured him. Dictatorially protecting the illegitimate power he always fears to lose, he surrounds himself with fire and thunderbolts, and makes up ugly stories about the Queen to explain human suffering under his rule. In due time, however, the Queen has another son who teaches people gentleness and compassion and alerts them to the fact that the King's priorities are seriously distorted. "He taught them that wisdom was not found in learned books nor in secret ceremonies, but in the heart of the child and the simple justice of nature."[2] A similar feminist myth is retold nine years later as the preface to Rosemary Ruether's *Sexism and God-Talk*. In her version, God the Father bellowing "I am the Lord thy God" from his high throne is contrasted with the iconoclastic teacher who speaks of a kingdom for the poor and the meek.[3]

There are several problems with this dualistic depiction of two natures of God, the most serious of which is that it projects a tension that exists *within* both Judaism and Christianity as a conflict *between* Judaism and Christianity. In the so-called Old Testament, God is fully developed as a God of justice *and* a God of mercy, and both these aspects of God are elaborated by rabbinic Judaism which also considers and problematizes the relation between them. In the Rosh Hashonah and Yom Kippur liturgies the thirteen attributes of God from Exodus 34 are repeated over and over again as the congregation prays for mercy on the (annual) day of judgment, "The Lord, the Lord is a merciful and gracious God, slow to anger and abounding in kindness and truth. He keeps kindness to the thousandth generation, forgiving iniquity and transgression and sin, and acquitting the penitent." The contrasting aspect of God, present in

Exodus but dropped from the liturgy—"but who will by no means clear the guilty, visiting the iniquity of the fathers upon the children..."— appears indirectly in numerous rabbinic *midrashim* and discussions that seek to make sense of Jewish suffering in light of belief in a merciful God. Indeed, Rosemary Ruether, in her myth, acknowledges the complexity of the God of the Hebrew Bible when her jealous God the Father remembers other ways of being God, such as vindicating the oppressed and freeing captives.[4] But then, as a Christian conscious of the history of anti-Judaism, why does she not portray a liberating God who is tempted by dominance rather than playing off the traditional stereotypes while hinting that they don't fully apply?

If the God of mercy is present in the Hebrew scriptures, then the God of wrath is also present in the New Testament, although often more as a background threat than as a vital presence. "He who believes and is baptized will be saved," says the risen Christ in the gospel of Mark (16:16), "but he who does not believe will be condemned." Judgment as the left hand of conversion and repentance is fully developed in the book of Revelation, a book that Christians playing out the contrast between the God of love and the God of wrath conveniently ignore. Moreover, the later Christian notion of the eternal damnation of masses of humanity—and the vigorous depiction of that damnation in Christian sculpture and painting—has no parallel in Judaism, which can think of no worse fate for the wicked than that they will be forgotten.

Often linked to the image of the jealous and dominating God of the Old Testament is the notion that this God is responsible for the death of the Goddess. While this theme has been most fully elaborated by post-Christian feminists as an implicit assumption of their historical reconstructions, it also plays a role, interestingly enough, within Christian feminism. In Sheila Collins's myth, God becomes King of the universe by turning against his wife/mother, the Queen of heaven who is presumed to have reigned over the whole earth until overthrown by the God of the "Old Testament." God's need for absolute dominion is a product of both his guilty conscience and his continuing fear of the mother whose power he usurped, but who always impinges on the margins of his consciousness. In Ruether's myth too, God thinks, "'The Queen of Heaven. Why does She still appear in my head? I crushed her rule a millennium ago.'"[5] Ruether's use of this theme is particularly surprising, given her insistence in other contexts that Goddess religions themselves were often patriarchal.

The feminist origin of the idea that biblical religion struck the death-blow to the Goddess is not difficult to see. As Carol Christ pointed out in her paper, "Not Blaming the Jews for the Death of the Goddess,"[6] it must come as a shock to any feminist brought up reading the Bible that the "idols" repeatedly vilified by the prophets were not mere sticks and stones, but the gods and goddesses of another religion—among them goddesses whose images and histories feminists are trying to reclaim. The realization that the biblical writers helped to suppress female imagery comes with a sense of betrayal that easily attaches itself to traditional anti-Jewish themes. Now the Jews have not one deicide on their hands, but two. Their perfidy in betraying Christ, not a comfortable theme in feminist circles, echoes their earlier banishment of the Goddess whose rightful rule was usurped by Yahweh, the upstart son.

That this theme should find its way into Christian feminist myth-making is ironic, given the role that Christianity played in the suppression of Goddess worship after the conversion of Constantine. It seems that in this case, as with the image of the wrathful God, it is easier for Christian feminists to point the finger at problematic aspects of the Christian tradition as they also appear within Judaism than it is to deal with them within Christianity itself. Beyond examining the antipaganism in Christian history, however, feminists must also realize that it is not Judaism or Christianity, separately or together, that bear the whole guilt for the death of the Goddess. As scholars of the Ancient Near East have pointed out, patriarchal societies and religions began to emerge throughout the Near East and Mediterranean worlds in the fourth through second millennia BCE. The struggle documented within the Hebrew Bible between advocates of exclusive worship of Yahweh and a larger population of Hebrew polytheists was just one facet of an older and much larger struggle between what some have depicted as Goddess-centered, matrifocal societies and emerging patriarchal societies with ascendant male gods.[7] As the evidence for such a wide-scale social transformation grows and becomes clearer, Jewish and Christian feminists will be able to locate the particular contributions of Hebrew and Christian patriarchy to this larger process.

The contrast between the God of love and the God of wrath and the condemnation of Jews for the death of the Goddess represent two areas in which feminist treatments of God continue traditional anti-Jewish themes. Anti-Judaism still seems most entrenched, however, in relation to the figure of Jesus, and in particular, feminist attempts to articulate his uniqueness and significance. I find the persistence of anti-Judaism in this area especially significant, given the profound ambivalence of many Christian feminists about the nature and role of Jesus. In the U.S. context, Christian feminist anti-Judaism certainly does not take the traditional forms of reproaching the Jews for rejecting the Messiah or accusing Jews of deicide, for Christian feminists are not always sure who they want to say Jesus was and is. Indeed, the charge of deicide is much more comfortably made in the Goddess context, for the Goddess at least is a clear representation of the sacred, even if not one Christian feminists wish to adopt. Yet in wanting to hold on somehow to the centrality and specialness of Jesus without necessarily making ontological claims about his nature, feminists are forced to focus on his human uniqueness, and this uniqueness is most easily established by contrasting him with his Jewish context.

I first made this point many years ago in relation to the still-popular claim that Jesus was a feminist. As I argued then and still would insist, this claim depends on wrenching Jesus out of his Jewish context and depicting the Judaism of his period in unambiguously negative terms. As one writer on this topic put it, "At the historical moment when Jesus was born into the world, the status of Jewish women had never been lower...By the time of Jesus's birth, many decades of rabbinic commentary and custom had surrounded Old Testament literature. And these rabbinic traditions considerably lowered the status of women."[8] The author then goes on to quote a series of misogynist Talmudic passages that may date anywhere from before the time of Jesus to five centuries later.

Such polemical use of rabbinic material to document Jesus's feminism shows no interest in the serious examination of Jesus's actual context. Aside from the fact that the Talmud is much more appropriately compared with the church fathers than with the sayings of Jesus, rabbinic literature is as varied as the New Testament in its comments about women and its legal treatment of women's issues. As Judith Wegner points out in her book *Chattel or Person? The Status of Women in the Mishnah*, the Mishnah, a second-century legal text that lays the basis for the Talmud, is perfectly comfortable treating women in some contexts as full legal persons with the rights and responsibilities of Jewish males, and in other contexts as virtual chattel.[9] To cite one side of this contradiction without the other is like quoting 1 Timothy 2 on women with the implication that it represents the entire New Testament.

Ignoring the complexities of rabbinic literature is just one problem with the Jesus-was-a-feminist argument, however. A more curious aspect of the strategy of contrasting Jesus with his Jewish background is that it simultaneously acknowledges and negates the fact that Jesus was a Jew. He was a Jew sufficiently that his supposed difference from other Jews is significant and noteworthy, yet he was not a Jew in the sense that his behavior counts as evidence for the nature of first-century Judaism. If we acknowledge that the Jesus movement was a movement within Judaism, however, then whatever Jesus's attitudes toward women, they represent not a victory *over* Judaism but a possibility *within* early Judaism—a Judaism that was in fact so diverse and pluralistic that it is impossible to state its normative position on anything. The notion of a normative Judaism is a later rabbinic construct that Jewish feminists are trying to free ourselves from, and that we would urge Christian feminists not to adopt in the first place.

The argument that Jesus was a feminist is theologically very interesting for its simultaneous radicalness and conservatism. Obviously, its intent is to awaken the Christian tradition to self-transformation, yet it does so on the basis of an un-nuanced and uncritical reading of the New Testament and early Judaism that seeks to proof-text in the service of feminism. It assumes, to use Krister Stendahl's phrase, that contemporary Christians are called upon to "play 'First Century Bible-Land'" and to do as Jesus did, however Jesus's actions are understood.[10] Moreover, though the Jesus-was-a-feminist argument does not depend upon explicit claims about Jesus's unique ontological status, it leaves these traditional claims unexamined in the background as a buttress to the feminist cause. It is perhaps not surprising then that traditional anti-Jewish attitudes work their way into this argument, along with other traditional assumptions.

I find it especially disturbing, therefore, that the tendency to define Jesus as unique over against Judaism remains even in feminists who do not make use of the Jesus-was-a-feminist argument, who are quite aware of Christian anti-Judaism, who are freely critical of Christian sources, and who have gone very far in deconstructing notions of Jesus's divinity. Carter Heyward's view of Jesus, for example, as a man of passionate faith who shows Christians the way to live their own lives in relationship to God, but who cannot do it for them, seems to provide very little grounding for traditional anti-Jewish themes. And yet when Heyward tries to state the meaning of the "dynamic relatedness we call Christ," she says that Jesus "seemed to perceive his own work would involve a radical shift in consciousness...from an emphasis on ritual to right-relationship; from salvation as 'deliverance-from-enemies' to salvation as 'right-relationship-with-God' which might involve deliverance into the hands of enemies."[11] Here we have the conventional law/gospel, carnal Jew/spiritual Christian dichotomies clearly stated in feminist form—a form that I must say is utterly astounding to me as a Jewish feminist, for what is *Judaism about*, if not right-relation?

It seems as if the feminist struggle with patriarchal christologies itself generates a dilemma that leads back into the trap of Christian anti-Judaism. If Jesus is not the Messiah and the incarnate son of God on any traditional interpretation of these terms, then how does one articulate his uniqueness in a way that makes sense out of remaining a Christian? If one is unwilling to make statements about Jesus's ontological status or about God's work in and through him, then maybe it is necessary to make some claim about his specialness as a human being—and how does one do that except by contrasting him with his Jewish context? This is why I said earlier that confronting anti-Judaism forces Christians to re-define the self. Must Jesus be different from every other human being who ever lived in order for Christianity to make sense? Can Christians value Jesus if he was just a Jew who chose to emphasize certain ideas and values in the Jewish tradition but did not invent or have a monopoly on them? If claims about Jesus's specialness are intrinsic to Christianity, then is there any way to make these claims that does not end up rejecting or disparaging Judaism as their left hand?

I think the persistence of anti-Judaism in feminist work—some-times even in the writing of feminists who have explicitly addressed the problem—is clear enough. Since, as I said earlier, I see the issue of anti-Judaism as one aspect of the larger issue of how we create communities that honor diversity, I must at least touch on the complex political context in which Jewish and Christian feminists of good will approach this issue.

In discussing three loci of Christian anti-Judaism in relation to the question of God, I tried to speak in a way that would not deny the kernel of truth in the issues concerning Judaism Christian feminists have raised. The image of a dominating, angry, father God is a problem for Jewish feminists as much as for Christian feminists. Jews *have* contributed to the suppression of the Goddess. The early Christian movement was open to women, whether we see that openness in contrast to Judaism or as part of it. Given these kernels of truth, even if Christian feminists engage in a continuing process of consciousness-raising and self-monitoring with regard to anti-Judaism, there always will remain gray areas in the anti-Judaism discussion that will need to be openly talked through with the utmost sensitivity. Christian and Jewish feminists need to be very aware of how we *talk about* and *hear* feminist criticism of Judaism and discussion of Jesus in light of the past and present history of Christian anti-Judaism.

This history, and efforts to begin grappling with it, raise very different dilemmas for Jewish and Christian feminists. On the one hand, it is very difficult for Jewish feminists to critique Judaism in a non-Jewish context when we know that what we say as internal criticism may appear against us in Christian work. On the other hand, it is obviously essential to our health and well-being as Jewish feminists that we do critique Judaism and seek to transform it. On the one hand, the Hebrew

Bible *is* the Christian Old Testament, and Christian feminists have a right to explore and critique the Old Testament—including images of God in the Old Testament—as part of their tradition. On the other hand, Christianity has a history of using the Hebrew Bible in a way that belittles and discredits the people who wrote it, and Christian feminist criticism cannot but be read in that context. On the one hand, Christian feminists have every reason to explore and value Jesus' openness to women. On the other hand, in doing so, they need to take account of the difficulty of talking about Jesus's relations with women without evoking in the hearer negative comparisons with Judaism. On the one hand, I as a Jewish feminist could write a feminist critique of modern Protestant theology without ever having anyone suggest I was anti-Christian. On the other hand, a Christian feminist whose field is Judaism might well find herself in very uncomfortable waters if she chooses to do work on documenting the patriarchal character of Judaism.

I do not have answers to the questions of exactly when critique or historical research veers into anti-Judaism or exactly who should speak and when. I do find it helpful, however, to keep in mind a joke that addresses the sometimes delicate boundary between self-critique and something else. What is the difference, the joke asks, between an anti-Semite and a prophet? The answer is, an anti-Semite says, "Jews are terrible," and a prophet says, "Jews are terrible, oy." This joke suggests to me that if Christian feminists want to say "Jews are terrible," they had better first have said the "oy" loudly and clearly in their work and in their lives. The absence of that "oy" is not simply a matter of a missing syllable. It is a matter of lending aid and comfort to those persons and institutions wedded to a society that excludes Jewish difference.

Finally, however, no awareness of feminist anti-Judaism and its relation to a long history, no effort to weed it out of one's thinking and writing, no sensitivity to the power imbalance in the relations between Jews and Christians can replace knowledge of Judaism as a living religion as the best antidote to anti-Judaism. Certainly, Jews have been oppressed. Certainly, Christianity's contribution to that oppression is something every Christian should be aware of. But Jews are not defined by our oppression. It is not what makes us Jews. It is not what makes our identity valuable and our difference worth asserting. To know Judaism primarily through anti-Judaism, to see anti-Judaism as the central issue confronting Jews, is itself another manifestation of anti-Judaism. If there is a role for Jewish-Christian dialogue in a feminist context, perhaps its most important function is this: to foster awareness of Judaism as defined by Jews, as a complex, varied, and evolving tradition.

ANTI-JUDAISM IN FEMINIST CHRISTIAN INTERPRETATION

Anti-Jewish themes in Christian writing are deep-rooted and tenacious, but there are ways in which feminists can address, rather than reproduce, this sorry aspect of Christian self-understanding. With prodding from women of color, feminists are beginning to grapple with the idea that racism and classism are dimensions of texts and social structures that must be confronted if feminism is to become a movement committed to the liberation of all women. Given the continuing presence of anti-Semitism as a structural element in Christian culture, this insight must also be extended to anti-Judaism in a thoroughgoing way.

1. The first step in eradicating anti-Judaism is becoming aware of its existence, and this means becoming educated about the dimensions of the problem. Fortunately, there are a number of good general histories of anti-Semitism, and also narrower studies of anti-Judaism in Christian history, thought, and practice. The critical discussion of anti-Judaism taking place in the feminist community has antecedents in many Christian scholarly works...

2. Once Christian feminists recognize anti-Jewish patterns, it is essential that they begin systematically to problematize anti-Judaism in the Christian tradition *as part of a feminist analysis* of Christian texts. Again, just as womanist scholars have taught white feminists that looking at racism and race relationships between women is a feminist task, so feminists must analyze "women's relational history" in terms of anti-Judaism and religious difference.[12] This means that it is not enough for feminist interpreters to avoid allying themselves with the anti-Judaism in Christian sources or even to raise in general terms the problem of anti-Judaism in feminist interpretation. Rather, it is necessary to signal the existence of anti-Judaism in Christian texts *wherever it appears* so that the problem of traditional Christian anti-Judaism becomes a dimension of feminist consciousness, and feminists begin to examine the dynamics of the relationship between sexism and anti-Judaism in Christian sources.

Explicit discussion of anti-Judaism is a task for feminist writers, but it is also important in the context of the classroom. Feminist teachers of New Testament can raise questions about the anti-Jewish story line of the gospels, just as they would raise questions about the roles and status of women in those texts. They can help students to reflect on the anti-Jewish "rules of formation" present in Christian historical materials, and their continuing impact on Christian self-understanding. Sometimes with a class that is resistant to feminist issues, it is tempting to gain student attention by claiming that "Jesus was a feminist" or was especially open to women. Teachers' attempts to avoid negative comparisons with Judaism in this context, however, cannot prevent students from appropriating such material in the framework of an anti-Jewish heritage. That is why, in discussing women in the early Christian movement or Jesus' attitudes toward women, it is essential to raise the problem of anti-Judaism explicitly and to examine its strategies and effects.

3. Addressing the anti-Judaism in Christian sources, because it is consciousness-raising for all parties, is probably the most important next step Christian feminists can take in dealing with the problem of feminist anti-Jewish interpretation. But sensitivity to anti-Judaism cannot of itself effect a transformation of anti-Jewish attitudes. The long history of anti-Judaism will finally be transcended only on the basis of an appreciation of Judaism as an autonomous, changing, and diverse tradition. In the specific context of feminist New Testament interpretation, this means it is impossible fully to discuss or evaluate the Jesus movement in relation to women without knowledge of feminist approaches to first-century Judaism.

Feminist exploration of Jewish women's history is a very new field. Just as feminist scholars have moved from addressing the sexism in Christian sources to recovering the complex reality of women's lives within Christian history, so they have begun to reconstruct the history of women within Judaism. While it is impossible to discuss here all the methodological issues the new feminist scholarship raises for Christian interpretation, probably its most important finding is that rabbinic literature is not an accurate reflection of the diversity of women's roles within first-century Judaism. To cite just two examples: the "Jesus-was-a-feminist" argument maintains that women played no role in the ancient synagogue, contrasting this exclusion with women's discipleship in the Jesus movement. But inscriptions from diaspora synagogues referring to women as elders, leaders, and synagogue presidents suggest that women could have played liturgical or administrative roles in the synagogues of Jesus' time. This inscriptional evidence is particularly significant when combined with the absence of any ancient literary or archaeological evidence for special women's sections or galleries in the synagogues of this period.[13] Second, the assumption that only men could initiate divorce in Judaism is challenged by a number of documents from the first centuries CE that depict individual women as divorcing their husbands or reserving the right of divorce in their marriage contracts. These documents suggest that there were two strands of thought and practice concerning divorce in ancient Judaism. One—which became normative Jewish practice—accorded only men the right of divorce, but the other also allowed women to initiate divorce.[14]

4. Two pieces of evidence for this second strand of Jewish practice are Mark 10:11–12 and 1 Corinthians 7:10–11. This fact points to another important strategy in overcoming anti-Judaism in feminist New Testament interpretation: reading the New Testament not as the antithesis or refutation of "Judaism," but as an important source for Jewish women's history.[15] If the gospels are seen as reflecting part of the continuum of first-century Jewish practice with regard to women, they tell a very different story about Jewish women's lives than if they are read oppositionally. The absence of any overt challenge to Jesus' treatment of or teachings about women suggests that his relation to women and gender norms might not have been so different from the relations of his contemporaries. Perhaps Jewish women sometimes divorced their husbands, moved freely in the streets and conversed with strangers, were visible in the synagogue and temple, and paid visits and received visitors.[16] Such a reconstruction may not provide a simple warrant for contemporary Christians to become feminists, but it both avoids perpetuating Christian anti-Judaism and yields a more nuanced and interesting picture of women's religious lives in the ancient world.

5. Finally, it is important to mention an institutional dimension to the persistence of anti-Judaism in Christian feminist interpretation. While feminists often celebrate the ways in which women's criticism and reconstruction of religion have opened up new areas of interreligious dialogue, the reality is that much Christian feminist work takes place in isolation from the Jewish feminist agenda. Christian institutes, workshops, panel discussions, and other projects deal with key feminist issues, either without including Jewish feminists working on the same questions or inviting Jewish participation on Christian terms. Whatever the rationale for this institutional isolation, it would seem to reflect and perpetuate a lack of awareness of the Jewish "Other" that necessarily makes it more difficult to recognize and grapple with anti-Judaism in a scholarly context. Appreciation of Judaism as an independent tradition must include an openness to Jewish feminist concerns—concerns that in their similarities and differences from Christian feminism challenge Christian feminists to develop a more critical perspective on a hegemonic tradition.

Notes

1. bell hooks, *Feminist Theory: From Margin to Center* (Boston: South End Press, 1984); Cherrie Moraga and Gloria Anzaldua, eds., *This Bridge Called My Back: Writings By Radical Women of Color* (1981; reprint, Latham, NY: Kitchen Table: Women of Color Press, 1983); Gloria Hull, Patricia Bell Scott, and Barbara Smith, *All the Women Are White, All the Blacks Are Men, But Some of Us Are Brave* (Old Westbury, NY: Feminist Press, 1982); Elizabeth V. Spelman, *Inessential Woman: Problems of Exclusion in Feminist Theory* (Boston: Beacon Press, 1988).

2. Sheila Collins, *A Different Heaven and Earth* (Valley Forge, PA: Judson Press, 1974), 25–30; quotation, 28f.

3. Rosemary Ruether, *Sexism and God-Talk: Toward a Feminist Theology* (Boston: Beacon Press, 1983), 1–11, esp. 1, 5–6.

4. Ruether, 3.

5. Collins, 27ff.; Ruether, 2.

6. Carol P. Christ, *Laughter of Aphrodite: Reflections on a Journey to the Goddess* (San Francisco: Harper & Row, 1987), 84.

7. See, e.g., Mary Wakeman, "Ancient Sumer and the Women's Movement: The Process of Reaching Behind, Encompassing, and Going Beyond," *Journal of Feminist Studies in Religion* 1 (Fall 1985): 7–27.

8. Virginia Ramey Mollenkott, *Women, Men, and the Bible* (Nashville: Abingdon, 1977), 10.

9. Judith Romney Wegner, *Chattel or Person? The Status of Women in the Mishnah* (New York and Oxford: Oxford University Press, 1988), esp. chapter 7.

10. Krister Stendahl, *The Bible and the Role of Women* (Philadelphia: Fortress Press, 1966), 40.

11. Carter Heyward, *Our Passion for Justice: Images of Power, Sexuality, and Liberation* (New York: Pilgrim Press, 1984), 17.

12. The term "women's relational history" is Delores Williams's ("Women's Oppression and Lifeline Politics in Black Women's Religious Narratives," *Journal of Feminist Studies in Religion* 1 [Fall 1985]: 69; see also Clarice Martin, *Journal of Feminist Studies in Religion* 6 [1990]: 41–43).

13. Bernadette Brooten, *Women Leaders in the Ancient Synagogue: Inscriptional Evidence and Background Issues* (Brown Judaic Studies 36; Chico, CA: Scholars Press, 1982); Brooten, "Early Christian Women," 89.

14. Bernadette Brooten, "Could Women Initiate Divorce in Ancient Judaism? The Implications for Mark 10:11–12 and I Corinthians 7:10–11" (The Ernest Cadwell Coleman Lecture, School of Theology at Claremont, April 14, 1981); and Brooten, "Early Christian Women," 73.

15. Brooten, "Could Women Initiate Divorce in Ancient Judaism?" esp. 9–12.

16. Von Kellenbach, "Anti-Judaism," 87–89.

III

A SYMPHONY OF VOICES

Christology has appeared to be central to women's theology. In the person and praxis of Jesus Christ, women of three continents (Africa, Asia, Latin America) find the grounds of our liberation from all discrimination: sexual, racial, social, economic, political, and religious. By reflecting on the incarnation, that is, the life, death, and resurrection of Jesus, we have come to realize the need to contextualize our Christology in the oppressed and painful realities of our continents. This means that Christology is integrally linked with action on behalf of social justice and the defense of each person's right to life and to a more humane life...

We remark also that many Christians in our continents are seeking to see in Jesus' own suffering, passion, death, and resurrection a meaning for their own suffering. This explains the great devotion our people have to the mysteries of the passion and the cross. Nevertheless, we have a mission to announce that Christ brought a new life for humanity and that this was the whole point of his suffering. Suffering that is inflicted by the oppressor and is passively accepted does not lead to life; it is destructive and demonic. But suffering that is part of the struggle for the sake of God's reign is redeeming and is rooted in the paschal mystery, evocative of the rhythm of pregnancy, delivery, and birth. This kind of suffering is familiar to women of all times, who participate in the pains of birth and the joys of the new creation.

Final Document on *Doing Theology from Third World Women's Perspective,* Ecumenical Association of Third World Theologians, Mexico 1986.

8
WHO IS JESUS FOR ASIAN WOMEN?

Chung Hyun Kyung (Korea/USA)

TRADITIONAL IMAGES

In order to express their experiences of Jesus, the majority of Asian women use the traditional titles that they received from missionaries. Since many Christian churches in Asia are still dominated by Western missionary theologies and androcentric interpretations of the Bible, some Asian women's theologies on the surface look similar to Western missionary or Asian male theologies. However, when we look closely at the Asian women's usage of the traditional titles of Jesus, we can find the emergence of new meaning out of the old language. The following are examples of traditional images of Jesus which have gone through the welding of meaning by the experiences of Asian women.

Jesus as Suffering Servant
The most prevailing image of Jesus among Asian women's theological expressions is the image of the suffering servant. Asian Christian women seem to feel most comfortable with this image whether they are theologically conservative or progressive. In light of their lives filled with suffering, it seems natural to meet Jesus in the experience that is most familiar to them.

When Asian women live through the hardship of suffering and obedience their family, society, and culture inflict upon them, they need a language that can define the meaning of their experience. The image of a suffering Jesus enables Asian women to see meaning in their own suffering. Jesus suffered for others as Asian women suffer for their families and other community members. As Jesus' suffering was salvific, Asian women are beginning to view their own suffering as redemptive. They are making meaning out of their suffering through the stories of Jesus' life and death. As Jesus' suffering for others was life-giving, so Asian women's suffering is being viewed as a source of empowerment for themselves and for others whose experience is defined by oppression.

However, making meaning out of suffering is a dangerous business. It can be both a seed for liberation and an opium for oppression. These two conflicting possibilities shape Asian women's experience of encounter with Jesus. For example, their fathers are supposed to be the protectors, the ones who give Asian women safety in an oppressive world, providing food, shelter, and clothing. But too often Asian women are beaten by their fathers or sold into child marriage or prostitution. Asian women's husbands are supposed to love them, but frequently they batter their wives in the name of love and family harmony. Asian women's brothers are supposed to support and encourage them, but they instead often further their own higher educations by tacitly using their Asian sisters, ignoring the reality that their sisters are selling their bodies to pay for tuition. The promises of safety, love, and nurturing have not been fulfilled. Asian women have trusted their beloved men, but their men have often betrayed them. Yet Asian women still hope, still believe that, "Maybe someday, somewhere, somebody will love me and nurture me as I am." Is Jesus that somebody?

The church's teachings about Jesus are very similar to what Asian women's fathers, husbands, and brothers say to them, rather than what Jesus actually says in the gospels. The church tells Asian women: "Be obedient and patient as Jesus was to his heavenly father. He endured suffering and death on the cross. That is what good Christian women are supposed to do. When you go through all the suffering, you too, like Jesus, will have a resurrection someday in heaven. Remember, without the cross, there will be no resurrection. You must die first in order to live."[1] This is a hard and confusing teaching for Asian women. They are asking, "Why should we die in order to gain Jesus' love? Can't we love Jesus while being fully alive?" Self-denial and love are always expected of women in the church as in the family. But why isn't this teaching applied to men?

Western colonialism and neo-colonialism have created an added burden to Asian women's belief in Jesus. When Western Christians brought Jesus to Asia, many also brought with them opium and guns. They taught Asians the love of Jesus while they gave Asians the slow death of opium or the fast death of a bullet. When the soldiers of the United States of America raped Vietnamese women and children and killed many Vietnamese people with Agent Orange, guns, and bombs in the name of democracy, the people of the United States still sang,

"God Bless America." Death and love are connected in missionary acts whether they are religious or secular.

Some Asian women have found Jesus as the one who really loves and respects them as human beings with dignity. It remains the case, however, that Asian women have believed in Jesus *in spite of* many contradictory experiences they receive from their families, churches, and societies. Believing *in spite of* great contradictions is the only option for many Asian women who are seeking to be Christian.

Some brave Asian women proclaim a resounding no to this endlessly confusing love game defined by "in spite of." They say they love Jesus *because of* and not *in spite of* who he is. They refuse to accept old, familiar ways of relating to their loved ones, which were based on forced sacrifice by women. Rather, they choose the *respect* of self. Jesus is only good for these Asian women when he affirms, respects, and is actively present with them in their long and hard journey for liberation and wholeness. Asian women are discovering with much passion and compassion that Jesus takes sides with the silenced Asian women in his solidarity with all oppressed people. This Jesus is Asian women's new lover, comrade, and suffering servant. He is neither a masochist who enjoys suffering nor a father's boy who blindly does what he is told to do. On the contrary, Jesus is a compassionate man of integrity who identified himself with the oppressed. He "stood for all he taught and did"[2] and took responsibility for the consequences of his choice even at the price of his life. This image of Jesus' suffering gives Asian women the wisdom to differentiate between the suffering imposed by an oppressor and the suffering that is the consequence of one's stand for justice and human dignity.

Korean theologian Choi Man Ja makes this liberative aspect of Jesus' suffering clear in her presentation on feminist Christology. She asks this question: "How do women, who are in the situation of suffering under and obeying oppressive power, take on significance as suffering and obeying servants?" Her answer is: "Suffering is not an end in itself... [It] has definite social references of divine redemptive activity. Suffering exposes patriarchal evil. Jesus endures the yoke of the cross against the evil powers of this patriarchal world. This obedience is different from simple submission to the worldly authority."[3] Servanthood is not mere submission or obedience. It is instead a powerful witness to evil and a challenge to the powers and the principalities of the world, especially male domination over women.

The suffering servant who is undergoing passive suffering with powerless Asian women and who is also accompanying them in their struggle for liberation by doing liberation is the prophetic Messiah who creates a new humanity for oppressed Asian women. Through Jesus Christ, Asian women see new meaning in their suffering and service. They see life-giving aspects in their suffering and service that create a new humanity for the people they serve.

Jesus as Lord

If the liberative dimension of the suffering servant image frees Asian women from imposed suffering and empowers them to accept suffering as a consequence of their own choice for liberation, the liberative dimension of the Lord image of Jesus frees Asian women from the false authority of the world over them and empowers them to claim true authority which springs from life-giving experiences.

Yet like the image of the suffering servant, the image of Lord also has been used against Asian women, perpetuating their submissive and oppressed status in Asian society and the church. Traditionally Asian women have not been the owners of themselves under mainline patriarchal culture. In the East Asian context where Confucianism was the dominant social and religious ideology, women have had to obey the men in their lives: fathers before marriage, husbands in marriage, and sons in widowhood. The Asian woman's man was her lord. In addition to Confucianism, feudalism and the emperor system did not give much space for the self-determination of women. Even though women could not actively participate in any public or political affairs, they did, of course, suffer from the results of the hierarchical social system (in such concrete ways as lack of food due to oppressive taxes).

Western colonialism used Jesus' image as Lord to justify political and economic domination over many Asian countries. To become a Christian meant obeying the Lord Jesus and the colonial power that brought him to Asia. This ruler image of Lord Jesus became especially strong in countries like the Philippines that were colonized by Spain. The Spanish conquistadores put Lord Jesus over all the indigenous spirits in the Philippines and put their king over the tribal leadership of the Filipino people. In their recent research many Filipino women theologians have demonstrated that the lordship ideology of colonial Christianity domesticated the vibrant pre-colonial Filipino women's self-understanding and power in the community. According to Mary John Mananzan's research, even some male scholars believe that Filipino society was based on a matriarchal culture before colonization.[4] This active image of the power of Filipino women was diminished as Christianity was spread along with the feudal ideology of the colonial power. The ideal image of the Filipino woman became one of passivity, submissiveness, obedience, and chastity.

Under this historical reality many Asian women who were seeking women's liberation and self-determination have become suspicious of the Lord image of Jesus. Yet they also see the liberative power of the image of Jesus as Lord of poor and oppressed women in Asia. According to Park Soon Kyung, the title *Kyrios* (Lord), which was the word for ruler in Hellenistic culture, transformed its meaning radically when it was used to name the power of Jesus. While patriarchal lordship of this world means the ruling power that oppresses people, lordship of Jesus means the power that liberates people. All lordship in this world becomes relativized in relation to this power with its origin in God:

> The Lordship of Christ means that his Lordship is [the] exact opposite of patriarchal Lordship and he eschatologically places the rule of the evil powers in this world under God's judgment. Jesus put a period to the power of patriarchal history by obeying to the righteousness of God as a male even to his death. His Lordship is the Lordship of the righteousness of God which is established by his suffering and death. This Lordship destroys the principality and power of the world and returns all the power and authority to God.[5]

Jesus' lordship, then, says no to patriarchal domination, freeing Asian women from false authority and empowering them to obey only God and not men.

Jesus as Immanuel (God-with-us)
Jesus, who became the Lord of the universe through his suffering and service for humanity, also shows Asian women God's presence among them. Many Asian women cherish the mystery of the incarnation through Jesus' person and work. Both the human and divine nature of Jesus are important for Asian women's identity and mission. Their understanding of Jesus' humanity and divinity, however, is very different from that of Nicene-Chalcedonian theological definitions stressing the Son's relationship to the Father and the two natures of his person. Two distinguished voices that articulate the meaning of incarnation (Logos becoming flesh in Jesus) come from India and Korea.

Noting that "every New Testament book attributes deity/divinity to Jesus either by direct statement or by inference,"[6] Indian theologian

Monica Melanchthon writes that this Jesus also shares human finitude with us by "lying in the cradle, growing, learning, feeling the pangs of hunger, thirst, anxiety, doubt, grief, and finally death and burial."[7] Through his incarnation Jesus becomes the representative of a new humanity, not only of men, who are just one-half of the human race, but of women too. The institutional church, however, distorted Jesus' image by emphasizing his maleness rather than his humanity. His gender became a constitutive factor used to exclude women from full participation in the church. Melanchthon warns that emphasizing the maleness of Jesus is a pagan act: "If we ascribe maleness to Jesus Christ, we are also committing the mistake of ascribing the pagan/Hindu notions of sexuality to our God who transcends this. The Church in India needs to recognize the personhood of Jesus Christ and the fact that Christ is the representative human being for all people including Indian women."[8] For her, Jesus' humanity embraces all people. The Christian God transcends sexuality and therefore frees Indian women from the stereotypical role assignments in Indian culture. Jesus as the Immanuel (God-with-us) transforms Hindu culture.

Drawing on a popular Korean format of the hero story, theologian Lee Oo Chung shows how Korean women experience the mystery of incarnation and "God-with-us" by becoming like Jesus.[9] Many Korean Christians in the movement claim that we should become "little Jesuses" in order to become true Christians. For many Korean women, Jesus is not the objectified divine being whom people must worship. Rather, Jesus is the one we relive through our lives. The meaning of Immanuel, then, has been changed through Korean mythological symbols and language from God-*with*-us to God-*among*-us, and finally to God-*is*-us in our struggle to reclaim our full humanity.

NEW EMERGING IMAGES

New images of Jesus have emerged from Asian women's movements for self-determination and liberation. The freer Asian women become from the patriarchal authorities of their family, church, and society, the more creative they become in naming their experience of Jesus Christ. Sometimes the images of Jesus are transformed to the degree that they show the radical discontinuity between the ones found in the Jewish and Christian culture and those from the Asian women's movement. Some Asian women have become confident enough in themselves to name the presence of Jesus Christ in their own culture, indigenous religions, and secular political movements. This is a *christological transformation* created out of Asian women's experiences as they struggle for full humanity. The old christological paradigms are transformed, new meanings are achieved, and diverse images of Jesus Christ emerge. Asian women as meaning-makers jump into an unknown open future shaping a new Christianity out of their own experience that never before existed in history. The following are examples of new, emerging images of Jesus Christ derived from Asian women who believe in their historical lived experience more than [in] imposed authority.

Jesus as Liberator, Revolutionary, and Political Martyr
Jesus Christ is portrayed as liberator in many writings of women from various Asian countries such as India, Indonesia, Korea, the Philippines, and Sri Lanka. The reason why Jesus as liberator is the most prominent new image among Asian women is a consequence of their historical situation. The liberation from colonialism, neo-colonialism, poverty, and military dictatorship, as well as from overarching patriarchy, has been the major aspiration of twentieth-century Asian women.

In the composite paper of the EATWOT Asian Women's Consultation, entitled "Women and the Christ Event," Jesus is defined as "the prototype of the real liberator." [The document also claims] that Jesus as liberator is evident "in the image of liberators in other non-Christian religions and movements."[10] This image of Jesus Christ as liberator is made concrete as revolutionary or political martyr in the Filipino women's reflection on the Christ event presented at the same consultation. According to Lydia Lascano from the Philippines, Filipino women who participate in the people's struggle for liberation "live out with their lives the Christ event—Jesus' life, passion, death and resurrection—leaving the mark of their womanhood in the Philippine liberation project, the project of God."[11]

Filipino women have suffered under more than three hundred years of Spanish and American colonialism and military dictatorships and have survived to reclaim their human dignity as a people. Filipino women find Christ's suffering, death, and resurrection *in* the suffering, death, and resurrection of Filipino women themselves. In their organized action for liberation, Filipino women have been arrested, raped, tortured, imprisoned, and displaced from their homes. Many have even been killed in their struggle toward self-determination for their people. Their names are today remembered by women in protest movements:

> Lorena Barros, a freedom fighter; Filomena Asuncion, a deaconess who offered her life for the conscientization of peasants; Leticia Celestino, a factory worker shot in the picket lines while demanding for a just wage; Angelina Sayat, a freedom fighter who died while in the custody of the military; Puri Pedro, a

catechist who served the farmers, was tortured and killed while being treated in a hospital.[12]

Unlike the women of Jerusalem in Jesus' time, Filipino women are not just comforting or shedding tears for Jesus on his way to the cross. They are bearing the cross and shedding blood for their people. Sister Lascano explains the political martyrdom among Filipino women:

> Today, the passion of Christ in the Filipino people is fashioning women disciples who would accompany the suffering Christ alive among the people, not merely to comfort and support but even to die with them. In the passion for social transformation, death takes on a new level of meaningfulness...Today many Filipino women do not merely accompany Christ to Calvary as spectators. They carry the cross with him and undergo his passion in an act of identification with his suffering.[13]

The resurrection of Jesus comes alive in the resurrection of these martyrs. The Filipino women's resistance movement makes the spirit and vision of these martyrs come alive by persistent organized action and active waiting and watching for the future victory of the struggle. When poor Filipino women are awakened to see the root cause of their suffering in structural evils, they begin to claim for themselves land and rights as human beings. And they take political action. This discovery has stirred hope in their hearts, believing that the liberating God of the Exodus has become alive in the resurrected Christ, now alive among them as the *Bagong Kristo,* the New Christ.

Jesus as Mother, Woman, and Shaman

Many Asian women portray Jesus with the image of mother. They see Jesus as a compassionate one who feels the suffering of humanity deeply, suffers and weeps with them. Since Jesus' compassion is so deep, the mother image is the most appropriate one for Asian women to express their experience of Jesus' compassion. Hong Kong theologian Kwok Pui-lan explains this point in her essay "God Weeps with Our Pain": "Jesus cried out for Jerusalem. His sorrow was so deep Matthew had to use a 'feminine metaphor' to describe what he actually felt: How often would I have gathered your children together as a hen gathers her brood under her wings (Matt 23:37)."[14] Like a mother who laments over her dead son who died in the wars in Indochina, like many weeping Korean mothers whose sons and daughters were taken by the secret police, Jesus cries out for the pain of suffering humanity.

This compassionate, sensitive mother image of Jesus was shared by the Indonesian theologian Marianne Katoppo. She illustrates her point by quoting a prayer of Anselm and a poem from the Indian poet Narayan Vaman Tilak:

"And thou, Jesus, sweet Lord, art Thou not also a mother?
Truly, Thou art a mother, the mother of all mothers
Who tasted death, in Thy desire to give life to Thy children"
—Anselm

Tenderest Mother-Guru mine,
Saviour, where is love like thine?
—Narayan Vaman Tilak

This mother image of Jesus demolishes "the paternalistic, authoritarian and hierarchical patterns" in our life and builds the "maternal, compassionate, sensitive, bearing and upbearing" relationship among people.[15]

Another female image of Jesus comes from the image of the shaman. Under oppressive political and economic oppression, and under the added burden of the Confucian system of ethics which inculcates male domination, Korean women's life experience is *han* itself. The resentment, indignation, sense of defeat, resignation, and nothingness in *han* make many Korean women brokenhearted and physically sick. In this situation, what would be the significance of Jesus Christ for them? "If Jesus Christ is to make sense to us, then Jesus Christ must be a priest of Han."[16] For the *minjung* women, salvation and redemption means being exorcised from their accumulated, many-layered *han*. Since Korean indigenous religion is shamanism, Korean women easily accept the Jesus of the Synoptic gospels, who healed the sick and exorcized the possessed like a Korean shaman.

In Korea the majority of shamans are women. Shamanism is the only religion among the various Korean religious traditions where women have been the center all through its development. Women shamans have been "big sisters" to many deprived *minjung* women, untangling their *han* and helping them cope with life's tribulations. When Korean women, therefore, see Jesus Christ as the priest of *han*, they connect with the female image of Jesus more than the male image of Jesus. They take Jesus as a big sister just as they take the shaman as a big sister in their community.

The female image of Jesus Christ is expressed most vividly by a theologian in India, Gabriele Dietrich. In a powerful poem she makes a connection between women's menstruation and Jesus' shedding of blood on the cross and in the Eucharist:[17]

> I am a woman
> and my blood cries out:
> Who are you
> to deny life
> to the life-givers?
> Each one of you
> has come from the womb
> but none of you
> can bear woman
> when she is strong
> and joyful and competent.
> You want our tears
> to clamour for protection.
> Who are you
> to protect us
> from yourselves?
>
> I am a woman
> and my monthly bloodshed
> makes me aware
> that blood
> is meant for life.
> It is you
> who have invented
> those lethal machines
> spreading death:
> Three kilotonnes of explosives
> for every human being
> on earth.
>
> I am a woman
> and the blood
> of my abortions
> is crying out.
> I had to kill
> my child
> because of you

who deny work to me
so that i cannot feed it.
I had to kill my child
because i am unmarried
and you would harass me
to death
if i defy
your norms.

I am a woman
and the blood
of being raped
is crying out.
This is how you keep
your power intact,
how you make me tremble
when i go out at night.
This is how you keep
me in place
in my house where
you rape me again.
I am not taking this
any longer.

I am a woman
and the blood
of my operation
is crying out.
Even if i am a nun
you still use my body
to make money
by giving me a hysterectomy
when i don't need it.
My body is in the clutches
of husbands, policemen,
doctors, pimps.
There is no end
to my alienation.

I am a woman
and the blood
of my struggles

is crying out.
Yes, my comrades,
you want us
in the forefront
because you have learnt
you cannot do without us.
You need us
in the class struggle
as you need us
in bed and to cook
your grub to bear
your children to dress
your wounds.
You will celebrate
women's day
like mother's day
garlands
for our great supporters.
Where would we be
without our women?

I am a woman
and the blood
of my sacrifices
cries out to the sky
which you call heaven.
I am sick of you priests
who have never bled
and yet say:
This is my body
given up for you
and my blood
shed for you
drink it.
Whose blood
has been shed
for life
since eternity?
I am sick of you priests
who rule the *garbagriha,*
who adore the womb
as a source for life

and keep me shut out
because my blood
is polluting.

I am a woman
and i keep bleeding
from my womb
but also from my heart
because it is difficult
to learn to hate
and it might not help
if i hate you.

I still love
my little son
who bullies his sister.
He has learnt it outside,
how do i stop him?
I still love
my children's father
because he was there
when i gave birth.
I still long
for my lover's touch
to break the spell
of perversion
which has grown
like a wall
between women and men.
I still love
my comrades in arms
because they care
for others who suffer
and there is hope
that they give their bodies
in the struggle for life
and not just for power.
But i have learned
to love my sisters.
We have learned
to love one another.
We have learned

even to respect
ourselves.

I am a woman
and my blood
cries out.
We are millions
and strong together.
You better hear us
or you may be doomed.

Dietrich questions the hypocrisy of the patriarchal church and society which "deny life to the life-givers" and "adore the womb as a source" but shut out women from full participation in life. Jesus shed blood on the cross due to his solidarity with the poor, oppressed, and alienated. He bled so as to give others everlasting life. Like Jesus, women's blood has been shed from eternity. Women's menstruation is a holy Eucharist through which the renewal of life becomes possible. Jesus joins women in his life-giving bleeding.

Jesus as Worker and Grain
Female images of Jesus Christ enable Asian women to image Jesus on the earth. The revelation of God they have heard from the church is usually the revelation from above. Theology based on the revelation from above can easily be distorted into a theology of domination because this theology is based on the abstract thinking of the head and not on the concrete experience of the body. It is based on distant (and largely male) intellectualism and not on the everyday, experiential reality of Asian women. Some Asian women find Jesus in the most ordinary, everyday experience. They see the revelation of God from below, the bottom, the earth. They refuse any kind of heroism. They are not looking for great men and women to worship. Rather, they want to find God, the saving presence within their daily lives.

A witness of faith from a Korean factory worker shows the meaning of Jesus Christ among the ordinary poor people:

I don't know how to live a Christ-like life. But I am discovering and awakening to the meaning of it little by little in my daily life. This is a cautious and mysterious process. [In order to explain this point,] I would like to talk about my mother. She is a woman full of "Han." She describes herself like that. She was married when she was seventeen. She gave birth to three children. Then her husband died even before she became thirty. Now my mother gets up 4:30 AM every morning and goes to marketplace for banding. There are too many people in the marketplace. It is hard to walk there. I think that marketplace is truly our context of life...

Whenever I see my mother, her face reminds me of the tired faces of my friends in the factory who are working eighteen to twenty-four hours a day without even any facial expression. Workers do not stop their work even when they are overwhelmed by despair and disgust. Since they experience despair, are humiliated by the rich and endure miserable situations, they know how to love the people in despair under every circumstance—even though we are in despair all the time. The world is constructed out of these hearts.

When I see workers, I feel the breath and heart-beat of history and the meaning of humanity and Christ in them. I wonder how Jesus the Christ will look when he comes back again. When I was young, I dreamt about Jesus wearing silvery white clothing, accompanying many angels with bright light and great sounds of music. But now I wonder. If Jesus comes again, he may come to us wearing ragged clothing and give my tired mother, who even dozes off while she is standing, a bottle of Bakas, or he may come to me, working mindlessly in the noisy factory, and quietly help my work while wearing an oily worker's uniform. I think our Christ is the ground of life, and my faith is in the midst of this working life and workers.[18]

This factory worker sees her Christ in workers and their hard struggle for survival. Another image of Jesus Christ which emerges from the earth is found in a poem from an Indian woman. She meets her Jesus Christ when she receives two hundred grams of gruel in a famine-stricken area. For her, Christ, God's beloved Son, is food for hungry people.

> Every noon at twelve
> In the blazing heat
> God comes to me
> in the form of
> Two hundred grams of gruel.
>
> I know Him in every grain
> I taste Him in every lick.

I commune with Him as I gulp
For He keeps me alive, with
Two hundred grams of gruel.

I wait till next noon
and now know He'd come:
I can hope to live one day more
For you made God to come to me as
Two hundreds grams of gruel.

I know now that God loves me—
Not until you made it possible.
Now I know what you're speaking about
For God so loves this world
That He gives His beloved Son
Every noon through You.[19]

Without food, there is no life. When starving people eat the food, they experience God "in every grain." They "know" and "taste" God when they chew each grain. When God gives them food through other concerned human beings, God gives them God's "beloved Son," Jesus Christ.

In conclusion, we have observed that there are *traditional* images of Jesus, which are being interpreted in fresh, creative ways by Asian women, largely based on their experiences of survival in the midst of oppression and on their efforts to liberate themselves. We also have observed *new* images of Jesus that offer a direct challenge to traditional Christologies. These new images of Jesus are also based on Asian women's experiences of survival and liberation. Because Jesus was a male, however, some Asian women think there is a limit to how much he can be transformed to meet the needs of Asian women. This is the main reason why Asian women theologians have emphasized the importance of Mary in their recent writings.

Notes

1. This is the common teaching Asian women receive from the institutional, male-dominated churches.

2. Virginia Fabella, "Asian Women and Christology," *In God's Image* (September 1987): 15.

3. Choi Man Ja, "Feminist Christology," Consultation on Asian Women's Theology, *In God's Image* (1988–1989): 6.

4. Mary John Mananzan, "The Philipino Woman: before and after the Spanish Conquest of the Philippines," in *Essays on Women* (Manila: Woman's Studies Program, Saint Scholastica's College, 1987), 7–36.

5. Park Soon Kyung, "Hankook Minjok Kwa Yeosung Shinhak eu Kwajae [*The Korean Nation and the Task of Women's Theology*], 47.

6. Monica Melanchthon, "Christology and Women," Consultation on Asian Women's Theology, *In God's Image* (1987): 1.

7. Ibid.

8. Ibid., 6.

9. Lee Oo Chung, "Korean Cultural and Feminist Theology,"*In God's Image* (September 1987): 36.

10. "Women and the Christ Event," *Proceedings: Asian Women's Consultation* (Manila: EATWOT, 1985), 131.

11. Lydia Lascano, *Proceedings: Asian Women's Consultation*, 121–29.

12. Ibid., 127.

13. Ibid.

14. Kwok Pui-lan, "God Weeps with Our Pain," in *New Eyes for Reading: Biblical and Theological Reflections by Women from the Third World*, ed. J. Pobee and B. von Wartenberg-Potter (Oak Park, IL: Meyer Stone Books, 1986), 92.

15. Marianne Katoppo, "Mother Jesus," in *Voices of Women: An Asian Anthology*, ed. Alison O'Grady (Singapore: Asian Christian Women's Conference, 1978) ,12.

16. Fabella, "Asian Women and Christology.

17. Gabriele Dietrich, *One day i shall be like a banyan tree* (Belgium: Dileep S. Kamat, 1985). G. Dietrich is of German origin. Since 1972 she has been working in South India. I include her as a theologian in India due to her commitment and her identification with Indian women and her acceptance by other Indian women in the movement.

18. Suh Nam Dong, *In Search of Minjung Theology* (Seoul, Korea: Kankil Sa, 1983), 355–56.

19. Anonymous, "From Jaini Bi—With Love," in O'Grady, p. 11. The editor explains that the Jaini Bi stands for all people who suffer extreme deprivation in a seemingly uncaring world but who receive a spark of hope from humanitarian concerns and actions.

9

CHRISTOLOGY FROM AN ASIAN WOMAN'S PERSPECTIVE

Virginia Fabella (Philippines)

Asian women are beginning to articulate their own Christologies. For too long, what we are to believe about Jesus Christ and what he means for us have been imposed on us by our colonizers, by the Western world, by a patriarchal church, and by male scholars and spiritual advisers. But now we are discovering Jesus Christ for ourselves. What we say may not be anything new; what is important is now we are saying it ourselves. To the question posed by Jesus "Who do people say that I am?" we are giving answers that reflect not only what we encounter in scriptures but also our reality and experience as Asian women. Thus our Christologies are not only interpretations of Jesus but confessions of our faith in this Jesus who has made a difference in our lives, and not only as a speculative activity, but as active engagement in striving toward the full humanity Jesus came to bring.

Although educated women doing theology and constructing Christologies have experienced discrimination and "tokenism" in both church and society, ours is a life of privilege compared to that of other women in Asia. The reality, backed by cases and statistics, is that "in all spheres of Asian society, women are dominated, dehumanized and de-womanized...viewed as inferior beings who must always subordinate themselves to the so-called male supremacy...treated with bias and condescension. In Asia and all over the world, the myth of the subservient, servile Asian women is blatantly peddled to reinforce the dominant male stereotype image."[1] Thus, even while writing from a Christian viewpoint, I take into account these countless women, whether they believe in Jesus Christ or not. Jesus' liberating message has meaning for all women struggling for full humanity and their rightful place in history.

120

I

Christology is at the heart of all theology, for it is Jesus who has revealed to us the deepest truths about God. In his humanity, Jesus revealed God as a loving God who cares for the weakest and lowliest and wills the full humanity and salvation of all, men and women alike. In his humanity, Jesus has shown us what it means to be truly human, to have life abundantly, to be saved. This Christology is central and integral to any talk about the human-God relationship and to any discussion about salvation and liberation.

There are important issues that any Christology must deal with. However, here I will only touch on those that have a bearing on my being Asian and woman, those that are more pertinent to the Asian context and the issue of gender. Feminist theologians in the U.S. have raised the question of the maleness of Jesus. Among Asian women, the maleness of Jesus has not been a problem for we see it as "accidental" to the salvific process. His maleness was not essential but functional. By being male, Jesus could repudiate more effectively the male definition of humanity, challenging both men and women to change their life patterns. Historically, however, Christology has been patriarchalized and has been the doctrine of the Christian tradition most used against women.[2] Thus the feminists' question stands.

An issue facing Christology pertinent to our Asian context is the way salvation/liberation takes on different meanings within the reality of massive poverty and multiple oppression on the one hand, and of religious, cultural, and ideological plurality on the other. In a continent where 97 percent of the people are not Christian, can we claim Jesus Christ as the savior of the whole world? How is he the unique and universal savior when the majority in Asia alone have never heard of him or have even ignored him in their quest for a better world? Some of the Asian faiths offer salvation which relates more closely than Christianity to the soteriological depths of our cultures and to the desire for liberation from both individual and organized greed.[3] Have we listened to what other major faiths have had to say about Jesus, especially those [that] have seriously grappled with his mystery, or have we as Christians tended to be "protective" and exclusive about Jesus?

These and other pertinent issues need to be addressed in the process of constructing an Asian Christology, a process which is just beginning. Theologians like Aloysius Pieris have indicated guidelines for this effort,[4] but these have not included anything that speaks directly to women's reality. Though the Christology be educed from the depths of our cultures and expressed in Asia's soteriological idiom, the result will not be relevant unless it takes into account women's experience, perspective, and contribution.

II

Every Christology focuses on the life and significance of Jesus Christ; therefore, the historical Jesus plays a central role. It is necessary to return to the Jesus of history, to the man Jesus who was born and who lived on our continent, whose life was rooted in Jewish culture and religious tradition. To bypass this history is to make an abstraction of Jesus and thus to distort his person, mission, and message of love and salvation. Moreover, it is only in reference to the historical Jesus that we can test the authenticity of our Jesus images and see how closely they relate to the reality.

Jesus' core message centered on the kingdom of God: "The reign of God is near; repent and believe in the good news" (Mark 1:15). His central message focused not on himself but on God and our response to God's gift of the kingdom. The notion of God's kingdom was a familiar one to the people, for it is contained in Hebrew scriptures and intertestamental literature, although by Jesus' time it had acquired a variety of interpretations. For this reason, Jesus aligned himself with John the Baptist and accepted John's baptism, for John preached the same message to the "crowds," the ordinary men and women, demanding repentance.

As an itinerant preacher/healer, Jesus drew a following for he performed signs and spoke with authority, and what he taught he practiced. He chose twelve apostles whom he instructed in the way of the kingdom. Although his message was for all, the people he attracted most were those on the fringes of society, those who were in "most need of salvation." However, not everything Jesus taught and practiced in terms of the kingdom was familiar or easy to understand, accept, or follow. His message included what others have never taught: the inclusive character of God's reign. Jesus lived out his teaching by freely associating with, and showing preference for, the poor and marginalized —sinners, outcasts, women. They were the last who had become first, the humble who had become exalted.

Jesus' attitude towards women and treatment of them was most uncommon even for a "good" Jew of his day, for he was not only considerate of them and treated them with deep respect, but even acted contrary to the prevailing customs and practices. Women were among the non-persons in society, mere chattel. But Jesus never ignored them when they approached him for healing; they were human beings worth making whole again. They were entitled to "life in abundance"; they were worthy of learning the Torah. He not only valued them as friends but affirmed their trustworthiness and capability to be disciples, witnesses, missionaries, and apostles.[5]

Jesus taught something else that was new and more difficult still: that love of God and neighbor must include love of enemies. From the time of Ezra, Jews and Samaritans had become irrevocable enemies. Yet by parable and example, Jesus made his point to "love your enemies; do good to those who hate you" (Luke 6:27). The Samaritan woman who gives him water to drink becomes his missionary to her people. Jesus likewise showed compassion on the foreigner, allowing himself to be challenged by the entreaties and confidence of a Syrophoenician woman. Thus Jesus showed that to live a truly human life, one lives a life-in-relation, demonstrated by care and service even to the least: the women, the enemy, the outsider.

But this was not all. Jesus spelled out what it means to "love one another" in practice: there is no lording it over others; even masters shall serve; right relation to one's neighbor has priority over temple worship; discipleship is above blood relationship; only by losing one's life shall one find it. What a liberating message for the women; they were the dominated, the taken for granted, the one-sided servers, the "mother of" or "daughter of." Jesus made clear what being human means; only thus can one enter the kingdom of God. And the invitation is open to all.

Jesus' words and deeds brought him into conflict not only with the Jewish religious authorities but also with the Roman leadership. When Jesus was arrested, tried in two courts, found guilty of sedition by the Romans and sentenced to death by crucifixion, he did not resist. He understood the consequences of his word and works in fidelity to God's call.

III

For the apostles, Jesus' death was a shame and a scandal which shook their faith and shattered their hopes. In fact, afraid of Roman reprisals, they dispersed, and only a few disciples, mostly women, remained with Jesus as he died on the cross, to all semblances a failure. But then, the unexpected happened. The disciples, beginning with the women, started to report appearances which they gradually began to identify with Jesus as they experienced peace and forgiveness. He had "risen from the dead!" Their new experience of Jesus radically transformed them into people of courage and faith, impelling them to continue Jesus' ministry and spread his message of salvation as they witnessed to him as their Lord and God. By his rising, Jesus is confirmed as the Christ and God's true son, the model of redeemed humanity, the incarnation of true divinity, no longer limited to the particularities of his maleness and Jewishness. Jesus Christ lives and continues to affect, renew, and give hope to the millions all over the globe who would believe and follow him. Jesus Christ is alive and we encounter him in our sisters and brothers.

The community's resurrection faith enabled them to interpret Jesus' death differently. The apostles had taken Jesus' death as a disappointing, shameful end of an eschatological prophet whose life failed to bring about the kingdom he preached. Their Easter faith, however, told them that Jesus' death was not a failure but a fulfillment. Jesus is the suffering servant who died for our sakes. The cross acquired a religious cultic significance, celebrating Jesus who died as "a ransom for many, whose shedding of blood expiates sins." From a negative event, the cross acquires a positive meaning.

In the course of time and movement across cultures, the positive meanings of Jesus' death became lost or distorted. In the Philippines, we have developed (or inherited) a dead-end theology of the cross with no resurrection or salvation in sight. Most of the women who sing the "pasyon" during Holy Week look upon the passion and death of Jesus as ends in themselves and actually relish being victims. This attitude is not uncommon among other women outside the "pasyon" singers, and it is not helped when priests reinforce the attitude through their homilies. One of them said not long ago that he does not preach the resurrection as "the people are not prepared for it."

In India, the theology of sacrifice thrust upon women is of no purpose. Indian women theologians tell us that their women silently bear taunts, abuse, and even battering; they sacrifice their self-esteem for the sake of family honor, subject themselves to sex determination tests, and endure the oppressive and even fatal effects of the dowry system. A woman who is raped will invariably commit suicide rather than allow her husband and family to suffer the ignominy of living with a raped woman. While we seek in Jesus' passion, death, and resurrection a meaning for our own suffering, we cannot passively submit ourselves as women to practices that are ultimately anti-life. Only that suffering endured for the sake of one's neighbor, for the sake of the kingdom, for the sake of greater life, can be redeeming and rooted in the paschal mystery. "On the cross of Jesus God himself is crucified...In this ultimate solidarity with humanity, he reveals himself as the God of love, who opens up a hope and a future through the most negative side of history."[6]

IV

The nature of Jesus' relationship to God was only reflected upon and gradually formulated after the resurrection. At first it was simply the application of the biblical titles to Jesus in the light of the resurrection experience: the Christ, Son of Man, Suffering Servant, Son of God, Lord, Son of David. Initially functional, the designations gradually took on a confessional dimension. Eventually, with increasing association with the Hellenistic world, ontological implications were drawn out. Thus through a process of historical growth and theological development, the identity of Jesus in terms of divinity was recognized and accepted by the early church, paving the way for the doctrine of the incarnation, the doctrine of the Word made flesh.

Intensive debates ended with authoritative formulations by the Council of Nicea (325 CE) and later the Council of Chalcedon (451 CE). The language and substance of these christological doctrines betray their historical and cultural conditionings, addressing as they did the disputes of another time and place which do not relate to the vital problems of present-day Asia. These doctrines are no longer of the greatest importance for many Asian theologians, for, taken as they are, they are largely unintelligible to the Asian mind. Thus the true significance of these councils is not so much their content, but the underlying challenge they pose to us to have our own contemporary culturally based christological formulations. And that is what small groups of Asian theologians, both men and women, are doing—having their own mini and informal Niceas and Chalcedons to determine, based on their context and concerns, who Jesus Christ is for them.

Just as the formulations of Nicea and Chalcedon have placed barriers in our efforts to have an honest dialogue with people of other faiths, so have our claims about Jesus as the universal savior. In Asia we experience dialogue on two levels, a more formal one commonly referred to as "interreligious dialogue" and a less formal one we refer to as "dialogue of life." Our experience in the latter where we share the life conditions, pain, risks, struggles, and aspirations of the Asian poor (the majority of whom are of other faiths or even of "no faith") has made us aware of our common search for a truly human life, our common desire for liberation from whatever shackles us internally and externally, and our common thrust toward a just society reflective of what we Christians term "the kingdom." In the struggle that binds us, there is an implicit acknowledgment and acceptance of our religious differences and our different paths to "salvation."

Theologians proclaiming that Jesus is wholly God but not the whole of God, or that Jesus is the Christ but the Christ is not Jesus,[7] should in no way lessen our own personal commitment to Jesus whom we Christians have personally known and experienced as revealer, savior, truth, way, and life. It should in no way disaffirm for us that the vision and power of Jesus of Nazareth is an effective, hope-filled, universally meaningful way of bringing about God's kingdom. We believe and confess that Jesus has brought us total salvation; others, however, are making similar claims about their own mediators with the same Ultimate Source of life's meaning whom we call God.

V

In view of what I have written, it would be inconsistent to hold on to the title and image of "lord" in reference to Jesus, because of the overtones of the word as used today. In Asia, the word "lord" is connected with the feudal system which in my own country is one of the root causes of the poverty, injustices, inequalities, and violent conflicts that exist there today, many of the victims being women. It is also a colonial term for the British masters, [a term] which is still used in countries like Pakistan for those who have taken their place. "Lord" connotes a relationship of domination, which is opposite to what Jesus taught and exemplified. "The rulers of the gentiles exercise lordship over them...but not so with you" (Luke 22:24). Asian women have been "lorded over" for centuries and all the major religions including Christianity have contributed to this sinful situation. The title "lord" would not be in keeping with a liberating Jesus.

In the light of Asian women's reality in general, a liberational, hope-filled, love-inspired, and praxis-oriented Christology is what holds meaning for me. In the person and praxis of Jesus are found the grounds of our liberation from all oppression and discrimination: whether political or economic, religious or cultural, or based on gender, race, or ethnicity. Therefore the image of Jesus as liberator is consistent with my Christology. In my own culture, however, not many women would be familiar with the figure of a liberating or liberated Jesus. They know him as the suffering or crucified Jesus who understands their own suffering which they passively or resignedly endure. Many remain unaware of their class and gender oppression and simply live on with a "status quo" Christology. Nevertheless, an increasing number of women are becoming aware of our subordinate place and exploited state in a patriarchal church and society, and see this as contrary to the will of a just and loving God, who created both men and women in God's own image. As these women strive to change this inequitable situation within the overall struggle against economic, political, and social injustices, they, too, see Jesus as their hope and liberator.

In our quest for a world of right human relationships, Jesus has shown us the way, and therefore Jesus is the norm for our action in reforming our lives and renewing society. Jesus never spoke of human rights or the common good or liberation from oppressive structures, yet his whole life, teachings, and actions embodied all of them, manifesting what it meant to be human and to act humanly. He showed us that we cannot work toward true liberation unless we seek the true humanity, the true liberation, of all. Thus, efforts to transform the existing structures and patterns of domination that prevent the least of our sisters and brothers from living truly human lives and enjoying just, reciprocal relationships, are moral actions.

Just as this Christology has implications for ethics, so it has implications for ecclesiology. To be a credible sign of salvation and to witness to Jesus' universal love, the church as institution has to rid itself of its non-liberating structures and non-loving practices, its exclusive, hierarchical mode of operation. It would do well to retrieve the egalitarian spirit of the early Christian communities. Unfortunately some of today's new experiences of being community are construed as a threat by the institutional church, instead of as an attempt to live out that spirit which grew from a faithful following of Jesus. If the church is indeed following in the steps of Jesus, then it should focus, as Jesus did, on preaching and living out the truths of the kingdom rather than on maintaining itself. If the church is serious in following Jesus, then it should encourage and support all efforts toward inclusiveness and full humanity.

Jesus intended this full humanity for all, not just for men, or less for women. Men and women have the same human nature and are endowed with the same potentials for "fullness." Men do not image God more than women do. Yet patriarchy has distorted these truths to promote a hierarchical and complementary model of humanity, which puts women in second place. Women's inferior status has become part of the working definition of being human in Asia, buttressed by the doctrines and practices of the major religions. This has had degrading and dehumanizing consequences for women in all areas of life down the ages, stark evidence of which is still present on our continent today. One of the deplorable consequences is the very internalization of this "ideology" of women's inferiority by women themselves as part and parcel of our cultures. Part of the work of an Asian Christology would be to determine the emancipating and enslaving elements of cultures and religions, to discern which ones foster and which ones impede the creation of a more human and humane life and a more just society.

VI

Lastly, there are certain implications of my Christology for mission ministry. The understanding of mission has undergone changes over the years and especially of late when the church has been present in almost all parts of the world. Transmission of the message in a transcultural milieu has acquired new modalities. Besides direct evangelization, missionaries are engaged in other activities: "witness" on behalf of the gospel, "prophetic" communication in word and sign, and involvement in personal and social transformation.

Throughout the past centuries, there has been such an urgency about planting the church that in preaching Jesus Christ, the stress has been given to the church he "founded" and its doctrine rather than the reign of God he proclaimed. But if our mission is an extension of Jesus' own mission, then we need to refocus on preaching the good news of God's reign which Jesus has already inaugurated and will come in its fullness in the future as God's gift. To make Jesus' message (its core and not its cultural overlays) comprehensible to Asians, we Christians need to engage in sincere and humble dialogue with people of other faiths, a dialogue which is as open to receive as to give, that in so doing we ourselves may come to grasp a fuller meaning of God's revelation. To make Jesus' message credible to Asian women, it must directly touch their everyday lives. Interreligious dialogue that is silent on women's oppression and thus simply perpetuates their subordinate status in religion and society is contrary to Jesus' saving word.

While many mission societies still insist on the primacy of first evangelization in mission, others have moved on to works of incultura- tion and liberation, both urgent tasks in Asia. While these are primarily the tasks of Asians themselves, they invite the support and collabora- tion of others, and missionaries have responded to this invitation. Missionaries are taking seriously what the Synod of Bishops said in 1971, that the mission of preaching the gospel demands our participa- tion in the transformation of the world.[8] Thus active solidarity with the people against sexism, racism, ethnic discrimination, and economic in- justice is truly missionary. For women missionaries all over the world, there is need to explore new mission ministries among, and on behalf of, women who need other women's support, presence, defense, sisterly help, friendship and active solidarity as they awaken to their reality and struggle for their full humanity. In Asia these women are numberless.

I have reflected on the significance of Jesus' life, death, and resur- rection from a specific horizon. It was my concern, however, that Christology not only express who Jesus is for me, but also recapture Jesus' life and message in such a way that it can be liberating and em- powering for other women. Hopefully this Christology will form part of the collective effort of Asian Christian women in search of a Chris- tology that is meaningful not only to us but to our Asian sisters whose life's struggles we have made our own. For now this is what I submit as my Christology as an Asian woman, knowing that it is subject to ad- ditions and revisions, and aware of the fact that the task of Christology is ongoing and never really finished.

Notes

1. "Proceedings of the Asian Women's Consultation," Manila, Philippines, November 21–30, 1985. Mimeographed.

2. Rosemary Radford Ruether, "Feminist Theology and Spirituality," in *Christian Feminism: Vision of a New Humanity*, ed. Judith L. Weidman (San Francisco: Harper & Row Publishers, 1984), 20.

3. Some Asian women question this claim as coming from a male perspec- tive. What Asian women need liberation from is not inordinate greed but exces- sive self-effacement.

4. Aloysius Pieris, "Speaking of the Son of God in Non-Christian Cultures, e.g. in Asia," in *Jesus, Son of God, Concilium* 153, ed. E. Schillebeeckx and J. B. Metz (New York: Seabury Press, 1982), 65–70.

5. Paul's claim to be an apostle because he had seen the risen Jesus and received a direct commission to preach the good news applies equally to Mary Magdalene (cf. John 20:16–18).

6. Jon Sobrino, *Christology at the Crossroads* (Maryknoll, NY: Orbis, 1978), 224.

7. Paul F. Knitter, *No Other Name?* (Maryknoll, NY: Orbis, 1986), 152, 156.

8. Synod of Bishops 1971, "Justice in the World," in *Renewing the Earth*, ed. David J. O'Brien and Thomas A. Shannon (Garden City, NY: Image Books, 1977), 391.

10

JESUS CHRIST AND THE LIBERATION OF WOMEN IN AFRICA

Teresia M. Hinga (Kenya/USA)

In the emergent and emerging theologies of liberation, both in the West but particularly in the Third World, the question of Christology has gained significant proportions. Theologians are trying to analyze and articulate the implications of Christianity and belief in Christ for their particular and often quite personal situations. A central question has been: Who is Christ? And what does belief in him mean, particularly for those who find themselves caught up in conditions of oppression?

This article attempts a reflection, however preliminary, on the implications of belief in Christ in the context of African women's search for liberation. It seeks to point out the ambivalence apparent in prevailing Christologies, and the need for the evolution of an African feminist Christology—or at least the need to create pointers in the right direction.

In recognition of the fact that feminism in Africa is a relatively novel extension of feminism in the West, and also of the fact that Western feminist theologians have reflected to a considerable depth, though without seeming to reach an unequivocal consensus, on the relationship between Christology and women, it is useful to reflect on what kind of ideas they have come up with so far.

A broad sweep of the Western feminist theologians' literature on the issue of Christology reveals that there are at least two perspectives. On the one hand, there is what may be referred to as the radical feminist view, which is probably best epitomized in the works of Mary Daly. On the whole, this view holds that cultural and social institutions, including religion, are so irredeemably warped by patriarchy that they can hardly be considered as allies of women as they try to liberate themselves. On the contrary, patriarchal culture and other social institutions help to engender their oppression and subjugation. This goes both for religion and received theology articulated largely by people who are perceived to be sexist and "misogynist" in their approach.

Thinking specifically of Christology, the doctrine of Christ, and the way it relates to women's liberation, Mary Daly, for example, advocates a rejection of the dogmas concerning Christ that have hitherto been formulated as largely oppressive of women. In her words:

> The distortion in Christian ideology resulting from and confirming sexual hierarchy [is] manifested not only in the doctrines of God and of the Fall but also in doctrines concerning Jesus. A great deal of Christian doctrine has been docetic, that is, it has not seriously accepted the fact that Jesus was a limited human being. A logical consequence of the liberation of women will be a loss of plausibility of christological formulas which reflect and encourage idolatry in relation to the person of Jesus.[1]

Mary Daly is also highly critical of the way Jesus has been presented as a model of emulation for Christians, including women. Given women's quest for liberation, Mary Daly suggests that imitating Christ as a model would only lead women to becoming more entrenched in the quagmire of subjugation. She argues that, insofar as received theology presents Christ as the primordial scapegoat, one who lives and dies entirely for another, his emulation would lead women to take on a role which they already are playing, for women, in any case, fulfill the role of victims and scapegoats in their various cultures. As she observes:

> The qualities that Christianity *idealizes*, especially for women, are also those of a victim: sacrificial love, passive acceptance of suffering, humility, meekness, etc. Since these are the qualities idealized in Jesus "who died for our sins," his functioning as a model reinforces the scapegoat syndrome for women. Given the victimized situation of the female in sexist society, these "virtues" are hardly the qualities that women should be encouraged to have. Moreover, since women cannot be "good" enough to measure up to this ideal, and since all are by sexual definition alien from the male savior, [Jesus] is an impossible model.[2]

Consequently, Mary Daly proposes that for women to succeed in their quest for liberation, they should learn not to look up to any models, least of all that of Jesus in his role as victim. In fact, Daly suggests that, for women to achieve their freedom, they will need to cultivate confidence in themselves, such that their actions spring from themselves, rather than being motivated by imitation of any role models.[3]

On the less extreme side of Western feminist theological discourse lie the thoughts of those who, for want of better terminology, I would call "reformist." These represent the view that social institutions are not distorted beyond repair. It is felt that aspects of culture and religion are salvageable, and that theology can help women in their struggle for emancipation and justice. In this category fall feminist theologians like Rosemary Ruether, Elisabeth Moltmann, Phyllis Trible, and Elisabeth Schüssler Fiorenza, among others.

Rosemary Ruether well exemplifies our theme here, for she has reflected specifically on the implications of Christology for women's liberation as she ponders on the question: Can a male savior save women?[4]

Ruether is mainly concerned with exposing the sexism embedded in some of the received Christologies that have been handed down to society through the ages—a sexism that would be an obstacle in women's search for justice and liberation. Such sexism is, according to Ruether, manifest in some of the works of the great church theologians. In particular, she cites the works of Thomas Aquinas who presented the view that women are malformed males and therefore constitute the abnormal half of the human species. With his own peculiar logic, he went on to argue that this is the reason why the incarnation of God could only be in a male, Jesus. The "maleness" of Jesus is, therefore, for Aquinas, not incidental but arises out of (ontological) necessity. The male reflects through Jesus the fullness of the image of God. By the same logic, woman is naturally second-rate and, therefore, naturally subordinate to man. This kind of theologizing has led to a fixation on the "maleness" of Christ as a decisive factor in Christology. It is a view often emphasized, for example, by those who oppose the ordination of women. The physical resemblance—that is, maleness[5]—is considered a necessary condition for those who represent Christ. Hence, priests are necessarily male!

However, as Ruether has rightly pointed out, the overfixation on the maleness of Jesus is a distortion of the truth as she sees it. For, indeed, it misses the whole point of the incarnation, namely, that Jesus became human in order to effect the redemption of humanity, both male and female. In this way, Jesus represented God who, in Hebrew thought, was perceived as their liberator and their redeemer par excellence.

Despite the essential "misogynism" of the dominant Christology in Western theological thought, Ruether goes on to show that there did occasionally emerge in Western Christianity alternative though less pervasive

Christologies. Some of these she isolates and highlights as potentially useful for women, because they are more inclusive and less sexist.[6]

In general, the above two perspectives reflect Western women's views concerning Jesus Christ and their specific context of a search for emancipation. At best, they reveal a certain ambivalence in their encounter with Christ. To [what] extent could these views be said to be universal? Could the same be said of the encounter between Christ and African women?

To be able to answer these questions, it is important to take into account the realization among contemporary theologians that Christ encounters people in various contexts. He has also been presented and appropriated in a variety of images or "faces," as Bonino prefers to call them. We have noted in this context that Ruether, for example, has isolated at least two such "faces" of Christ and has analyzed their implications for the women's cause. Another Latin American theologian[7] has discussed five images of Christ as appropriated by the Latin American masses, and their effects in engendering their oppression and powerlessness.

It would seem that in Africa, also, more than one image of Christ has been presented to and appropriated by Africans, including women, with, as I endeavor to show, mixed results.

Going back to history, we recall that during the period of colonial and imperial expansionism, the prevailing image of Christ was that of Christ the conqueror. Jesus was the warrior king, in whose name and banner (the cross) new territories, both physical and spiritual, would be fought for, annexed, and subjugated. An imperial Christianity thus had an imperial Christ to match. The Christ of the missionaries was a conquering Christ. Conversely, winning Africa for Christ was a major motivating factor in missionary zeal. Africa was the booty to be looted for Christ. What were the implications of this perception of Christ for the Africans?

The conquest of Africa often implied an erasing of most of what Africans held dear. The missionaries, in the name of Christ, sought to create a spiritual and cultural *tabula rasa* upon which they could inscribe a new culture, a new spirituality. This attempt at "erasing" was not all that successful, and, instead of creating a clean slate, the missionaries more often than not managed to create an identity crisis in the African minds—a sense of gross alienation. This is the kind of alienation and confusion that is lamented, for example, in Ngugi wa Thiongo's *The River Between*, or Chinua Achebe's *Things Fall Apart*.[8]

The cultural and spiritual imperialism[9] of the missionary endeavor has had some dire consequences. In dealing with some of what they deemed to be obstacles in their battle for Africa on behalf of Christ, in their zeal the missionaries often did not pause to reflect adequately on the consequences for the persons they sought to convert. Many examples can be given here, but I will highlight only two.

In treating the issue of polygamy, for example, the missionaries acted in a manner that was largely detrimental to the welfare of the women concerned.[10] Only the polygamist would be asked to abandon all but one of his wives as a condition for baptism. The policy of "disciplining" polygamists in this way undoubtedly brought untold pain to women and children thus discarded.

Another example which I give, because it comes from a culture I know well, is the issue of female circumcision encountered by missionaries in Kenya. Again, in their unilateral decision to stamp out what they considered to be a barbaric African custom, they ended up causing the women involved to suffer tremendously. Many a Protestant father was forced to sign, on pain of excommunication, that he would not circumcise his daughters. Meanwhile, the daughters continued to be exposed to a barrage of derision and ridicule for failing to undergo the rite that culturally defined them as women.[11] Many uncircumcised Protestant girls could not withstand the psychological torture, abuse, and social ostracism that was poured upon them, and they were secretly circumcised anyway.

No doubt, however, many missionaries would not have agreed with the above interpretation of their actions. This is because at the overt and conscious level, they expressed the desire to liberate the Africans from what they perceived to be the clutches of the devil. They were ostensibly motivated by the zeal to save Africa from the evils of slave trade, and to redeem her people from the state of savagery and apparent godlessness. They thought that by so doing they would be implementing the gospel of Christ the liberator—for they would be "proclaiming liberty to captives" and opening the prison for them that are bound.[12]

Thus, missionaries with a lot of commendable zeal were in the forefront, for example, of the movement for the abolition of slave trade, the freeing of captured slaves, and their rehabilitation.[13]

When the missionaries ventured into the African interior, they established mission stations which often functioned as centers of refuge or, in the view of the missionaries, "centers of Christianity and civilization." It is illuminating in this context to note that, at least initially, the people who were attracted to the mission were the socially disadvantaged. Thus, the White Fathers, for example, established their missions as orphanages, in which ransomed slave children could be taught self-reliance and "be brought up in the faith, away from the dangers of heathen environment."[14] In the same vein, another author observes that the people who were often attracted to the mission stations in Kikuyuland were from poor families. These people saw the mission community as a possible avenue for social and economic mobility and, for a time, sending children to school was an admission of poverty![15]

Moreover, the missionaries used education as a strategy for proselytization. This was welcomed by Africans as a means of social mobility, especially when education came to be correlated with a high economic status in the new secular sector.[16]

It was probably the perception of the emancipatory impulses within missionary Christianity, at this point, which led to the positive response given to Christianity by many Africans. We read in history books of mass conversions, and of the spectacular phenomenon in Uganda where within seven years of missionary work there were African Christians ready to die for their newfound faith.[17]

It is apparent that women also perceived these emancipatory impulses of the new religion and responded accordingly. Among the "refugees" who took shelter in mission stations were women, some of whom were trying to break away from unsatisfactory marriages or harsh parental control. Thus, it has been noted that a major component of the adherents to the AIM mission among the Kamba of Kenya were girls who revolted against parental control and fled to the missions.

It could be said, then, that these two images of Christ, that of Christ the conqueror who seemed to legitimize the subjugation of whole races, and Christ the liberator, glimpses of whom could sometimes be seen in some of the charity work that missionaries were doing for Africans, found expression in missionary praxis. The Christ of the missionary enterprise was, therefore, an ambivalent one. His encounter with Africans, including women, had ambiguous results, an ambiguity that many an African writer has not failed to notice and to highlight.

SOME ALTERNATIVE IMAGES OF CHRIST IN AFRICA
AND THEIR IMPLICATIONS FOR WOMEN

While the above is a description of the Christology that found expression in missionary praxis, it cannot be said to be coterminous with

Christ as expressed through missionary teaching. In their presentation of Christian doctrine, for example, the missionaries often made reference to the Bible as the authoritative source of the doctrine.

Consequently, Africans gained access to the various "images" of Christ enshrined in the New Testament. Through the Bible, Africans caught glimpses of who Christ was, and what loyalty to him implied for his followers. They appropriated one or several of these images of Christ and made them their own, despite the distortions apparent in missionary praxis. By way of illustration and conclusion, I will discuss here three quite "common" perceptions of Christ as understood by Africans, and their implications for women.

First, there is the very popular conception of Jesus Christ as the personal savior and personal friend of those who believe in him. Quite contrary to the view that Christ demands their subjugation—whether politically, socially, or culturally—many Africans have come to perceive that Jesus desires to accept them as they are, and to meet their needs at a very personal level. They have come to accept Jesus as the friend of the lonely and healer of those who are sick, whether spiritually or physically.

To some cynics, the view that Jesus is a personal friend, savior, or healer, [smacks] of an unwarranted "privatization" of the person of Jesus to fit a highly subjective context. To others, a confession of Christ as "personal" savior is an indication of pharisaism and gross pretentiousness on the side of those who make such claims. However, I would suggest that, while not ruling out the possibility of some pharisaism, the image of Jesus as a personal friend has been one of the most popular among women, precisely because they need such a personal friend most. (Thus, the image of Christ who helps them to bear their griefs, loneliness, and suffering is a welcome one indeed.)

Second, another also popular image of Christ is that which seems to blend Christology with pneumatology. Jesus is seen as the embodiment of the Spirit, the power of God, and the dispenser of the same to those who follow him. This image of Christ is particularly popular in the so-called independent churches. In our search for a feminist Christology, it may be pertinent to note that, by and large, the patrons of these movements are women, among other marginalized peoples. It is also noteworthy that, in these movements, where the power of the Spirit (of Christ) is accentuated, women are peculiarly articulate and much less inhibited and muted than in established churches. In the "pneumatic Christology," then, Christ becomes the voice of the voiceless, the power of the powerless. Women, as victims of oppression and muteness in society, would, no doubt, find this image of Christ useful in their quest.

A third face of Christ, also derived from the New Testament, is the conception of Christ as an iconoclastic prophet. Jesus stands out in scripture as a critic of the status quo, particularly when it engenders social injustices and marginalization of some in society. This is the kind of Christ whose "function" of "iconoclasm" is thought by many participants in the African independent churches to be "incarnated" in their founder members [whom] they sometimes hail as "Black Messiahs." These prophetic leaders in Africa have emerged in continuity with the prophetic role of Christ as the champion of the cause of the voiceless and the vindicator of the marginalized in society.

In conclusion, I would suggest that in African women's quest for a relevant Christology, aspects of the above three images of Christ would form some of the defining characteristics of the Christ whom women confess.[18] For Christ to become meaningful in the context of women's search for emancipation, he would need to be a concrete and personal figure who engenders hope in the oppressed by taking [women's] side, to give them confidence and courage to persevere.

Second, Christ would also need to be on the side of the powerless by giving them power and a voice to speak for themselves.[19]

Third, the Christ whom women look for is one who is actively concerned with the lot of victims of social injustice and the dismantling of unjust social structures. Christ would, therefore, be expected to be on the side of women as they fight for the dismantling of sexism in society, a sexism that has oppressed them through the ages.

It goes without saying that, along with formulating a relevant Christology, women would also need to be on the alert, and to be critical of any "versions" of Christology that would be inimical to their cause. They would have to reject, like others before them, any Christology that [smacks] of sexism, or that functions to entrench lopsided gender relations. Only in so doing would African women be able confidently to confess Christ as their liberator, as a partisan in their search for emancipation.

Notes

1. Mary Daly, *Beyond God the Father* (Boston, MA: Beacon Press, 1973), 69.

2. Ibid., 77.

3. Ibid., 67ff. In this context, Daly seems to propose a spirituality for women that not only goes "beyond God the Father" but also beyond Christ. The sentiments of women who share Mary Daly's view have, therefore, been aptly described as post-Christian.

4. This is a question to which Ruether has addressed herself in her books *Sexism and God Talk* (Boston: Beacon, 1983, 116ff.), and *To Change the World* (New York: Crossroad, 1983, 45ff.).

5. As one feminist wit has observed, it is interesting to note that no one insists that priests also be Jews and thirty-three years old, to complete the physical resemblance with Jesus of Nazareth.

6. See Ruether, *Sexism*, 127–34. Here she isolates two traditions of Christology, namely, androgynous Christologies and spirit Christologies.

7. See Dia Aranjo, in J. M. Bonino, *Faces of Jesus* (Maryknoll, NY: Orbis, 1984), 30–38.

8. See also Jean-Marc Éla, *African Cry* (Maryknoll, NY: Orbis, 1986), 9ff., and F. Ebousi-Boulaga, *Christianity without Fetishes* (Maryknoll, NY: Orbis, 1984).

9. This is, of course, not to mention that missionary Christianity seemed to provide the legitimating ideology for colonization and the exploitation of Africans that went with it. The alliance apparent between missionary religion and colonialism was not lost to Africans. Among the Agikuyu, for example, a telling adage was recounted, to the effect that there is no difference between the missionary priest and the colonial settler (*Gutiri muthungu na mubea*). An African lament reflects the same perception: "When the missionaries first came, they had the Bible and we had the land. Now they have the land and we have the Bible!"

10. This kind of tendency is still implicit in the ongoing debate about the merits or demerits of the institutions of polygamy in Africa. Many of the arguments are still given over women's heads; women are hardly consulted for their views.

11. For a detailed account of the upheaval that this particular problem occasioned in the relationship between missionaries and the Agikuyu, see Kamuyu wa Kang'ethe (1981). This work also records in detail the abusive song *Muthirigu*, which was purposely composed to wage psychological war on opponents of circumcision. The girls of Protestant families were particularly targeted in this song, and the psychological torture they underwent must have been tremendous.

12. Roland Oliver, *The Missionary Factor in East Africa* (Great Britain: Longman, 1966), 33.

13. Ibid., 31f.

14. Ibid., 47.

15. Robert Strayer et al., *Protest Movements in Colonial East Africa* (Syracuse, NY: Syracuse University Press, 1973).

16. Robert Strayer, *Inquiry into World Cultures—Kenya Focus on Nationalism* (New York: Prentice-Hall, 1973).

17. W. B. Anderson, *The Church in East Africa, 1840–1974* (Central Tanganyika Press, 1977), 23ff.

18. These three perceptions of Christ are discussed by way of illustration, and do not preclude the possibility of other "images" of Christ. These are discussed because of their prevalence and direct implications for the women's cause. It is the task of feminist theologians to analyze systematically further

images of Christ prevailing in Africa to see whether they are "useful" or inimical to women's search for liberation. It would be interesting to analyze, for example, the relationship between Mariology and Christology and its implications for women in African Catholicism.

19. This view is directly derived from the gospel narratives of the life of Jesus, for they depict Jesus as a friend and a "pal" of the marginalized in his contemporary society. In his public ministry, Jesus is also depicted as a compassionate friend of the lonely and the suffering, whose liberation he undertakes.

11

JESUS CHRIST

Mercy Amba Oduyoye (Ghana)

THE CONTEXT

African Christian theology is decidedly contextual, and this contribution on Jesus by an African woman will stay in that mode and reflect the faith of African Christian women in the African context. Jesus Christ yesterday, today, and tomorrow requires that each generation declare its faith in relation to its today. It is, therefore, natural that the Christologies African women were fed should reflect the faith of those who brought Christianity to Africa and the African men who did most of the interpretation and transmission. Having heard all this, African women today can announce in their own words the one in whom they have believed.

The intention of this chapter is to survey the language of African Christian women about Jesus and, through that, to build up a profile of the Jesus in their Christianity. We begin with a note on sources, as the expected "library study" of this subject will yield very little that is of the provenance of women. We then sample the oral Christology which is our key source, as most of what is written by African women began as oral contributions to study groups and conferences. The third section is this writer's assessment of what is being said about Jesus and why.

In the past thirty years or so, several christological models have appeared in books written by men theologians of Africa.[1] They share the emphases of the Western churches but several go beyond these. They are grounded in the classical Christian approach that identifies "Savior myths" with biblical narratives and attempt to answer the question: "Who is the Savior?" The classical divine-human motif is stated as a matter of faith and not debated, as was common in the early church. African theologians transmit as an article of faith the divine human person whose sacrifice on the cross is salvific. As a human being, the Savior is a pastor and an example for human life. As a human being, his role is like that of royalty in traditional African communities, a representative and leader, but it is as divine that the Savior is victorious over death.

The divinity of the Christ experienced through the Bible is that of one in control of the universe and history. The Christ controls evil and is a wonder-worker. In times of crisis, the Christ is expected to intervene directly on the side of the good, for God is the giver of good. In the gospels, the Christ is seen as a healer, an exorcist, and a companion. All these notions feature in African Christologies and influence what women, too, say about Jesus.

In dealing with Christologies in Africa, one finds two major trends, the inculturationalist and the liberationist. The first type is that of those who consciously appropriate Africa's traditional experience of God. We note that the Greek Bible imagery that forms the foundations of traditional Christologies has appropriated beliefs and language from Jewish religion, as well as Greco-Roman paradigms. To talk intelligently about new experience, one cannot but build upon what is known. African religion and culture furnish the language of Christologies that describe Jesus as an ancestor, a king, or elder brother. These carry notions of mediatorship and authority. It is as an ancestor that Jesus stands between humanity and God as the spokesperson, as the *Okyeame*; Jesus is interpreter and advocate. We name ourselves Christians after his being the Christ, just as we name our children after our worthy forebears.

We say Christ is king and we see the lives of royal leaders who were compassionate and brave community builders. We see the royal leaders of the Akan, who bear the title *Osagyefo*, the one who saves the battle, the victorious warrior, and we see Jesus as *Nana*, both ancestor and royalty. In several African traditional cultures, the rulers are regarded as hedged by divinity, and so one is able to talk about the Christ being both divine and human without raising the philosophical debates of early Christianity. So, praying to and through Jesus follows naturally and is practiced as the spirituality of the religion that enables Christians to face the daily realities of life.

Women have employed cultural paradigms to describe their belief in Jesus, but those that are most favored are the cultural ones that are also liberative. They employ myths of wonder-workers who save their communities from hunger and from the onslaught of their enemies, both physical and spiritual. The women's Christology in large measure therefore falls within the category of the liberationist types. Jesus is the brother or kin who frees women from the domination of inhuman husbands. Women relate more easily to the Christ who knew hunger, thirst, and homelessness, and see Jesus as oppressed by the culture of his own people. Jesus the liberator is a paradigm for the critique of culture that most African women theologians do.

The faith in and the language about Jesus that is reviewed here has become written theology within the last two decades or so; nonetheless, they are of African hue and have their roots in African Christianity in particular. The language about Jesus is heard in songs with lyrics created by both women and men and sung lustily in churches and in TV drama. There are several women's singing groups that have recorded cassettes sold on our streets, and songs are sung by people at work, at play, or while traveling. The name of Jesus is therefore on the lips, in the ears, and before the eyes of all, including those of other faiths.

Ghana, the country of my birth, today wears many placards bearing slogans that contain the name of Jesus. When you greet anyone in the streets and ask, "How do you do?" they will profess their faith by telling you, *"Yesu adom"*—"by the grace of Jesus." This version replaces the traditional "by the grace of God," which has become insufficient, as God was in Ghana before Christianity came and our Muslim sisters and brothers punctuate all hopes and plans and inquiries after their state of being with *"Insha Allah"*—by the will of Allah (God). Specifying the name of Jesus, therefore, properly claims Christian particularity. Who Jesus is to Ghanaian Christians is written largely in their songs, prayers, and sayings. The first full text of individual spirituality anchored in Jesus and coming from an African woman with no formal schooling is a publication with the English title *Jesus of the Deep Forest*.[2]

THE TEXTS

Jesus of the Deep Forest signifies the place of Jesus in the life of people both rural and urban. It is the prayers they pray to Jesus and the praises they give to him. One could almost say that, of the women "writing theologians" of Africa, Afua Kuma is the first, and she paved the way by pointing to the central theme of Christology. She will be our first source, and she represents the women who weave lyrics about Jesus and pour their hearts out in prayer and praise at all times and in all places, the women whose theology gets "reduced" into writing by those who can write.

Our second source is the writings of the women who belong to the Ecumenical Association of Third World Theologians (EATWOT) or to the Circle of Concerned African Women Theologians (the Circle). In the 1980s, EATWOT called attention to the Christologies of the Third World and generated many studies on the subject of Jesus. It is in this context that African women members of the association contributed to the publication, *With Passion and Compassion: Third World Women Doing Theology*.[3] The Circle, with its initial focus on religion and culture, had ecclesiology as its main theological schema, but naturally the subject of Jesus looms large in its members' reflection. The first publication of the Circle, *Talitha Qumi!*, features two Bible studies (on Luke 8:40–46, and 1:42) and one article on that subject that can aid us in our study. The series of *Circle Books* and reflections published in the newsletter *Amka* also provide relevant references.[4]

Our third source will be the writings of individual African women in other anthologies. An example of this is Anne Nasimiyu's "Christology and an African Woman's Experience" in Robert Schreiter's *Faces of Jesus in Africa*.[5] Individually authored books on the subject by women are rare, but there is a chapter on Jesus in this writer's *Hearing and Knowing*. Teresa Okure's opus on mission can, of course, be read from the perspective of Christology and so can Christina Landman's *The Piety of South African Women*.[6]

ORAL CHRISTOLOGY

In *Jesus of the Deep Forest* by Afua Kuma, our example of oral Christology, one encounters numerous astonishing reversals of so-called natural laws and unexpected outcomes of simple actions. Jesus is the one who catches birds from the depths of the ocean and fish from the heights of the trees. These reversals are then reflected in magnificent types of deeds in the lives of people. Jesus, the Great Provider under all circumstances, brings wealth to widows and orphans and is the friend of the aged. Jesus frees children from the fear of *kakae* (the monster) and breaks the will of the murderer. It is Jesus who has accepted the poor and given them glory. Jesus clears the forest of all evil spirits, making it safe for hunters. Imagery that is in keeping with the stilling of the storm abounds in oral Christology.

The motif of Savior and liberator is very strong in this and other reflections on Jesus by women. For Afua Kuma, the Exodus becomes another motif. Jesus is Yahweh of the Exodus, who defeated Pharaoh and his troops and becomes the sun ahead of Israel and lightning behind them. He is given the Akan title "*Osagyefo*, the one who saves the battle," and so we can depend on him to win life's battles. Other biblical images, like good shepherd, healer, and the compassionate one, are seen together with cultural ones such as "the mighty edifice that accommodates all corners," while provision of hospitality common to both serves as the very antidote to death. Whatever the situation, Jesus has the last word. There are no life challenges for which the power of Jesus is found unequal to the task of achieving victory. The following excerpt from *Jesus of the Deep Forest* illustrates the ethos of this publication:

> All-powerful Jesus who engages in marvelous deeds, he is the one called Hero *Okatakyi*! Of all earthly dominions he is master; the Python not overcome with mere sticks, the Big Boat which cannot be sunk.

> Jesus, Saviour of the poor, who brightens up our faces! *Damjo-Adu*: the clever one. We rely on you as the tongue relies on the mouth.

> The great Rock we hide behind: the great forest canopy that gives cool shade: the Big Tree that lifts its vines to peep at the heavens, the magnificent Tree whose dripping leaves encourage the luxuriant growth.[7]

Several images in Afua Kuma come from gospel-events involving Jesus and women. "Women recognize his uniqueness and put their cloths on the ground for him. A woman anoints him as Messiah, friend and Saviour."[8]

Reflecting on Jesus is not simply an intellectual task or one of personal spirituality. Afua Kuma, like many African women theologians, speaks as an evangelist. "Follow Jesus," she says, and not only will you witness miracles, but for you will come grace, blessings, eternal life, and peace. The cross of Jesus, she says, is like a net with which Jesus gathers in people; it is the bridge from this life to eternal life. The word of Jesus is the highway along which we should walk. She therefore prays to Jesus: "Use us to do your will for you have cleansed us with your blood."[9] This saving blood motif is featuring more and more frequently in song and in prayers in this period of deliverance-seeking. The royal blood of Jesus, precious and potent, has given us health and happiness, for it has overcome and kept at bay the power of demons. This living faith is proclaimed daily in the churches, in store fronts, on vehicles, and even in the designs of clothes people wear.

WRITTEN CHRISTOLOGY

"There is a concrete history that is lived which is prior to the history that is recounted. That lived history in all its concreteness is the ultimate ground of all the history that is written."[10] Christologies, therefore, are the results of questions asked by succeeding generations of theologians, the interpreters of the history of Jesus. The vocabulary of African women's theology is focused on Jesus, rarely on Christ or Christ Jesus. Few questions are asked beyond that of the human response to that history. The oral affirmations ask hardly any questions, but Rosemary Edet insists that some women do ask questions of this Jesus-story. As a Nigerian woman she could ask: "Who is the Christ to the Nigerian Woman? What type of Christ does she know? How does she relate to this Christ?"[11] The spirituality of the majority of African women moves us to conclude that it is the personality of the one about whom the gospel speaks that draws prayer and praise from them. The songs about Jesus proclaim royalty, king of kings. Jesus is the first and the best of all that is counted good in humanity, and best and first of all good professionals who keep human beings and human communities in a state of health and general well-being. Predominant is Jesus the wonder-worker. Essentially, what we get from African women is an affirmation of faith such as is stated by Rosemary Edet: "Jesus is the Son of God, son of Mary, sent by the Father to our planet to redeem mankind from sin and death and to restore them to grace."[12]

Snippets from the contributors to this volume follow the same train of reflections as in "Christ and the Nigerian Womanhood" in Edet and Umeagudosu's book.[13] In the same publication, A. E. Kwazu writes, "Jesus was born on earth to reform man who has completely deviated from God's call to being good."[14] Akon E. Udo affirms, "God has sent Jesus Christ to the world to break the barriers of culture and sexism, that is why the names of women appear in the genealogy of Jesus Christ."[15] This inclusiveness of the mission of God is then illustrated by Jesus' example of giving women the mandate to "Go and tell" of the resurrection (Mark 16:7).

In response to this inclusive mission, African women are heard loud and clear singing the redemptive love of Jesus the liberator. Jesus accomplishes God's mission by setting women free from sexism, oppression, and marginalization through his death and resurrection, and both women and men are made members of God's household and of the same royal priesthood as men.[16] In *Talitha Qumi!*, we read: "The ultimate mission of Jesus was to bring healing, life and dignity to the suffering. Jesus came to give voice to the voiceless."[17]

Teresia M. Hinga's contribution in *The Will to Arise: Jesus Christ and the Liberation of Women* offers a section on "Christology and African Women: The Ambivalence of the Encounter." She discusses two faces of Christ that are prevalent in African Christologies—the Colonial Christ who is a warrior-king, whose followers sang "Soldiers of Christ Arise" as they battled against other religions and cultures and indeed races, and the Imperial Christ, the conquering Christ of the missionaries who did battle for Africa, on behalf of the missionaries. Africans embraced this version of Christianity as a "means of social and economic mobility" —hence the reports we have of mass conversions in some parts of Africa. Hinga states that African women were among those who perceived the emancipating impulses of Christianity and turned to it. Women were among those who took refuge at the mission stations. The early missionary period in Africa presented a Christ who had two faces, the conqueror who inspires the subjugation of people and their cultures while promoting the liberation of individuals from the oppression generated by their environment. The Jesus of missionary praxis in Africa was an ambiguous Christ. Thus it is that he has acquired many faces on the continent.

The Christ of missionary teaching, based mostly on the Bible, adds complexity to this scenario. Hinga discusses three of its dimensions. The first is that of personal Savior and personal friend—accepting people as they are and meeting their needs at a very personal level—Jesus "friend of the lonely" and "healer of those who are sick, whether spiritually or physically."[18] The title "friend" is "one of the most popular among women, precisely because they need such a personal friend the most." Thus the heightened image of Jesus as the Christ who helps them to bear their griefs, loneliness, and suffering is a welcome one indeed.[19] Women's oral Christologies reflect this history and have been translated into the written ones.

Hinga observes that, in African women's theology, the "Image of Christ is a blend of Christology with pneumatology. Jesus is seen as the embodiment of the spirit, the power of God, and the dispenser of the same to all who follow him."[20] This "pneumatic Christology" is very popular among women, for here Christ is the voice of the voiceless and the power of the powerless on the models sculptured by Afua Kuma. African women do need such a Christ, for they are often expected to be mute and to accept oppression. The Spirit empowers them to enjoy a lively spiritual life that cannot be controlled by the official powers of the church. In this way they are able to defy unjust authority and repressive structures and to stand against cultural demands that go against the spirit of Jesus.

The Christ, the iconoclastic prophet-critic of the status quo that "engenders social injustices and marginalisation of some in society" illustrates "some of the defining characteristics of the Christ whom women confess":

> For Christ to become meaningful in the context of women's search for emancipation, he would need to be a concrete and personal figure who engenders hope in the oppressed by taking their [women's] side, to give them confidence and courage to persevere.[21]

Jesus has to be the Christ on the side of the powerless to empower them, the one who is concerned with the lot of victims of social injustice and with the dismantling of unjust social structures. However, the concern most heard these days is deliverance from "Satanic Bondage," and from demons who seem to have become very active in the Africa of the last decades of the twentieth century. The need for deliverance has revived traditional religious methods. Most especially, the importance of blood in African religions is reflected in the central place given to the blood of Jesus in women's theological imagery and, indeed, in much of "deliverance spirituality" of contemporary African Christianity. Just one example should suffice.

Grace Duah, a "deliverance Minister," in her book, *Deliverance: Fact or Fantasy?* includes puberty rites for girls that open the doors for demon possession, to demonstrate how easily people can come under the influence of demons and so need deliverance. She writes in her introduction:

> Jesus came not only to give us the highest form of deliverance, i.e., Salvation—Deliverance from a Kingdom of sin and darkness into a Kingdom of Righteousness and light—but also to give us deliverance from demonic obsession, demonic oppression, and demonic possession, as well as all forms of fleshly enslavement.[22]

Rosemary Edet, a foundation member of the Circle, reflects this in her contribution to the Circle's inaugural conference. Looking at the life of Jesus, she points out that "Christ has triumphed over illness, blood taboos, women's rituals and the conventions of society."[23] She is, of course, referring to rituals and conventions that are inimical to women's well-being. These are the ones that Grace Duah is referring to as providing opportunities for demons to possess women.

Jesus has become for us a liberator by countering misogynist culture. After all, says Edet, Jesus' humanity is the humanity of a woman; no human father contributed. The touch of the "bleeding woman" has become a very important image not only for healing, but also for total liberation from all that oppresses women culturally and makes Jesus

Savior *par excellence*, as we saw in the oral Christology. Therefore Margaret Obaga, commenting on the salvific role of the Christ, puts her emphasis on the breaking down of walls of hostilities created by religion and culture. She writes: "The breaking of the wall therefore meant the abolishing of all external customs and taboos of Judaism which created and perpetuated a state of enmity between Jews and Gentiles."[24] In her discussion of Ephesians 2:15, she calls attention to contemporary gender issues that are a source of subjugation for women in Africa.

In Afua Kuma, as in most of the writings under review, salvation comes to women and men alike. Even so, Afua Kuma does have feminist consciousness. In Edet, this consciousness is explicit in the very title of her paper, but even here the starting point is the universal appeal. She notes that Jesus is "sensitive to the oppression of the weak and the helpless, took them on in his incarnation," as a carpenter's son from a nondescript town.[25] This is heightened by his interpretation of Messiahship, which he portrayed "not as king but as a servant by contradicting in his life and person, the messianic expectation of Israel." Jessica Nakawombe is even more explicit with regard to this. She states bluntly that:

> Jesus was born of Mary, a good and godly woman. She was the obedient vessel through which Christ was conceived of the Holy Spirit. She was given a unique part to play in the outworking of God's plan for the salvation of humankind, for the Incarnation and the virgin birth have had a tremendous significance for Christology.[26]

The women cling to the full humanity of the Christ in order to honor their own humanity and to insist on the link between the human and the divine in all persons as it was in Jesus. The church's imagery of Jesus, which marginalizes women, is therefore non-biblical, and contemporary women theologians of other continents have traced the history of this state of affairs. For Edet, this process was most evident in the Constantinian era, with its return to the royal ideology of the Davidic Messiah that made the Christ the "pantokrator," reinforcing the distance between Christ and the feminine.[27] The Jesus of African women's Christology is the Jesus of the Bible and of whatever scholarship aids the identification of this Jesus and the context in which he lived his earthly life.

Another historical development highlighted by Edet is the Aristotelian desecration of womanhood. This desacralization of the feminine has succeeded in making the totality of the *imago dei* male, says Edet. Consequently, women have had to lead the Christian community toward a "return to the Christ of the gospels, his Person and his words and deeds."[28] It is in this tradition that African women's Christology stands:

> Africans in general have a holistic view of life which demands a Christ who affects the whole of life for there is nothing that is not the realm of God if it is true that God made everything and keeps them in being. God as father is beneficent but there are good and evil forces operating in the world. These affect humanity. In short, a Nigerian woman is a victim of evil forces like witches, hunger, infant mortality as well as the triple oppression of culture, religion and socio-economy. How does Christ function within this situation? If Jesus did take on himself our weakness and injustice at his incarnation, then he is a suffering Christ, a liberating Christ and a friend.[29]

Continuing with the christological texts of African women, we call attention now to *With Passion and Compassion*. In this publication, Térèsa Souga from Cameroon, writing on "The Christ Event," introduces her reflections with what she titles, "My Act of Faith." She has as her opening sentence, "Jesus Christ means everything to me … Christ is the true Human, the one who makes it possible for all persons to reach fulfillment and to overcome the historic alienation weighing them down."[30] Similarly, Afua Kuma would recite the traditional praise of enablers saying: Jesus is the big tree that makes it possible for the climbing plant to reach the sun. Souga's theology is deeply informed by Philippians 2:9–11, an affirmation of faith that enables her to link the suffering and resurrection of Jesus with women.[31] This, she says, is the source and motivation of African women's spirituality. She writes: "The realism of the cross every day tells me, as a woman of the Third World, that the laws of history can be overcome by means of crucified love."[32] Jesus bears a message of liberation for every human being and especially for those in social categories that are most disadvantaged.

Jesus "delivers women from every infirmity and suffering."[33] Souga has in view Africa's threefold captivity—cultural, spiritual, socio-economic—when she writes, "there can be no understanding of Jesus Christ outside of the situation in which we seek to understand ourselves."[34] "It is by way of these situations that Jesus bears on his person the condition of the weak, and hence that of women" (Luke 2:6–7, 22–24; John 2:46).[35] In the light of Christ, if Jesus is the God who has become weakness in our context, in his identity as God-Man, Jesus takes on the condition of the African woman. Souga surmises that the correlation between women's experience and liberation in Jesus Christ "leads us to discover that Jesus reveals God in the various kinds of bonds connecting him to women throughout the Gospels." Paul emphasizes the realism of the incarnation with a legacy of faith saying, "When the times were fulfilled, the son of God was born of a woman."[36] Afua Kuma would have said Jesus is the royal one who chooses to live as the common poor so that the common poor might appropriate the dignity of being human:

> Looking at Africa, I wondered how I could write on a subject that suggests or points towards hope and renewed life in a continent that for decades has witnessed unending violence, suffering and death. A critical reflection on the resurrected Christ, the one Paul knew and wrote about in the epistles, however, reminded me of the crucified and suffering Christ who faced violence and death. The awareness gave me the courage to write about the labour pains experienced by all creation in Africa as a Christian woman.[37]

The image of Jesus as the suffering servant is very prominent in the writings of African women theologians. Most, like Rosemary Edet and Nyambura Njoroge, describe Jesus as identifying with the suffering of humanity, especially that of women. In this vein, Edet describes Jesus as "the revelation of God's self-giving suffering and enduring love to humanity."[38]

This suffering love moves into healing the hurts of humanity and so Christ the healer is very popular with church women. Ada Nyaga brings out the results of this love among human beings when she writes:

> Similarly, Jesus calls us to revise our ways of thinking and asks us to reconsider what it means to be a woman in our new understanding. Just as Jesus forced the ruler of a synagogue to reconsider what it means to work on the Sabbath, when he showed his compassion for a crippled woman by healing her (Luke 13:10–17), there is an obvious need today to awaken women and free them from socio-cultural and theological restrictions based on a false understanding of the Bible.[39]

Suffering love operating in the incarnation wipes off the dirt that hides the glory of our true humanity, that which we believe is of the *imago*

dei. Healing here includes liberating women from all evil and life-denying forces, enabling the fullness of all we know of perfect womanhood
to be revealed. Jesus is the friend who enables women to overcome the
difficulties of life and restores to them the dignity of being in the image
of God, having annulled the stigma of blood taboos used as a separation of women's humanity. Akon E. Udo affirms that Jesus Christ has
broken the barriers of distinction between men and women and used
his precious blood to seal the broken relationships and to make men
and women one in himself.[40] Mercy Amba Oduyoye and Elizabeth
Amoah state in *With Passion and Compassion* that:

> the Christ for us is the Jesus of Nazareth who agreed to be
> God's "Sacrificial Lamb," thus teaching that true and living
> sacrifice is that which is freely and consciously made; and who
> pointed to the example of the widow who gave all she had in
> response to God's love. Christ is the Jesus of Nazareth who ap-
> proved of the costly sacrifice of the woman with the expensive
> oil, who anointed him (king, prophet, priest) in preparation for
> his burial, thereby also approving all that is noble, lovely, lov-
> ing and motivated by love and gratitude.[41]

Louise Tappa of Cameroon in *With Passion and Compassion*, states that
"the task of Christology is to work out the full meaning of the reality of
the Christ-event for humankind." Doctrinal Christology, which reduces
the Christ to a positive but sublime abstraction, can be and is ignored
"when the time comes to translate it into the life of our communities."
Tappa continues: "that is why even to the present it has been possible to
interpret the doctrines of the incarnation (liberation) and of expiation (reconciliation) in terms that leave intact the social structures and models of
our communities, including the church."[42] Like Afua Kuma, Tappa proposes another procedure, which she says is much simpler but no less
christological. It is to put more emphasis on the praxis of Jesus himself,
even though she occasionally refers also to Jesus' teaching.

SUMMARY AND REFLECTIONS

These works and words of Jesus, culled from the reflections of African
women on Jesus, constitute the Christologies that they are developing
and which embolden them to work and to speak for Jesus toward the
liberation of the world in fulfillment of the *missio dei*. "The Christ of

history is the one who defined his mission as a mission of liberation" (Luke 4:18–19). The Christ of dogma therefore plays only a marginal role in the women's affirmations about Jesus, who defined liberation by his quotation from Isaiah 61, and whose actions revealed that "the truly spiritual is that which embraces all the material and physical life of the human being and our communities" (Mark 5:21–34).[43]

Elizabeth Amoah and Mercy Amba Oduyoye, writing on "The Christ for African Women," point out that Jesus, the Messiah, is God-sent and the anointed of God. The messianic imagery is very powerful in Ghana and is reflected in Afua Kuma's praises that make references to what priests are teaching when they speak of deliverance. The influence of male theologians is evident in how large the cross looms in the theology of women like Afua Kuma. As noted earlier, she points out that the cross "has become the fishing net of Jesus. It is also the bridge from which Christians can jump into the pool of saving blood that leads to everlasting life."[44] The emphasis of women, however, is not that we emulate the suffering, but that it become the source of our liberation. We do not only admire Jesus, but we are caught in the net of liberation which we believe will bring us into fullness of life:

> The Christ whom African women worship, honor and depend on is the victorious Christ, knowing that evil is a reality. Death and life-denying forces are the experience of women, and so Christ, who countered these forces and who gave back her child to the widow of Nain, is the African woman's Christ.[45]

Ghana must have great hunger in its history, as is evidenced in folktales and legend. The more recent 1983 drought revives this reality, and so a Savior is certainly the one who can keep us whole, integrating body and soul and enabling us to enhance the quality of our lives. Jesus of Nazareth was all of this; his earthly life and today his name and spirit keep the liberative ministry alive. With Jesus we do not need guns and bullets to make the enemy disappear, since, as Afua Kuma points out, we only need to "tell Jesus." "I'm going to tell Jesus about it, today my husband is a lawyer. How eloquent he is!"[46]

Deliverance from death into life is often discussed by African women in the context of aspects of cultural practice that they experience as negative in their quest for fullness of life:

> This Christ is the liberator from the burden of disease and the ostracism of a society riddled with blood-taboos and theories of

inauspiciousness arising out of women's blood. Christ liberated women by being born of Mary, demanding that the woman bent double with gynecological disorders should stand up straight. The practice of making women become silent "beasts" of societies' burdens, bent double under racism, poverty, and lack of appreciation of what fullness of womanhood should be, has been annulled and countered by Christ. Christ transcends and transforms culture and has liberated us to do the same.[47]

African women's experiences lead them into christological language that does not come to African men. Hence Tappa can say: "I am convinced that Jesus died so that the patriarchal God might die and that Jesus rose so that the true God revealed in Jesus might rise in our lives, and in our communities."[48]

Souga and others have reiterated that it is by self-emptying that we become filled with the spirit of Jesus. What African women reject is the combination of cross and sacrifice laid on them by people who have no intention of walking those paths themselves. They would argue that the calls to take up the cross and to self-emptying are directed to all who would be called Christians; those calls are not sensitive to gender, race, or class. Amoah and Oduyoye, commenting on Kuma, highlight the same point.[49]

The vividness of this drama of jumping from bridges into pools of blood, even when blood has been the main source of women's marginalization, signifies the intensity of their spirituality of relating their lives to what the life of Jesus means to them. For them, Christology is not words or reasoning about Jesus, but an actuality in their lives. This is a life of faith, not of theological debates. It is a spirituality to overcome evil and oppression and to lift up constant thanks to God.

It is difficult to say whether the language of intimate relationships with Jesus, as used by African women, is to be read as eroticism or mysticism. What is clear, however, is that their spirituality is the result of this type of Christology. They find an affirmation of their personhood and worth in the person of Jesus, born of a woman without the participation of a man. The significance for them is that "womanness" contains the fullness of "humanness." By this they counter earlier assertions that a woman by herself is not fully human. This eroticism-mysticism enables them to understand suffering as related to crucified love with an anticipation of transformation and shalom.

Hinga has suggested that it is the lack of male companionship that drives women into the near-erotic language of Jesus as husband. Afua Kuma relies on Jesus, her husband, who is a lawyer who liberates her from the hands of oppressive legal procedures with his eloquence. The only time Jesus appeared in the diary of Dutch-Afrikaans woman, Alie Badenhorst (1866–1908), was when even God "The Strong One, the Powerful Father in heaven" had seemed impotent to deliver her. When she thought her last hour had come, "she left a message for her husband with her son, that she was going to Jesus and that she would wait for him there."[50] Thus for her—as for many African women, products of the same European missionary theology—Jesus is the last sure haven. While life lasts, however, African women theologians would suggest that Christology should be about reclaiming and reasserting the role of "Jesus Christ as Liberator and a saviour of women."[51]

> I am married to Jesus, Satan leave me alone.
> My husband is coming
> To take me away
> Into everlasting love.[52]

Afua Kuma is not afraid of court cases, for her "husband" Jesus is a most eloquent lawyer. Christina Landman, who has documented *The Piety of South African Women* from diaries, has several examples of this type of language from both African and Afrikaner women of South Africa under the influence of European Calvinism. In the context of "racial persecution (black women) and suburban boredom" for white women, pious women escaped "into the arms of Jesus," who suffered for them and continues to suffer with them. Landman comments: "Where there is suffering, a woman is in control,"[53] and oh, how Africa suffers. It is African women's experience that, where there is suffering, the powers that be, usually men, would allow women to take control. Women derive power from caring and being caregivers, a role that puts them on the side of the Christ. The hallowing of suffering, however, is rejected in the theology of several African women theologians who see this as a source of patriarchal domestication. The cross and suffering of Jesus are not to be perpetuated but rather decried and prevented.

The victorious Christ of Afua Kuma is clearly the Jesus of the writing theologians. Jesus turns death into life and overcomes the life-denying forces that dog our way. He conquers death and restores life to all who believe in him. Having triumphed over death, he has become our liberator by countering women-denying culture. After all—is his own humanity not that of a woman?[54]

My reading of African women's theology is that they have had no problem particularizing the "Christ of God" in the man of Nazareth. They know of saviors in their own histories; some are men, others are women. Their stance is that the maleness of Jesus is unjustly capitalized on by those who want to exclude women, but that does not detract from the fact that in Jesus' own practice, inclusion is the norm. What Rosemary Edet says about the humanity of Jesus is that it is the humanity of woman, and African women should and do claim Jesus as their liberator. They claim the soundly constructed so-called feminine traits they find in Jesus—his care and compassion for the weak and excluded. The anti-hunger ministry, healing, and the place of children in his words and works—all go together to create a bonding around women's lives that African women feel with Jesus. He is one of us, knows our world, and can therefore accompany us in our daily joys and struggles.

What alienates some African women is the interpretation of revelation that suggests that before Jesus Africans had not encountered God and that without Jesus all are doomed. Christian exclusiveness is in large measure not biblical and must therefore not be allowed to become an obstacle in the multi-religious communities of Africa. African women theologians have often reinterpreted the exclusiveness of John as a directive to walk in the path of Jesus. Elizabeth Amoah would say, "Jesus is the only way" is a call to the recognition that to make salvation a reality for all, we all should walk in the way of Jesus and live the truth of the implication of a kenotic life.[55]

There has been no need to insist on the Christ as the wisdom of God. The biblical references to *Sophia* as eternally with God have not played a significant role in this theology. What is clear is that wisdom language would be associated with fairness in dealings among humans and fidelity to the will of God that Jesus exemplified. Thus Christology is reflected in spirituality.

African Christian women attribute the positive outcome of their endeavors to God or Jesus and to the guidance and protection of the Holy Spirit. They learn from biblical narrators and from stories of liberation that others have attributed to their faith in Jesus. They cling to their own faith in the liberating powers of Jesus and expect them to work in their own lives. Living under conditions of such hardship, African women and men have learned to identify the good, attribute it to God in Christ, and live a life of prayer in the anticipation that the liberative potential of the person of Jesus will become a reality in their lives.

The victory of Jesus is not over other nations and cultures. It is over death and life-denying forces. The Jesus "who countered these forces and gave back her child to the widow of Nain, is the African woman's Christ." Jesus of Nazareth, by the counter-cultural relations he established with women, has become for us the Christ, the anointed one who liberates, the companion, friend, teacher, and true "Child of Woman" —"Child of Woman" truly, because in Christ the fullness of all that we know of perfect womanhood is revealed. The Christ for us is the Jesus of Nazareth who agreed to be God's sacrificial lamb, thus teaching that true and living sacrifice is that which is freely and consciously made. Jesus of Nazareth, designated "the Christ," is the one who has broken down the barriers we have erected between God and us as well as among us. The Christ is the Reconciler calling us back to our true selves, to one another, and to God, thereby saving us from isolation and alienation which is the lack of community that is the real experience of death.[56]

"The Christ of the women of Africa upholds not only motherhood, but all who like Jesus of Nazareth perform 'mothering roles' of bringing out the best in all around them." The present profit-centered economies of our world deny responsibilities to bring life to the dying and to empower those challenged by the multitude of impairments that many have to live with. Justine Kahungu Mbwiti, in a study of Jesus and a Samaritan woman (John 4:1–42), draws out several of the images of Jesus that empower African women. As rural women, they see the scandal of the incarnation, the appearance of God in the hinterlands of the Roman Empire, as God coming to their rural and slum situations. They relate to Jesus who deliberately shakes what was customary as a sign of renewal that opens for them the space to put critical questions to what is traditional. They refer to the scandalous action in the temple (John 2:13–16), and the many violations of the Sabbath (John 5:1–18) as affirmations that life is to be lived consciously and conscientiously. Jesus becomes therefore not just the one by whom God saves; He is Himself the Savior.[57]

We may conclude with another survey treatment of Christology in African women's theology, in Mabel Morny's contribution to *Talitha Qumi!* "Christ Restores to Life." She states: "When I think of liberation, a vision comes into my mind. A vision of a fuller and less injured life in a world where people can say 'I' with happiness; a vision is a means of restoring life."[58] Morny tries to develop an understanding of Christ as the liberator of all people; she writes as an African woman within the context of situations in Africa—cultural, social, religious, economic, and political. She writes in a context in which women resort to Jesus as the liberator from bondage, all that makes them less than what God intended them to be. Christology becomes a study of the Jesus who responds to African women's experiences of fear, uncertainty, sickness, illiteracy, hunger, spousal aggression, and distortion of the image of their humanity.

African women theologians think in inclusive terms, hence the emphasis on Jesus for all people, in every particular context and in all situations. At the same time, these theologians wish to maintain the relations the individual can establish with the Christ, as each is unique, and each is a child of God. My reading of African women's Christology, as it appears in the writings of the Circle of Concerned African Women Theologians, may therefore be summed up in the words of the workshop on "Jesus Christ and the Liberation of Women":

> Jesus Christ is liberator and a saviour of women from all the oppressive contexts discussed and empowerer of women in their contexts of powerlessness, and their friend and ally in the context of alienation and pain that women may be confronted with.[59]

Notes

1. In this series one finds J. N. K. Mugambi and Laurenti Magesa, eds., *Jesus in African Christianity: Experimentation and Diversity in African Christology* (Nairobi: Initiatives Ltd., 1989); John S. Pobee, ed., *Exploring Afro-Christology* (New York: Peter Lang, 1992); Enyi Ben Udoh, *Guest Christology: An Interpretative View of the Christological Problem in Africa* (New York: Peter Lang, 1988).

2. Afua Kuma, *Jesus of the Deep Forest*, ed. and trans. Peter Kwasi Ameyaw, Fr. Jon Kirby, SVD, et al. (Accra: Asempa Press, 1980). The rendering here is by Mercy Amba Oduyoye.

3. Virginia Fabella and Mercy Amba Oduyoye, eds., *With Passion and Compassion: Third World Women Doing Theology* (Maryknoll, NY: Orbis Books, 1988).

4. Since the initiation of the Circle of Concerned African Women Theologians in 1989, the following anthologies and four issues of *Amka* have been published: Mercy Amba Oduyoye and Musimbi R. A. Kanyoro, eds., *Talitha Qumi!: Proceedings of the Convocation of African Women Theologians* (Ibadan: Daystar Press, 1989 and 1990); idem, eds., *The Will to Arise: Women, Tradition and the Church in Africa* (Maryknoll, NY: Orbis Books, 1992); Rosemary N. Edet and Meg A. Umeagudosu, eds., *Life, Women and Culture: Theological Reflection; Proceedings of the National Conference of the Circle of African Women Theologians 1990* (Lagos: African Heritage Research and Publications, 1991); Justine Kahungi Mbwiti and Couthon M. Fassinou, et al., *Le canari d'eau Fraiche au L'hospitalité Africaine* (Lubumbashi: Éditions de Chemins de Vie, 1996); Musimbi R. A. Kanyoro and Nyambura J. Njoroge, eds., *Groaning in Faith: African Women in the Household of God* (Nairobi: Acton Publishers, 1996); Elizabeth Amoah, ed., *Where God Reigns: Reflections On Women in God's World* (Accra: Sam Woode Ltd., 1997); Grace Wamui and Mary Getui, eds., *Violence Against Women: Reflections by Kenyan Women Theologians* (Nairobi: Acton Publishers, 1996); Mercy A. Oduyoye, ed.,

Transforming Power: Women in the Household of God. Proceedings of the Pan-African Conference of the Circle of Concerned African Women Theologians (Accra: Sam Woode Ltd., 1997).

5. Robert J. Schreiter, ed., *Faces of Jesus in Africa* (Maryknoll, NY: Orbis Books, 1988); Denise Ackermann, et al., eds., *Women Hold Up Half the Sky: Women in the Church in South Africa* (Pietermaritzburg: Cluster Publications, 1991).

6. Mercy Amba Oduyoye, *Hearing and Knowing: Theological Reflections on Christianity in Africa* (Maryknoll, NY: Orbis Books, 1986); Teresa Okure, *Johannine Approach to Mission: A Contextual Study of John 4:1–42* (Tübingen: J. C. B. Mohr/Paul Siebeck Verlag, 1988); and Christina Landman, *The Piety of South African Women* (Pretoria: C. B. Powell Bible Centre, UNISA, 1999).

7. Kuma, *Jesus of the Deep Forest*, 5.

8. Ibid.

9. Ibid.

10. Rosemary Edet, "Christ and the Nigerian Womanhood," in Edet and Umeagudosu, *Life, Women and Culture*, 177.

11. Ibid.

12. Ibid. Note that inclusive language, even on the horizontal level, is not common with African women, most of whose mother tongues have non-gendered pronouns and words for humanity.

13. Edet, "Christ and the Nigerian Womanhood," 177–93.

14. A. E. Kwazu, "Church Leadership and the Nigerian Woman," in Edet and Umeagudosu, *Life, Women and Culture*, 94.

15. Akon E. Udo, "The Emerging Spiritualities of Women in Nigeria," in Edet and Umeagudosu, *Life, Women and Culture*, 102.

16. Akon E. Udo, "Women in God's World: Some Biblical Affirmations," in Amoah, *Where God Reigns*, 20–25.

17. Musimbi R. A. Kanyoro, "Daughter, Arise: Luke 8:40-56," in Oduyoye and Kanyoro, *Talitha Qumi!* 59.

18. Teresia M. Hinga, "Jesus Christ and the Liberation of Women in Africa," in Oduyoye and Kanyoro, *The Will to Arise*, 190.

19. Hinga, "Jesus Christ," 191; See also Christine Landman, *The Piety of South African Women*, 19, 51.

20. Hinga, "Jesus Christ," 191.

21. Ibid., 191–92.

22. Grace Duah, *Deliverance: Fact or Fantasy?* (no publication details available).

23. Rosemary N. Edet, "Christianity and African Women's Rituals," in Oduyoye and Kanyoro, *The Will to Arise*, 26–29.

24. Margaret K. Obaga, "Women are Members of God's Commonwealth," in Kanyoro and Njoroge, *Groaning in Faith*, 69.

25. Edet, "Christ and the Nigerian Womanhood," 178.

26. Jessica Keturah Nakawombe, "Women in the Kingdom of God," in Kanyoro and Njoroge, *Groaning in Faith*, 47. See also Betty Govinden on the link between Christology and Mariology in Kanyoro and Njoroge, *Groaning in Faith*, 122–23.

27. Edet, "Christ and the Nigerian Womanhood," 183. Note, however, that it seems that, for women like Afua Kuma, this "pantokrator" is not a distant emperor, but the African ruler into whose courts all can run for refuge, for food, for fairness, and for fair-play.

28. Edet, "Christ and the Nigerian Womanhood," 184.

29. Ibid., 184–85.

30. Térèsa Souga, "The Christ Event from the Viewpoint of African Women: A Catholic Perspective," in Fabella and Oduyoye, *With Passion and Compassion*, 22.

31. Ibid., 28–29.

32. Ibid., 22.

33. Ibid., 24.

34. Ibid., 26.

35. Ibid., 28.

36. Ibid.

37. Nyambura Njoroge, "Groaning and Languishing in Labour Pains," in Kanyoro and Njoroge, eds., *Groaning in Faith*, 4.

38. Edet, "Christ and the Nigerian Womanhood," 185.

39. Ada Nyaga, "Women's Dignity and Worth in God's Kingdom," in Kanyoro and Njoroge, *Groaning in Faith*, 81.

40. Akon E. Udo, "Emerging Spiritualities of Women in Nigeria," in Edet and Umeagudosu, *Life, Women and Culture*, 105.

41. Mercy Amba Oduyoye and Elizabeth Amoah, "The Christ for African Women," in Fabella and Oduyoye, *With Passion and Compassion*, 44. The sacrifice involved in the widow's mite, however, does raise a question. Is Jesus only approving her action or also illustrating how religious obligations can rob the poor of even the little they have for sustaining their lives?

42. Louise Tappa, "The Christ-Event: A Protestant Perspective," in Fabella and Oduyoye, *With Passion and Compassion*, 31.

43. Ibid., 31–32.

44. As quoted by Oduyoye and Amoah in "The Christ for African Women," 43.

45. Ibid.

46. Kuma, *Jesus of the Deep Forest*, 42.

47. Oduyoye and Amoah, "The Christ for African Women," 43.

48. Tappa, "The Christ-Event," 34.

49. Oduyoye and Amoah, "The Christ for African Women," 44.

50. Landman, *The Piety of South African Women*, 63.

51. Oduyoye and Kanyoro, *Talitha Qumi!* 206.

52. Conversations on Christology with Pastor Pamela Martin, Baptist from Cameroon, November 1999.

53. Landman, *The Piety of South African Women*, 29.

54. Edet, "Christ and the Nigerian Womanhood," 187.

55. Conversations on Christology with Dr. Elizabeth Amoah, June 1999.

56. Landman, *The Piety of South African Women*, 34.

57. Justine Kahungu Mbwiti, "Jesus and the Samaritan Woman," in Oduyoye and Kanyoro, *Talitha Qumi!* 63–76. At the time of this writing, the name of the country was Zaire; it is now the Democratic Republic of the Congo, a nation still crying for shalom.

58. Mabel S. Morny, "Christ Restores to Life," in Oduyoye and Kanyoro, *Talitha Qumi!* 145–49.

59. Workshop on "Jesus Christ and the Liberation of the African Woman," in Oduyoye and Kanyoro, *Talitha Qumi!* 206.

12

AUSTRALIAN ABORIGINAL WOMEN'S CHRISTOLOGIES

Lee Miena Skye (Palawa, Australia)

Australian Aboriginal women were pursued by a paradoxical Christology through the missiology of colonialism. The paradox intended to save, but instead brought about spiritual, cultural and physical, actual genocide. The Aboriginal people of Australia were considered to be less than human and, therefore, were not treated as if they were human. Hence, there was a meager attempt to understand the meaning of their culture and ways by a common *Weltanschauung* (worldview) shared by a colonialist church and state. A new paradox has occurred in the present day, however, when there is an intense interest in understanding the Aboriginal tribal ways and culture in order to save this world. The Aboriginal scientific system, which allows people to fit into rather than outside of the ecology, has been and is being investigated because, unlike the Western world and in M. J. Christie's words, it does not place "humanity apart from and above the natural world."[1] Consequently, the Indigenous people of Australia will be the messengers of a new ecological vision and ecotheology / creation theology for the new millennium.

Aboriginal people's *Weltanschauungen* are being investigated by the Western world for all possible answers for survival in a world in crisis: the environment; the threat of nuclear war; poverty; disease; the lack of mental, spiritual, and physical wholeness of humanity. Westerners look to a race of people who have "survived" since time began, with very few of these aspects of crisis in their history. The study of racial ontology and epistemology reveals a race with a deeper "spiritualness" than Western ontology and epistemology. A study of the genetics of memory helps to support this theory. Hence, this ontological quality is what, significantly, separates Australian Aboriginal and Western ontology;

therefore, it seems an intense study of this major aspect of Australian Aboriginal ontology is where the core of knowledge for human survival will be found.

Such an ontology with a central characteristic of deeper spiritualness reveals a culture that does not have a work-ethic ideology, as is the case with Western culture, but works only to survive, and "balances" the rest of existence with rest and recreation. The gender structure within the traditional cultures is balanced and egalitarian; men and women see their role as one of partnership. Aboriginals were constantly referred to as "savages" by the colonialists, but that has not been my experience of my Tasmanian Aboriginal culture. Aboriginal children were never physically hit as a part of chastisement; if any chastisement was necessary, it occurred only after initiation. The children were treated as extremely precious, as gifts from God, to be celebrated and cherished. This is my memory of the treatment I received from my Aboriginal grandfather; it is impossible for me to perceive my ancestors in white terms. The Aboriginal culture places little value on the material things of life, only on what contributes to human "happiness"—being: wholeness, harmony, physical survival, and love. Hence, these cultural ways that arise out of a deep spiritualness give a strong message to the generations of the future regarding what is essential for survival and quality existence.

The phenomenon is that, in spite of a paradoxical, phantom, intrinsically violent and unhealthy Christology inherited from colonialism, some Aboriginal people became Christian, as did many generations that followed. None were more exploited, from then until now, than Australian Indigenous women; they are on the lowest rung of the Australian social order and experience a "quadric-dimensional" oppression of racism, classism, sexism (including heterosexism), and naturism. The answer to the phenomenon seems to be that, in spite of the legacy of a violent Christology and the multilayered oppression these women experience, they have found a gentle Christ who tenderly and solidly comforts, identifies with, supports, and empowers them in their *Sitz im Leben* (settings in life). This I see as one of the most important messages Australian Aboriginal women give to future generations, white, black, and of color—the "real and true" insight they have into the being of Christ, born out of the incredible depths of their suffering; in this, they are significantly the *kerygmatics* of the new millennium in their Christologies.

While interviewing the women in order to document their Christologies, I became aware of their remarkable "benevolence," even in a state of suffering virtually incomprehensible to white people. This benevolence toward their oppressors, I believe, contains a message to future generations. Thus, combined with their real and true insight into Christ came an expression of benevolence. This charitable attitude was displayed in the interest in "education," as a means of helping Aboriginal people be able to communicate with white people and thus assist in bringing about reconciliation. White people, however, do not seem to have seen a need to initiate the learning of Aboriginal peoples' languages for mutual benefit. A positive activity in the area of education has been the training of Indigenous teachers for Indigenous students; this can be effective if the teachers are allowed to employ their own methodologies for teaching and are not hindered by the hegemonic bureaucracy. Indigenous support for and interest in education is something that I think is of value for future generations to contemplate and consider.

One of the interviewees of my research, who is a teacher, remarked on how she preferred a teaching methodology that was designed to educate her students about the "spiritual" things of life, and she liked to put this into practice by being guided spiritually. This teaching methodology would be very alien to a white culture that possessed an ontology strongly anchored in the intellect. The emphasis on the *spirit* in all areas of their lives would have to be the strongest characteristic of Australian Aboriginal ontological and epistemological expression. Even their perception of Christ is centered on his spiritual reality. There are healing methods that are centered on a combination of Aboriginal and Christian spirituality; these methods display a common, accepted practice among Australian Aboriginal Christian women to inculturate the spirituality of Christ into Aboriginal spirituality. In the area of Western psychology and practice in Australia, physicians have begun to recognize the power Aboriginal elders have in healing Indigenous people with diagnosed mental health problems. The elders bring these people into the life of the spirit and help to establish their Aboriginal identity. The fundamental message the Aboriginal Christian women are offering here to others is that wholeness requires mental, physical, and spiritual balance. Fortunately, the Western world is beginning to look at Aboriginal *Weltanschauung* to aid in mental health, as it knows its Western philosophies and medicines are limited in establishing mental wholeness.

Aboriginal spirituality is diverse in its healing concepts and practices from tribe to tribe, but there are major common healing concepts such as stillness, a natural closeness to God, and an intimate relationship with nature. The Aboriginal elders will bring those of their people who are ill in contact with these concepts. In the stillness, you come in touch with the spirit within you. This is how you come in touch with the Spirit of God within you. It is only in that stillness that you become aware of the Spirit of God within you also existing without. You then become aware that the Spirit of God existing without is "one" with all that is living. This is the first important step in healing, coming to know what the Spirit is; this method can be followed by anyone, of any culture, who wants to get in touch with their spiritual-self and spiritual reality, and to begin the process of balancing the mental, physical, and spiritual, which is very important for human wholeness. The next important step in healing is the establishing of Aboriginal identity, coming to know one's roots and uniqueness, as an individual and as part of a community; this creates a sense of "belonging," which is extremely important, and the building up of self-esteem.

The majority of Australian Aboriginal women interviewed suggested that the activities that would be of the greatest value to Indigenous people of the future were to establish Aboriginal "identity" and to walk close to God. The importance of establishing Aboriginal identity cannot be over-emphasized. These people are dispossessed, mentally, physically, and spiritually in their *Sitz im Leben* due to the effects of white hegemonic culture; this has to be reversed. The message of establishing identity is an important one for other Indigenous cultures throughout the world who have suffered at the hands of other hegemonic cultures.

When Aboriginal women are encouraging other people to walk close to God, it is God as seen through their eyes; that perception is one that is unique, intimate, and powerful, reflected in their Christologies. To them, God and Christ are one and the same. This characteristic of their Christologies they share with the Christologies of other black women and women of color from throughout the world. There are other attributes of their Christologies that are shared with the Christologies of these women from other cultures. They share a view of Christ who identifies with and supports them in their liberation from a quadri-dimensional oppression of racism, classism, sexism (including heterosexism), and naturism. Australian Aboriginal Christian women are not interested in issues centered around the gender of Christ, as is the case with white Christian feminists; their interest is centered more on his "humanity" and "saving power." This aspect of their Christologies they also share with the Christologies of their black sisters and sisters of color. Hence, there are "universal" attributes that Australian Indigenous Christian women share with other black women and women of color from throughout the world in their Christologies. In this, Australian Aboriginal Christian women are contributing to the universal academic area of womanist theology, strengthening its foundation for the generations to come and, thus, building a more solid foundation for universal healing of Christian Indigenous women struggling in hegemonic cultures.

There are other attributes of their Christologies that they do not necessarily share with their black sisters and sisters of color in the area of Christology. The understanding of the "sacredness" of life and land, and especially land, is very strong in their Christologies in comparison to the Christologies of their sisters from other black cultures and cultures of color. The strong connection Australian Aboriginal women have to land/nature/creation and to the source of creation is a unique aspect of their Christologies and calls for a methodology for doing Christology within this context. The majority of Australian Aboriginal Christian women interviewed inculturate the Spirit of Christ into their Indigenous spirituality. A Creation/Identity methodology[2] for doing Christology helps to articulate this inculturation. The methodology affirms the sacredness of creation and allows for the flourishing of identity with the Creator/Source and the natural environment. Thus, Christ becomes "one" with creation. I see this methodology as the most valuable contribution Australian Aboriginal Christian women make to the generations of the new millennium. This contribution will have benefits not only for Aboriginal women, but also for all people of black cultures and cultures of color, and for white people as well, doing Christology. A Creation/Identity methodology anchors Christ in creation, uniting spirit and nature, which is a major negative dualism that has existed for too long in Western culture. The end of this dualism in Western consciousness will help in shaping human attitudes toward the environment; the importance of this cannot be overstated in our state of universal environmental crisis. A Creation/Identity methodology for doing Christology allows Christ to be inculturated into whatever conception one has of God in one's culture; if the conception of God is female, then Christ becomes One-with-the-feminine-principle, hence, helping to end the male/female dualism, another major negative dualism in Western consciousness.

There is a relationship that exists between church and state in the Western world in the areas of morality and ethics; the changes in Christology in the church, therefore, will in turn affect the moral and ethical conscience of society. Thus, a Creation/Identity methodology for doing Christology can have resounding positive effects on church, and then state, in the Western world of the future.

Australian Aboriginal women doing Christology by using a Creation/Identity methodology will produce "new" Christologies that reflect their individual tribal spirituality/culture. The Christologies, therefore, will reflect differing images of Christ after being inculturated into their creation and religious stories, beliefs, and ways. The common characteristics that these Christologies will share, however, is that they will be ecowomanist, contextual, ecumenical, and inclusive. In their ecowomanist aspect, they are fighting for liberation from the oppression of naturism, an oppression exercised by white hegemonic culture; in this characteristic of their Christologies they contribute to the academic area of creation theology, which is and must be a domain of social ethics. Their Christologies will be contextual because the uniqueness of their *Sitz im Leben* demands such a perspective; this demand was the influence behind the development of Creation/Identity methodology for doing Christology, and in this they are liberated from Christologies written for women of a different *Sitz im Leben* and *Weltanschauung*. They will expound Christologies that reflect their Indigenous theologies with strong links to the Source of Creation and land/nature/creation. In this, they contribute to creation spirituality because their Christology is done through the study of creation and its interrelating spiritual relationships.

The ecumenical aspect of the Christologies comes about by the willingness of the women to inculturate Christ, a God brought to them by a hegemonic culture and spirituality, into their Aboriginal spirituality. This ecumenical aspect is significant in that it displays a great closeness to the Spirit of Christ, even if the vehicle for this savior is their oppressors. Their depth of closeness to Christ and their benevolent attitude toward their oppressors are strong messages indeed, now and in the future, for generations dealing with the plight of imposed Christianity. The inclusive aspect of their Christologies expounds their interest in keeping harmony in human relationships; to these women, Christ is inculturated into all of humanity; there is no hierarchical manifestation, no male/female dualism, only humankind being united in Christ. This aspect of their Christologies reflects Aboriginal culture's egalitarian and community outlook.

This inclusive aspect as well as all the other aspects of Australian Aboriginal women's Christologies just discussed, utilized in a Creation/Identity methodology, make critical contributions to liberation theology and spirituality while witnessing to the depth of the reality of Christ and the attitude to hold while experiencing oppression and encouraging the seeking of peace and harmony in all one's relationships with humankind and creation. This is a collective message of justice/wholeness/truth/peace being found for the Australian Indigenous Christian woman, and an encouragement for others to seek and find the same within the uniqueness of their *Sitz im Leben* and *Weltanschauung*.

Australian Aboriginal women using a Creation/Identity methodology for doing Christology will be aware of the common conception in Aboriginal spirituality of the sacredness of life, an attitude that encompasses all of creation. By the inculturation of the sacredness of the Spirit of Christ into the sacredness of all life, there is a unification of both Aboriginal and white spirituality; this activity witnesses in turn the inculturation of Christ, linked to the sacredness of all life, into white culture. This means a witness to the liberation of the oppressor from destructive Christologies that separate spirit from matter, people from each other, and humankind from nature. In the spiritual concept of the sacredness of all of life, a contribution is made to earth-based spiritualities, the theology of the Creator Spirit, and Christian sacramentalism. Therefore, Australian Aboriginal women doing Christology, using a Creation/Identity methodology, contribute to spiritualities and theologies that emphasize the sacredness of life: the earth, individuals, communities, the cosmos.

The aspect of Aboriginal spirituality that understands the earth as mother when it is united with the Spirit of Christ not only is the uniting of the feminine and masculine principles but also is the joining of the living Spirit of Christ with the living spirit of the earth. In this activity, Creation/Identity Christological methodology contributes to Gaia Spirituality, which sees the earth as a female, living, spiritual entity.

In this Earth Mother spirituality, along with all other aspects of Australian spirituality inculturated with the Spirit of Christ, is the witness to the end of the dualism of black and white spirituality; hence, Australian Aboriginal women using a Creation/Identity Christological methodology will help to create new Christologies that contribute to universal health and harmony, and to display the possibility that such positive things can be achieved in future generations.

Australian Aboriginal women using a Creation/Identity Christological methodology will contribute to theologies and spiritualities that are seeking the right mind-set, philosophy, or religious practice for the salvation of our world, in human and earth wholeness, in its permanent, unchangeable, symbiotic relationship. The importance of this contribution is urgent in a world at war with the earth and with itself. In light of this important contribution on a global scale, and all the other extremely valuable messages Australian Aboriginal Christian women can give to the generations of the new millennium, the value of the womanist perspective for interpreting one's *Sitz im Leben* is undeniable. I hope this thesis will encourage Australian Aboriginal Christian women to adopt this perspective in their cognitive thinking and to receive the benefits it will bring in liberation and wholeness to them, individually, and to the community.

The message Australian Aboriginal Christian women interviewed for this thesis and those Christian women who are part of the Australian Aboriginal community of women of my lived experience give to the church of the future is the need for its indigenization and for a holistic ministry that will help contribute to the mental, physical, and spiritual wholeness of Aboriginal people. Fundamentalism is responsible for Australian Aboriginal people receiving an incorrect biblical hermeneutic, and through the indigenization of the church we hope to see a rereading of scripture in the Australian Indigenous context. This reading done by Australian Aboriginal women in the contexts of their individual tribal theologies, racial and gender ontologies and epistemologies, in the view of Will Coleman, will offer theologies that will help reformulate all theological languages;[3] the women, as Matthew Fox suggests, in being an authentic source of revelation, are the primary spiritual directors for future generations.[4]

This thesis has taken us on a journey from the times of colonialism when Australian Aboriginal women received a violent Christology, through the development of their own Christologies that reveal the "real and true Christ," born out of the depths of their suffering, which is their legacy for the generations to come. I have the honor of documenting their Christologies for the first time in history. I hope that anyone who takes this journey while reading this thesis will be overwhelmed, as I have been, by the immense healing value the documentation and evaluation of these Christologies will have not only for Australian Aboriginal women but also for anyone from any culture or gender who is seeking healing for our earth and its people.

As a *Palawa*, a Tasmanian Aboriginal, I have grown up in a community of Indigenous women who have constantly questioned "why" this tremendous suffering occurred, and why it still occurs to our people. I hope this thesis has helped to answer this question in some way, and provided a path for healing. Mostly, I hope that this thesis helps first of all to ensure that the physical genocide of my people will never be forgotten and, second, to provide ways of healing for Australian Aboriginal Christian women experiencing the effects of genocide. The most powerful message Australian Aboriginal Christian women give to the generations of the new millennium is to please let there be no more genocide in the history of humanity! Please let the pain that is expressed in this poem, written by a *Palawa* woman, never occur again:

Why?

Across the Strait is Tasmania
A place that was once *Koorie* Land
A place that belonged to our people
As they wandered with love of their land

They roamed the hills and the mountains
Swam in the vast flowing sea
LIVED on this land of beauty
Land that was happy and free

They didn't need houses to live in
Their home was the land it was free
They didn't need medical treatment
Their medicine came from the Tree

No prison was there to hold them
For they were all happy and free
Our people the Tasmanian *Koories*!
Who lived on their land so free

They didn't have clocks to remind them
They knew what the weather should be
As they looked up above it would tell them
What the forecast for tomorrow would be

Then without warning it happened!!!
A tragedy no-one wanted to see
As they watched from the shore
A ship came sailing to their land
The land of the free

With fear in their eyes they stood watching not knowing
What was to be—
As the guns fired death lay all around them
The horror no one wanted to see
Killed by the guns of the white man
Killed on their own sacred Land

They didn't hurt anybody
They didn't take any land

After 200 years they have waited
And still they cannot understand

Why did they kill our people? ...
Why did they take our land? ...
Why? ...
—Brenda Campbell (1983)

Notes

1. M. J. Christie, "Aboriginal Science for the Ecologically Sustainable Future," *Aboriginal Science Teachers Journal* 37, no. 1 (March, 1991): 26–31.

2. This concept was given to the author in an oral communication by Anne Pattel-Gray.

3. Will Coleman, "Tribal Talk: Black Theology in Postmodern Configurations," *Theology Today* 50, no. 1 (April, 1993): 68–77.

4. Matthew Fox, *Original Blessing: A Primer in Creation Spirituality Presented in Four Paths, Twenty-Six Themes, and Two Questions* (Santa Fe, NM: Bear & Company, 1983), 267–70.

13

LORD OF THE INSIGNIFICANT: A CHRIST FOR NI-VANUATU WOMEN

Judith Vusi (Vanuatu)

THE LEGEND OF WAGERRIE

In Ni-Vanuatu myths and legends in my native tongue, the name *Wagerrie* refers to a very small man. He is seen as a member of a group of people who served *Budkolkol,* a native god. He could be described in English as a dwarf-like figure, who is always looked down upon because of his small size. He is considered unimportant, and yet the power and effectiveness of what he does stands out very clearly and is spoken of by everyone. A symbol of Wagerrie's character is the strong identity seen in the color of the root vegetables which he grows in his little garden. There are many legends concerning his character. One of the legends about him goes as follows:

> Once upon a time, Budkolkol and his group of followers, including Wagerrie, decided to plant a new garden of taro, which they did. Even though Wagerrie was present, he was not counted or included, but he managed nevertheless to clear some bush and to plant one tiny garden. When the taro was ready to be harvested, a big feast was held. When the men collected their big taro, Wagerrie also collected his. His taro were tiny in size, but he still contributed them. The others laughed at his taro and said that they were worth nothing at all. Still, when the taro were grated to make a big pudding (*laplap*), the tiny taro of Wagerrie were also grated, and their color was a bright red. The *laplap* was baked in the bush-oven, and when the leaves were unwrapped, to everyone's surprise and amazement the color of the whole *laplap* was red, taking on the color

172

from the tiny taro that Wagerrie had contributed from his little garden.

If Wagerrie had given up and looked down on himself as being of no value, he would have had no identity or effect. Yet he persisted to contribute what he could. Although small in size, and seemingly small in terms of contribution, he added "color" to the feast and helped to transform everyone else's contributions.

WAGERRIE AND CHRIST

Jesus came into the world to fulfill God's plan of salvation for the whole world. When he demonstrated his power, healing all kinds of diseases, feeding multitudes of people with the very small amount of food that was available, and teaching the people about the Kingdom, some people could not accept him. They would say things such as, "Is he not the carpenter's son, and are not his brothers here with us?" The public did not recognize him and refused to see and accept who he really was. His society regarded him as an ordinary man. The people looked down on him. Many did not want to have anything to do with him, and they ended up crucifying him. "He came unto his own, but his own received him not" (John 1:11). Yet, despite this rejection, Jesus' story and his mighty work of salvation for the whole world is told in every nation throughout history and is still continuing to be told and to empower people today.

WOMEN IN VANUATU SOCIETY

The status of women in my society fits well with the status of the legendary figure of Wagerrie and with that of Jesus in his society. Women make valuable contributions in society today which are not recognized. Women's ministries are silent ministries, seen by society as insignificant and small. Yet I am proud of the way in which women in my culture handle many things to the best of their abilities—in their homes, communities, mission fields, parishes, schools, government, and many other institutions. These contributions demonstrate that women possess many capabilities and gifts. They have a strong determination to press on, no matter what the obstacles in their path.

Wagerrie endured the cruel discrimination of his group members. Jesus Christ tolerated the cruel treatment that the public meted out to him in his time. Yet both of them have been remembered for their service to others. Women can take courage that, in their spirit of Christlike service, they are also being remembered by God.

This legend is also an excellent analogy for women as we weave our theology together. Each of us can add our own distinctive "colors" and "flavors" to make the whole work of our weaving a work of beauty.

WOMEN'S SERVICE IN THE BIBLE

It may be helpful for us to reflect at this point on some of the women in the Bible whose use of their gifts can be an example for women today. Rahab, for instance, was very brave to do what she did to protect the lives of the spies, and it was recommended that her action be told to the world. The woman who anointed Jesus' feet with a precious ointment at Bethany was seen by others as insignificant, but Jesus indicated to his disciples that what she did then would be retold in memory of her, wherever the gospel was to be proclaimed throughout the world (Matt 26:6–13). It is also encouraging to read from Luke the account of the women who contributed much to support Jesus and the other disciples out of their own households. In their appreciation of Jesus for his healing and empowerment of their own lives, they in turn shared in his wider ministry to others.

We women in our communities in Vanuatu and the Pacific today also have resources within ourselves and our own households—gifts of various kinds which we can contribute toward the development and well-being of our people, our churches, and the world. Although society may not view these gifts as significant, in Jesus' eyes they are of great value.

CONCLUSION

In the legendary figure of Wagerrie we see that, although he was underestimated in every way by his society, the contributions he made proved to be valuable, even in comparison to what others were doing. It was not easy for him, but his determination enabled him to do great things, for which he was remembered.

Jesus was bruised from being despised and ill-treated by his own people, who regarded him as the lowly son of Mary and Joseph, despite his empowering ministry of healing, caring, and teaching. Yet he persisted in his ministry, even to the point of enduring the cruelty of crucifixion to fulfill God's plan for him. "He humbled himself and was obedient unto death, even death on the cross. God exalted him and gave him the name that is above every other name. Even heaven and earth bow to this name and every tongue can confess that he is Christ" (Phil 2:9–11).

We Ni-Vanuatu women are made in the image of God. We have special qualities and abilities because we are part of God's image. Let us continue to prove ourselves to the world by using the variety of gifts and talents we have been given—big or small—as we weave them together in God's service. The outcome of this weaving will show to the world who we are and what we possess as part of God's image. Let us aim to give glory to God as we weave our theology and develop our people, society, and world to grow in the knowledge and worship of God, the Creator of the universe and Sustainer of us all.

14

MASCULINITY, FEMININITY, AND THE CHRIST

Maria Clara Lucchetti Bingemer (Brazil)

Among the various facets of theology that are seeking fresh expression on the basis of the gender perspective, Christology is perhaps one of the most important and certainly one of the most polemical. The reason for this is that, while on the one hand Jesus Christ is the central focus of Christian faith and theology, the point of convergence and of our—men's and women's—possibility of accessing the salvation offered by the living God and so the fullness of life this God represents, on the other, many women find that the masculinity of Jesus—the historical-theological fact, that is, that the God of all glory and majesty became incarnate in the person of a male in Palestine 2000 years ago—is not without its problems.

In this article I propose to reflect on this question and the christological challenge it poses, starting with the thinking some major recent feminist theologians have devoted to it. Next, I turn my attention to the gospels, seeking to discover how Jesus' relations with women are described there and the significance of this attitude in a markedly patriarchal society such as his. Then, I shall seek to reflect theologically on the biblical data considered in tandem with psychology, which questions the separation and firm differentiation between the masculine and the feminine in human persons. Finally, I try to examine the data in a trinitarian setting, in fidelity to the principle that should guide all Christian theological reflection.

I. JESUS: THE MAN FROM NAZARETH AND THEOLOGICAL FEMINISM

Many feminist theologians, endeavoring to ponder on revealed mystery from their standpoint of human beings of the feminine gender, find an obstacle in the person and mystery of Jesus Christ.[1] The centrality and lordship of this masculine God strikes them as having been employed—doctrinally, politically, psychologically, and structurally—in the service of a fellowship of brothers and fathers, the church, whose female members were always counted as auxiliaries or underlings or, in special cases, as so like men so that they could be relatively easily accepted into their company.[2]

The main thrust of feminist critique, nevertheless, does not cover the use made of masculine images to describe God. These, in themselves, can serve as finite points of reference pointing in the direction of God. The problem lies rather in the fact of these images being understood in a literal sense, identifying the mystery with a He, a masculine being. Besides this, there is the problem of utilizing masculine images modeled on a patriarchal outlook. The feminine dimension is simply incorporated artificially into an overall symbol that remains firmly masculine.[3]

Christology has also been viewed by many women as the doctrine in Christian tradition that has most often been used against them. Some statements by great theological masters such as Augustine of Hippo and, in the high Scholastic era, Thomas Aquinas, have been interpreted as saying that the male is the generic sex of the human species. The male alone represents the fullness of human potential, in himself and as head of the woman. He is the totality of the image of God, while woman in herself does not represent the image of God or possess the fullness of humanity.[4]

If Christianity is basically following *of* and identification *with* Jesus Christ, if this constitutes salvation and the full realization of the longings of the human heart, how can women find their place in it, in full faithfulness to their feminine condition? How do they find the *way* to feeling themselves to be full citizens of the Kingdom put forward by Jesus? How do they find their space in the Revelation of a God with masculine characteristics and in a community made up of his followers that is structured and patterned on essentially male lines?

Although the church has always proclaimed that the incarnation of God in Jesus Christ is the Good News of Salvation for all: Jews and Greeks, slaves and free, men and women (cf. Gal 3:28), at all times and in all places, we still find that in most cases the practice does not live up to the pronouncement. All down the ages, women have suffered real and serious discrimination in the church community, not only at the ministerial level but also and above all at the theological level. I believe, nevertheless, that women's theological view of the saving events of the New Testament can uncover new aspects, which, investigated and worked out from a feminine perspective, can provide us with a better basis for stating that Christology has an irreplaceable word to speak in the process of liberating women here and now. The key to overcoming this difficulty is to be found, in my view, in a re-encounter with the Jesus of the gospels, seeking to perceive and contemplate the features of his personality and the steps of his journey just as the first witnesses did. The outcome of such an observation will be discovery of a man who displayed a special kinship and empathy for the women of his time, who founded a community and inaugurated a style of life in which they were welcomed and found their place. A man who, furthermore, showed a deep and harmonious integration between his *"animus"* and his *"anima,"* between the masculine and the feminine components of his personality.[5]

II. Considering Jesus . . .

What we can learn about Jesus of Nazareth from the gospel narratives shows him to have been the initiator of an itinerant charismatic group, to which men and women were admitted in a relationship of fraternal friendship. Unlike John the Baptist's movement, which laid marked stress on ascesis and penance, and unlike the Qumran sect, which admitted men only, the movement Jesus inaugurated was characterized—besides its central preoccupation with preaching the Kingdom as a real project in history—by joy, by sharing without preconditions in celebrations and meals to which sinners and marginal groups in general were admitted, and by the break from a number of taboos associated with the society of his time.

Among these differences, one of the most obvious is that involving relations with women.[6] Any woman of Jesus' time was considered socially and religiously inferior, "first for not being circumcised and, as a result, not belonging fully to the Alliance with God; then on account of the rigorous purification precepts to which she was obliged because of her biological condition as a woman; and finally because she personified Eve, with all the pejorative charge attached to her."[7]

The triple Judaic prayer that characterized Rabbinism of the second century came to reflect the mentality predominant in Judaism since Jesus' time—a prayer in which pious Jews gave thanks to God every day for three things: for not having been born a gentile, outside the Law, or a woman.[8] In this context, Jesus' actions proved not merely innovative, but also shocking. Despite not having left any formal teaching on the subject, Jesus' attitude to women was so unheard-of that it surprised the disciples themselves (John 4:27).

The fact that women formed part of the assembly of the Kingdom summoned by Jesus is common to all four gospels: in this assembly they were not simply accidental components but active and participatory (cf. Luke 10:38–42) and also privileged beneficiaries of his miracles (cf. Luke 8:2; Mark 1:29–31; 5:25–34; 7:24–30, etc.).[9]

This enhancement of women on Jesus' part has a double theological import for us today:

(1) It applies to a particular aspect of the gospel that shows it in its most essential form: the Good News proclaimed to the poor, freed by Jesus as a priority, the deserted, the rejected, pagans, sinners, and those suffering any manner of exclusion, among which women and children were grouped, not being counted as part of Jewish society. Jesus made all these the privileged recipients of his Kingdom, making them fully part of the community of children of God, because his divine vision, constantly informed by the impulses of the Spirit and by his filial relationship with the Father, enabled him to discern hidden values in all these poor, including women: "the precious life of the trampled reed or the smoldering fire in the still-smoking embers."[10]

Women played a major role in this evangelical vision of social reversal implied in Jesus' actions and words. It is the women who, among the various categories of the socially excluded, appear as the representatives of the little people and the oppressed. The first talk and recognition of Jesus as Messiah comes from a Samaritan woman (cf. John 4). It is a Syro-Phoenician (cf. Mark 7:24–30) or Canaanite woman (Matt 15:21–28) who makes Jesus carry out the prophetic gesture of proclaiming the Good News to the gentiles. Among the poor, whom Jesus calls blessed because they are capable of generosity in the midst of deepest need, the figure of the widow (Luke 21:3) stands out as the most destitute and most generous. Prostitutes are singled out as those most marginalized and beyond the law, who will nevertheless be among the first to enter the Kingdom of God (see Matt 21:31). Among the impure, denied access to religious rites and the whole structure of organized religion, the woman with a hemorrhage (Luke 8:40; Matt 9:20–22) is the prototype, permanently impure according to Jewish law (cf. Lev15:19) and rendering everything she touches impure.

Women are, then, a formative and principal part of Jesus' messianic vision and mission, and in it they appear as the most oppressed among the oppressed.[11] They are the lowest step on the social ladder, and are therefore seen as the last who will be first in the Kingdom of God. The burden on their shoulders is the double one of social and cultural, then classist and sexist, oppression. This makes them the favored recipients of

Jesus' liberating proclamation and praxis. This is also why the response of these sufferers from oppression and discrimination to the messianic message is so rapid and so radical. Because they were at the bottom of the heap of social relationships at the time, women were the ones who had most reason and were best placed to long and struggle for the non-perpetuation of the "status quo" that oppressed and enslaved them.

(2) Jesus' relationship with women carries another component that, closely linked to the first, enriches and complements the picture of the liberating promise of the Kingdom. This is his relationship with women's bodies, a central aspect and the cause of the discrimination to which they were subjected.[12]

With his liberating praxis in relation to women, accepting them just as they are, even with their bodies that were regarded as imperfect and impure in his culture, Jesus proclaimed an integral anthropology, valuing human beings in their dimension of bodies enlivened by the divine breath, as a whole in which spirit and corporeality form a single entity.

As women's biological make-up was, in the society of that time, the central point through which the exclusion to which they were subjected as persons passed, Jesus' actions as shown in the gospels were definitely and specifically liberating and saving, opening up possibilities and new horizons of communion to all whose whom society excluded and proclaiming the advent of a new humanity in which the original image created by God—"male and female" (Gen 1:27)—could be raised to its full stature (cf. Eph 4:13).

The gospels, then, do not present a dualism in which masculine and feminine are opposed, in conflict with one another, or even romantic "complements" to one another. They rather put forward a view of life in which the half of the human race that is still despised and discriminated against has the right of access to a human and egalitarian relationship, one that is adult and responsible. At the same time as preaching this integrated and integrating anthropology, Jesus demonstrates it in his own person and the way he lives his life.

Having looked at Jesus' attitude toward the feminine, we now need to turn our attention to the feminine in Jesus, to the presence of the feminine dimension that Jesus, as the human being he was, bore within himself. The insight of modern psychology—that every human being is, to varying degrees, at once *animus* and *anima,* masculine and feminine—gives us an opening on this point.[13] If this—accepted today as an uncontroversial part of contemporary culture—is true, then Jesus, a man in whom the masculine mode of being a person predominated, also included the feminine dimension in his constitution. Moving beyond the androcentrism of his time, "he incorporated within himself so many behavioral characteristics that he can be considered the first person to achieve a complete maturity."[14] The gospels show us Jesus as a man who did not display the widespread masculine "shame" at expressing his feelings. Just as he was capable of severely reproaching the Pharisees and his disciples, so he let his lips sing to the Father with joy and thanksgiving when asserting the revelation made to the little ones and hidden from the wise (Matt 11:25–7); he did not restrain the overflowing tenderness that seized him at the sight of "harassed and helpless" creatures disregarded by the society of his time (see Mark 9:36 and par.). Furthermore, Jesus experienced in his own person, in the very depth of his being, the emotions and sorrows that afflicted the "*rahamim*" (maternal bowels) of Yahweh in the Old Testament.[15] This can be seen when he weeps at the death of his friend Lazarus (John 11:35) and at the suffering of his beloved Mary of Bethany (John 11:33); when he delivers a bitter and heartfelt lament over the city that will be responsible for his martyrdom (Luke 19:41); when he cries "woe" to cities that would not accept salvation (Matt 11.21), and in his cry of frustrated maternal desire to gather the unwilling "brood" of Jerusalem "under [his] wings" (Luke 13:34).[16]

III. JESUS, SON OF GOD, HUMAN LIKE US IN ALL THINGS . . .

All this feminine nature in Jesus, made up of infinite tenderness, compassion, and mercy, of a delicacy that is not opposed to firmness, of a love that displays longings, gestures, and expressions that can be identified not just as paternal but as maternal as well, and fraternal in a fellowship that is no less a "sorority," was taken up eternally, definitively, hypostatically, by the Word: that is, by the Second Person of the Trinity.

If we declare that, in Jesus, God becomes "like us in all things but sin," we are thereby stating that, like any one of us, God lives that inner composition in which the predominance of one aspect of sexuality does not exclude the presence of the other. In Jesus, human, a man from Nazareth, the feminine is really and truly present. On the basis of this affirmation we can, then, go on to say that if God raised him and made him Lord and Christ, his whole personal identity, with all it contained, was divinely assumed. In the life, words, actions, and person of Jesus, the feminine is—finally—divinized in the deepest aspects of his being and so belongs to the innermost nucleus of the mystery of God's love.

Starting with Jesus' resurrection, the Spirit is poured out on all flesh, forming a new humanity, which is none other than the body of

Christ. It is this body of Christ, a new creation, collective and all-embracing, that the Spirit continues to form and bring to birth "groaning in labor pains" (cf. Rom 8:22–23) until now, making the original image of the Father's creation—a creation that is "male and female" (Gen 1:27)—present in the world. And this creation finds its prototype in Christ, the first-born of all creatures.[17] In this Christology, women are not only announcers of the risen Christ but also identified with his actual person. Women too speak, live, and act, in a very deep sense, "*in persona Christi.*" They too are an "*alter Christus.*"[18]

The early church assimilated all this in a profound and creative fashion. The New Testament contains many examples of prophetesses (Acts 19:8–9) and deaconesses (Rom 16:1). Later the church of the catacombs and martyrs of the first three centuries, in its turn, witnessed innumerable women—like men—shedding their blood for their faith in Jesus Christ, the embodiment of the dead and raised Lord.[19]

This Christology of the early centuries, developed under the powerful impact of experience of the Spirit and marked by eschatological expectation of the coming *parousia,* made no distinction between the past history of Jesus of Nazareth and the present time of the risen Christ. Nor did it separate these from the pre-existence of the Word that antedates creation. In it, Jesus Christ is the one who continues to reveal himself in persons—men and women—in an ever-expanding potential for a new humanity. The reality of Jesus Christ was not completed or closed off in the earthly life of Jesus but continued being present in the body of the risen Lord, made up of all those men and women who gave their lives, in one way or another, for the coming of the Kingdom.

We should not forget, however, that in this risen but still crucified Lord, rather than crucified then risen, creation re-acquires its original light. Made reality in Christ—the first-born of all creatures—the image of the divine community—Father, Son, and Holy Spirit—is made present in the world in the human community—men and women. The Christ who is the prototype of humanity is—also and equally—the prototype of women. The Second Person of the Trinity—the Word made flesh—is salvation for women too.

Women, victims of the dual social and religious oppression at the historical moment the Word became flesh, are, together with other outcasts awaiting Jesus' call, privileged representatives of a new social order in which the will of God will be made known and will fill the earth. Jesus Christ, who on the one hand cannot simply be reduced to the spatio-temporal dimensions of the man from Nazareth but at the same time has to be proclaimed and venerated as *Kyrios* (glorified and glorious Lord), cannot, on the other hand, be confined by Christology to the glorious lordship of the Risen Lord, forgetting that he who reigns at the Father's right hand is the same person who washed his disciples' feet, who showed himself as the servant who gave his life for his friends, obedient even unto death on a cross. He is the one who showed preference for the poor and oppressed, identifying himself as one of them. And he is the same person who treated the despised and downtrodden women of his time with affection and respect, proclaiming their full dignity as daughters of God and citizens of the Kingdom.

CONCLUSION: THE TWO FACES OF THE MYSTERY OF JESUS CHRIST

The glory of the resurrection is nothing other than the seal of approval given to the historical path taken by this Jesus—servant and brother—as the only path that leads to salvation. To forget this is to remove oneself from the center of the New Testament *kerygma* and so from faith in Christ itself.

The Christian community, made up of men and women, gives continuity to this all-embracing Christ, bringing about—with the assistance of the Holy Spirit—the full liberation of the cosmos and of humankind. Christology is thus still today—as ever and never more so than now—Good News of salvation for women seeking their space and their place, side-by-side with men, in society and in the church.

In the Son, God became flesh of men and women. The Son of the Father, pre-existing from all eternity and who gave us the power to be children of God and to call this God Father, is also the son of Mary (cf. Mark 6:3; Matt 13:55; John 6:42), born of woman (cf. Gal 2:4). This is the process of kenotic descent celebrated in the letter to the Philippians (2:5–8). The one in whom we believe as risen and glorious is in no wise different from the child who was born of Mary's flesh and from this Galilean woman received the body of God walking the ways of humanity's land. Having come from the womb of that young woman from Nazareth, he would grow in grace and wisdom and surprise his contemporaries, who, seeing the signs and wonders he performed, would say, "Is not this the carpenter's son? Is not his mother called Mary?" (Matt 13:55; cf. Mark 6:3; John 6:42).

At the center of the mystery of the incarnation, a mystery that is salvation for the whole human race, the New Testament places man and woman, Jesus and Mary, God who takes human flesh *in* and *through* the flesh of the woman—"born of woman." God does not become man and identify himself with just one half of humankind; God becomes flesh, flesh of man and woman, in such a manner that the way to the Father must necessarily lead through the overall human condition, which is masculine and feminine.

The mystery of the incarnation of Jesus in the flesh of Mary teaches us that human beings are not divided into a body of sin and imperfection and a spirit of greatness and transcendence. It is only in the weakness, poverty, and limitations of human flesh—flesh of men and women—that the ineffable greatness of the Spirit can be experienced, contemplated, and adored. And it is only here that theology can, finally, stammer its word.

—Translated by Paul Burns

Notes

1. The most balanced critiques are, among U.S. women theologians, in works such as E. Johnson, *She Who Is: The Mystery of God in Feminist Theological Discourse* (New York: Crossroad, 1992) and, among Europeans, K. E. Börresen, *Subordination and Experience: The Nature and Role of Woman in Augustine and Thomas Aquinas* (London: SCM Press, 1968); Börresen, ed., *Image of God and Gender Models in Judaeo-Christian Tradition* (Minneapolis, MN: Fortress, 1995). The most radical must include Mary Daly, whose *Beyond God the Father* (Boston: Beacon Press, 1973) became a sort of manifesto for the dawning feminist theology.

2. Cf. the question of the eternal feminine, so much criticized by feminism. On this see *Concilium* 2000/5, *In the Power of Wisdom*, especially the editorial by E. Schüssler Fiorenza, "Walking in the Way of Wisdom," 7–10.

3. E. Schüssler Fiorenza, *Jesus, Miriam's Child: Critical Issues in Feminist Theology* (New York: Crossroad, 1994); E. Johnson, "The Maleness of Christ," *Concilium* 1991/6, *The Special Nature of Women?* 108–16; Johnson, *She Who Is*; Johnson, *Consider Jesus: Waves of Renewal in Christology* (New York: Crossroad, 2001).

4. See, e.g., the commentary by R. Radford Ruether in *To Change the World: Christology and Cultural Criticism* (New York: Crossroad, 1983), 45. See also Börresen, *Subordination and Experience*.

5. Cf. the excellent article by R. M. Ceballos, "La masculinidad patriarcal y la masculinidad liberadora. El modelo de Jesús de Nazaret," *Anuario Pedagógico* 11 (Santo Domingo: Centro Cultural Poveda, 2007). In this he distinguishes the masculinity of Jesus from traditional patriarchal masculinity and argues that Jesus represents the true destiny of the male, in a liberating masculinity.

6. Cf. www.pucsp.br/rv_2005/p-kochmann.pd44 (accessed 6 Apr. 2008) and what R. S. Kochmann says on the place of women in Judaism through history.

7. L. Boff, *O rosto materno de Deus* (Petrópolis: Vozes, 1979), 77–78. See also my article "'Chiarete. Alegrai-vos' (Lc 15.8–10) ou a mulher não futuro da Teologia da Libertaçio," REB 48 (1988): 565–87.

8. Cf. R. S. Kochmann's words in the text cited above, n. 5, at p. 36.

9. See Boff, *O rosto materno*; A. M. Tepedino, *As Discípulas de Jesus* (Petrópolis: Vozes, 1990); C. Ricci, *Mary Magdalen and Many Others: Women Who Followed Jesus* (Tunbridge Wells: Burns & Oates, 1993); M. C. L. Bingemer, *O segredo feminino do Mistério* (Petrópolis: Vozes, 1991); M. P. Aquino, *Nuestro clamor por la vida. Teología latinoamericana desde la perspectiva de la mujer* (San José: DEI, 1992), among others.

10. R. Laurentin, "Jesus and Women: An Underestimated Revolution," *Concilium* 134 (1980), *Women in a Men's Church*, 80–92.

11. Cf. R. Radford Ruether, *Sexism and God-talk* (Boston: Beacon Press, 1993), 84.

12. I refer to what I said above on the fact of women being kept apart from public and religious life on account of their biological make-up, which led to them often being considered impure.

13. On this point, see Boff, *O rosto materno*, 102–3, strongly influenced by C. G. Jung. See also Boff, *Trinity and Society* (Tunbridge Wells: Burns & Oates, and Maryknoll, NY: Orbis Books, 1992).

14. J. Moltmann and E. Moltmann Wendel, *Dieu homme et femme* (Paris: Cerf, 1984), 58.

15. For a fuller consideration of this subject see my "A Trindade a partir da perspective da mulher," REB 46 (1986): 73–99 (re-worked and extended in 'Abbá: un padre maternal,' *Estudios Trinitarios* 36 [2002]: 69–102).

16. On this point I refer, *inter alia*, to S. McFague, *Models of God: Theology for an Ecological, Nuclear Age* (Philadelphia: Fortress, 1988); V. Molenkott, *The Divine Feminine. The Biblical Imagery of God as Feminine* (New York: Crossroad, 1987); also Johnson, *She Who Is*.

17. Cf. Börresen, *Image of God and Gender Models*.

18. These expressions, which in the Catholic Church are reserved to priests, can, I believe, justifiably be applied to all Christians, who, by virtue of their baptism, are made one with Christ in his paschal mystery. Therefore, such expressions are applicable to women too. Cf. what E. Johnson says on this in "The Maleness of Christ."

19. Cf. the "Letter from the Churches of Lyon and Vienne" describing the martyrdom of the young Blandina and the slave Felicity, where there are clear comparisons and analogies with Christ. Cf. P. Allard, *Histoire des persécutions pendant la première moitié du IIme siécle* (Paris, 1886), 73, cited by L. Bouyer (*Le Consolateur* [Paris: Cerf, 1980]), 127.

15

JESUS CHRIST:
LIFE AND LIBERATION
IN A DISCIPLESHIP OF EQUALS

María Pilar Aquino (Mexico/USA)

Saying who Jesus is for Latin American women today means taking up the question Jesus asked the men and women who shared his ministry: "Who do you say I am?" (Mark 8:27). The reply is in terms of the respondent's personal history and tries to express what Jesus means for her. Like many biblical characters, Latin American women Christians today feel *summoned* to share in a discipleship of equals in Jesus' ministry. An answer to Jesus' question is only possible in terms of a consciously adopted attitude about ourselves, that is, realizing that our own lives are deeply affected by the person of Jesus. The core of christological reflection from the perspective of women is that it is in Jesus—whose life, death, and resurrection was for the sake of the reign of God—that God's saving plan for humanity has been manifested. Through the power of the Spirit women feel called to share in the new world that has begun with Jesus.

PETER'S AND MARTHA'S REPLIES

New Testament hermeneutics usually takes for granted—erroneously, as feminist exegesis shows—that the central question put by Jesus to those who were disciples in his movement is addressed only to *twelve male* disciples, thus excluding women and other men.[1] This view is reinforced by the emphasis given, following the Synoptic tradition, to Peter's answer: "You are the Christ" (Mark 8:29). This shows the patriarchal prejudice of androcentric hermeneutics, which disregards the messianic profession of faith that John's theology places in the mouth of a woman, Martha of Bethany, who proclaims: "Yes, Lord, I believe that you are the Christ, the Son of God, the one who was to come into this world" (John 11:27). As Ana María Tepedino points out, by this proclamation Martha "crystallizes the messianic faith of the community, being its spokesperson in her capacity as the 'beloved disciple' of Jesus."[2] Neither of these replies excludes the other and should not do so; they share the same space of equal discipleship. The problem is that preeminence has been given to the one that expresses only the androcentric interest, with the object of legitimating religious power in the hands of men. But both replies taken together enable us to understand more fully not only the person of Jesus but also the nature of the inclusive discipleship he offered and his own experience of God in a sharing community.

As Nelly Ritchie points out, Latin American women take up the question and answer it in terms of their own interest in taking part in social and religious liberation movements and the protagonistic role they are now trying to play in history. For them,

> the statement: that Jesus is Christ! covers new dimensions. It does not have to do with an applied doctrine but with a truth to discover, with a response which, translated into words and deeds, takes on historical truthfulness and liberating force... This attempt to give answers happens within our context as Latin American women.[3]

Latin American women's Christology is based on our own experience of a historical reality, and this means our Christology is *contextual*. To do this Christology implies a commitment to the transformation of our own suffering and that of others, to joy, liberation, and justice. Women's discourse about Jesus Christ is nourished by liberating activities in the church base communities and the various social movements of struggle and resistance.

So, knowledge and understanding of Jesus Christ has to do with the historical experience of the struggle against oppression and for liberation. This knowledge consciously distances itself from the theoretical and tries to become *sentient knowledge*. Both the woman seeking knowledge and Jesus Christ are significant in this process; they relate in such a way that if either is left out the very identity of the other is radically affected and will have to be reformulated.

Christian women in Latin America experience faith in Jesus Christ as a vocation and a call to participate. As Nelly Ritchie writes:

> Our reality means that we are women, we belong to Latin
> America, and we are members of the body of Christ. We are
> setting out on an adventure which will bring together all our
> humble contributions. We do so with the confidence that to-
> gether we will enrich each other's lives, we will inspire one an-
> other, and share the work involved in liberating our continent
> ...What we hope to do is to provoke new questions and to
> open ourselves up to the marvelous revelations of God who, in
> Jesus, is shown to be the Liberator.[4]

Women's christological reflections express their vision and expectation
of a new earth to which they are called in the power of the Spirit.

SOME PRESUPPOSITIONS OF FEMINIST CHRISTOLOGY

Christology from the perspective of women welcomes the findings and
aims of Latin American Christology in general.[5] But it has different emphases and stresses aspects ignored by androcentric reflection. Among
others, we may mention women's active participation in Jesus' movement; their full membership in the community summoned together by
him; women's equal discipleship with men; Jesus' humanizing attitude
toward women; Jesus' criticism of patriarchal social and religious institutions; and the prophetic wisdom traditions in Jesus. Up till now these aspects have been peripheral in the Christology done by male theologians.
This Christology has failed to give the relationship between Jesus and
oppressed women the importance it should have in liberation hermeneutics and which is present in the gospel itself. This means that systematic
work on Christology today is not automatically inclusive; it is necessary
that the person doing it consciously choose that it should be so.

Those who believe that the new era of the reign of God initiated by
Jesus implies the end of women's oppression must deliberately include
this objective in their theology and make plain that the good news also
announces the end of women's current subordination.[6] In order to find
personal and social meaning in the gospel's liberating message for
women, it is essential to participate in the historical struggles for change
without reductionism or postponement of women's issues. Likewise, in
approaching Jesus as an object of our theological reflection, we must
clearly pay attention to the historical Jesus; at the same time we must
make a conscious effort not to add more androcentric weight to that already present in the biblical accounts. This critical position will give us a

broader access to the life and ministry of the historical Jesus. Our christological vision must not overlook fundamental aspects of Jesus' life and
activity, one of which is his relation to women. He clearly viewed
women not just as belonging to the impoverished masses, but simply as
women; not just as receivers of the good things brought by the messiah,
but also as actors contributing to the spread of the good news; not as ap-
pendices to do the housework, but as full members of the equal community he founded.[7]

Although Latin American Christology may be lacking in these respects, the work done by women lays equal emphasis on Jesus Christ
as liberator. It stresses Jesus' liberating mission in its historical, structural, personal, and eschatological dimensions. From the perspective of
women, historical liberation is not a closed circle but points to a future
still to be revealed. The present is only an anticipation of the fulfillment
to come in an abundance of life for the whole earth.[8]

There are certain classical questions for modern exegesis about the
liberation brought by Jesus. For example, the definitive gift of God's
reign, freely offered as a blessing for the poor and oppressed, requires *responsible human action* for the transformation of the reality that produces
inhumanity and oppression. As this liberation embraces all human relationships, it must change the unequal relationship between men and
women in daily life.[9] This is because Jesus' liberation does not support a
split between the personal and the social, private and public, the transcendent and the historical, men and women, above and below. Once
again the criterion is the one I mentioned earlier: women's special way of
seeing life as a single whole. Now I point out certain aspects of the
Christology elaborated by Latin American women.

From Patriarchal Christology to Jesus' Egalitarian Practice

One of the first things women's Christology does is to examine the patriarchalization of Christology, notorious in the New Testament texts
and in later elaborations of Christian theology. Rosemary Radford
Ruether has made a significant contribution here to the development of
Latin American women's Christology, as is noted in Bingemer's work.[10]
For Bingemer the patriarchal roots of Christology go back to the Old
Testament messianic expectations, in which the monarchical Davidic
messianism prevails over the Isaiah tradition of the Servant. Likewise
in New Testament times, the Greek *logos* prevails over the *hochmah*
(wisdom), culminating in the fourth century with the establishment of

Christianity as the official religion of the Roman Empire. The convergence of these two processes in Christology will have dramatic consequences for women in the fields of anthropology as well as Christology and soteriology.[11] With the final stage in the patriarchalization of Christology in the fourth century, Jesus became the image of the emperor—the *Pantocrator,* Judge, and Lord—like a temporal ruler. He thus becomes "the consolidation of the lordship of a masculine God, who can only have male representatives."[12]

The ensuing Christology, together with Greek androcentric patriarchal anthropology, not only placed women in a subordinate position but also damaged understanding of the God of Jesus Christ. Bingemer points out two particular problems that this Christology has passed on to the church today and that need to be solved. On the one hand, the exclusion of women from the ordained ministry appeals to the argument that women do not act *in persona Christi.* On the other hand, this Christology

> makes women second-class citizens in the order of creation and salvation. As well as being christological, the problem is soteriological. Many women (especially now that women's liberation is growing fast) find it difficult to see this man, "the one whom men killed, God made Lord and Christ" (Acts 2:23–24), as God's salvation offered to humanity.[13]

Women are seeking ways to solve these problems and create an alternative Christology that is also liberating for them. They are trying to reencounter the Jesus of the gospels in order to return to his relation with women and women's active participation in his movement.

A second feature in women's christological reflection is concerned with the primary link between Jesus and the poor and oppressed from the very beginning in the incarnation of God's eternal word. This link relates the person of Jesus with women, both as women and as oppressed. The undeniable fact, without which theology would cease to be Christian and without which Jesus Christ would lose his power as the savior and liberator of humanity, is that God's Word becomes flesh (*sarx*) (John 1:14) and chooses as its human dwelling place women and men, *not* primarily men. But the fact that really causes scandal is that God's Word does not just become human but becomes flesh in the humanity of the poor and oppressed, identifying with them in their life, destiny, and hope (Mark 9:37; Matt 8:20; 25:40, 45). Hence the acknowledgment made in the final document of the Latin American meeting on Women, Church, and Theology:

It seems important to recognize that the incarnation of the Son of God takes place in the humanity of the poor, and his resurrection is the victory of the new humanity over death. Jesus' special concern for women lies within the scope of this fact: God becomes poor before becoming man or woman and God conquers death to become new humanity, cancelling the divisions of class, race, and sex.[14]

Without this fundamental recognition we cannot understand Jesus' action for women as people in their own right or the scandal that his behavior provoked. At the same time this perspective enables us to understand that Jesus' good news to the poor and oppressed is not given to women *in addition* to men, but because God has taken on flesh and their cause.

The third important aspect is women's incorporation into Jesus' liberating plan, centered around God's reign. Unlike other Jewish groups and movements in the first century of our era,[15] Jesus' movement admitted women because of his special way of understanding of the reign of God and his experience of God. According to the gospel accounts, Jesus initiated an itinerant charismatic movement, whose central vision continues to be that God's reign has broken into history in Jesus' own person and ministry. This is a new reality that benefits the poor, sinners, and outcasts, for whom society offers no salvation. It is to this collection of needy men and women that God's reign belongs. It comes to them as a blessing and tells them that now is the time of salvation. It is the good news of liberation. The power of God's reign is already at work and will change the face of the earth. The triumph over the evils that deprive the poor and oppressed of life has already begun and can be seen in Jesus' activity, the signs of liberation created by him.

Characteristically, Jesus likes to express God's reign as restoring power in a common meal, shared by the most disconcerting groups of people: the poor, sinners, prostitutes, the impure, women. In short, he eats with those who are considered to be religiously and socially deficient by those occupying positions of religious power. For Jesus, God's reign means joy, superabundance of life and well-being, human relationships based on justice, solidarity, and constant human renewal. So God's reign proclaimed by Jesus and experienced by those who followed him is understood in terms of the fulfillment to which history, humanity, and the whole creation is destined.[16]

"Jesus embodied God's will to form a more human community by treating women as persons worthy to share in it together with men."[17]

From the beginning of Jesus' ministry women form part of the community that follows him. Indeed, says Bingemer,

> It is common to the four gospels that women form part of the assembly of the reign of God summoned by Jesus. They are not merely accidental components, but active participants (Lk 10:38–42) and special recipients of his miracles (cf. Lk 8:2; Mk 1:29–31; Mk 5:25–34; 7:24–30). So women are an integral and principal part of the vision and messianic mission of Jesus. They are the most oppressed of the oppressed. They are the lowest rung of the social ladder.[18]

> Jesus offers a different future, and women belong to his movement in a radical way.

> As they are at the bottom of the heap in the society of their time, bearing the weight of its contradictions, women are the ones who have the most reason to want to fight for the non-perpetuation of the status quo that oppresses and enslaves them.[19]

These women show the way in which Jesus turned society upside down.

THE RECOVERY OF WOMEN'S BODIES AS BELONGING TO THE REIGN OF GOD

Another fruitful line of reflection for Latin American women is the rediscovery of Jesus' relation with women and women's activities within the new community. Women are not only recipients of messianic benefits, but of the power of God's reign, begun by the person of Jesus and his ministry, which is at work in them. There is no doubt about the active participation of women in Jesus' movement. They did not go along simply in their traditional role of suppliers of domestic needs, as the account in Luke appears to suggest (Luke 8:1–3). Just because Luke speaks about women does not mean he is speaking for them. In fact, Luke's own community kept up the traditional sexual division of labor.[20] Luke presents as a *public sinner* (Luke 7:37) a woman who was not a rich prostitute or a prostitute of any kind. Moreover, he appears to take a great interest in rich women.[21]

For Bingemer, Jesus' relation with women must be placed in the framework of the liberating project of the reign of God. And here it is important to describe Jesus' relation with women's bodies, given that it is precisely women's biological condition that causes their exclusion. According to patriarchal socio-religious laws, women are permanently in a state of impurity and do not belong to the *holy people* because they are not circumcised.[22] Ana María Tepedino points out that an inherent part of Jesus' project is the humanization of the person; therefore women's bodies are restored as the primary place for divine activity. This cancels the inhuman logic leading to women's oppression. Jesus restores the dignity of women's bodies and proposes equal relations with women and all the poor and oppressed, thereby showing what it means to bring abundant life (John 10:10).[23]

At this point we may look at certain situations given in the gospel showing the relation between Jesus and women.[24]

- Peter's mother-in-law is healed by Jesus (Mark 1:29–31). He comes up to her, takes her hands, and raises her up, restoring her to health and life. She recovers her full human powers and "served them." We should note that this serving by the women is analogous to Jesus' serving. He came "to serve, and to give his life as a ransom for many" (Mark 10:45).
- The woman who is bleeding and therefore impure (Mk 5:25–34) not only suffered economic want but also exclusion from the community. She touches Jesus and is cured, restored. She is also called to live fully and share in the community.
- The dead girl, Jairus's daughter (Mark 5:21–24; 35–43), feels the transforming power of God's reign in Jesus and herself. Death changes to life, and the child walks on her own feet. According to the purity codex (Num 19:11–13), Jesus would become impure by touching the dead girl. But through his action Jesus promotes the logic of fullness of life, which is the driving force of God's reign.
- The Syro-Phoenician woman and the wholeness of life restored to her daughter (Mark 7:24–30) demonstrate a supremely important attitude to women. Their condition as women, even foreigners, poor and impure, is no reason to justify their exclusion from the community initiated by Jesus. The Syro-Phoenician claims her right and her daughter's with firm determination, replying to Jesus' negative by making him see that the abundance of the reign of God was not just for male Jews. Jesus recognizes this argument and cures this foreign woman's daughter. The woman's behavior shows two important things: she represents a special moment in Jesus' self-understanding in relation to the humanizing project of the reign of God; that is, it must be open to all and

not just to the house of Israel. Moreover, it is she as a woman who has opened the way to integrity, freedom, and fullness for her daughter, for women, and for all races. "The Syrophoenician woman whose adroit argument opened up a future of freedom and wholeness for her daughter has also become the historically-still-visible advocate of such a future for gentiles. She has become the apostolic 'foremother' of all gentile Christians."[25]

- In an argument about marriage (Mark 10:2–12) Jesus defends women's humanity and integrity and criticizes the patriarchal structure of marriage. Jesus points out that a man must leave his patriarchal household for the man and woman to be joined as an equal couple united by love. The coupling by God "from the beginning of creation" (v. 6) of two equal persons is a relationship that no human being can break.

- The poor widow woman, who, Jesus told his disciples, put into the treasury everything she possessed, everything she had to live on (Mark 12:41–44), represents the poverty among Jesus' people. On the other hand, there are the rich who put in only from what they do not need. In Jesus' time widowhood was considered to be a state of absolute privation. But for Jesus this woman is the typical example of what it means to be *poor* and therefore one to whom the beatitudes of God's reign are addressed.

- The anonymous woman who anoints Jesus on the head with a very expensive perfume (Mark 14:3–9), as the kings of Israel were anointed by the prophets, is the one who through her symbolic action explicitly recognizes Jesus as the awaited messiah. Of this woman Jesus says, "Wherever throughout all the world the gospel is proclaimed, what she has done will be told as well, in remembrance of her" (v. 9).

- The experience of human fullness and spiritual betrothal experienced by women sharing the discipleship of equals promoted by Jesus did not disappear even after the arrest and crucifixion of Jesus (Mark 15:40–41). In contrast to the fear and paralysis manifested by the male disciples, the women resisted strongly to the end. They shared in Jesus' ministry from Galilee to Jerusalem, they resisted persecution, at the cross and sepulcher. Therefore it is not surprising that they were the first to receive the good news of the resurrection (Mark 16:1–6). Women are called to extend the humanizing process they have experienced with Jesus beyond Jerusalem and Galilee. For them it is certain that God has raised Jesus and that God is on their side.

After this general consideration of how Latin American women perceive Jesus' relation to women, and in particular to women's bodies, I
shall now point out the most significant features of a Christology from
the perspective of women.[26]

FEATURES OF JESUS IN A CHRISTOLOGY FROM THE PERSPECTIVE OF WOMEN

The principal feature in a Christology from the perspective of women is
Jesus' compassion and solidarity with those who have least. This solidarity becomes action to restore what is lost (see Luke 7:11–15). This
restoration anticipates the fulfillment to which the whole of creation is
called. At the same time it condemns those who grasp power over the
lives of others. Hence the decisive feature of this Jesus is as the Christ
of life. Jesus' whole life speaks of a God who is not indifferent to the
unjust misfortunes of the poor and oppressed. He is not a magic deity
trapped in ritual without any relationship to real life. Jesus proclaims
the good news of a God who embraces in love and mercy those who
according to the dominant religious system are out of favor with the divinity. In the new community men and women who suffer injustice can
experience that God is on their side and defends their cause. Jesus
shows a God who has inaugurated a new order, in which grace and
freedom offer the beginnings of a new life (Luke 7:36–50, 4:18–19). He
gives women abundant self-esteem so that they can choose a different
life for themselves and become part of the current of life-giving power
of the Spirit. Thus they discover Christ to be the Christ of grace.

Jesus challenges institutionalized religion, which claims to honor
God without this involving any commitment to justice. Jesus attacks
the false gods whose legal prescriptions damage people's lives. He sets
the God of life within reach of those who hope to be freed from these
imposed burdens (Luke 13:10–17). Many women laden with burdens
that even the religious leaders cannot bear experience the true God's
compassion and liberation. Jesus enables them to assume their proper
human condition and become persons with full rights. Jesus' activity,
person, and ministry free them and all the oppressed from the destructive power of sin and evil that enslaves them. In this way they discover
Jesus to be the liberating Christ.

All these features presuppose a clear option for life to the full for
those who suffer poverty and dehumanization, so that no one remains
outside the blessedness promised by God. This is indeed choosing the
better part, which will not be taken away (Luke 10:38–42). Following

Jesus means commitment, and discipleship also involves sorrow, struggle, hard work, sacrifice, and renunciation. But with it all goes the conviction that this cause is the cause of God. The vision that goes with this commitment is of a total renewal of the present order. It is an option to make God's reign present through daily struggle to restore women and men to lives that are fully human. In this commitment Jesus is discovered to be the Christ of God's reign.

Finally, Christology done by women in Latin America stresses Jesus' resurrection as the starting point for the experience of faith, just as it was for the early Christians. Women are the first witnesses of the resurrection and the first to meet the risen Christ (Mark 16:6–9; Luke 24:5–8; John 20:11–17), the first who are sent to proclaim the good news (Mark 16:10–11; Luke 24:9–10; John 20:17–18), and the first to proclaim the new life God is offering humanity. In spite of the androcentric character of the biblical accounts, the paschal witness shows the presence of women at Pentecost (Acts 1:14; 2:1, 17–18). They also played a crucial part at the birth of the church. Women belong to the sphere of the New Creation anticipated by Jesus. "From Jesus' resurrection," writes Bingemer,

> the Spirit is poured out on all flesh, creating a new humanity, which is the body of Christ. And this body of Christ, the collective new creation, which the Spirit continues to form and give birth to "in labor" (Rom 8:22–23) continues to make God's original creation present in the world—male and female (Gen 1:27). This is Christ the firstborn of every creature.[27]

So women's Christology stresses that both men and women constitute the new humanity and the body of Christ. Consequently, the writer continues, "in this christology women are not only spokeswomen for the risen Christ but also identified with the same Christ. They too speak, live and act *in persona Christi*. They too are *alter Christus*."[28] Jesus' resurrection has finally cancelled any form of inequality between persons, so that it cannot be said that only one part of humanity is destined to represent Christ in the world.[29] Otherwise the resurrection, and with it the whole foundation of the Christian faith, loses its power.

God's plan for fullness of life for humanity and especially those who lack it—as anticipated in the life, death, and resurrection of Jesus— must involve women as well as men. It is not possible to conceive of God's fullness when the great majority of women continue to occupy a subordinate position in the church and society. Accepting Jesus' liberation and proclaiming God's plan require us to commit ourselves to wiping out every form of suffering, sin, and death afflicting these women. Taking on their cause and that of the great oppressed masses anticipates the glory of the resurrection in constant hope of the day of total fulfillment. Thus, for Latin American women Christology becomes working to establish their own identity and develop spiritually as women and as members of the people struggling for life and liberation in the following of Jesus.

Notes

1. Elisabeth Moltmann-Wendell, *A Land Flowing with Milk and Honey: Perspectives on Feminist Theology* (Crossroad, New York, 1986), 82; Schüssler Fiorenza, *In Memory of Her*, 316–23.

2. Tepedino, "Feminist Theology as the Fruit of Passion and Compassion," 170. See also Schüssler Fiorenza, *In Memory of Her*, 323–33.

3. Nelly Ritchie, "Women and Christology," in *Through Her Eyes*, 82.

4. Ibid., 84.

5. The most relevant christological works in Latin America are: Jon Sobrino, *Cristology at the Crossroads* (Maryknoll, NY: Orbis, 1976); Leonardo Boff, *Jesus Christ Liberator* (Maryknoll, NY: Orbis, 1978); Juan Luis Segundo, *Jesus of Nazareth: Yesterday and Today*, 5 vols. (Maryknoll, NY: Orbis, 1985–1988); Hugo Echegaray, *The Practice of Jesus* (Maryknoll, NY: Orbis, 1984).

6. Echegaray, *The Practice of Jesus*, 82.

7. Thus the Final Statement of the Encuentro Comunidad de Mujeres y Hombres en la Iglesia declares, "We see in Jesus' historical activity the guidelines by which we should read the whole Bible" (Tamez et al., *Comunidad de mujeres y hombres en la iglesia*, 24). This is because Jesus' practice does not exclude women. For my methodological observations I have followed Julio Lois, *Jesucristo Liberador* (AA.VV., Pontifical University of Salamanca, 1988), 41–43.

8. Ritchie, "Women and Christology," 91.

9. For the reign of God as eschatological gift and human task, see Echegaray, *The Practice of Jesus*, 79–81.

10. María Clara Bingemer, "Mujer y Cristología: Jesucristo y la salvación de la mujer" in Aquino, *Aportes para una teología desde la mujer* (Madrid: Biblia y Fe, 1988), 80–93. From Rosemary Radford Ruether's works, I list the following: *To Change the World: Christology and Cultural Criticism* (New York: Crossroad, 1983); *Sexism and God Talk* (Boston: Beacon Press, 1983). Elisabeth Moltmann-Wendell also acknowledges a debt to Rosemary Radford Ruether in her research on the subject. Cf. Moltmann-Wendell, *A Land Flowing with Milk and Honey: Perspectives on Feminist Theology*, 117.

11. Bingemer, "Mujer y Cristología: Jesuscristo y la salvación de la mujer," 82–85.

12. Ibid., 84.

13. Ibid., 85.

14. Cora Ferro et al., *Mujer latinoamericana: Iglesia y teología* (MPD, Mexico, 1981), 216.

15. For a detailed investigation of the socio-religious movements in Jesus' time, see Echegaray, *The Practice of Jesus*, 39–67. On research into whether women participated in these movements or not, see Schüssler Fiorenza, *In Memory of Her*, 110–18.

16. Schüssler Fiorenza, *In Memory of Her*, 113 and 110–18; Echegaray, *The Practice of Jesus*, 79–88.

17. Tamez et al., *Comunidad de mujeres y hombres en la iglesia*, 24.

18. Bingemer, "Mujer y Cristología," 86–87.

19. Ibid., 87.

20. Moltmann-Wendell, *A Land Flowing with Milk and Honey*, 129.

21. Schüssler Fiorenza, *In Memory of Her*, 129, 140.

22. Bingemer, "Mujer y Cristología," 86–87.

23. Tepedino, "Jesús e a recuperação do ser human mulher," 274.

24. The commentaries on the biblical texts are found in Tepedino, "Jesús e a recuperação do ser humano mulher," 273–82.

25. Schüssler Fiorenza, *In Memory of Her*, 138; also quoted by Tepedino in "Jesús e a recuperação do ser humano mulher."

26. The features I point out from here onward are those mentioned by Nelly Ritchie, "Women and Christology," in Tamez, *Through Her Eyes*, 81–95.

27. Bingemer, "Mujer y Cristología," 90.

28. Ibid.

29. I have pointed out this aspect elsewhere. Cf. Aquino, "Praxis ministerial hoy: La respuesta del Tercer Mundo," *Revista de Teología Blblica* 46 (1990): 116–39.

16

BLACK WOMEN'S SURROGACY EXPERIENCE AND THE CHRISTIAN NOTION OF REDEMPTION

Delores S. Williams (USA)

Often, African-American women in church and society have character-ized their oppression as unique. Some black female scholars define this uniqueness on the basis of the interfacing of racial, class, and gender op-pression in the experience of black women. However, this interfacing of oppressions is not unique to black women's experience. Jewish, His-panic, Asian, and other women of color in America can also experience this reality. My exploration of black women's sources has revealed a heretofore undetected structure of domination that has been operative in African-American women's lives since slavery. This structure of dom-ination is surrogacy, and it gives black women's oppression its unique character—and raises challenging questions about the way redemption is imaged in a Christian context.

Two Faces of Surrogacy

On the basis of African-American women's sources it is possible to identify two kinds of surrogacy that have given rise to the unique char-acter of black women's oppression. They are *coerced surrogacy* and *vol-untary surrogacy*. Coerced surrogacy, belonging to the pre–Civil War period, was a forced condition in which people and systems more pow-erful than black women and black people forced black women to func-tion in roles that ordinarily would have been filled by someone else. For example, black female slaves were forced to substitute for the slave owner's wife in nurturing roles involving white children. Black women were forced to take the place of men in work roles that, according to the larger society's understanding of male and female roles, belonged to men. Frederick Law Olmstead, a northern architect writing in the nineteenth century, said he "stood for a long time watching slave women repair a road on a South Carolina Plantation" (quoted in White, 41). During the antebellum period this coerced surrogacy was legally supported in the ownership rights by which slave masters controlled their property, for example, black women. Slave women could not exercise the choice of refusing the surrogacy role.

After emancipation the coercion associated with antebellum surrogacy was replaced by social pressures that influenced black women to continue to fill some surrogacy roles. But surrogacy in the antebellum period differed from surrogacy in the postbellum period. The difference was that black women, after emancipation, could exercise the choice of refusing the surrogate role. Because of this element of choice, postbellum surrogacy can be referred to as voluntary surrogacy, even though social pressures influenced the choices black women made as they adjusted to life in a "free" world.

A closer look at these two modes of surrogacy in the two different periods (antebellum and postbellum) provides an in-depth view of the differences between the two modes.

COERCED SURROGACY AND ANTEBELLUM REALITIES

In the period before the Civil War, coerced surrogacy roles involving black women were in the areas of nurturance, field labor, and sexuality.

The mammy role was the direct result of the demands slavocracy made upon black women's nurturing capacities. Standing in the place of the slave owner's wife, mammy nurtured the entire white family. A long and respected tradition among many southern whites, mammy was an empowered (but not autonomous) house slave who was given considerable authority by her owners. According to the existing scattered reports of mammies and how the tradition operated, we know many southerners thought "mammy could do anything, and do it better than anyone else. Because of her expertise in all domestic matters, she was the premier house servant and all others were her subordinates" (White, 47). According to White, Eliza Riply, a southern white woman who received nurture from a mammy, remembers her as

a "supernumerary" who, after the children grew up...managed the whole big and mixed household. In her [Eliza Riply's] father's house, everyone was made to understand that...all applications were to go through Mammy Charlotte. Nobody thought to go to the judge or his wife for anything. (White, 47)

The testimony of ex-slaves themselves also attests to the value and power of mammies in the slaveholders' household. Drucella Martin remembers "that her mother was in full charge of the house and all marse children" (White, 47). Katherine Epps of Alabama said that her mother "worked in the Big House, 'aspinnin and 'anussin de white chillun" (White, 47). Epps also claimed that the slave owner's wife was so fond of her mother "that when she learned ... the overseer had whipped the woman whom everyone called 'Mammy,' she dismissed him and gave him until sundown to remove himself and his family from the plantation" (White, 47).

Mammy was not always so well treated, however. Frederick Douglass tells of his grandmother, who was mammy to a white family. When she became too old and frail to work, "they took her to the woods, built her a little hut with a mud chimney, and left her there to support and care for herself." As Douglass put it, "they turned her out to die" (White, 56). And there is the awful fate of one mammy told by ex-slave Jacob Stroyer. This mammy was named Aunt Betty. "She nursed her master through infancy, lived to see him become a drunk, and then became his victim when, during one of his drunken rampages, he took his shotgun and killed her" (White, 55). Nevertheless, the mammy role was probably the most powerful and authoritative one slave women could fill. Though slave women in their coerced roles as mammies were often abused, they were also empowered.[1]

This was not the case for slave women laboring beyond the "big house," that is, the slave owner's dwelling. In the area of field labor, black women were forced into work usually associated with male roles.[2] Feminist scholar bell hooks claims that on large plantations "Women plowed, planted ... harvested crops. On some plantations black women worked longer hours in the fields than black men" (hooks, 23). What this amounted to, in terms of coerced surrogacy, was black female energy substituting for male energy. This resulted in what hooks refers to as the masculinization of the black female (hooks, 22).

In their autobiographies some ex-slave women describe the masculine work roles black women were forced to fill. Bethany Veney tells of helping her cruel slave owner haul logs, drive out hogs, and set posts into the ground for fences (Veney, 12–13). Louisa Picquet told of slave women who drove ox wagons, tended mills, and plowed just like men (Picquet, 17). Another ex-slave, Mary Prince, tells of a slave woman who drove cattle, tended sheep, and did general farming work in the fields (Prince, 6).

Unlike the mammy role of the female house slave, the masculinized roles of the female field slave did not empower black women in the slave structure to the extent that mammies were empowered. In the fields the greatest amount of power a slave could hold was in the position of slave driver or overseer. Usually, only males could ascend to these roles. Thus the driver was a male slave. Though a few black males served as overseers, this role was usually filled by white men of lower social class than the slave owner. Females who filled the masculinized roles in the fields were less respected than mammies and drivers. Field women were not often given recognition for their service, seldom realized the endearment of the white folks as did some of the mammies, got worse food and clothing, and often received more brutal punishment. These masculinized female field slaves were thought to be of a lower class than the female house slaves, who usually did "women's work" consisting of cleaning, spinning, cooking, sewing, and tending to the children.

More than in the areas of nurturance and field labor, coerced surrogacy in the area of sexuality was threatening to slave women's self-esteem and sense of self-worth. This is the area in which slave women were forced to stand in the place of white women to provide sexual pleasure for white male slave owners. The Victorian ideal of true womanhood (for Anglo-American women) supported a consciousness which, in the area of sexual relations, imagined sex between free white men and their wives to be for the purpose of procreation rather than for pleasure. Many white males turned to slave women for sexual pleasure and forced these women to fulfill needs which, according to racist ideology concerning male-female relations, should have been fulfilled by white women.

In her narrative *Incidents in the Life of a Slave Girl*, Linda Brent presents a vivid description of her slave owner Dr. Flint, who tried to force her into one of these illicit female slave/slave master sexual liaisons. Brent escaped his advances by fleeing from his house and hiding for seven years in a crawl space in the roof of her grandmother's home (Brent, 6–36). The octoroon slave woman Louisa Picquet was not as fortunate as Linda Brent. Louisa was purchased by a Mr. Williams when she was about fourteen years old. He forced her into sexual relations with him. From these relations four children issued (Picquet, 18–21). Another slave woman, Cynthia, was purchased by a slave trader who told her she would either accompany him home and become his "housekeeper" or he would sell her as a field worker to one of the worst plantations on the Mississippi River. Cynthia thus became the slave trader's mistress and housekeeper (Brown, 194–95).

There was in the antebellum South a kind of institutionalizing of female slave/slave master sexual liaisons that was maintained through the "fancy trade." This was a special kind of slave trading involving the sale of what were thought to be beautiful black women for the exclusive purpose of becoming mistresses of wealthy slave owners. Though New Orleans seems to have been the center of this trade, it also flourished in Charleston and Columbia, South Carolina; St. Louis, Missouri; and Lexington and Richmond, Virginia (White, 37–38). The famous octoroon balls that occurred in New Orleans allowed rich white men to meet and purchase these black women, who became their mistresses and often bore children by these slave owners.

Beyond this special kind of arrangement, slave owners also frequented the slave quarters and established sexual relations with any female slave they chose. The slave woman in either kind of arrangement had no power to refuse this coerced surrogacy in which she stood in the place of the white woman. Sometimes these slave women hoped for (and were promised) their freedom through sexual liaisons with the slave master. But more often than not their expectations were futile, and they were "sold off to plantations where...[they] shared the misery of all slaves" (White, 15).

All three forms of coerced surrogacy illustrate a unique kind of oppression only black women experienced in the slavocracy. Only black women were mammies. Only black women were permanently assigned to field labor. Only black women permanently lost control of their bodies to the lust of white men. During slavery, black women were bound to a system that had respect for neither their bodies, their dignity, their labor, nor their motherhood except as it was put to the service of securing the well-being of ruling class white families. In North America fierce and violent struggle had to afflict the entire nation before southern slave women could experience a measure of relief from coerced surrogacy roles.

VOLUNTARY SURROGACY AND POSTBELLUM REALITIES

When the American Civil War ended and the master-slave relation was officially terminated in the South, black people tried to determine for whom or what black women *would not* stand in place. They were especially anxious to relieve black women from those coerced surrogacy roles related to fieldwork and to black women's sexuality involving black female/white male sexual liaisons. Ex-slave women themselves are reported to have said "they never mean to do any outdoor work, that white men support their wives and the [black women] mean that their husbands shall support them" (Giddings, 62). Black men were just as anxious for black women to quit the fields. According to historians Carter G. Woodson and Lorenzo Greene, "The Negro male when he worked for wages...tended to imitate the whites by keeping his wife and daughters at home" (Woodson and Greene, 31).

Of even greater concern to black males and females were their efforts to terminate the forced sexual relations between black women and white men that existed during slavery. Inasmuch as marriage between African-American women and men became legal after freedom and droves of black women and men came to official locations to be married (Giddings, 57–58), sexual liaisons between white men and black women could be curtailed, although white men (without regard for black marriage) still took advantage of some black women. bell hooks points out that after black reconstruction (1867–77) "black women were often...[pressured] into sexual liaisons with white employers who would threaten to fire them unless they capitulated to sexual demands" (hooks, 37).

Nevertheless, there was not nearly as much sexual activity between black women and white men after slavery because black women themselves could refuse to substitute for white women in providing sexual pleasure for white males. Nancy White, a contemporary black female domestic worker, testified about refusing this role of playmate to white male employers:

> I've had to ask some [white male employers] to keep their hands off me and I've had to just give up some jobs if they got too hot behind me...I have lost some money that way, but that's all right. When you lose control of your body, you have just about lost all you have in this world. (Gwaltney, 146–47)

Nancy White makes it clear that some white female employers approved of black women standing in their places to provide sexual favors for their husbands. White says:

> One day that woman [her white female employer] told me that she wouldn't be mad if I let her husband treat me the same way he treated her. I told her I would be mad...if he tried to treat me like I was as married to him as she was. (Gwaltney, 151)

Nancy White goes on to describe her method of declining this surrogate role her female and male employers wanted to assign her. Says White: "I had to threaten that devil [the white male employer] with a pot of hot grease to get him to keep his hands to hisself" (Gwaltney, 150).

While black women and men did realize a small measure of success in determining the surrogate roles black women would not fill after emancipation, certain social and economic realities limited black women's power to choose full exemption from all surrogacy roles. Poverty and the nature of the work available, especially to southern black families, demanded black women's participation in some of the most strenuous areas of the work force. There was also the attempt among newly freed black families to adopt some of the values of the people they took to be "quality white folk" during slavery.[3] This meant that efforts were made to influence black women to choose to continue in two of the surrogate roles they had filled during slavery: substituting female power and energy for male power and energy, and acting in mammy capacities.

After emancipation black women chose to substitute their energy and power for male energy and power in the area of farm labor. Greene and Woodson tell of urban Negro male laborers in 1901 who saved money and invested in farms. "It was not uncommon...to see Negro mechanics owning well-kept farms, which were cared for chiefly by wives and families" (Woodson and Greene, 61). The United States Census of 1910 reported that 967,837 black women were farm laborers and 79,309 were farmers (Foner and Lewis, 55). Also in 1910 Addie W. Hunton reported that

> More than half of the 2,000,000 wage earning women of the [black] race are engaged in agriculture from its roughest and rudest form to its highest and most attractive form...The 15,792,579 acres owned and cultivated by Negroes, which with buildings and equipment and rented farm lands reach a valuation approaching a billion dollars, represent not only the hardihood and perseverance of the Negro man but the power for physical and mental endurance of the woman working by his side. Many of the farms owned by colored men are managed entirely by the women of the family while these men give themselves to other employment. (Foner and Lewis, 55)

It was, however, the surrogate role of mammy that some black males and white people consciously tried to perpetuate into the future beyond slavery and reconstruction. In Athens, Georgia, in the early twentieth century, Samuel Harris, the black principal of Athens Colored High School, dreamed up the idea of starting the Black Mammy Memorial Institute in that city. With the help of prominent white citizens this institute was chartered on September 19, 1910, and was authorized to operate for twenty years. According to a brochure published by the Black Mammy Memorial Association, the institute was to be

> a memorial where men and women learn...how to work and to love their work; where the mantle of the "Old Black Mammy" may fall on those who go forth to serve; where the story of these women will be told to the generations that come and go; where better mothers for homes will be trained; a building from which those who go forth in life may speak louder in their works than their words...The MONUMENTAL INDUSTRIAL INSTITUTE to the OLD BLACK MAMMY of the South will be devoted to the industrial and moral training of young Negro men and women. The work that is to receive special emphasis is the training of young women in Domestic Art. (Patten, 153)

Obviously the prominent white citizens wanted to perpetuate the mammy roles so that the comfort of the white family could be assured by a type of black female servant who (after slavery) was properly trained in the skills of nurturing, supporting, and caring about the well-being of white children. Not so obvious, but probable, is the suggestion that to the black man Mr. Harris, black women trained in the mammy skills could learn to organize and manage the black households in the same way that the slave owners' households were organized and managed. This meant that the black family had to become more patriarchal in its structure and values in order to resemble the slave owners' households.

Mammy had a variety of skills that could accommodate this process. She was skillful at exerting authority in the household while being careful not to offend or usurp the power of the patriarchal authority figures: the slave master and his wife. Mammy was skilled in about every form of what was thought of as women's work: sewing, spinning, cooking, cleaning, tending to children, and so on. Hence she could train female children in this work. According to Deborah Gray White, mammy was often the advisor of the slave master in business matters. With regard to the quality of relationships in the master's family, she knew how to be a diplomat and a peacemaker who often healed relations that had gone awry. The mammy skills could promote and support black males as they became the patriarchal heads of the black household after slavery. And the black family could therefore resemble the patriarchal model of family sanctioned in mainline American society.

One could also suggest that the institution of Mothers of the Church, which developed in some black churches after emancipation, has kinship with the mammy tradition. Like the antebellum mammy, a mother of the church exerts considerable authority in the church family. But more often than not she uses her power in such a way that it does not challenge the power and authority of the patriarchal head of the church, usually a male preacher. She is sometimes called upon to be a healer of relationships within the congregation. She is well versed in and knows how to pass along the church's highest values for living the Christian life. Her power and influence often extend beyond the church into her community because she has been empowered by one of the central authority agents of the community (the black church) to provide care and nurture for the children of God.

Black women's history of filling surrogacy roles has fed into negative stereotypes of black women that exist until this day. From the mammy tradition has emerged the image of black women as perpetual mother figures, religious, fat, asexual, loving children better than themselves, self-sacrificing, giving up self-concern for group advancement. The antebellum tradition of masculinizing black women through their work has given rise to the image of black women as unfeminine, physically strong, and having the capacity to bear considerably more pain than white women. These kinds of ideas helped create the notion of black women as superwomen. The sexual liaisons between white men and slave women created the image of the black woman as Jezebel, as one "governed almost entirely by her libido...the counterimage of the mid-nineteenth-century ideal of the Victorian lady" (White, 29). Hence the surrogacy roles black women have filled during slavery and beyond are exploitative. They rob African-American women of self-consciousness, self-care, and self-esteem, and put them in the service of other people's desires, tasks, and goals. This has serious implications for Christian theologians attempting to use black women's history as a source for constructive theology.

From Black Woman Surrogate to Surrogate-Jesus

One of the results of focusing upon African-American women's historic experience with surrogacy is that it raises significant questions about the way many Christians, including black women, have been taught to image redemption. More often than not the theology in mainline Christian churches, including black ones, teaches believers that sinful humankind has been redeemed because Jesus died on the cross in the place of humans, thereby taking human sin upon himself. In this sense Jesus represents the ultimate surrogate figure standing in the place of someone else: sinful humankind. Surrogacy, attached to this divine personage, thus takes on an aura of the sacred. It is therefore altogether fitting and proper for black women to ask whether the image of a surrogate-God has salvific power for black women, or whether this image of redemption supports and reinforces the exploitation that has accompanied their experience with surrogacy. If black women accept this image of redemption, can they not also passively accept the exploitation surrogacy brings?

This essay recognizes that reflection upon these questions causes many complex theological issues to surface. For instance, there is the issue of the part God the Father played in determining the redemptive, surrogate role filled by Jesus, the Son. For black women there is also the question of whether Jesus on the cross represents coerced surrogacy (willed by the father) or voluntary surrogacy (chosen by the son) or both. At any rate, a major theological problem here is the place of the cross in any theology significantly informed by African-American women's experience with surrogacy. Even if one buys into Moltmann's notion of the cross as the meeting place of the will of God to give up the Son (coerced surrogacy?) and the will of the Son to give up himself (voluntary surrogacy?) so that "the spirit of abandonment and self-giving love" proceed from the cross "to raise up abandoned men" (Moltmann, 31–35), African-American women are still left with this question: Can there be salvific power in Christian images of oppression (for example, Jesus on the cross) meant to teach something about redemption?

Theologians since the time of Origen have been trying to make the Christian principle of atonement believable by shaping theories about it in the language and thought that people of a particular time understood and were grounded in. Thus most theories of atonement, classical and contemporary, are time-bound (as well as ideologically bound with patriarchy) and do not respond meaningfully to the questions of people living beyond the particular time period. For instance, Origen (183–253 CE), capitalizing on people's belief in devils and spirits, provided what Alan Richardson speaks of as a ransom theory, claiming that the death of Jesus on the cross was a ransom paid by God to the devil for the sins of humankind (Richardson, 96–113). This view of atonement declined when another age dawned. Thus Anselm emerged in the eleventh century and spoke of atonement using the chivalric language and sociopolitical thought of his time. He shaped a theory describing sin as the human way of dishonoring God. People owed honor to God just as peasants and squires owed honor and loyalty to the feudal overlord. However, men had no power to render satisfaction to God for their massive disloyalty to God through sin. According to the codes of chivalry in Anselm's time, one atoned for a crime either by receiving punishment or by providing satisfaction to the injured person. Since God did not want to punish humans forever (which the sin deserved) and since humans had no means to render satisfaction to God's injured honor, the deity, Godself, made restitution for humanity. God satisfied God's own violated honor by sending the Son to earth in human form ultimately to die on the cross.

There were also the theories of atonement associated with Abelard (1079–1142). Since the church in Abelard's time put great stress upon the penitential life of believers, it was reasonable for Abelard to see Calvary as "the school of penitence of the human race, for there men of all ages and races have learned the depth and power of the love of God" (Richardson, 21). Often referred to as the moral theories of atonement (Richardson, 21), these emphasized God's love in the work of atonement and claimed that, when humans look upon the death of Jesus, they see the love of God manifested. The cross brings repentance to humankind and shows simultaneously God the Father's love and the suffering inflicted upon that love by human sin. The moral theories of atonement taught that the cross was "the most powerful moral influence in history, bringing to men that repentance which renders them able to be forgiven" (Richardson, 21).

As the Renaissance approached and the medieval worldview collapsed, the Anselmian and Abelardian ways of understanding the atonement began to fade. The Renaissance was a time of great interest in the revival of ancient law. So it was reasonable to expect the reformers to work out their theories of atonement in legal terms grounded in the new political and legal thought of the sixteenth century. Thus Calvin and others spoke of the justice of God the judge, of the divine law of punishment that could not be ignored, and of the infinite character of human sin that deserved infinite harsh punishment. But, according to the Reformers, God is both just and merciful. Therefore, in infinite mercy God provided a substitute who would bear the punishment for human sin. Jesus Christ came to offer himself as a substitute for humans. He took their punishment upon himself. Thus the Reformers provided a substitution theory of atonement.

While these ransom, satisfaction, substitution, and moral theories of atonement may not be serviceable for providing an acceptable response to African-American women's questions about redemption and surrogacy, they do illustrate a serviceable practice for female theologians attempting today to respond to this question. That practice (as shown by the theologians above) was to use the language and sociopolitical thought of the time to render Christian principles understandable. This fits well the task of the black female theologian. For that task is to use the language and socio-political thought of black women's world to show them that their salvation does not depend upon any form of surrogacy made sacred by human understandings of God. This means using the language and thought of liberation to liberate redemption from the cross and to liberate the cross from the "sacred aura" put around it by existing patriarchal responses to the question of what Jesus' death represents. To find resources to accomplish this task, the black female theologian is led to the scriptures.

The Synoptic gospels (more than Paul's letters) provide resources for constructing a Christian understanding of redemption that speaks meaningfully to black women, given their historic experience with surrogacy. Jesus' own words in Luke 4 and his ministry of healing the human body, mind, and spirit (described in Matthew, Mark, and Luke) suggest that Jesus did not come to redeem humans by showing them God's love "manifested" in the death of God's innocent child on a cross erected by cruel, imperialistic, patriarchal power. Rather, the spirit of God in Jesus came to show humans *life*—to show redemption through a perfect *ministerial* vision of righting relationships. A female-male inclusive vision, Jesus' ministry of righting relationships involved raising the dead (for example, those appearing to be lost from life), casting out demons (for example, ridding the mind of destructive forces prohibiting the flourishing of positive, peaceful life), and proclaiming the word of life that demanded the transformation of tradition so that life could be lived more abundantly. Jesus was quick to remind his disciples that humans were not made for the Sabbath; rather, the Sabbath was made for humans. God's gift to humans, through Jesus, was to invite them to participate in this ministerial vision ("whosoever will, let them come") of righting relations. The response to this invitation by human principalities and powers was the horrible deed that the cross represents—the evil of humankind trying to kill the ministerial vision of life in relation that Jesus brought to humanity. The resurrection does not depend upon the cross for life, for the cross only represents historical evil trying to defeat good. The resurrection of Jesus and the flourishing of God's spirit in the world as the result of resurrection represents the life of the ministerial vision gaining victory over the evil attempt to kill it. Thus, to respond meaningfully to black women's historic experience of surrogacy-oppression, the theologian must show that redemption of humans can have nothing to do with any kind of surrogate role Jesus was reputed to have played in a bloody act that supposedly gained victory over sin and/or evil. Black women are intelligent people living in a technological world where nuclear bombs, defilement of the earth, racism, sexism, and economic injustices attest to the presence and power of evil in the world. Perhaps not many people today can believe that evil and sin were overcome by Jesus' death on the cross, that is, that Jesus took human sin upon himself and therefore saved humankind. Rather, it seems more intelligent to understand that redemption had to do with God, through Jesus, giving humankind new vision to see resources for positive, abundant relational life—a vision humankind did not have before. Hence, the kingdom of God theme in the ministerial vision of Jesus does not point to death; that is, it is not something one has to die to get to. Rather, the kingdom of God is a metaphor of hope God gives those attempting to right the relations between self and self, between self and others, between self and God as prescribed in the sermon on the mount and the golden rule.

Though space limitations here prohibit more extensive reconstruction of this Christian understanding of redemption (given black women's surrogacy experience), there are a few things that can be said about sin in this kind of reconstruction. The image of Jesus on the cross is the image of human sin in its most desecrated form. This execution destroyed the body but not before it mocked and defiled Jesus by publicly exposing his nakedness and private parts, by mocking the ministerial vision as they labeled him king of the Jews, by placing a crown of thorns upon his head mocking his dignity and the integrity of his divine mission. The cross thus becomes an image of defilement, a gross manifestation of collective human sin. Jesus, then, does not conquer sin through death on the cross. Rather, Jesus conquers the sin of temptation in the wilderness (Matt 4:1–11) by resistance—by resisting the temptation to value the material over the spiritual ("Man shall not live by bread alone"); by resisting death (not attempting suicide; "if you are the son of God, throw yourself down"); by resisting the greedy urge of monopolistic ownership ("He showed him all the kingdoms of the world and the glory of them; and he said to him, 'All these I will give you, if you will fall down and worship me'"). Jesus therefore conquered sin in life, not in death. In the wilderness he refused to allow evil forces to defile the balanced relation between the material and the spiritual, between life and death, between power and the exertion of it.

What this allows the black female theologian to show black women is that God did not intend the surrogacy roles they have been forced to perform. God did not intend the defilement of their bodies as white patriarchal power put them in the place of white women to provide sexual pleasure for white men during the slavocracy. This was rape. Rape is defilement, and defilement means wanton desecration. Worse, deeper and more wounding than alienation, the sin of defilement is the one of which today's technological world is most guilty. Nature—the land, the seas, the animals in the sea—are every day defiled by humans. Cultures such as Native American and African have been defiled by the onslaught of Western, patriarchal imperialism. The oceans are defiled by oil spills and human waste, destroying marine life. The rain forest is being defiled. The cross is a reminder of how humans have tried throughout history to destroy visions of righting relationships that involve transformation of tradition and transformation of social relations and arrangements sanctioned by the status quo. The resurrection of Jesus and the kingdom of God theme in Jesus' ministerial vision provide black women with the knowledge that God has, through Jesus, shown humankind how to live peacefully, productively, and abundantly in relationship. Humankind is therefore redeemed through Jesus' life and not through Jesus' death. There is nothing of God in the blood of the cross. God does not intend black women's surrogacy experience. Neither can Christian faith affirm such an idea. Jesus did not come to be a surrogate. Jesus came for life, to show humans a perfect vision of ministerial relation that humans had forgotten long ago. However, as Christians, black women cannot forget the cross. But neither can they glorify it. To do so is to make their exploitation sacred. To do so is to glorify sin.

Notes

1. This is not to suggest that such empowerment led to autonomy for slave women. Quite to the contrary. Slave women, like slave men, were always subject to the control of the slave owners. And as historian Deborah Gray White's description of mammy reveals, the empowerment of mammy was also directly related to the attempt of pro-slavery advocates to provide an image of black

women which proved that the institution of slavery was vital for molding some black women in accord with the maternal ideals of the Victorian understanding of true womanhood.

2. Some scholars estimate that about eighty percent of slave women worked in the fields. Twenty percent worked as house servants. See Fogel and Engerman 1974, 38–58.

3. Historian Joel Williamson discusses this in relation to a process of acculturation he says existed among slaves and continued into and beyond the reconstruction. Williamson refers to the slaves as trying to "become more white." See Williamson's article.

Works Cited

Brent, Linda. *Incidents in the Life of a Slave Girl.* Boston: By the Author, Stereotype Foundry, 1861.

Brown, William Wells. "Narrative of William Wells Brown." *Puttin' on Ole Massa.* Ed. Gilbert Osofsky. New York: Harper and Row, 1969.

Fogel, Robert, and Stanley Engerman. *Time on the Cross.* Boston: Little, Brown and Company, 1974.

Foner, Philip S., and Ronald L. Lewis, eds. *The Black Worker,* vol. 5. Philadelphia: Temple University Press, 1980.

Giddings, Paula. *When and Where I Enter.* New York: William Morrow and Company, 1984.

Gwaltney, John Langston. *Drylongso.* New York: Random House, 1980.

Hooks, Bell. *Ain't I a Woman?* Boston: South End Press, 1981.

Moltmann, Jürgen. "The 'Crucified God': God and the Trinity Today." *New Questions on God.* Ed. Johannes B. Metz. New York: Herder and Herder, 1972.

Patten, June O. "Document: Moonlight and Magnolias in Southern Education: The Black Mammy Memorial Institute." *The Journal of Negro History* 65, no. 2 (Spring 1980): 153.

Picquet, Louisa. *Louisa Picquet, the Octoroon: A Tale of Southern Slave Life.* Ed. Reverend H. Mattison. New York: 1861. Reprinted in *Collected Black Women's Narratives,* the Schomburg Library of Nineteenth-Century Black Women Writers. Series ed. Henry Louis Gates, Jr. New York: Oxford University Press, 1988.

Prince, Mary. *The History of Mary Prince, A West Indian Slave.* Ed. F. Westley and A. H. Davis. London: 1831. Reprinted in *Collected Black Women's Narratives,* the Schomburg Library of Nineteenth-Century Black Women Writers. Series ed. Henry Louis Gates, Jr. New York: Oxford University Press, 1988.

Richardson, Alan. *Creeds in the Making.* London: Student Christian Movement Press, 1951.

Veney, Bethany. *The Narrative of Bethany Veney a Slave Woman.* Ed. Henry Louis Gates, Jr. Boston: The Press of George H. Ellis, 1889. Reprinted in *Six*

Women's Narratives, the Schomburg Library of Nineteenth-Century Black Women Writers. Series ed. Henry Louis Gates, Jr. New York: Oxford University Press, 1988.

White, Deborah Gray. *Ar'n't I A Woman?* New York: W. W. North's Company, 1985.

Williamson, Joel. "Black Self-Assertion Before and After Emancipation." In *Key Issues in the Afro-American Experience,* ed. Nathan I. Huggins, Martin Kilson, and Daniel M. Fox. New York: Harcourt Brace Jovanovich, 1971.

Woodson, Carter G., and Lorenzo J. Greene. *The Negro Wage Earner.* Washington, DC.: The Association for the Study of Negro Life and History, Inc., 1930.

17

SUBJECTIFICATION AS A REQUIREMENT
FOR CHRISTOLOGICAL CONSTRUCTION

Jacquelyn Grant (USA)

CONTEXT AND COMMITMENT

As a collective "I," Black women have been saddled with labels and definitions. They have been called matriarchs; they've been blamed for the ills of the Black community; they've been considered sexually promiscuous; and to facilitate the needs of whites, they were reduced to maids, mammies, and other service workers. Zora Neale Hurston conveys through the words of one of her characters in *Their Eyes Were Watching God*[1] that Black women function as the mules of the world, that is, they carry the burdens of the world. They are among the poorest of the poor and among the most oppressed of the oppressed. This is my context.

Black women have moved beyond these definitions by defying time and space. This tradition has been known as the strong Black woman tradition. It is the one which we now call the womanist tradition.

My commitment is to the unearthing of the lost, forgotten, or ignored traditions of Black women, so that we might be able to develop more holistic theologies which are truly reflective of liberation of humanity. Within the development of the theological arms of both the Black liberation movement and the feminist liberation movement, the particular experiences of Black women have not been represented.

Hull, Scott, and Smith critique these two movements in the very title of their book, *All the Women Are White, All the Blacks Are Men, But Some of Us Are Brave.*[2] Who are these brave women? Mari Evans describes them as she names herself in this way:

I

Am a Black Woman

tall as a Cypress

Strong
beyond all definitions still
defying place
and time
and circumstances
Assailed
impervious
indestructible
Look
on me and be
renewed[3]

CONSTRUCTION

When Jesus asked the disciples the question, "Who do you say that I am?" (Mark 8:29), he began what was to become an endless debate and discussion on a central doctrine in Christian theology. The one who posed the question was Jesus of Nazareth. Historical and biblical records give us limited details about who Jesus of Nazareth was. We know of him from birth to twelve years of age and then from age thirty to thirty-three. We have records that bear out certain data.

Yet when Jesus asked this question, could he have been referring to something other than biographical details? Perhaps he was confronting the disciples with the question, "Who am I to *you*? What's the significance of my work for *you*?" "Who do *you* say that I am?" focuses the question on the ones giving the answers—the disciples.

Recognizing this possibility, then, we must at some point focus our attention on the disciples. This subjectification of the disciples relocates the central subject of this passage. No longer is it Jesus, but the one(s) who answer.

If so, it is important to discuss the context in which Jesus is encountered by people, for this context shapes the answers to Jesus' question. When John asks Jesus, "Are you the one or shall we look for another?" the subject is called upon to identify himself. Jesus in turning the question around to the disciples makes them the subjects. "Who do you say that I am?" This question is posed anew in each new generation and in each context. Just as the disciples were called to answer, to be subjects, so we must also be subjects.

Historically the power to be subjects has been carefully and conveniently kept out of the hands of nonwhites and to a lesser extent out of the hands of women. The continual objectification of Blacks and women in recent history has meant that essentially they have been defined by the (political and theological) status quo. It has been within this status quo that many theologians have presumed, in the interest of truth and universality, to answer the christological question in a once-and-for-all fashion, that is, for all times and for all peoples. Consequently, they taught Blacks that Jesus meant docility, meekness, and mildness in the face of the physical brutalities of racial oppression. Then when white people (subjects) answered Jesus' question for Black people (victimized objects): they said Jesus was the one being honored when Black people obeyed their earthly masters and accepted their prescribed roles as servants in the society.

At the same time these same self-proclaimed subjects taught women that Jesus' maleness meant that he was to carry out the patriarchal mandates of all times—that women are to subject themselves to male authority, for God chose to reveal *himself* in a male person—Jesus the *God man*.

In more recent years Blacks and women have forged movements designed to take control of their lives by becoming the primary definers, the subjects, in theological and other discussions. This is particularly significant in that both the Black experience and women's experience represent realities from the underside of history—that is, they are nonnormative experiences. They represent experiences in which one normally would not expect to find subjects in the christological debate. White male theologians representing the normative experience—the topside of history—have customarily assumed the subject role in this debate.

The experience of Black women is one of triple jeopardy; their lived reality is at least three times removed from the so-called normative culture, placing them on the underside of history. Though Black women are victimized by racism, sexism, and classism, I will focus primarily on racism and sexism, both of which have consequent implications for social class. In this section we will give glimpses of some perceptions of Jesus Christ from the underside.

The Subjectification of Black People

Since the beginning of their presence in the United States, Black people have been objects of control for the service of the needs and desires of white people. Institutional slavery rendered them less than human, and even when a measure of humanity was given them, they (Black men) were counted as only three fifths of a white man (a fraction of a man) and that was only for political (specifically for apportionment) purposes. In actuality they were still considered nonhuman.

History records some of the varied attempts of Blacks to affirm their human dignity, from David Walker's appeal in 1829 to James Forman's *Black Manifesto* in 1969. At various historical moments Blacks have raised the issue in its theological context. Each of these political and theological statements is part of the struggle of Blacks to become subjects—that is, masters of their own destiny. They recognized that this would not be easy. In bare political terms it meant that in order for Blacks to gain control of their own destiny, whites had to be disempowered. And as Frederick Douglass pointed out, no one gives up power without a struggle. This meant therefore that the insurrections and other rebellious acts of Harriet Tubman, Denmark Vesey, and many others were attempts to break the power base to the white establishment and in effect to become subjects.

The passing of the thirteenth, fourteenth, and fifteenth amendments to the Constitution were steps in the subjectification of Black people, but as history demonstrates, Blacks were still legally disenfranchised, economically impotent, socially dehumanized, and religiously insignificant. The battle to become subjects continued. In the 1920s and 1930s, Carter G. Woodson identified the problem as more than just political, economic, and social control of Blacks by whites. He described how whites maintained that control through effective oppressive miseducation of Blacks. This miseducation has manifested itself both in the political and the religious life, so that white people controlled Black minds through oppressive educational systems and religious symbols. Woodson argued for self-reliance and self-determination. Though the odds were against it, he believed it possible.[4]

The Civil Rights and Black Power movements of the 1950s, 1960s, and 1970s were direct actions designed to change the power balance in the United States. That period represented a consistent challenge for self-reliance and self-determination and for political, economic, and social freedom. In other words, to some degree Blacks were finally becoming subjects.

Who Do Black People Say Jesus Christ Is?

It is the thesis of Black theologians that Christology is constructed from the interplay of social context, scripture, and traditions.[5] The significance of social context is addressed in the first chapter of James Cone's book, *God of the Oppressed.* Cone crystallizes the issue in the following way: "The focus on social context means that we cannot separate our questions about Jesus from the concreteness of everyday life. We ask, 'Who is Jesus Christ for us today?' because we believe that the story of his life and death is the answer to the human story of oppression and suffering."[6]

The social context for Black Christology is the Black experience of oppression and the struggle against it. Christology is irrelevant if it does not take this into account, because historically Christology has been constructed in the context of white superiority, ideology, and domination. Christ has functioned to legitimate these social and political realities. Essentially, Christ has been white. For "white conservatives and liberals alike...Christ is a mild, easygoing white American who can afford to mouth the luxuries of 'love,' 'mercy,' 'long-suffering,' and other white irrelevances, because he has a multibillion dollar military force to protect him from the encroachment of the ghetto and the 'communist conspiracy.'"[7]

To counteract this historical and theological trend, what the late Bishop Joseph Johnson called "the tragedy of the white Christ,"[8] Black theologians have called not only for a new departure in theology but more specifically for a new christological interpretation. This white Christ must be eliminated from the Black experience and the concept of a Black Christ must emerge.

The claims for the blackness of Christ are argued by Black theologians in several different ways. Albert Cleage's position leaves no room for guessing his meaning. Postulating actual historical Blackness, Cleage argues that Jesus was a Black Jew.[9] From Cleage's perspective it is simply impossible to believe that Jesus could have been anything but Black, given the established fact of "the intermingling of races in Africa and the Mediterranean area."[10] James Cone...finds that Blackness clarifies the incarnation in its specificity.[11] Wilmore finds the meaning of "the Black Messiah" to be "the relevance of the Person and Work of Christ for existence under the condition of oppression."[12] Rejected, despised, and acquainted with grief—both biblically and on the contemporary scene—this is the christological symbol: God loves the outcast.[13]

The Subjectification of Women

If Blacks were objectified as slaves and chattels, women have been objectified as sexual commodities and relegated to domestic affairs, specifically the upkeep and maintenance of the family. As such, women's reality was defined by men and accommodated by both men and women for the purpose of securing patriarchal structures in both public and private areas. In nineteenth century American life, this culminated in the notion of the "true woman."[14] Barbara Welter says of this concept of true woman, "Women were inherently more religious, modest, passive and domestic."[15] Barbara Andolsen continues the thought, "Women were also nurturing, pure, sweetly persuasive, and self-sacrificing."[16] For women, biology was indeed destiny: women were constrained to the private sphere and were to be content with family affairs, specifically motherhood and wifely duties. Their place was in the home.

Women began to move toward self-definition in the context of the women's movement for liberation in the nineteenth century. They recognized that the patriarchal structures under which women lived functioned for the empowerment and independence of men and the impotence and dependence of women. Hence, women began to organize around issues such as suffrage, wages, personhood, and marriage. Though all of the issues were interrelated, suffrage captured the attention of the majority of women in the movement from 1848 to the 1920s when the nineteenth amendment, giving women the vote, was passed.

In the area of religion, though women were thought to be innately more religious, they were not permitted the authority to define religion. The church with remarkable success resisted the impact of the women's movement. The resistance took the form of teachings on the virtues of womanhood, lauding the feminine qualities of women as godly and God given. Nancy Cott described the indoctrination which women received regarding their role in the church and family. Women populated the church by a majority as early as the mid-seventeenth century. They were kept in line, however, by the constant teaching that they had special "female values." Being seduced by the minister's teachings that they were of "conscientious and prudent character, especially suited to religion," women became well indoctrinated in what was expected of them.[17]

In spite of their ecclesiastical and religious oppression, however, women from time to time did challenge the church about its role in perpetuating such oppression. The speeches of Sarah and Angelina Grimké, directed to Christian women and advocating the equality of the sexes, elicited angry reactions from the clergy. One church body responded to the work of the Grimké sisters with a proclamation that God condones the "protected" and "dependent" state of women. The General Association of the Church wrote the following: "The power of woman is her dependence, flowing from the consciousness of that weakness which God has given her for her protection, and which keeps her in those departments of life that form the character of individuals and of the nation."[18] In spite of these kinds of "divinely-inspired" attacks, women began to claim and articulate revelations to the contrary. Sarah Grimké affirmed that the appropriate duties and influence of women are revealed in the New Testament. In her words, "No one can desire more earnestly than I do that woman may move exactly in the sphere which her creator has assigned her; and I believe her having been displaced from that sphere has introduced confusion into the world."[19] Grimké felt that the New Testament in its untarnished form can be used as a guide for women. Having been contaminated by the interpretations and translations of men, the Bible and commentaries thereupon have been distorted especially with regard to women.

Who Do Feminists Say That Jesus Christ Is?

Twentieth-century women were aware of the significant oppressive impact of religion and theology in their lives. This is perhaps why religion and theology have been consistently addressed in the contemporary women's movement. More importantly, they specifically recognized the special functions of Jesus Christ in the maintenance of the subordinate status of women. For this reason women began to see themselves as subjects to whom Jesus directed the question, "Who do you say that I am?" The question has been answered in many different ways. Three answers are explored here.

Recognizing the relationship between the patriarchal structures of the church and society and the male presence in the divine, some seek to empower women by affirming the female presence in the divine. Consequently, they argue that Jesus Christ was and is an androgynous person, embracing both masculine and feminine traits. In Jesus we find the reasonableness, self-confidence, and security often associated with the masculine person. In addition we find the emotions, peacefulness, and humility often associated with the feminine person. They see Jesus as "emphatically androgynous."[20] Some say that Jesus Christ was and is a feminist.[21] He is believed to be so because of his documented actions and reactions toward women.

Many feminists have interpreted Jesus' frequent affirmations of women (Luke 7:36ff., Mark 9:20ff., John 4:5ff., Matt 28:9ff., etc.) and other actions of Jesus as a rejection of patriarchy and an affirmation of women's experience.[22] Swidler concludes his analysis by reiterating that "it should be clear that Jesus vigorously promoted the dignity and equality of women in the midst of a very male-dominated society; Jesus was a feminist and a very radical one. Can his followers attempt to be anything else—*de imitatione Christ?*"[23]

Rosemary Ruether addresses the topic of feminist Christology in an article entitled "Feminism and Christology: Can a Male Savior Help Women?"[24]; in the same article revised under the title "Feminism and Christology: Can a Male Savior Save Women?"[25]; and in her book, *Sexism and God-Talk: Toward a Feminist Theology.*[26] In the article, Ruether puts the primary critical question in its most simple, yet profound, way. Given the realities of what maleness and femaleness mean in the church and in society, the question brings into focus elements of the very basic conflict in contemporary male/female relationship. Traditional understanding of the "nature of man" consisted of a dualism that kept man as "protector." Woman's sphere was limited in order to maintain consistency with this social dualism. Women have begun to challenge the motives of such an arrangement—that is, they have questioned whether men have been protecting women, or, in fact, protecting the "sacredness" of their privileged position. A male Christology, developed in the context of a Christian theology which itself perpetuates the socio-theological dualism, is met with the same suspicion by feminists. If the male Christ has like investments in the socio-theological status quo, then he cannot be trusted to help women. Thus Ruether asked "Can a Male Savior Help Women?"

When published in her book *To Change the World,* the question becomes more pointedly theological and specifically soteriological: "Can a male savior save women?" Salvation in a patriarchal system would be comparable to accepting one's designated place in the order of creation. This male Christ figure would merely put its stamp of approval upon the patriarchically defined place of women. It is here where Ruether prepares the way for her liberation approach to Christology when she poses the question, "Can Christology be liberated from its encapsulation in the structure of patriarchy and really become an expression of liberation of women?"[27] In both essays Ruether provides a positive response to the question. In her first essay, the concepts of service and conversion are elevated. Service must not be confused with servitude. In her view, "service implies autonomy and power used in behalf of others."[28] We are all called to service. Our conversion is to accept this call by abandoning previous, inaccurate notions of being called to hierarchical and oppressive leadership and power. The new

Christology which is to be developed, then, is one of "conversion and social transformation."[29] Ruether affirms the "liberating praxis" emphasis of liberation theologians, saying that "a starting point for feminist christological inquiry must be a reencounter with the Jesus of the Synoptic Gospels, not the accumulated doctrine about him but his message and praxis."[30] This way we are able to see the ways in which Jesus challenged the customs and laws of his time regarding women. Ruether stops short of saying that Jesus Christ was a feminist for his time, but she does claim "that the criticism of religious and social hierarchy characteristic of the early portrait of Jesus is a remarkable parallel to feminist criticism."[31] He seems to promote a more egalitarian form of relationship—lineal rather than vertical—perhaps one of brother and sister. Jesus elevated many who were at the bottom of the social hierarchy to a new level of equality. This trend is especially evident in his relationship to women.

There is a dynamic quality to the redemptive process. This dynamism not only exists between the redeemer and the redeemed community but also within the redeemer itself. For "the redeemer is one who has been redeemed, just as Jesus himself accepted the baptism of John."[32] As Jesus is paradigmatic, we become so when we liberate others as we have been liberated ourselves. Recognition of this dynamism moves us away from the traditional "once-for-all" notion of Jesus. Because the redemptive process still continues, we can experience the Christ as the historical Jesus and we can experience "Christ in the form of our sister."[33] This means that neither Christ nor humanity is imaged solely as male.

The historical Jesus was a man, but men do not have a monopoly upon Christ, and Eve was a woman but women do not have a monopoly upon sin. For "Christ is not necessarily male, nor is the redeemed community only women, but new humanity, female and male."[34]

As both Blacks and women have struggled from place of objects to subjects, they have more and more begun to answer Jesus' question for themselves. "Who do you say that I am?" You are the Black Messiah, the Liberator, the Redeemer. You are the Christ, the Savior, the Sister.

The Subjectification of Black Women

Even in the midst of the struggles for liberation, Black women still found themselves objectified indeed by white men, but also by Black men and white women. In the Black movement women were intimi-

dated into believing that sexism was not a reality in the Black community. Consequently, for some time most Black women did not publicly
address sexism. In the women's movement, Black women were ignored
in significant ways; consequently most Black women ignored the
movement. In other words, in the subjectification process, essentially
invisible Black women were left to fall through the cracks.

While Black women did not accept that imposed invisibility quietly,
they did fall through the cracks. For example, though neither the Bill of
Rights nor the amendments to the Constitution ensured Black women
(or Black men for that matter) their rights, this did not totally prevent
the rise of activism among Black women. Womanists such as Harriet
Tubman, Sojourner Truth, Fannie B. Williams, Ida B. Wells, Mary
McLeod Bethune, Fannie Lou Harper, and others were present to challenge in one way or another the racism, sexism, and classism of their
day, often at great cost to themselves. Being active both in the aboli-
tion/anti-racism movement and the women's liberation/anti-sexism
movement meant that these women were doubly burdened, doubly
taxed, and twice removed from the seat of power by virtue of being victims of both racism and sexism. In actuality they were thrice removed
from any real sense of self-control, for their control in the early days was
in the hands of white men and women and more recently also in the
hands of Black men.

For them, becoming subjects meant engaging in three battles: (1)
the battle against the ever-pervasive racism of the dominant culture; (2)
the battle against the sexism of the dominant male culture; and (3) the
battle against the sexism of nondominant cultures, including Black
men. Though the subjectification process has become less evident in
Black women's communities, we can still discern its presence as they
attempt to live out their response to the question "Who do you say that
I am?"

Who Do Womanists Say That Jesus Christ Is?

Black women have said and continue to say that Jesus Christ is one of
us. When we see Jesus Christ, we see both the particular Jesus of
Nazareth and the universal Christ of faith. In Jesus Christ, we see an
oppressed experience and at the same time we see liberation. When we
see Jesus Christ, we see concreteness and absoluteness, for in Jesus
Christ, the absolute becomes concrete.

Black women can identify with this Jesus Christ because the Jesus
Christ reality is so akin to their own reality. For it is in the context of

Black women's experience that we find the particular connecting with the universal. By this I mean that in each of the three dynamics of oppression which characterize their reality, Black women share in the reality of a broader community: they share race suffering with Black men; with white women and other Third World women they are victims of sexism; and with poor Blacks and whites, and other Third World peoples, especially women, they are disproportionately poor. To speak of Black women's tridimensional reality, therefore, is not to speak of Black women exclusively, for there is an implied universality which connects them with others.

Similarly, there was an implied universality with Jesus Christ, which made him identify with others—the poor, the women, the stranger. To affirm Jesus' solidarity with the "least of the people" (Matt 25:31–46) is not an exercise in romanticized contentment with one's oppressed status in life. For the resurrection signified that there is more to the life of Jesus Christ than the cross. For Black women, the resurrection signifies that their triply oppressive existence is not the end. It represents the context in which a particular people struggle to experience hope and liberation. Jesus Christ thus represents a threefold significance: first, he identifies with the "little people"—Black women— where they are and he accompanies them in their struggles.[35] Second, he affirms the basic humanity of these, "the least," and in affirming them he empowers them to gain "more." Third, he inspires active hope in the struggle for resurrected, liberated existence. Christ's empowerment effects liberation.

Identification with "Little People"

To locate the Christ in the experiences of Black people as Black theology has done is a radical and necessary step. An understanding of Black women's reality challenges us to go further. Christ among the least must also mean Christ in the community of Black women. William Eichelberger was able to recognize this as he further particularized the significance of the Blackness of Jesus by locating Christ in a Black women's community. He was able to see Christ not only as Black male but also as Black female: "It is my feeling that God is now manifesting Himself, and has been for over 450 years, in the form of the Black American Woman as mother, as wife, as nourisher, sustainer, and preserver of life, the Suffering Servant who is despised and rejected by men, a personality of sorrow who is acquainted with grief."[36] Granted, Eichelberger's categories for God and woman are very traditional. Nevertheless, the significance of his thought is that he was able to conceive of the divine reality as other than a Black male messianic figure.

The possibility that Christ is in the experiences of Black women high-lights the notion that Christ accompanies the people in their pain and suffering and loneliness.

In the experiences of Black people, Jesus was "all things."[37] Chief among these, however, was the belief in Jesus as the divine co-sufferer, who empowers them in situations of oppression. For Christian Black women in the past, Jesus was their central frame of reference. They identified with Jesus because they believed that Jesus identified with them. As Jesus was persecuted and made to suffer undeservedly, so were they. His suffering culminated in the crucifixion. Their crucifixion included rape, their babies being sold, and their men being castrated. But Jesus' suffering was not the suffering of a mere human, for Jesus was understood to be God incarnate. As Harold Carter observed of Black prayers in general, there was no difference between the persons of the trinity, Jesus, God, or the Holy Spirit. All of these proper names for God were used interchangeably in prayer language. Thus, Jesus was the one who speaks the world into creation. He was the power be-hind the church.

Black women's affirmation of Jesus as God meant that white peo-ple were not God. One old slave woman clearly demonstrated this as she prayed: "Dear Massa Jesus, we all uns beg ooner [you] come make us a call dis yere day. We is nutting but poor Ethiopian women and people ain't tink much 'bout we. We ain't trust any of dem great high people for come to we church, but do' you is de one great Massa, great yoo much dan Massa Likum, you ain't shame to care for we African people."[38]

This slave woman did not hesitate to identify her struggles and pain with those of Jesus. In fact, the common struggle made her know that Jesus would respond to her beck and call: "Come to we, dear Massa Jesus. De sun, he hot too much, de road am dat long and boggy [sandy] and we ain't got no buggy for send and fetch Ooner. But Massa, you 'member how you walk up Calvary and ain't weary but tink about we all dat way. We pick out de thorns, de prickles, de brier, de backslidin' and de quarrel and de sin out of you path so dey shan't hurt Ooner pierce feet no more."[39] As she is truly among the people at the bottom of humanity, she can make things comfortable for Jesus, even though she may have nothing to give him—no water, no food—but she can give tears and love. She continues: "Come to we, dear Massa Jesus. We all uns ain't got no good cool water for to give you when you thirsty. You know, Massa, de drought so long, and the well so low, ain't nutting but mud to drink. But we gwine to take de 'munion cup and fill it wid de tear of repentance and love clean out of we heart. Dat all we hab to gib you, good Massa."⁴⁰ Isn't it interesting that the women here have faith that Jesus will join them in the drought (presumably a metaphor for their condition)? In spite of the mud (again a metaphor for their possessions), you will find rightness of heart, love, and repentance.

Affirmation of Humanity

For Black women, the role of Jesus Christ was demystified as they encountered him in their experience as one who empowers the weak. Jesus Christ dwells with the people in their survival struggles, and the Christ projects faithful followers forward into meaningful liberation praxis. In this vein, Jesus was such a central part of Sojourner Truth's life that all of her sermons started with him. When asked by a preacher if the source of her preaching was the Bible, she responded, "No honey, can't preach from de Bible—can't read a letter."⁴¹ Then she explained: "When I preaches, I has jest one text to preach from, an' I always preaches from this one. My text is, 'When I found Jesus!'⁴² In this sermon Sojourner Truth recounts the events and struggles of her life from the time her parents were brought from Africa and sold "up an' down, and 'hither an' yon"⁴³ to the time that she met Jesus within the context of her struggles for the dignity of Black people and women. Her encounter with Jesus brought such joy that she became overwhelmed with love and praise: "Praise, praise, praise to the Lord! An' I begun to feel such a love in my soul as I never felt before—love to all creatures. An' then, all of a sudden, it stopped, an' I said, 'Dar's de white folks that have abused you, an' beat you, an' abused your people—tink o' them!' But then there came another rush of love through my soul, an' I cried out loud—'Lord, I can love *even de white folks!*'"⁴⁴ This love was not a sentimental, passive love. It was a tough, active love that empowered her to fight more fiercely for the freedom of her people. For the rest of her life she continued speaking at abolition and women's rights gatherings, condemning the horrors of oppression. In this regard, she was a true incarnation of the Christ.

Empowerment for Liberation

James Cone argues that the christological title "the Black Christ" is not validated by its universality, but, in fact, by its particularity. Its significance lies in whether or not that christological title "points to God's universal will to liberate particular oppressed people from inhumanity."⁴⁵ These particular oppressed peoples to which Cone refers are characterized in Jesus' parable on the Last Judgment as "the least." The least in America are literally and symbolically present in Black people.[46] This notion of "the least" is attractive because it descriptively locates the condition of Black women. "The least" are those people who have no water to give, but offer what they have, as the old slave woman says in her prayer. Black women's experience in general is such a reality. Their threefold oppression renders their particular situation a complex one. They are the oppressed of the oppressed, and therefore their salvation represents "the particular within the particular."

The Christ understood as the stranger, the outcast, the hungry, the weak, the poor, makes a traditional male Christ less significant. Even our sisters, the womanists of the past, had some suspicions about the effects of a male image of the divine, for they did challenge the oppressive use of it in the church's theology. In so doing, they were able to move from a traditional oppressive Christology, with respect to women, to an egalitarian Christology. This kind of Christology was operative in Jarena Lee's argument for the right of women to preach. She argued "the Savior died for the woman as well as for the man."[47] The crucifixion was for universal salvation, not just for male salvation or, as we may extend the argument, not just for white salvation. Because of this Christ came and died, no less for the woman than for the man, no less for Blacks than for whites. "If the man may preach because the Savior died for him, why not the woman? Seeing he died for her also. Is he not a whole Savior, instead of half one?—as those who hold it wrong for a woman to preach seem to make it appear."[48] Lee correctly perceives that there is an ontological issue at stake. If Jesus Christ were a Savior of men then it is true the maleness of Christ would be paramount. But if Christ is a Savior of all then it is the humanity—the wholeness—of Christ which is significant.

Sojourner Truth was aware of the same tendency of some scholars and church leaders to link the maleness of Jesus and the sin of Eve with the status of women. She challenged this notion in her famous speech "Ain't I a Woman?"

> Then that little man in black there, he says women can't have as much rights as men, 'cause Christ wasn't a woman! Where did your Christ come from? Where did your Christ come from? From God and a woman. Man had nothing to do with Him. If the first woman God ever made was strong enough to turn the world upside down all alone, these women together ought to be able to turn it back, and get it right side up again! And now they is asking to do it, the men better let them.[49]

CONCLUSION

I would argue, as suggested by both Lee and Sojourner Truth, that the significance of Christ is not his maleness, but his humanity. The most significant events of Jesus Christ were the life and ministry, the crucifixion, and the resurrection. The significance of these events, in one sense, is that in them the absolute becomes concrete. God becomes concrete not only in the man Jesus, for he was crucified, but in the lives of those who will accept the challenges of the risen Savior—the Christ. For Lee, this meant that women could preach; for Sojourner Truth, it meant that women could possibly save the world; for me, it means that today, this Christ, found in the experience of Black women, is a Black woman.

At last! Black women are indeed becoming subjects. More and more they are resisting the objectification by those whose histories and herstories continue to render them invisible. And, so to the question, "Who do *you* say that I am?" Black women say that you are the one who is with us and among us in our community as we struggle for survival. You are the one who not only is with us, but you are one of us. "Who do you say that I am?" You are the Christ, the one who affirms us, the one who accompanies us as we move from mere survival to redemptive liberation. "Who do you say that I am?" You are indeed the Christ.

Notes

1. Zora Neale Hurston, *Their Eyes Were Watching God* (Philadelphia: Lippincott, 1939).

2. Gloria T. Hull, Patricia Bell Scott, and Barbara Smith, eds., *All the Women Are White, All the Blacks Are Men, But Some of Us Are Brave: Black Women's Studies* (Old Westbury, NY: Feminist Press, 1982).

3. From the poem "I Am a Black Woman," in *I Am a Black Woman: Poems by Mari Evans* (New York: Morrow, 1970), 12.

4. Carter G. Woodson, *The Mis-Education of the Negro* (Philadelphia: Hakim, 1922).

5. James H. Cone, *God of the Oppressed* (New York: Seabury, 1975), 108–9.

6. Ibid.

7. James H. Cone, *A Black Theology of Liberation* (Philadelphia: Lippincott, 1970), 198.

8. J. A. Johnson, "The Need for a Black Christian Theology," *Journal of the I.T.C.* 11 (Fall 1974): 25.

9. Albert Cleage, *The Black Messiah* (New York: Sheed and Ward, 1968), 3.

10. Ibid.

11. Cone, *Black Theology*, 214–15.

12. Gayraud Wilmore, "The Black Messiah: Revising the Color Symbolism of Western Christianity," *Journal of the Interdenominational Theological Center* 2 (Fall 1974): 13–14.

13. William Eichelberger, "Reflections on the Person and Personality of the Black Messiah," in C. Eric Lincoln's *The Black Church Since Frazier* (New York: Schocken, 1974), 6, 61.

14. Barbara Hilkert Andolsen, *Daughters of Jefferson, Daughters of Bootblacks: Racism and American Feminism* (Macon, GA: Mercer University Press, 1986), see chap. 3.

15. Quoted in Andolsen, *Daughters of Jefferson*, 17.

16. Ibid.

17. Nancy Cott, *The Bonds of Womanhood: Women's Sphere in New England, 1780–1835* (New Haven, CT: Yale University Press, 1972), 126ff.

18. "The General Association of Massachusetts (Orthodox) to the Churches Under Their Care, 1837," in *Feminist Papers: from Adams to de Beauvoir,* ed. Alice Rossi (New York: Columbia University Press, 1973), 305.

19. Sarah Grimké, "Letter on the Equality of the Sexes and Condition of Women," in Rossi, *Feminist Papers*, 107. Both Grimké sisters were active women's rights advocates (as well as abolitionists). They spoke out for the rights of women, including the right to speak on any issue—be it Negro or women's suffrage. See also Angelina E. Grimké, *An Appeal to the Christian Women of the South* (New York: American Antislavery Society, 1836).

20. Leonard Swidler, *Biblical Affirmation of Women* (Philadelphia: Westminster, 1979).

21. Leonard Swidler, "Jesus Was a Feminist," *South Asia Journal of Theology* 13 (1971): 106.

22. See Kathleen Storrie, "New Yeast in the Dough: Jesus Transforms Authority," *Daughters of Sarah* 10 (January/February 1984). In this article Storrie draws on the work of Elisabeth Schüssler Fiorenza, *In Memory of Her* (New York: Crossroad, 1983), and Dorothee Soelle, *Beyond Mere Obedience* (Minneapolis, MN: Augsburg, 1970).

23. Swidler, "Jesus Was a Feminist," 103.

24. Rosemary Radford Ruether, "Feminism and Christology: Can a Male Savior Help Women?" in *Occasional Papers* (Nashville, TN: United Methodist Board of Higher Education and Ministry, 1976), 1–9.

25. Rosemary Radford Ruether, in *To Change the World: Chrislology and Cultural Criticism* (New York: Crossroad, 1981), 47.

26. Rosemary Radford Ruether, *Sexism and God-Talk: Toward a Feminist Theology* (Boston: Beacon, 1983), 135.

27. Ruether, *To Change the World*, 47.

28. Ruether, "Feminism and Christology."

29. Ibid.

30. Ruether, *Sexism*, 135.

31. Ibid.

32. Ibid., 138.

33. Ibid.

34. Ibid.

35. This word was used by El Salvadoran activist Marta Benarides in describing the need for a theology of accompaniment vs. empowerment. For Black women, I would argue, as I see evidence in Black women's religious experiences, for both a theology of accompaniment and empowerment.

36. William Eichelberger, *The Black Church*, 54.

37. Harold A. Carter, *The Prayer Tradition of Black People* (Valley Forge, PA: Judson, 1976). Carter, in referring to traditional Black prayer in general, states that Jesus is revealed as one who is "all one needs!"

38. Ibid., 49.

39. Ibid.

40. Ibid.

41. Olive Gilbert, ed., *Sojourner Truth: Narrative and Book of Life* (1850, 1875; reprint, Chicago: Johnson's, 1970), 118.

42. Ibid., 119.

43. Ibid.

44. Ibid., 122.

45. Cone, *God of the Oppressed*, 135.

46. Ibid., 136.

47. Jarena Lee, *Religious Experiences and Journal of Mrs. Jarena Lee* (Philadelphia, 1849), 15–16.

48. Ibid., 16.

49. Sojourner Truth, "Ain't I a Woman?" in *Feminism*, ed. Miriam Schneir (New York: Vintage, 1972), 94.

18

FROM *SATAS* TO *SANTAS*—
SOBRAJAS NO MORE:
SALVATION IN THE SPACES OF THE EVERYDAY

Loida I. Martell-Otero

INTRODUCTION: *ABUELITA* THEOLOGIES

I grew up in the church. My earliest memories centered on the life of the church and scripture at home. Religion established the patterns and rhythms of my childhood through my adolescence, marked by the activities surrounding Sunday school, church services, visiting the sick, evangelistic forays into the streets of Spanish Harlem, and even summer camp. My initial theological views were forged not only through the sermons I heard, but more importantly by the extraordinary women of my childhood congregation. Through their teaching of the Bible, prayers, and *testimonios* (witnessing), as well as through hymns and *coritos* (musical refrains), I learned about the God who inhabited our *vida cotidiana* (daily lives). The common theme throughout these teachings was that in Jesus Christ and through the power of the Spirit, God was a saving God. These wise women did not simply pass on the gospel (*el evangelio*) as a set of accepted dogmatic statements. They nurtured us with a keen sense of the Spirit's ability to create anew, to empower prophetic words, and to awaken our responsibility to seek and hear them.

As a growing number of Latina Protestant (*evangélica*) women have become teaching and writing theologians, we draw on this tradition. What defines us in the first place are the theologies we have inherited from our *abuelas, madres, comadres*, and *tías* (grandmothers, mothers, godmothers, and aunts), the wise women of our faith communities who gave us a firm foundation of the gospel and taught us to love the

Lord and demonstrate that love in the world. From this starting point, our work is a collaborative, critical effort to uncover how certain aspects of our inherited tradition have been colonized by imperial powers. It is also a creative, constructive effort to interpret this tradition anew in view of the situation of our community today, characterized more often than not by marginalization and poverty.

Who are Latinas? They are women from a Latin American or Latin Caribbean background who were born in or now reside in the continental United States. As such, they form an essential part of distinct communities of Mexican, Puerto Rican, Cuban, Dominican, and other Caribbean groups as well as various ethnic, cultural, or national enclaves that stem from Central or South America. Latinas are part of this broad community that, though disparate, nevertheless share common experiences of bilingualism, multiculturalism, popular religious faith, migration, and cultural alienation. For the most part they are undereducated, underemployed, and exploited. They lack access to quality housing and proper health care. The likelihood that they are poor is double that of white women.

Arising from this cultural matrix, this essay endeavors to speak about the meaning of salvation from an *evangélica* perspective. Yet its audience is not so narrowly circumscribed. Contextual theologies have made clear that all theologies arise from specific social locations, and consequently have both creative insights and painful blind spots. The various viewpoints should allow for an enriching conversation. Until recently the absence of Latina *evangélica* voices, all too easily dismissed as marginal and derivative, has impoverished this overall discourse. However, with their interpretation and praxis of salvation as *santidad* (vocation), *sanidad* (wholistic healing) and *liberación* (freedom from oppression and for living), *abuelita* theologies make a distinctive contribution to Christian discourse as a whole.

CHRISTIAN TRADITION AND THE MEANING OF SALVATION

The study of salvation or soteriology has traditionally been defined in ways that link it closely with the doctrine of Jesus Christ, that is, with Christology. For example, Daniel Migliore defines soteriology as the "doctrine of the saving work of Jesus Christ."[1] William Placher echoes a similar understanding when he defines soteriology as "the study of how Jesus acts as *sōter*, or Savior."[2] However, unlike disputes over the person and nature of Jesus Christ which resulted in definitive doctrine, the early church did not undergo a soteriological controversy that led to a creedal statement defining salvation in a specific way. Thus, there is no single definition for the term salvation.

A cursory examination reveals that salvation has meant different things at different times in the Jewish and Christian traditions. In the First Testament, salvation is understood as God's intervention in concrete and historical events that saves the people from hunger, illness, famine, military incursions, and political oppression. Above all, salvation was *shalom*, God's outpouring of peace, well-being, and rich blessings so that the community as a whole could flourish in harmony with God, creation, and each other. The Second Testament maintains this understanding, albeit within an eschatological framework that understands Jesus Christ to be the embodiment of the reign of God. God's reign is by no means simply a transcendental event. As in the First Testament, the reign represents justice, mercy, and communal wholeness for all of creation within human history.

By the patristic era, this understanding had shifted. In the Eastern Church salvation was viewed as *theosis* or divinization. Jesus Christ was God become human so that we could become like God: incorruptible and in eternal communion with divine glory. The incarnation was crucial for this view of salvation, as the axiom "what was not assumed could not be saved" attests.[3] The Western Church eventually became deeply influenced by Anselm of Canterbury's satisfaction theory of the atonement, expressed in later Protestant notions of sin. Salvation took on juridical connotations. Humankind had violated the divine law and consequently became indebted to God. Jesus' vicarious death was the means to pay this debt. Jesus' crucifixion, rather than the incarnation, took center stage in what came to be known as atonement soteriologies. In the wake of Pietism and Holiness movements, salvation lost its communal implications. As salvation became an increasingly interiorized, individualistic, and privatized event, greater emphasis was placed on its transcendental dimension: Jesus died "for *me*" so that I could "go to heaven."

An *evangélica* soteriology differs from these more traditional approaches because in the first place the social-historical location from which Latinas do theology is different; they theologize from the periphery, from places of powerlessness and voicelessness. In addition, an *evangélica* understanding of salvation tends to be functionally trinitarian, rather than solely christocentric, because of the prominent role accorded to the Holy Spirit. Unlike traditional atonement soteriologies with their emphasis on Christ's suffering and death as a means to satisfy and appease what is at times depicted as a wrathful God, an *evangélica* understanding is more incarnational. That is to say, Jesus' life and ministry and the Spirit's outpouring are salvific in very concrete ways *en lo cotidiano* (in the spaces of the everyday). This historical concreteness implies that salvation must include an inherent ethical imperative that leads to the holistic humanization of the oppressed and disenfranchised. To paraphrase a famous dictum: without justice there can be no salvation.

EVANGÉLICAS AS SATAS: STANDING AT THE PERIPHERY AS SOBRAJA

In general Latinas are perennial outsiders, treated as nobodies within racist, classist, and sexist structures that permeate U.S. society. Most Latinas live in neighborhoods where one must daily struggle for the basic staples of life: fresh and sanitary food, quality education, safe homes, heat and hot water, and myriad other details that contribute to a decent quality of life. Women in my congregation have shared how they sought to shield their babies from rats in dilapidated buildings, or how they covered up broken windows with cardboard in the dead of winter, fearing for the health of their children. Many deal with domestic as well as institutional violence. Adequate medical care is often beyond reach. Life is a perennial struggle. They struggle not just for themselves, but also for their families and communities.

Thus, Latinas exist at the periphery of U.S. society as "other." They are treated as *satas*. In Puerto Rico, *sata* was originally slang for a mongrel dog, considered ugly and a carrier of vermin, tainted by the very fact of being a mixed breed. In contemporary Puerto Rican society, the meaning of this term has expanded. It denotes an unsavory character, a person of low morals, or someone who has behaved indecently. Many Latinas, particularly immigrant and poor women residing in the United States, understand this experience, having been called "spics," "illegals," and "wetbacks." I use *sata* as a theological metaphor to connote the existential pluriform and peripheral experience of Latinas. It underscores their status as *sobraja*, a people who are treated as if they have no inherent worth and who are consequently relegated to the bottom rungs of society. Latinas are the nobodies who are shooed away: dehumanized, stereotyped, exploited, and marginalized.

JESÚS JÍBARO: CHRIST OUTSIDE THE GATE

In traditional form, incarnational Christologies often set about asking ontological questions, i.e., *what* is Christ rather than *who* is Jesus. Perhaps this is why so many traditional soteriologies that purport to regard highly the event of the incarnation have ironically said so little about Jesus' attention to the bodily afflictions of the oppressed of his time. Perhaps this also explains why most contemporary theologians from the center have been blind to or silent about the constant disregard, abuse, and misuse of marginalized bodies. In contradistinction, the shift to a more holistically incarnational Christology, as seen in Virgilio Elizondo's paradigm of *mestizaje* and Orlando Costas's view of Jesus as *jíbaro* (a distinctively Puerto Rican term for peasant or country bumpkin), has led to the articulation of soteriologies that address real issues facing Latinas.[4] From such a perspective, Jesus is saving because in him God has come to reside as a marginalized cosmological and human *sato*. That is to say, Jesus is a vehicle of God's salvation because he lived, and continues to live, at the periphery, challenging those who wish to follow him to "go outside the gate" (Heb 13:12–13).

To refer to him as *"Jesús sato"* or *"Jesús jíbaro"* is to acknowledge that historically he is a peripherally-placed person who faces the struggles of his very humanity in the midst of a colonized and peripherally-placed people. This is no idealized or disembodied Messiah. This person, whom *evangélica* tradition readily acknowledges as God-become-human, weeps, gets angry, chastises, and tires. He is a *sato* because of his questionable parental lineage: he is an illegal by birth! He is marginalized because of his cultural and religious background as well as his geographical location in Galilee.

El evangelio (the good news) that *evangélicas* can claim is that in this *Jesús sato*, who is truly Immanu-el, God has intentionally chosen to be with the *satas* and *sobrajas* of the world. In this Jesus, they encounter the one who is present *en sus vidas cotidianas* (in their daily lives) and *en sus sufrimientos* (in their sufferings). He began his ministry empowered by the Holy Spirit. *Evangélicas* know this Jesus, whose fundamental vocation is to be with "the least of these": those considered to be *sobrajas* and *sata/os*, such as women, children, prostitutes, tax collectors, publicans, lepers, and Samaritans. Jesus heard and knew the needs of those on the periphery of his time, and *evangélicas* believe that he knows them today. Jesus' foundational good news was not that they would go to heaven but rather that "the reign of God is in the midst of you" (Mark 1:15).

For *evangélicas*, then, *Jesús sato* is not an appeasement for a wrathful God. Rather, he is the embodied evidence that God knows them and loves them because, like them, God in Jesus has experienced and confronted the sinful structures of the world. They recognize that through

Jesus, God understands what it means to be wounded and to suffer. Like them, *Jesús jíbaro* suffered death and abandonment. Like them, he was dehumanized, *tratado como un perro* (treated like a dog). The good news for *evangélicas* is that God faced the worst of the world, but was not overcome by the sin of the world. Suffering, abandonment, cruelty, and death do not have dominion. The resurrection is God's "No" to the rejection of the *satas* of this world. It is God's resounding "No" to death-dealing institutional forces, whether social, political, economic, religious, or familial, that destroy bodies and communities. The resurrection of *Jesús sato* is evidence of the faithfulness of God, who sends the Spirit to bring life, and life abundant. The resurrection is evidence that in the eyes of God, those whom the world rejects as *satas*, God considers *santas* (saints). They are not *sobraja*, persons of no worth, but children of the Living God. For those who "stand outside the gate" of hope and justice, this is good news indeed.

HOLY SPIRIT: SALVATION AS PRESENCE AND PERSONHOOD

Jesus' salvific ministry did not end with his resurrection. *Evangélicas* continue to affirm his presence in their midst. They believe that God, who is present in Jesus, continues to save through the Holy Spirit. In contradistinction to more traditional pneumatologies, *evangélica* pneumatology does not perceive the Spirit to be a force, an energy, or simply a "bond of love," but a Person, the Wild Child, God made palpably present in all the spaces of the daily lives of *evangélicas*.[5] As lay leader Linda Castro testified before her congregation, the Spirit's presence allowed her to affirm that "God is not on a throne but by my side" when she faced a potentially catastrophic illness.[6]

This abiding presence of God is a powerfully salvific event in the lives of those who are treated as *sobraja*, abandoned by spouses, family, or community, and left with no visible means of societal support. To assert that God is with us when others have discounted our very humanity is prophetically subversive good news for the abandoned. The Spirit who is Person affirms our personhood and showers upon us the bounty of God's grace and *hesed* (faithful love). In the Spirit we experience *santidad* (holiness), *sanidad* (healing), and *liberación* (liberation). In the Spirit we receive *shalom* and joy. The voiceless speak in tongues and prophecy. We dream dreams of a better life. We envision a better world. Anointed by the Spirit we go forth with a mandate to transform our lives, communities, and world. Just as the Spirit empowered *Jesús sato*, so we are given courage to go into marginalized, poor, and dangerous areas too often eschewed by those from the centers of power.

Thus empowered, *evangélicas* resist the ecclesial structures that reject our calling simply based on our gender or ethnicity. When we sing *"Dios está aquí"* ("God is here"), we are affirming the palpable presence of *Jesús sato* and the Spirit. This experience of the Spirit's saving presence prevents an *evangélica* understanding of salvation from being solely christocentric. It is a functionally trinitarian event.

NARRATIVES OF SALVATION IN THE SPACES OF THE EVERYDAY

In contradistinction to *mujerista* claims, scripture is an important theological tool for *evangélicas*.[7] When interwoven with prayers, *testimonios* (witnessing, or telling personal stories), and *coritos* (short refrains based on scriptural texts, or indigenously generated songs of lamentation and joy), biblical texts provide *evangélicas* with a sense of self and agency. These interweavings articulate an experiential faith, a historical encounter with God from the margins that narrates a holistic experience of salvation in everyday life. Given the role of scripture in these interweavings, I have chosen three biblical narratives that I believe demonstrate that *santidad, sanidad*, and *liberación* are integral to an *evangélica* understanding of salvation.

Santidad: the unnamed Samaritan woman in John 4:1–42. The protagonist of this pericope faces discrimination as both a Samaritan and a woman. Even modern patriarchal exegetes have misrepresented and stereotyped her from pulpits and in academic writings as a loose woman, a harlot, a sinner, though the text does not necessarily support such a reading. Encountering Jesus at the village well, she engages in rich theological conversation. The world may reject her, but *Jesús sato* acknowledges her personhood and sees her as one called by God. She is neither *sata* nor *sobraja* but rather *santa*, a saint called and transformed by God. As *santa*, she goes forth with a deep sense of vocation, announcing good news to those considered *satas/os* by the world.

The story of *la Samaritana* is the story of so many Latinas, particularly undocumented migrants. Invisible, faceless, and voiceless, they reside at the periphery of a society that knows how to exploit them and to deny them their human rights. Those from the centers of power often impose their distorted views on these women, accusing them of wantonness, criminal actions, and a number of other sins. Exploited in the domestic spheres of their existence as well as in the larger society, they are modern-day *Samaritanas* who struggle against almost insurmountable odds to provide for their families.

Jesús sato goes out to find them. He sees them, values them, and gives them purpose. They are no longer *satas* but *santas:* the impure are truly saints, imbued with a full sense of humanity and a deep sense of vocation. In the eyes of God they are not *sobraja*, ignorant, superstitious, uneducated women who can be scoffed at or ignored. Rather, they are deeply religious and astutely theological women who have much to contribute. The Spirit of God is poured out on them, restoring their sense of personhood; from a deep place of restful peace, they become empowered to speak on behalf of the poor and oppressed who for so long have been voiceless. No longer exploited, they can now rest. On Sunday mornings they gather and joyfully sing, "*Venid a mi todo el que estáis trabajado . . . y os haré descansar*": "Come to me all you that are weary and carrying heavy burdens, and I will give you rest" (Matt 11:28).

Sanidad: the woman with a hemorrhage in Mark 5:25–33. *Evangélicas* resonate with biblical stories of healing, and in particular that of the hemorrhagic woman. Nameless and faceless, she too is the object of much speculation of contemporary scholarship. Yet little is known other than that she had been suffering for twelve years and "had endured much under many physicians, and had spent all that she had." Like many *evangélicas* who could claim this woman's story as their own, she had no one to intercede on her behalf. She had to seek relief for her chronic condition on her own. She approaches Jesus with fear and trembling, as so many in the Latina community, particularly undocumented workers, approach hospitals and health care facilities. Latinas are not strangers to physical abuse by many in the medical field. Like so many abused women, she hopes that Jesus' touch will not harm but heal: "If I but touch his clothes, I will be made well."

While pressed by others to continue, Jesus stops for her. He stops to look deeply into her life and situation, and then declares that her faith had saved/healed her. She moves from being ill, victimized, silenced, and invisible to being made whole. No longer a walking curse, she could have faith in her body again, in herself. She is no longer *sobraja*. Rather, Jesus declares her to be "daughter"; she is part of a community; she is *familia*. In Jesus' words to the hemorrhagic woman *evangélicas* hear a word of promise and hope for themselves and for their communities, which suffer violence from powerful institutions that organize the world for their own benefit. The world cannot heal us or make us whole, but God is able. The God of *Jesús sato* is the One who pours out a healing Spirit, mending the complex fractures that rend not only their bodies but also their communities.

Liberacíon: the perennially stooped woman in Luke 13:10–17. Bent over for eighteen years, this unnamed woman is ignored by those assembled in the place of prayer. Her suffering and silence are matters of indifference; she is socially disvalued. Her presence is an anomaly in a sacred space. Yet while she may be *sobraja* to others, to Jesus she is a "daughter of Abraham." He approaches her, proclaiming the necessity to set her "loose"; whereupon he lays hands upon her and she is "straightened." Synagogue leaders may protest, but set free she is able to claim her identity and give voice to her faith in God. Salvation is liberation where God *hace acta de presencia* (God is present, acting in decisive ways).

While Latinas may not necessarily be physically fused in such a position, they often spend many hours of each day bent over sewing machines, gathering the harvest as migrant workers, caring for children (whether their own or those of others), cleaning houses and public facilities, or engaged in menial labor for sub-living wages. They know what it is to be treated with disrespect, what it feels like to be invisible, with very few caring what happens to them or to their communities. They have also experienced the swift vituperation of those who protest when they perceive their sacred spaces of privilege being invaded. The response can be violent personally (death at the hands of border patrols) or institutionally (English-only laws). Yet like the once-stooped and now-straightened woman, *evangélicas* know that thanks to *Jesús sato* who sees them and liberates them, they are *mujeres dignas* deserving of respect. It is through the saving power of the Spirit that they can stand straight, and through the Spirit's charisms that they are empowered to speak and sing, glorifying God. Salvation as liberation is thus a reversal of unjust conditions. This is truly a Sabbath moment and word of good news.

CONCLUSION

A Latina *evangélica* soteriology challenges soteriologies from the center. When seen through the lens of liminal spaces of survival, salvation must by necessity become an incarnational event that responds to the daily suffering of forgotten people. From such a perspective one can only ask: how can theologians speak about heaven and rewards, crosses and sacrifice with such disincarnate passion when faced with the reality of so many whose bodies are literally abused, exploited, and disfigured? How can we so glibly take the cup and bread of Eucharist on Sunday mornings, while excluding so many from the table that is God's grace to the excluded? How can the Western Church place so much emphasis on the forgiveness of debt through Jesus Christ, while being complicit with economic institutions that demand exorbitant fees from the poor? In light of the scope of dehumanization that takes place, how can Christians "go to sleep so peacefully despite the millions around them who live and suffer...in the world?"[8]

Any soteriology that does not incorporate a radical call to serve those at the periphery is, in Dietrich Bonhoeffer's words, "cheap grace."[9] It is a disincarnate Christianity that allows its adherents to exploit the poor, ignore the suffering, and smugly await a heavenly reward at no cost to themselves. Only a soteriology of the privileged can ignore God's call to go "outside the gate." This is why the locus of salvation is never at the centers of power, which are blind to their inherent sin of injustice. To truly experience God's salvation, one must begin at the periphery, where *Jesús sato* beckons us to follow.

A Latina *evangélica* soteriology is not disincarnate, devoid of the concrete day-to-day realities of the poor and suffering, or focused solely on going to heaven. Its themes of *santidad, sanidad,* and *liberación* remind us through the embodied witness of Jesus' life and ministry that salvation is about the triune God's reign, and thus about incarnational justice. Jesus' death and resurrection underscore that while a grace, it is a costly grace. Salvation as integral wholeness means not just the healing of persons but of whole communities that have been fractured by complex socioeconomic, religious, political, and cultural factors. Salvation is the outpouring of God's Spirit, and therefore of abundant life that gives hope to those without hope, and frees those bound and made powerless by the powers and principalities of our day. Those considered nobodies are now somebodies because they are re-formed as community and *familia*. In Christ and through the Spirit, *las satas ya no son sobrajas, sino santas,* a people called by God.

Notes

1. Daniel Migliore, *Faith Seeking Understanding* (Grand Rapids: Eerdmans, 1991), 140.

2. William Placher, ed., *Essentials of Christian Theology* (Louisville: Westminster John Knox, 2003), 188.

3. Gregory of Nazianzus, "To Cledonius Against Apollinaris," 218.

4. Virgilio Elizondo, *Galilean Journey: Mexican-American Promise* (Maryknoll, NY: Orbis, 2000); Orlando Costas, *Christ Outside the Gate: Mission beyond Christendom* (Maryknoll, NY: Orbis, 1982).

5. Zaida Maldonado Pérez, Loida Martell-Otero, and Elizabeth Conde-Frazier, "Dancing with the Wild Child: *Evangélicas* and the Holy Spirit," in *Latina Evangélicas*, 14–32.

6. "Dios no está en un trono, sino a mi lado." *Testimonio* by Linda Castro, First Baptist Church of Caguas, Puerto Rico, September 26, 2010.

7. Ada María Isasi-Díaz, *En la Lucha/In the Struggle: Elaborating a Mujerista Theology* (Minneapolis: Fortress, 1993), 46–47.

8. Orlando Costas, *Liberating News* (Grand Rapids: Eerdmans, 1989), 69.

9. Dietrich Bonheoffer, *The Cost of Discipleship* (New York: Collier/Macmillan, 1959), 45–47.

19

CHRIST, THE MAN FOR OTHERS

Dorothee Soelle (Germany)

The spirit of our time raises many questions of the Christian faith. Some are posed with words, in conversations and discussions. But more frequently they are posed, so to speak, with feet in either secret or open withdrawal from the church. It is these latter questions that concern me here. Though most are not articulated, they are quite critical questions in a deeper sense.

When I try to explain to non-church-going people why I am "still," as they usually say, a Christian, I begin to reflect back over three phases of my own religious development which seem to me to be typical of the behavior of people in industrial culture.

Most of us go through the first phase during childhood if we are brought up according to the religious norms and customs as well as the beliefs and practices of our ancestors. The religious sensibility of our ancestors arose in the cultural climate of the small town or village, where the church stood at the center of social and intellectual life. Myths and legends, values and ethical norms, were rooted and centered in traditions which were simply accepted. I call this religious phase that of the village. Even today there are still people who spend their whole religious life "in the village." But the great majority emigrate to the big city, if not in reality then at least from the standpoint of feeling: they have ceased to pray and to go to church.

In this second phase, religion slowly but surely loses its power over people. It either falls into oblivion or becomes the focus of a conscious critique in which people ask themselves how they can be freed from a religion which was thrust upon them or how they can be healed from "God poisoning" (Tilmann Moser). In this second phase most throw off their religious heritage and live as post-Christian citizens in a secular city.

The history of religion, however, does not end with this departure, this urbanization, this industrialization. The contradictions of life in the city, the rootlessness, the disintegration of rituals and customs which are necessary for life make many people insecure and send them on a search for *religio* (binding back), for undamaged roots. Where should they turn? Back to the village perhaps, as churches often recommend? Back to the worn-out authorities and rules? To the pipe organs and confirmation rites? I think that there is yet a third phase. After the religious security in the village, after the religion-free departure into the cold city, people decide consciously for new forms of religion. Today they are still in the minority, but the number of those who are devout—albeit not in the sense of the old village—will grow. Two things seem to me important for this third phase of religious consciousness. First, it is a *conscious* religious decision. The religion of the village was inherited; one was born into it. But the new forms of religion—whether they be Christian or Eastern or from some other cultural horizon—are consciously chosen. That religion today can no longer be inherited is a result of the Enlightenment and of this human migration into the city.

A second element is closely connected with this: the decision in favor of a religious conviction happens critically, not naively. We do not accept everything; we act selectively, making choices. Gottfried von Lessing already understood this when he asked: "Should I then swallow the carton with the medicine?" Must I believe and follow each word in the Bible? The answer to this is a clear no. Even the strictest Bible believers do not marry the wife of their brother when he dies! With the departure from the religious village, authority—of the pastor, scripture, or the official church—is gone; it cannot be reinstituted. Anyone who comes to a critical affirmation of faith after an intensive debate in the second phase is now also struggling for the development of new forms of religious life.

I suspect that many today are on the way from phase two to phase three. Within the Christian women's movement and feminist theology, above all, there is a search which cannot be dismissed as authoritarian, as back to the village, to paternal or clerical authority. But also outside of the Western Christian horizon, many people are involved in a search for a new religious house, for new forms and rituals, for spirituality in a completely different language, for new models and new forms of expression. I know a number of young people whose parents still had to struggle with the transition from phase one to phase two and who then at first were relieved to settle into the largely religion-free big city. Their sons and daughters no longer have anything to do with these clashes; they tell me enthusiastically about Zen meditation, about a Sufi master, and so forth. They look for gurus, teachers, masters, models. Often they identify Christianity so much with the village of their grandparents that they consider it to be beyond hope. I then try to tell them and the other inhabitants of the secular and boring city something about Jesus—the rigidified cliché, yet completely unknown master, guru, teacher, model, liberator of the Christian tradition. I try to make them appreciate devotion to Jesus and also the teachings about Jesus.

The technical term for reflection about Jesus Christ is Christology, and so I have chosen three common questions which I have experienced as personal probings. By proceeding through them I want to try to present a Christology which, I am convinced, can emerge today only in dialogue with Christians of other regions of the world, that is, ecumenically. Because I believe I have learned something from these Christians of the poor world, it will have to be a Christology "from below."

Many years ago, when I was still a small, shy student, I asked a man at a construction site, "Do you happen to know what time it is?" He gave me such a strange answer that at that time I was completely speechless. "Am I Jesus?" he said in a kind of good-humored mockery. Always when I reflect on who this Jesus, let alone this Christ is supposed to be for us today, this man with his question gets in my way. Am I Jesus?!

For this worker, Jesus is from another world. A heavenly being who has nothing to do with us, who sees, hears, knows, and can do everything. The churchly language, which has called him Messiah, Lord, Son of God, the Christ, gets its due here. That's what you get, I would like to say to the thinkers and fathers of the faith, when you make Jesus into an unreachable, completely other Superman, indeed into God! That is precisely what comes out below from your steep Christology which celebrates the Godness of Jesus at the expense of his humanness so that nothing reasonable is left over, at most a Sunday outing of the heavenly being who stopped by for a short visit in Bethlehem. Christology from above, which starts with the Godly side of Jesus and makes of him an all-knowing immortal, ends in "docetism," as that false teaching is called in technical theological language, which recognizes Jesus' humanness and above all his suffering as appearance only.

This false manner of deifying Jesus is quite common among us. As a young teacher of religion I once asked the schoolchildren whether they thought the baby Jesus also had wet diapers. Most children rejected that decisively. Jesus, already even as the Christ child, must be different, higher, purer. My own children believed for a long time that the Christ child was a girl. This kind of children's religion is indeed gratifying in the feeling that Jesus incorporates both the masculine and the feminine. But it also suggests the image of an unreal, genderless being—as if Jesus were something other than a true, ordinary person like all of us. Martin Luther insisted on drawing Christ "into the flesh," and it was for just that reason that I spoke of wet diapers! But high Christology draws Jesus away from this world; he becomes unreachable, incomparable. And above all we cannot live as he lived—we shouldn't even try, because it's impossible anyway. How would we ever manage to feed the hungry? When we ourselves don't have much more than five loaves and two fishes? How would we ever manage not to serve the industry of death? Or how would we manage to heal the lepers? Are we Jesus?!

Today I would answer the worker at the construction site a little more openly and take the initiative. "Naturally," I would say, "you are Jesus, man! What else would you want to make of your life?! Being yourself alone isn't sufficient—you know that already! You too are born and have come into the world to witness to the truth. Don't make yourself smaller than you are. We have enough fellow-travelers already. Just imagine: you and I and your mother-in-law and your boss—are Jesus. What would change? There's something in us...of God."

That is how I would talk today and in so doing think about what the Quakers with their strange expression call "that of God in you." Because in actuality we cannot understand Christ if we do not believe and accept "that of God" in each person. "If Christ is born a thousand times in Bethlehem / And not in you / You remain still eternally lost," writes Angelus Silesius. To the question "Am I Jesus?" the answer can only be: "Yes, why shouldn't I be?"

I want to mention a second kind of modern inquiry into the role of Jesus. Once when I was preparing for Christmas, an American non-Christian woman asked me: "What is so special about Christmas? That a man comes into the world and regards himself as God—what's new about that?" In this remark there are two important critiques of the Christianity that has been handed down. One is a critique of patriarchy, the other of its hero worship. The main lie of patriarchy consists in confusing man with human being. Many have still not yet understood that the likeness of God in the Bible was not a man, Adam, but two human beings, Adam and Eve. According to this religion, therefore, God's characteristics must be just as feminine as masculine. Would Jesus have come to divert us from this truth? Would he want to give his blessing to the adulation of men and sanctify three male symbols in the name of "Father, Son and Spirit"?

Yet even this critique of the theology and doctrine of Jesus thinks "from above." The real Jesus in the gospels did not regard himself as God unless perhaps in the sense of the mystics, to which I just alluded. Jesus was a devout Jew who lived and spoke out of the power of God. He did not use his consciousness of God to hold himself up as something better, to let himself be served, to shove himself into the foreground. He was not equipped with miraculous powers that always functioned; in Nazareth, where no one believed in him, he was not able to heal. It was no easier for him to believe in God than it is for us. He did not inherit any psychological lead.

But within the critique of the man who comes into the world and regards himself as God there lies still another question which can be called that regarding christolatry, or idolizing of Christ. Why do we need heroes, gurus, wise men, or leaders anyhow? How is someone who lived two thousand years ago supposed to be the decisive occurrence for everyone, those who live later and, in many speculations about Christ, also those who lived earlier? Do we really need a savior, a king, a conqueror, a redeemer? Someone who does everything that we cannot, who loves when we can no longer love, hopes when we give up, lives when we die? This question is difficult to answer, and I believe in fact that we need more for living than just ourselves. The individualism which lies behind the question must be criticized. But again the tradition of a Christology from above is more of an impediment. We do not need another conqueror, judge, or hero. Nor is a redeemer needed if the word means that some overpowering person transplants me out of the miserable position in which I find myself into a good, unscathed other world without my cooperation. These caricatures of being saved through Christ surely cannot be what is intended!

To redeem in the Bible amounts to the same as to liberate or save or heal. Christ is not the superhero who suddenly and magically makes cancer or nuclear weapons go away. But he does free us from the fear of being possessed by evil, and he heals by taking away our anxiety, which blocks our healing power. To redeem means to set free the power of God, "that of God" in us; therefore the redeemed are those who insist on their human dignity. "When I get to heaven," sang the black slaves in the South, "then I'm going to run around freely everywhere; no one will throw me out." The liberating Christ of these people kept their human dignity, their hunger and thirst for righteousness alive.

The goal of the Christian religion is not the idolizing of Christ, not christolatry, but that we all "are in Christ," as the mystical expression goes, that we have a part in the life of Christ. This savior is a wounded healer, and he heals so that we may become as he is. Be as he is, laugh as he laughs, weep as he weeps. Heal the sick, even those who without knowing it have contracted the great neuroses of our society, who know no mercy with themselves and their children when they consent to the nuclear state and technologies inimical to life. To feed the hungry means to do away with militarism. To bless the children means to leave the trees standing for them.

Christolatry is the opposite of what it means to be "in Christ." Søren Kierkegaard practiced this distinction between those who esteem Christ and those who follow him. If I esteem him then I lift him ever higher and have nothing to do with him; I use my admiration to keep myself free of Christ. He is big, I am dependent on him, yet I do not want to go his way. But if I try to follow him, then he never calls to me saying, "Leave well enough alone; you can't do anything anyway. I have already settled everything once for all time." His language is completely different from that of the dogmaticians: "Come along," he says, and that above all. "Come along into God's kingdom—to our home country, where no one is beaten, no one is thrown out and shoved away. Look and see," he says to me and shows how the lame begin to walk. He does not say, "Close your eyes; I'll do everything."

My relationship to Christ is thus not that of a personality cult à la Joseph Stalin or Adolf Hitler. I am with him on the way, but here I must more correctly say "we," because that corresponds to my experience of resistance and working for God's kingdom. We who get involved in him and regard his as the right way are with him on the way. We do not marvel; we go with him. He is our "first-born brother," as Paul says. Latin American devotion expresses this nicely: less is being said today about Christ the King (*Cristo rey*), and more about *compañero cristo*.

In a certain sense the word "Christ" thus expresses a collective meaning. If Jesus of Nazareth was the poor man from Galilee who was tortured to death, then Christ is that which cannot be destroyed, which came into the world with him and lives through us in him. When I say Christ, I always think also of Francis of Assisi and Hildegard of Bingen and Martin Luther King, Jr., and of Ita Ford, the American nun who was murdered in El Salvador—as well as of all resistance fighters who are sitting in prison today. Christ is a name which for me expresses solidarity, hence suffering with, struggling with. Christ is the mysterious power which was in Jesus and which continues on and sometimes makes us into "fools in Christ," who, without hope of success and without an objective, share life with others. Share bread, shelter, anxiety, and joy. Jesus' attitude toward life was that it cannot be possessed, hoarded, safeguarded. What we can do with life is to share it, pass it along, get it as a gift and give it on.

With this I am at a third inquiry from outside regarding the enthusiasm for Jesus which lives in the church as correctly understood. Once in a theological-political discussion I referred to Jesus, at which point an older man who had been silent up to this point entered in: "What do you want with this Jesus? He didn't accomplish anything! I have nothing at all against him, but he didn't succeed. He was killed, like many others before and after him. I don't understand why you want to follow him. Do you want to be on the cross, too?" This man was a skeptical, non-believing Jew. I tried to say: "The killing didn't completely work, as you see. He still lives here and now, too." But it was one of the conversations in which skepticism and faith, tangled up together, wrestle with each other without result.

Naturally my conversation partner was correct in his historically based skepticism. Not only was Jesus condemned and murdered at that time, but Christ still dies over and over again before our eyes. He has been buried in our churches, corrupted to the point of being unrecognizable within the political parties that decorate themselves with his name, and distorted in the symbols, like the sign of the cross, that have been used to murder the innocent. Yet I want to hold on to this Jesus in and with the community of believers. And actually I would like to win for him the three persons about whom I have written: the worker who says, "Am I Jesus?" the woman who despairs of the male management in the male church, and the Jewish skeptic for whom the course of history refutes Jesus and shows his plan a failure. Not because I consider the questions of these contemporaries wrong—I am just as distrustful of docetism and christolatry as they—but rather because this Jesus has a secret which makes him strong and has given me strength again and again. In what does this secret consist? Why can he not be killed either by his enemies or even by his friends?

Christian tradition has tried to formulate this mystery with the words "the Anointed of the Lord," "Messiah," "Son of God!" "God the Son"; and it has named Christ in a paradox "true man" and "true God" at the same time. But when we proceed from "true God," there is danger that we will lose the "true man." If, on the other hand, we think "from below," completely different things than "Messiah," "Lord," "Savior," and "Redeemer" become important. Then it is possible to see who this Jesus really was: the illegitimate son of a poor girl, a teenager; a worker who belonged to the landless; a poor man in every sense of the word, living among poor, insignificant people, a nobody from a provincial town; a crackpot who was "out of his mind," as his family decided; a subversive who was sought by the authorities; a political prisoner who was tortured and finally condemned to death. The picture which arises in this way from the actual social history of the gospels does not resemble the victor or judge who is crowned with signs of imperial power. It is more like the emaciated peasant of the great German Peasants' War, as Matthias Grünewald depicted Jesus. The mystery of Christ is the mystery of the suffering, the impoverished, the landless of the Third World, whom we in the rich lands sell into debtors' slavery for generations. Without this affiliation with the poor, without having taken up the fate of the poor to be arrested arbitrarily, interrogated meticulously, tortured and killed—as happens to the *campesinos* in Latin America, the textile workers in Taiwan or South Korea, the black children in Soweto and many other places—one cannot understand Jesus. One cannot hear the call, "Come follow me!" if one's ears are closed to the cry of the poor and their demands for justice.

In what does the mystery of Jesus consist? How can we name that which could and cannot be destroyed? I think that different times have necessarily coined different formulas in order to discover this contagious power in the midst of defeats and in despair. A christological formula that helps me was advanced by Dietrich Bonhoeffer. Bonhoeffer called Christ a "man for others." This is not meant as false selflessness, such as is often demanded of and forced upon women. This man-for-others could indeed say "I" in a tremendously provocative way, putting his "But I say to you . . ." against a tradition, pronouncing his "I am . . . the water of life, the light of the world." He meant God's water, he meant God's light. He let this light shine through himself, he did not hide it in the depths of his soul, he gave it out. He was the man-for-others because he was the man of God and knew himself to be so borne up by God that he did not fall out of God, not even when he felt himself abandoned by God. The old formula "true man" is rendered by Bonhoeffer as "man," whereas being "true God" is called by Bonhoeffer simply being there "for others," because God is for others the God of love. Thus the sentence, "Christ is the man for others," is the old christological formula "true God and true man" in contemporary speech which refers to God without using religious formulas. The man for others is the man after God's heart.

In the dark night of the cross, life, God's Spirit, of which we are also capable, was with him—in spite of his lack of success. There is a point in Christian understanding when the question of success has to take a back seat to that of truth. Thus I can—with the old skeptic—

doubt the success of Christ, but not his truth, which invites me to join him at his side. Thus we do not love this poor Jesus of Nazareth because he was victorious or left the world behind, but rather because his manner of being there as the man-for-others touches us to the bottom of our heart. Indeed that is the intent with us, too. "Love him who burns with love," one hymn reads. Every other reason, for example that he was God's Son, did many miracles, rose and will in the end be victorious, is too weak. The mystery of Jesus cannot be derived from God, but vice versa: his call, his "Come follow me!" or "Pick up your bed and walk!" draws us into God. Christ lets us see into God's heart. To believe the truth of the man-for-others and thus to take his God is the way of Christology from below.

IV

FRESH TAKES ON THE BODY OF CHRIST

By his resurrection from the dead, Jesus, as Paul says, became life-giving Spirit (1 Cor 15:45), the principle of life of his body which is the Church. As J. A. T. Robinson so well said, "One must be chary of speaking of the Body of Christ as merely a metaphor. Paul uses the analogy of the human body to elucidate his teaching that Christians form Christ's body. The analogy holds because they are in literal fact the risen organism of Christ's person in all its concrete reality."

In other words, the Christ is not simply the glorified Jesus, but the glorified Jesus animating his body which is the Church. Christ said to Paul, "Why do you persecute *me*?" (Acts 9:4) because the literal fact is that the Christ is composed of all the baptized. This means that Christ, in contrast to Jesus, is not male, or more exactly not exclusively male. Christ is quite accurately portrayed as black, old, Gentile, female, Asian, or Polish. Christ is inclusively all the baptized.

In baptism women, like men, put on Christ. But women do not thereby become male. Consequently, maleness, however constitutive of the historical Jesus, is in no way constitutive of "Christ-ness." If it were, women could not be baptized... Through baptism women share the identity of Jesus *as the Christ* in exactly the same way and to the same extent that men do. This theological fact points out again the heretical character of the attempt to make maleness a prerequisite for represent-ing the Christ in sacramental activity...

Sandra Schneiders, *Women and the Word* (New York: Paulist Press, 1986).

20

ENGENDERING CHRIST

Kwok Pui-lan (Hong Kong/USA)

When I was a doctoral student, I took a course entitled "Gospel Stories of Women" with Professor Elisabeth Schüssler Fiorenza. On a cold day in the spring of 1985, I went to her office to discuss my struggles in articulating an Asian feminist biblical hermeneutics. She anticipated my difficulties: my project, she said, would involve three paradigm shifts: first, from West to East; second, from male to female; third, from the middle class to the impoverished. It would take me many more years to understand the scope and depth of what she had told me that afternoon. It has been my privilege to have had Schüssler Fiorenza as mentor, friend, and colleague in the course of my intellectual journey. Together we have team-taught a course on feminist biblical interpretation, coedited a *Concilium* volume entitled *Women's Sacred Scriptures*,[1] and worked on many other projects. Currently, we serve as coeditors of the *Journal of Feminist Studies in Religion*, for which Schüssler Fiorenza served as cofounder. To pay tribute to her distinguished leadership in the fields of biblical hermeneutics and feminist theological and religious studies, I would like to reflect on the topic of "engendering Christ," taking into consideration Jesus and the politics of interpretation, an issue of central concern in her work.[2]

The year 1997 marked the end of 155 years of British rule over Hong Kong. The return of Hong Kong to China signified the closing of an important chapter of the British colonial era. In 1800 the British Empire consisted of 1.5 million square miles and 20 million people; by 1900 the Victorian empire was made up of 11 million square miles and about 390 million people.[3] From 1815 to 1914 European colonial domination expanded from 35 percent of the earth to about 85 percent of it.[4] As a postcolonial intellectual who was born in Hong Kong, I am interested in rethinking some of the categories of feminist theology, including the Bible, Jesus, sexuality, and "other religions," paying attention in so doing to the intersections of gender, race, class, culture, and colonialism in multiple ways.

POSTCOLONIAL FEMINIST RETHINKING OF JESUS/CHRIST

A postcolonial interpretation of Christ needs to push the boundaries and ask the following critical questions: How does belief in the uniqueness of Christ justify the superiority of Christianity and condone colonization as the "civilizing mission of the West," often seen as the "white man's burden"? Why did the image of Jesus sent by the missionaries look more like a white man with a straight nose and blue eyes than a Jewish man? How does the Aryan Christ contribute to the colonization of "the other" living outside Europe as well as the oppression of "the other" living inside Europe—the Jews? When feminist theologians such as Mary Daly and Rosemary Radford Ruether criticize the androcentric symbols of Christianity such as the maleness of Christ, why is it that only the gender of Jesus matters? What does Ruether's famous question, "Can a male savior save women?"[5] both reveal and suppress? In the liberation theological movements that emerged in the 1960s, why was the maleness of Christ revitalized to signify a "masculinist" liberator, without concomitant concerns about how such images might have marginalized women? What is at stake when the colonizers, the dominant theologians, and the Vatican all take for granted that the Christ-figure must be masculine? How has the masculinity of Jesus been constructed? Even if Jesus' masculinity is presupposed, why has Jesus' sexuality been regarded as taboo?

As these explosive questions indicate, a postcolonial female theologian cannot simply accept the dominant positions about Christology in mainline Christianity, and neither can she subscribe to white feminist or liberationist formulations without some serious rethinking. I believe the task of a critical theologian is not so much to provide answers as to raise new questions that have not been asked before or to point to new avenues of thought that may have been overlooked or suppressed. Indeed, the question of the gender of Christ has been so much a part of our common sense that "engendering Christ" has seldom been the substance of serious theological debate. Ruether's question, "Can a male savior save women?" implicitly consents to the fact that the savior is male, and the question then becomes what has a male savior to do with women. If we problematize the gender of the savior, what kind of questions will we ask?

To ask about the gender of Christ is to press on the discursive limits of sex, gender, and sexuality in Christianity. Such issues are at the heart of Christian symbolics. Since they are so powerful, they are often treated as taboo in Christian circles. In this essay I should like to experiment with thinking at the limits of conventional theology and listen to some of the emergent voices that are shaping the christological debate at the beginning of the new millennium. Sometimes, we need to get out of our comfort zone in order to encounter God anew and listen to the gentle voice of God coming from the whirlwind. It is often at the margin of our consciousness that something new can be discerned, which jolts us from our familiar habit of thinking. As postcolonial critic Homi Bhabha has pointed out, it is at the epistemological "limits" of some of the dominant and ethnocentric ideas that a range of other dissonant, and even dissident, histories and voices—of women, the colonized, and racial and sexual minority groups—can be heard.[6]

One of the most significant developments of liberation theology is that marginalized communities have begun to use their own cultural idioms and religious imaginations to articulate their own understanding of salvation and the role of Jesus Christ in the salvific process. Instead of a monolithic understanding of Christ as the liberator, a plurality of images of Jesus have been offered, including the Black Christ, Jesus the Crucified Guru, Jesus the Corn Mother, Jesus the Priest of *Han*, Jesus the Feminine *Shakti*, and Jesus the Sophia-God. Some of these images highlight the socioeconomic aspects of salvation, while others have more to do with its cultural-religious dimensions.

How can we, as theologians, begin to understand and theorize this seeming "sea of heteroglossia," as Mikhail Bakhtin would say, when people begin to use their own tongues and cultural idioms to speak about Christ? I think the concept of hybridity, as it has been vigorously debated among postcolonial theorists, offers some important pointers with which to think these issues through. First, hybridity is not simply the mixing of two languages or the juxtaposition of two cultures, as our liberal or "pluralistic" understanding presents it, as if the two were on equal footing. Rather, hybridity in postcolonial discourse deals specifically with the colonial authority and power of representation. As Homi Bhabha puts it: "Hybridity is a problematic of colonial representation and individuation that reverses the effects of the colonialist disavowal, so that other 'denied' knowledges enter upon the dominant discourse and estrange the basis of its authority—its rules of recognition."[7] Second, Stuart Hall and others have insisted that colonization is a double inscription process, affecting the metropolis as much as the colonies.[8] Thus, hybridity exposes the myths of cultural purity, monologic discourse, unitary enunciation, and collapse of difference that legitimize colonial authority. Third, hybridity destabilizes the frame of reference/ frame of mind which sees things as binary opposites: black and white, here and there, East and West, European and Native. It critiques rigid boundaries, challenges the construction of the center and the periphery, and speaks of "interstitial integrity."[9] The subtle, nuanced difference in between, the multidimensional temporalities, the pluriphonic voices of women and men, and the "fruitful ambiguity" offer new possibilities and open new space for creative scholarship and theological imagination.

JESUS / CHRIST AS HYBRID CONCEPT

The most hybridized concept in the Christian tradition is that of Jesus / Christ. The space between Jesus and Christ is unsettling and fluid, resisting easy categorization and closure. It is the "contact zone" or "borderland" between the human and the divine, the one and the many, the historical and the cosmological, the Jewish and the Hellenistic, the prophetic and the sacramental, the God of the conquerors and the God of the meek and the lowly. Jesus' question, "Who do you say that I am?" is an invitation for every Christian and local faith community to infuse that contact zone with new meanings, insights, and possibilities. The richness and vibrancy of the Christian community are diminished whenever the space between Jesus and Christ is fixed, whether, on the one hand, as a result of the need for doctrinal purity, the suppression of syncretism, or the fear of contamination from Native cultures, or, on the other hand, on account of historical positivism and its claims of objectivity and scientific truths about Jesus.

The images of Jesus/Christ presented in the New Testament are highly pluralistic and hybridized, emerging out of the intermingling of the cultures of Palestine, the Hellenistic Jewish diaspora, and the wider Hellenistic world. As George Soares-Prabhu, a biblical scholar from India, has noted:

New Testament christology is inclusive and pluriform. Every community evolves its own understanding of Jesus responding to its own cry for life. And because life changes christologies change too. The New Testament preserves all these christologies, without opting exclusively for any one among them, because it does not wish to offer us (as dogmatic theology pretends to do) a finished product, to be accepted unquestionably by all. Rather its pluralism indicates a christological open-endedness, inviting us to discover our own particular christology, that is, the specific significance of Jesus for our situation in the Third World today.[10]

However, such open-ended and fluid understanding of Christology became a threat to the expanding Roman Empire when imperial unity required some kind of doctrinal uniformity. Under political pressure and amid ecclesiastical rivalry, the early Christian councils sought to differentiate orthodoxy from heterodoxy. Yet it is important to remember that the christological formulae crafted in Nicaea, Ephesus, and Chalcedon were never accepted as normative by all Christians. These creedal and "orthodox" formulae never succeeded in silencing the debates or shutting out the voices of dissent. At a later stage, when missionaries promoted the interests of European empires and the United States through their so-called civilizing mission, their prepackaged and encapsulated Christ was also resisted and challenged. Bhabha relates an interesting story in this regard about how the Indians in the subcontinent could not understand the meaning of eating Jesus' body and drinking his blood because most of them were vegetarians.

One of the most important insights I have learned from postcolonial critics is that colonization is a double and mutually inscribing process. Much has been said about cultural hybridization in the colonies as a result of the forced imposition of European and American cultures onto others. Less attention has been paid to the equally profound hybridization going on in the metropolitan centers. In doing research on the relationship between Christology and the colonial imagination, I am fascinated by the fact that the quest for the historical Jesus always takes place in the metropolis. The quest for Jesus is a quest for cultural origin, national identity, and racial genealogy. The first quest could not have taken place without the new knowledge brought to Europe about the myths, cultures, and religions of the colonized peoples. Its epistemological framework was constructed out of a combination of Oriental philology, racist ideology, and Eurocentric study of other peoples' mythology and religions.

I have argued that the search for Jesus must be read against the search for "natives" who could be conquered.[11] The encounter with the natives created anxiety and necessitated the quest for European self-identity. David Friedrich Strauss's portrayal of Jesus as a hero, Ernest Renan's picture of him within French bourgeois culture, and the Anglo-Saxon Christ of social Darwinism represent examples of cultural hybridization, attempts to interpret the Christ symbol through the lenses of the culture of imperialism. Yet the ambivalence about one's origin and culture had to be concealed, split off, or displaced. These images of Jesus were thus offered as the results of the quest for scientific and objective truths, upon which the origin of Christianity could be established and the foundation of European civilization maintained.

However, the first quest for the historical Jesus took place not only in the search for the Native to colonize but also in the suppression of "the other" within—namely, the Jews. Jonathan Boyarin's work *A Storm from Paradise* has helped me to make the connection between colonialism, anti-Judaism, and feminism.[12] Susannah Heschel's important research on New Testament scholarship in nineteenth-century Germany has shown how the Jewishness of Jesus was downplayed by a variety of scholars who portrayed him as a rebel against Judaism, calling himself the Son of Man to avoid being associated with the Jews. Some even suggested that Jesus might not be Jewish in origin, while others actually tried to prove that Jesus was in fact an Aryan because he had come from Galilee rather than Judea. This Aryan Christianity wanted to distinguish itself from its Jewish roots and to justify the superiority of the Aryan race, following the racial theory current at the time.[13]

While the first quest took place in Europe, the newest quest has gathered momentum in the United States, as the United States is trying to create a Pax Americana. Because of the history of immigration, the natives are no longer outside but are already *inside* the metropolitan centers, and the dominant white culture does not know how to deal with the challenges of diversity and multiculturalism. The images of Jesus as the sage, the healer, the Spirit-filled person, promoted in the popular quest books, look much like the modern-day gurus in the age of self-help and New Age movements. Billed as the first interdisciplinary quest and the most scientific search for Jesus, this current quest may also be a displaced and repressed quest for white male identity at a time when the melting pot does not melt anymore. Stephen Moore has described this current quest for Jesus in a sarcastic way:

> Many of us have joined that manhunt for the Jew of Nazareth, many more of us cheering or yelling obscenities from the sidelines. Startled eyes turn as the hysterical Jesus suspects are dragged into the church by the triumphant band of scholars. To the dubious congregation in the pews, each Jesus seems more unlikely than the last. "Did you at any time claim to be the Christ, the Son of the living God?" each is asked in turn. "I did not," most of them reply.[14]

MARGINALIZED IMAGES OF JESUS/CHRIST

Theologians from marginalized communities have offered different images and understandings of Jesus/Christ, subverting the theological hegemony of Europe and white America and expressing little interest themselves in joining this manhunt for Jesus. I would like to discuss five such images that I find relevant to the topic of "engendering Christ": the Black Christ in the works of black and womanist theologians; Jesus as Corn Mother; Jesus as the Feminine *Shakti* in India; Jesus as the theological transvestite; and Jesus as the Bi/Christ. Afterwards, I will present a number of critical observations and reflections.

The Black Christ

The Black Christ became a concrete symbol of the civil rights and Black Power movements of the 1960s with the advent of the black consciousness era. In response to Malcolm X's challenges to Christianity as an oppressive religion in which black people worship a white Christ, black theologians formulated the hybridized concept of a Black Christ. The space between black and Christ has been hotly contested and debated among male black theologians, later joined by their womanist colleagues.

Albert Cleage, for example, advocated a literal blackness, arguing that Jesus of Nazareth was ethnically black.[15] James Cone opted for a symbolic blackness, for as he so eloquently puts it, "Christ is black, therefore, not because of some cultural or psychological need of black people, but because and only because Christ *really* enters into our world where the poor, the despised, and the black are, disclosing that he is with them."[16] More recently, Garth Kasimu Baker-Fletcher presents an even more hybridized version, with Jesus as an Afro-Asiatic Jew, and implores the black churches to affirm both Jesus' blackness and Jewishness.[17]

These black theologians have been challenged by their female counterparts, who claim that a one-dimensional focus on Jesus' racial and ethnic background is not sufficient as long as the maleness of Christ is left unexamined. The image of the Black Christ contests the power behind the symbol of the blue-eyed, pale-skinned Christ in order to restore the dignity and manhood of black men. The subjugated and enslaved black man wants to confront the white man's power, while preserving his male privilege intact. To understand Christ in the life and struggle of black women, womanist theologians insist that we must move beyond limiting the experience of Christ to the historical Jesus and risk seeing salvific acts in other persons and events. Jacquelyn Grant has no problem seeing Jesus in black women, and Kelly Brown Douglas states: "Christ can be seen in the face of a Sojourner Truth, a Harriet Tubman, or a Fannie Lou Hamer,"[18] as well as in male figures who help the entire black community to struggle for wholeness.

Trying to move beyond both androcentric and anthropocentric assumptions about the Black Christ, Karen Baker-Fletcher proposes a creation-centered Christology that focuses neither on color nor on race. For her, "Jesus is fully spirit and fully dust."[19] In her womanist eco-theological project, Jesus the incarnate, embodied in dust, reminds us of God's intimate relation to creation.

The Corn Mother

Similar to black and womanist theologians, George Tinker criticizes the oppression of white Christianity, its missionary conquest and its formulation of Jesus as Conqueror. He charges, "American Indian peoples were being co-opted into a cultural frame of reference that necessitated self-denial and assimilation to the language and social structures of the conqueror."[20] Instead of focusing on skin color, Tinker looks for symbolic and mythological structures in Indian culture to infuse new meanings into the understanding of Christ. In this regard he finds the preexistent Logos in the first chapter of the gospel of John helpful in bridging this mental and imaginative gap. Jesus is thus seen as one, albeit very powerful, occurrence of the Logos in human history. Consequently, American Indian people can add to Christianity's knowledge of salvation from their own experiences of healing throughout their history. Furthermore, Tinker argues that the Logos should not be construed as male, that the American Indian understanding of bi-gender duality entertains the possibility that Christ could be female. For him, therefore, the mythic image of the Corn Mother, whose suffering and self-sacrifice offer food and sustenance for her children, prevalent in many American Indian cultures, becomes a compelling image for Christ. This image, he further argues, overcomes anthropocentrism, for in dying she becomes identified with the earth. Reading John's gospel through Native eyes, Tinker powerfully asks: "Why should Indian people be coerced to give up God's unique self-disclosure to us? Why ought Indian people learn to identify after the fact with God's self-disclosure to some other people in a different place and time in a mythic tradition that is culturally strange and alienating?"[21]

The Feminine "Shakti"

While Tinker has recovered the mythic structure of Native people in the Americas, Asian feminist theologians articulate their understanding of Christ through a dialogue between Christian faith and Asian indigenous traditions and social contexts. Chung Hyun Kyung, for example, argues that theologians should shift their focus from institutional religions to people's religions, such as shamanism.[22] She points out that institutional dogmatic religions are usually male-centered and authoritarian, while people's religions may contain liberating elements that are expressions of their faith and daily struggles. She suggests that we listen to the people instead of turning to scripture and dogma as our primary source and data.

A concrete example of christological reformulation comes from India, where feminist theologians are reclaiming their cultural roots to understand the life and work of Christ. They have attached great importance to the Hindu concept of *Shakti*, the feminine principle that is the life energy of the universe. According to Aruna Gnanadason, *Shakti is* the source and substance of all things, pervading everything, and the creative principle of the universe.[23] The recovery of the feminine principle of *Shakti* has been crucial in ecological awareness in India, as is evident in the writings of noted scientist and ecologist Vandana Shiva.[24] For theologian Stella Baltazar, the transcended Christ can be imagined as the embodiment of the feminine principle, the *Shakti*, the energizer and vitalizer.[25] For her, it is a serious limitation to express the resurrected Christ in purely male or patriarchal terms. Using the Hindu concept of *Shakti*, the liberative potential of the cosmic Christ can then be expressed through the Indian cosmology of wholeness and interconnectedness.

The Theological Transvestite
My fourth example comes not from Christians who want to claim christological language on their terms but from a Jewish theologian who wants to "destabilize Christian theology and create a space of Jewish self-definition."[26] Susannah Heschel notes that the figure of Jesus stands at the boundary of Judaism and Christianity, so that the debate on the Jewishness of Jesus calls into question the self-understanding of both religions. Building on the insights of queer theory, she proposes to see Jesus as a theological transvestite. Just as the performative activity of a transvestite disrupts the easy categorization and identifiable essence of gender, the figure of Jesus destabilizes and questions the construction of boundary between Judaism and Christianity. She notes that there have been various attempts on the Jewish side to emphasize the Jewishness of Jesus and to deny that Jesus initiated a new religious movement. On the other hand, the historical quest for Jesus on the Protestant side tends to present an ahistorical Jesus by focusing on his uniqueness and his superior religious consciousness. Liberal theologians downplay Jewish influences on Jesus' teachings to safeguard the purity of Jesus as the ultimate cultural phallus for Western civilization. Heschel states, "As Jew and the first Christian, yet neither a Jew nor a Christian, Jesus is the ultimate

theological transvestite" that unsettles and queers the boundaries between Judaism and Christianity.[27]

It is interesting that Heschel does not spell out whether Jesus was a man who cross-dressed as a female or a woman who cross-dressed as a male. While she questions gender binarism in our thought patterns, her focus is not on the gender difference as it may apply to the Christ figure. Her work is based on the classical study of transvestites by Marjorie Garber, who suggests that the figure of the transvestite questions binary thinking and introduces the "third"—a mode of articulation, a way of describing a space of possibility.[28] Garber notes that the transvestite figure that does not seem "to be primarily concerned with gender difference or blurred gender indicates a *category crisis elsewhere,* an irresolvable conflict or epistemological crux that destabilizes binarity, and displaces the resulting discomfort onto a figure that already inhabits, indeed incarnates, the margin."[29] Unlike Eleanor McLaughlin, who uses Jesus as the transvestite to question gender binarism in support of women's ordination,[30] Heschel uses the transvestite figure to call into question *a category crisis elsewhere,* namely, the problematic and unsettling boundary between Judaism and Christianity.

Jesus as Bi/Christ

My last example comes from the provocative book *Indecent Theology* by Marcella Althaus-Reid, who grew up in Argentina and is teaching in Scotland.[31] With the argument that all theology is sexual, Althaus-Reid challenges theologians to come out from their sexual and theological closets. *Indecent Theology* argues that feminist theology has so far concentrated on gender and has rarely talked about sex and sexuality. While feminist and liberation theologies have emphasized the use of experience in theology, sexual stories have seldom been seen as data that could provide theological insights. Except in gay and lesbian theology, sexual theology has remained underdeveloped, marginalized, and has in fact been left in the closet of mainstream theology. Althaus-Reid counters that sexuality is not a middle-class concern, as it is often assumed to be, but is linked to the ways in which politics and economics are organized.

She contends that although liberation theology has shifted the theological subject to "the poor," it continues to share the masculinist and heterosexual assumptions of the dominant theology. As a result, most liberation theologians—male and female—support the sexual codification of both church and society. Likewise, Jesus is imagined to be a sexually safe celibate, while Mary assumes the role of the mother of the poor. The images of Christ and Mary that liberation theologians portray are decent and safe; these are images that will not disrupt conventional sexual norms. Jesus can be seen as a social radical, but only as an asexual or celibate figure. Althaus-Reid writes: "He has been dressed theologically as a heterosexually orientated (celibate) man(?)."[32] She offers a number of images for Christ in her book, one of which is that of a Bi/Christ. This Bi/Christ, for her, is not related to the sexual performances of Jesus but to two important points: people's sexual identity outside heterosexualism and "a pattern of thought for a larger Christ outside binary boundaries."[33]

CRITICAL OBSERVATIONS AND REFLECTIONS

I would now like to offer some observations and reflections of my own on the basis of these various attempts of de/reconstructing the symbol of Christ.

First, the notion of Jesus/Christ has been a very hybridized concept from the beginning, and, as Christianity has encountered diverse cultures, the formulations of Christology have continued to hybridize. There is no original or privileged understanding of Christ, whether at the beginning of the Christian religion or in the history of the church, that can be claimed as pure and foundational, not subject to the limitations of culture and history. The concept of hybridization may have advantages over the earlier notions of contextualization and indigenization, for the latter terms sometimes assume that there is a Christian essence to be transplanted, transposed, or indigenized in a foreign culture or context. Deconstructing the white and colonial constructs of Christ as hybrids allows marginalized communities to claim the authority to advance their own christological claims.

Second, there was an explosion of hybridized images of Jesus in the second half of the twentieth century because of the struggle for political independence and cultural identity of the formerly colonized and oppressed peoples. Thus, the Black Christ emerged in the Black Power movement, the Corn Mother in the struggle for sovereignty on the part of Native peoples, and the Feminine *Shakti* from the cultural and religious resources of Asian women. Each of these constructs critiques the mainstream and oppressive images of Christ yet draws from the biblical and theological traditions to imagine and speak about Christ in radically new ways. The identity formation of the marginalized group influences theologians' selection of data from the tradition as well as their work on particular facets of the notion of Christ. In effect: black male theologians focus on race and ethnicity; womanists explore the intersection of race, gender, and class; Tinker pays attention to mythic and symbolic structures; Asian women are interested in interreligious dialogue and mutual transformation.

As the understanding of the identity of a group becomes more fluid and diversified, a concomitant nuanced and diverse understanding of Christ emerges. This is most evident in the development of the notion of the Black Christ. In the beginning, blackness was reappropriated and embraced by black theologians in opposition to its disavowal and denigration by the white culture. When the notion of blackness was in danger of becoming essentialized to legitimate Afrocentrism and to exclude other viewpoints, black and womanist theologians infused the term with new meanings, and the image of the Black Christ became more nuanced and fluid. Similarly, Asian Christian women find that a rigid and stabilized differentiation between Asian religions and Christianity often works to support colonial power, and so they suggest a much more hybridized understanding of Jesus. The process of hybridization takes place not only between two cultures, languages, symbolic and mythic structures, but also, and increasingly, between divergent claims and identity formations within the same ethnic, religious, and cultural groupings.

Third, I suspect that one of the key debates concerning Christ will be in the interpretation of his passion and suffering. In her book *The Psychic Life of Power*, Judith Butler, a Jewish feminist theorist, has raised a poignant question in a different context: How can the subjection of a person become the most defining characteristic in the subject formation process?[34] Many white feminists have criticized the language of self-sacrifice and suffering in theories of atonement. Delores Williams has challenged the notion of the surrogate Christ and the focus on Jesus' death instead of on his life and ministry.[35] Yet, in the works of Grant, Brown Douglas, and Karen Baker-Fletcher, one finds renewed interest in exploring the relation between the suffering of black women and men and the suffering of Jesus. George Tinker also speaks of the important role of vicarious self-sacrifice in Native history and ceremonies. The suffering of the Corn Mother for the life of the community is at the heart of his reconstruction of Jesus. While we should not glorify suffering and senseless sacrifice, these theologians are looking for pastoral and theological insights to address the questions of suffering and healing that they see daily in their communities.

Fourth, in constructing the symbol of Christ, we have to guard against anti-Judaism, which has shaped much of the Christian imagination. The works of Judith Plaskow and Amy-Jill Levine have pointed to anti-Jewish tendencies in Christian feminist theology both in the

United States and in other parts of the world. They have asserted that Judaism is often presented as monolithically patriarchal as a negative foil, in order to show that Christianity is liberative for women or that Jesus was a feminist. Anti-Judaism was an integral part of the ideology undergirding empire building and the colonial expansion of Europe and was brought to the colonized world through the missionaries and theological educational institutions. It is also found in standard works and reference texts of the Bible used in the seminaries of the Third World. Some Third World feminist theologians have used the argument that Christianity "reformed" Judaism as a precursor to the argument that Christianity would also "transform" the patriarchal elements of their own cultures, without being conscious of the fact that such a statement may reinscribe both colonialist and anti-Jewish beliefs. Susannah Heschel's Jesus as a theological transvestite raises the question of the extent to which we need to attend to Jesus' Jewish identity when we transpose the Christ symbol into another cultural context. What are the implications of the deemphasis of Jesus' Jewishness when Jesus is interpreted as the Corn Mother, the feminine embodiment of *Shakti,* or seen in the images of the Black women?

Finally, colonialist representation and anti-Jewish ideology have much to do with gender and sexual stereotypes. In what way can an "indecent Christ"—that is, a Christ who challenges conventional norms of masculinity and heteronormativity—open new avenues for our thinking about Christ and salvation? Third World feminist theology has focused on sexual exploitation such as sex tourism, sexual discrimination in the church and in the workplace, and sexual taboos such as menstruation and pollution. Seldom have we written or imagined sexual stories as sources to think about Christ, as Althaus-Reid has suggested. Indeed, how can our deepest longings, intimate desires, and fantasies be resources for our knowing about Christ? How is the love of God related to our erotic connection with others and ourselves? Instead of talking constantly about the morality of sex, how can we recover the beautiful, the sublime, and the carnivalesque aspects of sex?

CONCLUDING COMMENT

I would like to conclude by sharing a powerful experience I had recently in Boston's Symphony Hall as I listened to a performance of Osvaldo Golijov's *La Pasión según San Marcos* (The Passion According to St. Mark). Sung in Spanish, the piece combined voice, strings and brass, drums and percussion, and Afro-Cuban dance. Golijov is Jewish, with a Central European heritage, and grew up in Argentina. What is most iconoclastic and nonconventional about the work is that the roles of Jesus, Pilate, Peter, and the people were sung by the soloists and the chorus without regard to numbers or gender. Thus, Jesus was sometimes a woman, sometimes a man, sometimes a group of voices, and sometimes a dancer. I found it deeply moving to hear a Latino female vocalist sing "Abba abba abba abba abba." These artists have ventured far ahead of us in their theological imagination. Why do we, theological faculty and students, lag so far behind and continue to find ourselves bound by the epistemological "limits" of our thinking about Christ?

Notes

1. Kwok Pui-lan and E. Schüssler Fiorenza, eds., *Women's Sacred Scriptures,* Concilium 1998/3 (London: SCM Press; Maryknoll, NY: Orbis, 1998).

2. This study is based on the Antoinette Brown Lecture I delivered at the Divinity School, Vanderbilt University, in March 2001. I thank the faculty and students for their warm reception.

3. S. P. Huntington, *The Clash of Civilizations and the Remaking of World Order* (New York: Simon & Schuster, 1996), 51.

4. E. W. Said, *Orientalism* (New York: Vintage Books, 1979), 41.

5. See R. Radford Ruether, *Sexism and God-Talk* (Boston: Beacon Press, 1985), 116–38.

6. H. K. Bhabha, *The Location of Culture* (London: Routledge, 1994), 4–5.

7. Ibid., 114.

8. S. Hall, "When Was 'the Postcolonial'? Thinking at the Limit," in *The Postcolonial Question: Common Skies, Divided Horizon,* ed. I. Chambers and L. Curti (New York: Routledge, 1996), 247.

9. R. Nakashima Brock, "Interstitial Integrity: Reflections toward an Asian American Woman's Theology," in *Introduction to Theology: Contemporary North American Perspectives,* ed. R. A. Badham (Louisville: Westminster John Knox Press, 1998), 183–96.

10. G. Soares-Prabhu, "The Jesus of Faith: A Christological Contribution to an Ecumenical Third World Spirituality," in *Spirituality of the Third World,* ed. K. C. Abraham and B. Mbuy-Beya (Maryknoll, NY: Orbis, 1994), 146.

11. Kwok Pui-lan, "Jesus/The Native: Biblical Studies from a Postcolonial Perspective," in *Teaching the Bible: The Discourses and Politics of Biblical Pedagogy,* ed. F. F. Segovia and M. A. Tolbert (Maryknoll, NY: Orbis, 1998), 75–80.

12. J. Boyarin, *A Storm from Paradise: The Politics of Jewish Memory* (Minneapolis: University of Minnesota Press, 1992).

13. S. Heschel, "The Image of Judaism in Nineteenth-Century Christian New Testament Scholarship in Germany," in *Jewish-Christian Encounter over the*

Centuries: Symbiosis, Prejudice, Holocaust, Dialogue, ed. M. Perry and F. M. Schweitzer (New York: Peter Lang, 1994), 215–40.

14. S. D. Moore, "Ugly Thought: On the Face and Physique of the Historical Jesus," in *Biblical Studies/Cultural Studies: The Third Sheffield Colloquium,* ed. J. C. Exum and S. D. Moore (Sheffield: Sheffield Academic Press, 1998), 378.

15. A. Cleage, *The Black Messiah* (Kansas City: Sheed & Ward, 1969), 42.

16. J. H. Cone, *God of the Oppressed* (New York: Seabury Press, 1975), 136.

17. K. Baker-Fletcher and G. K. Baker-Fletcher, *My Sister, My Brother: Womanist and Xodus God-Talk* (Maryknoll, NY: Orbis, 1997), 97–98.

18. K. Brown Douglas, *The Black Christ* (Maryknoll, NY: Orbis, 1994), 108.

19. Baker-Fletcher and Baker-Fletcher, *My Sister, My Brother,* 87.

20. G. Tinker, "Jesus, Corn Mother, and Conquest: Christology and Colonialism," in *Native American Religious Identity: Unforgotten Gods,* ed. J. Weaver (Maryknoll, NY: Orbis, 1998), 139.

21. Ibid., 152.

22. Chung Hyun Kyung, "Asian Christologies and People's Religions," *Voices from the Third World* 19, no. 1 (1996): 214–27.

23. A. Gnanadason, "Toward a Feminist Eco-Theology for India," in *Women Healing Earth,* ed. R. Radford Ruether (Maryknoll, NY: Orbis Books, 1996), 75.

24. V. Shiva, *Staying Alive: Women, Ecology and Development* (London: Zed Books, 1989).

25. S. Baltazar, "Domestic Violence in Indian Perspective," in *Women Resisting Violence: Spirituality for Life,* ed. M. J. Mananzan et al. (Maryknoll, NY: Orbis, 1996), 64.

26. S. Heschel, "Jesus as a Theological Transvestite," in *Judaism since Gender,* ed. M. Peskowitz and L. Levitt (New York: Routledge, 1997), 188–97.

27. Ibid., 194.

28. M. Garber, *Vested Interests: Cross-Dressing and Cultural Anxiety* (New York: Routledge, 1992), 11.

29. Ibid., 17.

30. E. McLaughlin, "Feminist Christologies: Re-Dressing the Tradition," in *Reconstructing the Christ Symbol: Essays in Feminist Christology,* ed. M. Stevens (New York: Paulist Press, 1993), 138–42.

31. M. Althaus-Reid, *Indecent Theology: Theological Perversions in Sex, Gender and Politics* (London: Routledge, 2000).

32. Ibid., 114.

33. Ibid., 117.

34. J. Butler, *The Psychic Life of Power: Theories in Subjection* (Stanford: Stanford University Press, 1997).

35. D. S. Williams, "Black Women's Surrogacy Experience and the Christian Notion of Redemption," in *After Patriarchy: Feminist Transformations of the World Religions,* ed. P. M. Cooey, W. R. Eakin, and J. B. McDaniel (Maryknoll, NY: Orbis, 1991), 1–14. [Note that the article also appears in this volume as chapter 16, p. 199.]

21

MARKING THE BODY OF JESUS, THE BODY OF CHRIST

M. Shawn Copeland (USA)

In the beginning was the Word, and the Word was with God,
and the Word was God . . . And the Word became flesh and lived among us.
(John 1:14)

The Word of God assumed humanity that we might become [like] God.
(Athanasius)

Focus on the body, on flesh, is no novelty in theology. Christian teaching long has struggled to understand and interpret the truth that the eternal Word, the *Logos*, became flesh, became the bodily, concrete, marked, historical being, Jesus of Nazareth; that Jesus died, rather than betray his mission, his love for God and for human beings; that fidelity, integrity, and love were vindicated, and his crucified body was raised glorious from the dead. This teaching promotes the value and significance of the body, which is never to be disregarded or treated with contempt.

Yet history shows how brutally and easily the value and significance of the body has been undermined. For bodies are marked, that is, made individual, particular, different, and vivid through race, sex and gender, sexuality, and culture. These marks delight as much as they unnerve. They impose limitation: some insinuate exclusion, others inclusion. Often, the body's marks become more complex through creolization, *mestizaje*, and hybridity. In every instance the marked body denotes a "boundary" that matters. In a finite and sinful context, some unnerved historical human beings violate in multiple vicious ways the marked bodies of others. Such violence overlooks just how these bodily marks ground intelligence, discovery, beauty, and joy; enable apprehension and response to sensible experience; and shape culture, society, and religion. Such violence ignores the ways in which society and religion in turn shape our bodies.

In theology the body is a contested site—ambiguous and sacred, wounded and creative, malleable and resistant—disclosing and mediating "more." Given the view of Christian faith that when God desires to manifest the divine presence, God does so in human flesh, the body can never be simply one element among others in theological reflection. Yet any formulation that takes body and body marks seriously risks absolutizing or fetishizing what can be seen (race and sex), constructed (gender), represented (sexuality), expressed (culture), and regulated (social order). Moreover, such attention to concrete, specific, nonetheless accidental, characteristics also risks fragmenting the human being. What makes taking that risk imperative, however, is the location and condition of bodies in empire. What makes such risk obligatory is that the body of Jesus of Nazareth, the Word made flesh, was subjugated in empire. In memory of his body, in memory of the victims of empire, in the service of life and love, theology must protest any imperial word that dismisses his body and seeks the de-creation of human bodies.

Three major sections follow. In the first, empire forms a principal context for thinking about the marked, i.e., raced, sexed, gendered, regulated body of Jesus of Nazareth. The second section considers marked bodies ensnared in an imperial order, in particular homosexual bodies, and points to the difference that embracing those bodies might make to the body of Christ. Finally, in order to be worthy of his name in which it gathers, the church cannot but open its heart and embrace those bodies that empire abuses, negates, and crucifies. Thus, the third section calls for a (re)marking of the flesh of the church.

JESUS AND EMPIRE

Jesus of Nazareth was born and died in subjugation to the Roman Empire. His flesh, his body, was and remains marked by race, gender, culture, and religion: he was a practicing Jew in a territory controlled by Roman political, military, and economic forces. His flesh also was and remains marked by sex, gender, and sexuality: he was male and, although we cannot speak about his sexual orientation, tradition assumes his heterosexuality.

Under the reign of Rome, Jesus in his body knew refugee status, occupation and colonization, social regulation and control. His life played out amid the breakdowns "in the social relationships and political conditions that prevailed in Jewish Palestine under Roman and

Herodian rule": military intimidation, exploitive taxation, displacement from ancestral lands, brutality as a means of control.[1] His mission cannot be understood apart from the palpable tension between resistance to empire and desire for *basileia tou theou*, the reign of God. Note how at the center of his praxis were the bodies of common people, peasants, economic and political refugees, the poor and destitute. They were the subjects of his compassionate care: children, women, and men who were materially impoverished as well as those who were socially and religiously marginalized or were physically disabled (the blind, paralyzed, palsied, deaf, lepers); those who had lost land to indebtedness, who were displaced through military occupation or religious corruption; those who were possessed and broken in spirit from ostracism and persecution.

Jesus did not shun or despise these women and men; he put his body where they were. He handled, touched, and embraced their marked bodies. He befriended them, not "to show his compassion in a detached, old-fashioned teaching mode," as Marcella Althaus-Reid observes, but in recognition that they were human beings like anyone else, at times with great troubles.[2] Through exorcisms and healings, men and women, shunned and isolated by demon possession or leprosy, hemorrhage or blindness, were restored to synagogue and family, kin and friends. Those lost to human conversation and interaction, physical and affective intimacy were found; those abandoned or hidden because of deformity were restored to family life.

Central to this mission was the audacious practice of the welcome table. Jesus ate and drank with sinners: tax collectors, who made the already hardscrabble life of peasants even more so; lepers, whose diseased bodies threatened the bodily boundaries of "others"; women, who were forced to sell their bodies for survival; women, who were accused of giving their bodies away in adultery. The parable of the Great Banquet (Luke 14:21–24, Matt 22:9–10) underscores the challenge this practice posed to social and religious conventions: "The host replaces the absent guests with anyone off the streets. But if one actually brought in *anyone off the street*, one could, in such a situation, have classes, sexes, and ranks all mixed up together. Anyone could be reclining next to anyone else, female next to male, free next to slave, socially high next to socially low, ritually pure next to ritually impure."[3]

Through his table practice Jesus acted out just how unrestricted neighbor love must be, just how much "other" bodies matter. The open table embodied egalitarianism, disrupted domination, and abolished the etiquette of empire. In the design of the reign of God, *all* are welcome. Jesus invites all who would follow him to abandon loyalties of class and station, family and kin, culture and nation in order to form God's people anew and, thus, to contest empire.

That Jesus carried out his passion for the reign of God precisely as a male human being raises another profound challenge to empire. This prophet from Nazareth had a human body; his was a male body; he had the genitals of a male human being. Through his preaching and practices, living and behavior, however, Jesus performed masculinity in ways that opposed patriarchal expressions of maleness through coercive power, control and exploitation of "other" bodies, exclusion, and violence. He confronted this system through lived example, intentionally choosing courage over conformity, moral conflict over acquiescence, and boldness over caution. Through his oppositional appropriation of masculinity, Jesus countered many gendered cultural expectations. He overturned the patriarchal family structure, releasing family members from their denotation as property of the male head of household. He stretched solidarity far beyond the bonds and ties of blood and marriage, insisting on love of enemies, of the poor, of the excluded, of the despised. He chose women as disciples and taught them as he taught the men, defending them against those who questioned, attacked, or belittled them. Overall Jesus' performance of masculinity was *kenotic*: he emptied himself of all that would subvert or stifle authentic human liberation. In these ways, his maleness stood as contradictory signification, undermining kyriarchy and its multiple forms of oppression.

A healthy appropriation of sexuality is crucial to generous, generative, and full living. A fully embodied spirituality calls for the integration of sexual energies and drives, rather than repression or even sublimation. Comfortable in his body, sexuality, and masculinity, Jesus lived out of a "creative interplay of both immanent and transcendent spiritual energies."[4] Understanding *eros* as these creative energies integrated into a dynamic life force, we can say that Jesus had an eros for others; he gave his body, his very self to and for others, to and for the Other. Jesus lived out, and lived out of a fully embodied spirituality, an *eros*. In spite of themselves, the suspicious, the timid, the broken-hearted were attracted to his energy and joy. In spite of themselves, the arrogant, the smug, the self-satisfied were drawn to his authority and knowledge. In spite of themselves, hesitant men and women felt intense hope at sharing his struggle for the reign of God. Children, women, and men were attracted to his eros, and found themselves lifted up, made whole and new, open to others.

Jesus of Nazareth is the measure or standard for our exercise of erotic power and freedom in the service of the reign of God and against empire. He is the clearest example of what it means to identify with children and women and men who are poor, excluded, and despised; to take their side in the struggle for life—no matter the cost. Through his body marked, made individual, particular, and vivid through race, gender, sexuality, religious practice, and culture, he mediates the gracious gift given and the gracious giving gift. His incarnation, which makes the Infinite God present, disrupts every pleasure of hierarchy, economy, cultural domination, racial violence, gender oppression, and abuse of sexual others. Through his body, his flesh and blood, Jesus of Nazareth offers us a new and compelling way of being God's people even as we reside in a new globalizing imperial order.

THE BODY IN THE NEW IMPERIAL (DIS)ORDER

Insofar as race and gender are co-constitutive in today's empire created by globalization, they are governed by political and economic displays of power; sexuality in this empire is particularly subjugated through commercial exchange. Red, brown, yellow, poorwhite, and black female bodies, violated and "occupied" in empire-building, poached in the process of globalization, function as exotic and standard commodities for trafficking and sex tourism, pornographic fantasy and sadomasochistic spectacle. Red, brown, yellow, and, especially black male bodies lynched and castrated in empire-building, mechanized in the process of globalization, now are caricatured as "sexually aggressive, violent, animalistic."[5] Empire's eager debasement of black flesh robs *all* human persons of healthy, dignified, and generative sexual expression. For in empire, the primary function of sex no longer entails human communication, embrace, and intimacy (not even procreation), but the heterosexual service of white male privilege. Sex is amusement; its imperial purposes are distraction, entertainment, dissipation.

Thus, homosexuality in empire undergoes particularly intense opprobrium. Empire entices and intimidates its *ordinary* subjects, and, perhaps especially, its most wretched subjects, to react to gay and lesbian people with panic, loathing, and violence (malevolent homophobia); empire permits its *privileged* subjects to respond with curiosity, experimentation, and tokenism (benign homophobia). In empire, self-disclosure and self-disclosive acts by gay and lesbian people are penalized by repression, expulsion, and sometimes death. The vulnerability and marginality of gay and lesbian people makes a claim on the body of Jesus of Nazareth, on the body of Christ.

Catholic Church Teaching

Catholic Church teaching on sex and sexuality manifests ambivalence and disquiet toward the body—female and homosexual bodies, in particular. Church teaching signals a preference for celibacy and promotes marriage chiefly as a means for procreation. Certainly, church teaching acknowledges the presence of gay and lesbian persons, accords them equal human dignity with heterosexual persons, and urges pastoral compassion in their regard.[6] Yet that teaching does little to contest the use and abuse of gay and lesbian people in empire. Church teaching distinguishes homosexual orientation from homosexual activity, and deems the latter "intrinsically disordered."[7] Homosexual acts are deemed contrary to the natural law, and the *Catechism of the Catholic Church* declares that such acts "close the sexual act to the gift of life [and] do not proceed from a genuine affective and sexual complementarity" (#2357). This teaching admonishes gays and lesbians to repress or sacrifice their sexual orientation, to relinquish genital expression, to deny their bodies and their selves. But, if the body is a sacrament, if it is the concrete medium through which persons realize themselves interdependently in the world and in freedom in Christ, then, on Catholic teaching, in and through (genital) bodily expression, gays and lesbians are compelled to render themselves disordered. For on Catholic teaching, the condition of homosexuality constitutes a transgression that approximates ontological status. Can the (artificial) distinction between orientation and act (really) be upheld? What are gays and lesbians to do with their bodies, their selves?

Consider the response of *Homosexualitatis problema* to these questions:

> Fundamentally [homosexuals] are called to enact the will of God in their life by joining whatever sufferings and difficulties they experience in virtue of their condition to the sacrifice of the Lord's Cross. That Cross, for the believer, is a fruitful sacrifice since from that death come life and redemption. While any call to carry the Cross or to understand a Christian's suffering in this way will predictably be met with bitter ridicule by some, it should be remembered that this is the way to eternal life for "all" who follow Christ.
>
> [The Cross] is easily misunderstood, however, if it is merely seen as a pointless effort at self-denial. The Cross is a denial of self, but in service to the will of God himself who makes life

come from death and empowers those who trust in him to practice virtue in place of vice.

To celebrate the Paschal Mystery, it is necessary to let that Mystery become imprinted in the fabric of daily life. To refuse to sacrifice one's own will in obedience to the will of the Lord is effectively to prevent salvation. Just as the Cross was central to the expression of God's redemptive love for us in Jesus, so the conformity of the self-denial of homosexual men and women with the sacrifice of the Lord will constitute for them a source of self-giving which will save them from a way of life which constantly threatens to destroy them.

Christians who are homosexual are called, as all of us are, to a chaste life. As they dedicate their lives to understanding the nature of God's personal call to them, they will be able to celebrate the Sacrament of Penance more faithfully and receive the Lord's grace so freely offered there in order to convert their lives more fully to his Way. (#12)

This is stern counsel: It calls for embrace of the cross, for bodily (sexual) asceticism, self-denial, and imposes strict abstinence. In a carefully argued analysis of the document, Paul Crowley affirms the meaningfulness of the cross not only for gay and lesbian people, but for *all* Christians since the cross is *the* condition of discipleship. Crowley rightly objects to the peculiar application of "crucified living" (enforced abstinence) to the (sexual) fulfillment of gays and lesbians. With regard to the last sentences quoted above, Crowley points out, "While penance is mentioned here as an aid to gay persons in attaining a chaste life, no mention is made of the graces accruing from one's baptism or from the life of the Eucharist."[8]

Regarding the command of abstinence, Xavier Seubert reasons that "to prescribe, in advance, abstinence and celibacy for the homosexual person simply because the person is homosexual is to say that, as it is, homosexual bodily existence stands outside the sacramental transformation to which all creation is called in Christ."[9] The writing of *Homosexualitatis problema* surely was motivated by deep pastoral concern. But it rings with what James Alison describes as a reproachful sanctioning ecclesiastical voice, which commands: "Love and do not love, be and do not be." He concludes: "The voice of God has been presented as a double bind, which is actually far more dangerous than a simple message of hate, since it destabilizes being into annihilation, and thinks that annihilation to be a good thing."[10] Church teaching repels gay and lesbian (anti)bodies to the periphery of the ecclesial body, and may well disclose just how afraid the church may be of the body of Jesus of Nazareth.

Moral theologian Stephen J. Pope calls the magisterium's teaching about homosexual orientation "powerfully stigmatizing and dehumanizing." This teaching, he continues,

> is also at least tacitly, if not explicitly, liable to be used to support exactly the kinds of unjust discrimination that the Church has repeatedly condemned. Describing someone's sexual identity as "gravely disordered" would seem to arouse suspicion, mistrust, and alienation...One can understand why observers conclude that the magisterium's teaching about homosexuality stands in tension with its affirmation that each gay person is created in the *imago Dei*.[11]

Church teaching on homosexuality exposes us to the manipulation of agents of empire, and coaxes our collusion in opposing and punishing gay and lesbian people who refuse to internalize homophobia and who live their lives without self-censorship. This teaching feeds innuendo and panic; it nudges us to discipline the body's phrasing and comportment, the curiosity and play of our children; it disturbs our families and relationships; it rewards our disingenuousness as we praise, then, mock women and men whose talents enrich our daily lives and weekly worship. Seubert poses a grave critique, one that incriminates the very mystery of the church: the "denial of the homosexual body as this group's basis of spiritual, relational, historical experience is tantamount to impeding access to the reality of Christ in a certain moment of human history."[12] This charge brings the church much too close to betraying the great mystery of love that suffuses it and stirs up continually a longing to realize itself as the marked flesh of Christ.

This situation provokes a most poignant, most indecent question, "Can Jesus of Nazareth be an option for gays and lesbians?" This question uncovers the pain, anguish, and anger that many gays and lesbians feel as we thwart their desire to follow Jesus of Nazareth, to realize themselves in his image. This question springs from "the deep-seated feeling among many gays and lesbians that Jesus Christ is not an option for them, that he, as the embodied representative of God, hates them, and that they have no place in either Christ's church or the kingdom of God he announced during his earthy ministry.

If Jesus of Nazareth, the Christ of God, cannot be an option for gays and lesbians, then he cannot be an option. An adequate response to this concern requires a different christological interpretation, one in which we *all* may recognize, love, and realize our bodyselves as his own flesh, as the body of Christ.

Marking the (Queer) Flesh of Christ

The words "queer" and "Christ" form a necessary if shocking, perhaps, even "obscene" conjunction. By inscribing a queer mark on the flesh of Christ, I *neither* propose *nor* insinuate that Jesus Christ was homosexual. By inscribing a "queer" mark, I recognize that this mark poses epistemological challenges for theology: Have we turned the (male) body of Christ into a fetish or idol? In an effort to discipline *eros*, have we disregarded "God's proto-erotic desire for us"?[13] Can a Christology incorporate all the dimensions of corporality?

These questions target some of the discursive limits of sex, gender, and sexuality in Christianity and disturb cherished symbols. Just as a black Christ heals the anthropological impoverishment of black bodies, so too a "queer" Christ heals the anthropological impoverishment of homosexual bodies. Because Jesus of Nazareth declared himself with and for others—the poor, excluded, and despised—and offered a new "way" and new freedom to *all* who would hear and follow him, we may be confident that the Christ of our faith *is* for gay and lesbian people. Conversely, if the risen Christ cannot identify with gay and lesbian people, then the gospel announces no good news and the reign of God presents no real alternative to the reign of sin. Only an *ekklesia* that follows Jesus of Nazareth in (re)marking its flesh as "queer" as his own, may set a welcome table in the household of God.

Robert Goss takes the experience of homophobic oppression of homosexual bodies in culture, society, and church as a starting point for a "queer" christological reflection. He grounds this articulation in the "generative matrix" of the *basileia* praxis of Jesus and in the real suffering of gay and lesbian people. The immanent and transcendent scope of that praxis allows Goss to detach the radical truth of Jesus Christ from all forms of hegemony and ideology—whether cultural, social, ecclesiastical, biblical, or theological—that might seek to master Infinite God present among us. Further, he constructs a "queer" biblical hermeneutics through which to unmask and discredit any heretical use of the Hebrew and Christian scriptures to justify bigotry and violence against gay and lesbian people. Goss challenges the abusive use of the cross to justify explicit or implicit oppression and violence against gay and lesbian people as well as gay and lesbian acquiescence to interiorized oppression.

The cross symbolizes the political infrastructure of homophobic practice and oppression. It symbolizes the terror of internalized homophobia that has led to the closeted invisibility of gay and lesbian people. It indicates the brutal silencing, the hate crimes, the systemic violence perpetuated against us. The cross now belongs to us. We have been crucified.[14]

Crucifixion was the response of imperial power to Jesus' "*basileia* solidarity with the poor, the outcast, the sinner, the socially dysfunctional, and the sexually oppressed." The death of Jesus "shapes the cross into a symbol of struggle for queer liberation" and Easter becomes the hope and fulfillment of that struggle. "From the perspective of Easter…God identifies with the suffering and death of Jesus at the hands of a political system of oppression. For gay and lesbian Christians, Easter becomes the event at which God says no to homophobic violence and sexual oppression…On Easter, God made Jesus queer in his solidarity with us. In other words, Jesus 'came out of the closet' and became the 'queer' Christ…Jesus the Christ is queer by his solidarity with queers."[15]

All Christology is interpretation and, in these passages, Goss articulates an understanding of the cross and resurrection from the perspective of the homophobic suffering of gay and lesbian persons. His theological analysis turns on the scandal of the body particular: Jesus of Nazareth in all his marked particularity of race, gender, sex, culture, and religion teaches us the universal meaning of being human in the world. In Jesus, God critiques any imperial or ecclesiastical practice of body exclusion and control, sorrows at our obstinacy, and calls us all unceasingly to new practices of body inclusion and liberation. In Jesus, God manifests an eros for us *as we are* in our marked particularity of race, gender, sex, sexuality, culture. Note that christological reflection from the perspectives of black, Mexican-American, Asian, African, Latin American, feminist, *mujerista*, womanist make this same appeal to particularity.

In contrast to christological formulations that avoid or distort sexuality and sexual desire, Goss's work offers an opportunity to honor what Sarah Coakley calls the "profound entanglement of our human sexual desires and our desire for God."[16] A "queer" Christ is not scandalized by human desire, but liberates that desire from cloying commonsense satisfaction, misuse, and disrespect. This liberation begins in regard and esteem for the body and comes to proximate fulfillment in authentic love of the body, as authentic love and loving. Thus, a "queer" Christ embraces *all* our bodies passionately, revalorizes them as embodied mystery, and reorients sexual desire toward God's desire for us in and through our sexuality. This is not a matter of fitting God into our lives, but of fitting our lives into God. Homosexual and hetero-sexual persons are drawn by God's passionate love for us working in us to bring us into God's love. To live in and live out of this reorienta-tion demands refusal of isolating egoism, of body denial, and of what-ever betrays spiritual and bodily integrity. Moreover, living in and out of this reorientation leads us, even if fitfully, toward virtue; helps us to grow lovable and loving; and, in fulfillment, we are gift and gifted with and in love.

In his relationships with women and men, Jesus embodied open-ness, equality, and mutuality. In his suffering and death on the cross, he showed us the cost of integrity, when we live in freedom, in love, and in solidarity with others. In his resurrection, Jesus became the One in whom "God's erotic power"[17] releases bodily desire from the tomb of fear and loathing, the One who fructifies all loving exchange, the One who, in his risen body, quiets the restless yearning of our hearts.

(RE)MARKING THE FLESH OF THE CHURCH

If theological reflection on the body cannot ignore a Christ identified with black, brown, red, yellow, poorwhite, and queer folk, neither can it ignore reflection on "the flesh of the Church."[18] For, as Gregory of Nyssa tells us, whoever "sees the Church looks directly at Christ."[19] And as the flesh of the church is the flesh of Christ in every age, the flesh of the church is marked (as was his flesh) by race, sex, gender, sexuality, and culture. These marks differentiate and transgress, they unify and bind, but the flesh of Christ relativizes these marks in the flesh of the church. These marks may count, but the mark of Christ, the baptismal sign of the cross, counts for more, trumps all marks. Acts of justice-doing, empire critique, love, and solidarity mark us as his flesh made vivid leaven in our world.

In a letter to followers of "the way" at Corinth, Paul hands over the gift he has been given: "For I received from the Lord what I also deliv-ered to you, that the Lord Jesus on the night when he was betrayed took bread, and when he had given thanks, he broke it and said, 'This is my body which is for you.' Do this in remembrance of me" (1 Cor 11:23–24). This is the Tradition: the body of the Lord is handed over to us, handled by us as we feed one another. Further on Paul declares: "You are the body of Christ and individually members of it" (1 Cor 12:27). We are the body raised up by Christ for himself within human-ity; through us, the flesh of the crucified and resurrected Jesus is ex-tended through time and space.

In the very act of nourishing our flesh with his flesh, Christ makes us women and men new again, emboldens us to surrender position and privilege and power and wealth, to abolish all claims to racial and cultural superiority, to contradict repressive codes of gender formation and sexual orientation. In Christ, there is neither brown nor black, neither red nor white; in Christ, there is neither Creole nor *mestizo*, neither senator nor worker in the *maquiladoras*. In Christ, there is neither male nor female, neither gay/lesbian nor straight, neither heterosexual nor homosexual (after Gal 3:28). We are all transformed in Christ: *we are his very own flesh.*

If my sister or brother is not at the table, we are not the flesh of Christ. If my sister's mark of sexuality must be obscured, if my brother's mark of race must be disguised, if my sister's mark of culture must be repressed, then we are not the flesh of Christ. For, it is through and in Christ's own flesh that the "other" is my sister, is my brother; indeed, the "other" is me (*yo soy tu otro yo*). Unless our sisters and brothers are beside and with each of us, we are not the flesh of Christ. The sacramental aesthetics of Eucharist, the thankful living manifestation of God's image through particularly marked flesh, demands the vigorous display of difference in race and culture and tongue, gender and sex and sexuality. Again, Gregory of Nyssa: "The establishment of the Church is re-creation of the world. But it is only in the *union of all the particular members* that the beauty of Christ's Body is complete."[20]

The body of Jesus the Christ, both before and after his death, radically clarifies the meaning of be-ing embodied in the world. His love and praxis release the power of God's animating image and likeness in our red, brown, yellow, white, black bodies—our homosexual and heterosexual bodies, our HIV/AIDS infected bodies, our starving bodies, our prostituted bodies, our yearning bodies, our ill and infirm bodies, our young and old and joyous bodies. To stand silent before war and death, incarceration and torture, rape and queer-bashing, pain and disease, abuse of power and position is to be complicit with empire's sacrilegious anti-liturgy, which dislodges the table of the bread of life. That desiccated anti-liturgy hands us all over to consumption by the corrupt body of the market.

The only body capable of taking us *all* in as we are with all our different body marks—certainly, the mark of homosexuality—is the body of Christ. This taking us in, this in-corporation is akin to sublation, not erasure, not uniformity: the *basileia* praxis of Jesus draws us up to him. Our humble engagement in his praxis revalues our identities and differences, even as it preserves the integrity and significance of our body marks. At the same time, those very particular body marks are relativized, reoriented, and reappropriated under his sign, the sign of the cross. Thus, in solidarity and in love of others and the Other, we are (re)made and (re)marked as the flesh of Christ, as the flesh of his church.

To sum up: Jesus of Nazareth was born of people subjugated by the Roman Empire; an itinerant and charismatic preacher and teacher, his strenuous critique of oppressive structures, whether political or religious or cultural, along with his fearless love of ordinary people provoked those in authority to brand him a criminal. Jesus mediated God's presence among us through a body marked by race, gender, sex, sexuality, culture, and religion. His radical self-disclosure constitutes the paradigm for all human self-disclosure in contexts of empire and oppression, exclusion and alienation, slavery and death.

The body of Jesus provokes our interrogation of the new imperial deployment and debasement of bodies. The flesh of his church is multilayered. Pulling back layer after layer, we expose the suffering and groaning, outrage and hope of the victims of history. In them we glimpse the flesh of Christ and we are drawn by that eros, his radiant desire for us, and we too seek to imitate his incarnation of love of the Other, love of others. The body of Jesus of Nazareth impels us to place the bodies of the victims of history at the center of theology. His love calls us to break bonds imposed by imperial design, to imagine and grasp and realize ourselves as his own flesh, as the body of Christ.

Notes

1. Richard Horsley, *Jesus and Empire: The Kingdom of God and the New World Disorder* (Minneapolis: Fortress, 2003), 15.

2. Marcella Althaus-Reid, *Indecent Theology: Theological Perversions in Sex, Gender, and Politics* (London: Routledge, 2000), 113.

3. John Dominic Crossan, *Jesus: A Revolutionary Biography* (New York; Harper & Row, 1994), 68; author's emphasis.

4. Jorge N. Ferrer, "Embodied Spirituality, Now and Then," *Tikkun* (May/June 2006): 42.

5. Dwight Hopkins, "The Construction of the Black Male Body," in *Loving the Body: Black Religious Studies and the Erotic*, ed. Anthony Pinn and Dwight Hopkins (New York: Palgrave Macmillan, 2006), 186–88, 185.

6. *Homosexualitatis problema*, "Letter to All Catholic Bishops on the Pastoral Care of Homosexual Persons," (1/11/1986); *The Catechism of the Catholic Church*, #2358.

7. *Persona Humana*, "Declaration on Certain Questions Concerning Sexual Ethics," CDF, (12/29/1975) #8; see also, "Considerations Regarding Proposals to Give Legal Recognition to Unions Between Homosexual Persons," (03/28/2003).

8. Paul Crowley, *Unwanted Wisdom: Suffering, the Cross, and Hope* (New York: Continuum, 2005), 109; see his "Homosexuality and the Counsel of the Cross," *Theological Studies* 65, no. 3 (September 2004): 500–29.

9. Xavier John Seubert, "'But Do Not Use the Rotted Names': Theological Adequacy and Homosexuality," *Heythrop Journal* 40, no. 1 (January 1999): 74, n.23.

10. James Alison, *Faith Beyond Resentment: Fragments Catholic and Gay* (New York: Crossroad, 2001), 94.

11. Stephen J. Pope, "The Magisterium's Arguments against 'Same-Sex Marriage': An Ethical Analysis and Critique," *Theological Studies* 65, no. 3 (September 2004): 550.

12. Seubert, "But Do Not Use the Rotted Names," 65.

13. Sarah Coakley, "Living into the Mystery of the Holy Trinity: Trinity, Prayer and Sexuality," *Anglican Theological Review* 80, no. 2 (Spring 1998): 230. Coakley cautions, "No language of eros is safe from possible nefarious application..." (231).

14. Robert Goss, *Jesus Acted Up: A Gay and Lesbian Manifesto* (San Francisco: HarperCollins, 1993), 83.

15. Ibid., 84.

16. Coakley, "Living into the Mystery of the Holy Trinity," 224.

17. Goss, *Jesus Acted Up*, 169.

18. The phrase comes from Jean-Marie Tillard, *Flesh of the Church, Flesh of Christ: At the Source of the Ecclesiology of Communion* (Collegeville, MN: Pueblo/ Liturgical Press, 1992/2001).

19. Gregory of Nyssa, "On the Making of Man," 13, 1049B-1052A, in *Gregory of Nyssa, Dogmatic Treatises*, ed. Philip Schaff and Henry Wace (Grand Rapids, MI: William B. Eerdmans, 1979).

20. Ibid., emphasis mine.

22

CHRISTOLOGY BETWEEN
IDENTITY AND DIFFERENCE:
ON BEHALF OF A WORLD IN NEED

Jeannine Hill Fletcher (USA)

Christology, like all theology, is a profoundly human enterprise. At the intersection of the human and the divine, Jesus Christ stands as symbol through which Christians have affirmed their most intimate intuitions of God and insights into their own human existence. The ways Christians have thought about the person of Christ have been influenced by the wider social context and location of the individuals from whom the theological thinking emerged. Recognizing Christology as an ongoing process, Christians today are invited to return to the person of Jesus and find resources for human living. In the words of Kwok Pui-lan, Jesus Christ is the locus of a

> "contact zone" or "borderland" between the human and the divine, the one and the many, the historical and the cosmological ...Jesus' question, "Who do you say that I am?" is an invitation for every Christian and local faith community to infuse that contact zone with new meanings, insights and possibilities.[1]

In the project of Christology, Christians articulate anew an understanding of their identity in and through Christ.

Accepting the invitation to Christology and striving toward relevance for today, Christians must approach the biblical text and tradition with an awareness that this identity in Christ is situated in a complex world. Our current condition is constituted by globalization, where systems of travel, information, migration, and economics (among others) have compressed our world to make it "a single place."[2] These technologies and systems bring us into ever-greater contact with difference—different ideas, different worldviews, different ways of being human, and different religions. But the systems of globalization also diversely impact human beings, heightening conditions of inequality and injustice. Our world is in need of healing, a healing that must not be confined by the borders of identity. While Christians will look to the person of Christ as the symbolic identity marker under which they might bring forth a new humanity, the salvation found in Christ must transgress the boundaries of difference. With the biblical witness of the book of Revelation, "salvation is only possible after all dehumanizing powers are overcome and a 'new heaven and a new earth' has come into being, because salvation means not only the salvation of the soul but of the whole person."[3] Carrying on the Christian vision for a world in need, we might seek a Christology that enables care and concern across boundaries of difference. We need a Christology that recognizes that humans do not exist in individual isolation; we need a Christology that reflects and encourages our human relatedness. Such a Christology, for many theologians, is at the heart of the Christian vision. In the words of Tina Beattie:

> Christianity is essentially relational both in its proclamation of a Trinitarian God and in its celebration of the incarnation as an event that continuously reveals itself in the space of creative symbolic encounter between God, Mary, Christ and the Church. So the story of Christ is the story of Mary is the story of the Church is the story of humanity is the story of God, and the prismatic vision thus revealed cannot be adequately expressed by any one symbol in isolation from the rest. To recognize this means developing a theological perspective that goes beyond the narrow Christological focus, to a more encompassing vision of incarnation that incorporates all of creation, including the male and female bodies and the natural world.[4]

From out of the creative symbolic encounter of God, Mary, Christ, and Church, a Christology of relationality might emerge.

CHRISTOLOGY OF RELATIONALITY

A Christology of relationality might begin from current insights into the human condition. From the perspective of psychoanalysis, relationality is evidenced as a fundamental characteristic of our humanity from the earliest forms of human development. We enter this world dependent upon those who have preceded us, and we walk through this world in complex networks of care, dependence, and fragile solidarity. We learn our first patterns of relationality in relation to the one(s) who will serve as "mother" (whether this is a biological mother or another mother). The 'm/other' (whether mothers, or father, or fathers, or caregiver, or grandparent, or sibling) calls the child forth into being through relationship. While the child's individuality emerges from the simultaneous identification with the other/mother and the recognition of a "separate" self,[5] some psychoanalysts posit that the act of individuation is never complete separation. Instead, separation includes the internalization of that first m/other relationship as well: "The loss of the other whom one desires and loves is overcome through a specific act of identification that seeks to harbor the other within the very structure of the self."[6] In this visioning of human development, the self is never alone, but internalizes the relationships that are formative. Such suggestions about the nature of human selfhood return Christians to the story of scripture to recognize a new importance to Mary of Nazareth. Far from a mere conduit for bringing a savior into the world,[7] as the first primary relationship for the one who will come to be identified as savior, she constitutes his very self. In the gospel accounts, she is the one who cradles and shelters the helpless newborn (Luke 2:7) and who very soon after introduces him to Jewish sacred ritual in his presentation in the temple (Luke 2:21–39). Along with Joseph, she continues his religious education, for example, marking together the feast of Passover by journeying to Jerusalem (Luke 2:41). While an important role is played in the early years of life, Mary's role in helping to shape Jesus' self-understanding is implicit throughout in her role in the gospel accounts and continuing influence on his ministry. It is Mary who calls Jesus into public ministry in John's account of the wedding at Cana (John 2:1–11). Was it perhaps Mary who instilled in Jesus a love for the weakest, the child, as she had once given her promise of a life of care in her response to the annunciation? Was it she who shaped him to experience outrage at the misuse of monies in their exchange at the temple? Did he draw strength in his trust of God's promised reign as, at the crucifixion, he encountered his mother who stood by her commitment to God throughout her life? A Christology rooted in relationality recognizes Jesus' self-giving pattern fostered by those closest to him, and in this, Mary is key.

But since the self is not a static entity moving through the world from childhood onward, this dynamic development of the self is constituted not by the primary relationship alone, but through a wide variety of relationships. The ties we have with others "constitute a sense of self, compose who we are."[8] As feminist theologian Catherine Keller has articulated, "For if 'I' am partially constituted by you even as you partially constitute me, for better or for worse, that is if I flow into, in-fluence you as you in-fluence me, then my subjectivity describes itself as radically open-ended in time as well as space."[9] If what it means to be human is to be constituted by relationships, and we are in multiple relationships, a sense of the self in multiplicity emerges. In the words of Morwenna Griffiths, "Identity [is] constructed, reconstructed and negotiated in relationships of love, resistance, acceptance and rejection."[10] Using this lens to understand the narrative of the gospels, Jesus' self emerges in relation to friends, strangers, and even adversaries. For example, Jesus is called into a sense of self through his relationships with Martha and Mary of Bethany (Matt 26:6–13; Mark 14:3–9; Luke 7:36–50; 10:38–42; John 11:1–4; 12:1–8). In an interreligious exchange with the gentile woman of Syrophoenician origin, Jesus' mind is changed in the theological engagement through which she lays claim on him (Matt 15:21–28; Mark 7:24–30). In looking at the stories of Jesus through the lens of dynamic identity, we can imagine the way that his own understanding of himself and his mission was constituted by his own "creative, agential negotiation of the intersecting currents and competing loyalties" that ran through him.[11] Even one's adversaries call forth the development of one's own identity as a self. For example, it is when a lawyer challenges Jesus, interrogating him on the necessary requirements for a life of wholeness and eternal life, that Jesus indicates the heart of his teaching: Love God with all your heart, mind, and soul; and your neighbor as yourself (Luke 10:25–37). The entire persona, mission, and ministry of Jesus seems to embrace the communal nature of what it means to be human—embedded in relationships, called in care for the least, and fulfilled [in] a vision of human being and becoming *together*.

As those around him call Jesus forth into new enactments of himself and his mission, he simultaneously transforms and empowers those who follow him. The very calling of disciples to follow indicates that his mission was not solitary. His teachings engaged his hearers in creative revisioning that drew them into the parables he used as vehicles. Jesus' vision of a reign of God had in mind not the well-being of an individual before God, but a holistic well-being for all. And he called his disciples into a relationality that empowered them as well: they were constituted and empowered by their encounter with him and with one another. In Jesus' presence, the broken are made whole, and in the dynamic exchange of the community, those who follow Jesus are empowered to do likewise, as the Acts of the Apostles is full of stories of those who carried on Jesus' mission, as they continued to share in his life-restoring power. The salvation that is announced in

Jesus of Nazareth is not a singular salvation resting on one individual. The salvific vision of Jesus of Nazareth is enacted in his life and in the lives of those who follow him. The transformation of the world toward its fullness in justice and relationship is a process that discipleship enables in the many and diverse human beings who seek it. As Schüssler Fiorenza has reconstructed, "Sophia, the God of Jesus, wills the wholeness and humanity of everyone and therefore enables the Jesus movement to become a 'discipleship of equals.'"[12]

Portrayed as an adult in the gospel accounts, Jesus has longed for such a community embodying the vision of wholeness, response, and responsibility, and he sees himself in the role of mother: informing and being mutually informed by the community in which he is embedded. In the gospel of Luke, the words put on Jesus' lips envision him in the role of mother hen, longing to gather her children together as "a hen gathers her brood under her wings" (Luke 13:34). Jesus is shaped by those who mother him into being, *and* he himself takes on the role of mother. As he steps into the subject-position of "mother," he is not suddenly entering relationality; rather, the relationships with family, friends, and the wider social networks continue to impact his subjectivity. Yet, in mothering, one takes on a new pattern of relationality, learning new ways of being in the world and realizing new dimensions of the self as one takes on responsibility for another. Stepping into the mother role, what did Jesus learn about himself from those to whom he extended care? Perhaps the most powerful experience he claimed in adopting the subject-position "mother" is that he understood that what it means to be human is not, in fact, to be autonomous, self-directed, and free, but rather, to be willingly restrained by those relationships to which one has committed—to be willing to embrace one's own vulnerability in care for the vulnerable other. In the ultimate act of vulnerability, Jesus responds with his very life, refusing to compromise his countercultural vision, and being murdered at the hands of those who found such a vision threatening.

Continuing the pattern of mother care, early Christian writings envision Jesus' self-giving modeled on a lactating mother where the "milk of Christ" is spiritual nourishment.[13] This symbolism was taken up with enthusiasm during the Middle Ages as Caroline Walker Bynum introduces us to the little known medieval devotion to Jesus our Mother. Anselm of Canterbury (d. 1109) points to the image of Jesus as mother hen, confessing, "Truly, master, you are a mother."[14] And Bernard of Clairvaux (d. 1153) entreats his readers to seek in Christ's breasts the milk of healing, when he writes, "If you feel the sting of temptation... suck not so much the wounds as the breasts of the Crucified. He will be your mother, and you will be his son."[15]

Aelred of Rievaulx (d. 1167) similarly draws on the lactating imagery when he writes,

> On your altar let it be enough for you to have a representation of our Savior hanging on the cross; that will bring before your mind his Passion for you to imitate, his outspread arms will invite you to embrace him, his naked breasts will feed you with the milk of sweetness to console you.[16]

The image of Christ as breastfeeding mother draws in his own maternal relationship (and painted images of Mary breastfeeding will become popular a few centuries later).[17] Popular imagery of Christ employed this physical nurturance as metaphor for the divine self-giving that sustains humanity. Humanity suckles at the breasts of Christ as Christ gives himself for the lives of many, and Christians are called to carry on that mother role for a world in need. While an increasingly androcentric Christian tradition wrests the image of nursing away from the embodied experience of women as breast-feeders, it is only with the help of actual women's experiences of breast-feeding that the insight into Christ's mother role can be illuminated.[18]

RECOGNIZING CHRIST'S MOTHER-LOVE AS SACRIFICE

Self-giving love in the pattern of a breast-feeding mother can be understood at three o'clock in the morning, when for the 180th night in a row a mother stumbles from her sleep to answer the call of her crying child. There is little romance in this sleep-deprived selflessness. It is night after night after night after night after night after night after night. Around the globe, in every culture, at every moment in time, women emerge from their sleep—interrupted and silent—and care for a crying child. And, to be purposefully colloquial, it sucks. The theological language of self-sacrifice can glamorize the process of self-giving through an image of actions satisfying in themselves, or be glorified under the banner of the ultimacy of the giving in light of a supra-human ideal, or be constructed romantically in a mutual interdependence that is of benefit even to the one who sacrifices. But, self-giving at three in the morning is none of these: it is not glamorous, self-satisfying, supra-human, or rooted in mutuality. It is a plain old exhausting pattern of being depended upon. And the self-giving in history of breast-feeding women does not end when the sun comes up. It requires commitment all night and all day to giving of the self to the needs of the other. It is an impossible balance, but one which women who have chosen this (or economically are required to) find themselves pursuing. They stop what they are doing, bare their breast, and give of themselves. Or, sometimes, they simultaneously complete the tasks at hand with baby on breast. There are times, however, when the needs of the child demand more than a woman can give. She has given all that she has and is literally emptied. Giving of herself when the child wants more, she continues to offer comfort and suckle even when she has nothing left to give. And when her breasts are broken from the constant sucking, the child takes from her both blood and milk at the same time. Having committed to this course of action, she continues . . . a life depends upon it. The woman who has committed herself to nurturing her child in this way must follow through on the giving. And she herself is the gift. All that sustains the child has been produced within her, and all that can satisfy the needs of the other must come from within. There is no other real alternative. This is sacrifice. It is self-giving that empties the self with no necessary return.

This is the pattern of self-giving that is the choice of many women, but it is also a pattern that has enslaved women as wet nurses in countless contexts. Also, it is a pattern required for women in families where economic resources are scarce. Further, when women who can choose whether or not to breast-feed make the choice to do so, they can become trapped in a process of unequal caregiving, when partners or others in the community relinquish responsibilities under the presumption of it being the breast-feeding woman's responsibility to care for the child. There is danger, clearly, in holding up breast-feeding as yet another ideal to which women must adhere. And yet, my aim here is not to set up breast-feeding as the only option or the only manner of nurturing.[19] Rather, I'd like to use the experience of breast-feeding as one lens through which to understand the depth of theological meaning communicated in the images of Christ as nurturing mother. If Christ is imagined as a nursing mother, his style of giving is what hers is: it is day after day, every two or three hours—sometimes more frequently— being asked again to give even when it hurts and sometimes when there is nothing left to give. If Christians desire a world reconciled to God that reflects ideals of justice, the restoration of creation requires this kind of sacrifice. It requires self-giving that is not easy, that is not glamorous, that offers few immediate rewards and, at times, little satisfaction. When theologians describe Christians patterning their actions on Jesus' self-giving love, they sound the prophetic call of patterning ourselves toward this restoration of justice. When coupled with the imagery of humanity feeding from the divine breasts, we are offered a physical experience of what that sacrificial pattern entails. It entails round-the-clock attentiveness to the needs of the other. It requires self-giving that is self-emptying in a real sense. It demands a pattern of self-denial that puts the needs of the other before one's own. But just as the lactating mother requires nourishment to produce milk, so too must care be taken for one's own well-being. The pattern of self-giving love that is *Christa Lactans* consists of a lifestyle of giving, not in discrete acts of charity, but in the self-giving that nurtures others to become fully human themselves. That's what Christians are called to in the pattern of Jesus' self-giving love.

Framing Christ in the role of breast-feeding mother must also be joined with the remembered rejection of a narrowly constituted motherly role. While breast-feeding may give insight into the motherly care necessary for healing a broken world, it is the healing that is important, with breasts as illuminative, although not exclusive, vehicles.

> While he was saying this, a woman in the crowd raised her voice and said to him, "Blessed is the womb that bore you and the breasts that nursed you!" But he said, "Blessed rather are those who hear the word of God and obey it!" (Luke 11:27–28)

In contemplating the mother role of Jesus, the early communities also were critical of the socially constructed mother role in its limitations. For example, in the story of Jesus' response to the approach of his mother and his brothers, we see a concern for the narrow mother care that social constructions enable.

> Then his mother and his brothers came; and standing outside, they sent to him and called him. A crowd was sitting around him; and they said to him, "Your mother and your brothers and sisters are outside, asking for you." And he replied, "Who are my mother and my brothers?" And looking at those who sat around him, he said, "Here are my mother and my brothers! Whoever does the will of God is my brother and sister and mother." (Mark 3:31–35; see also Luke 8:19–20)

What appears to be an affront to the mother love of Jesus' own mother is a reminder that it is not mothers who bring about the healing of the world, but *mothering*. And this mothering must extend beyond the bounds of familial care: "Whoever loves son or daughter more than me is not worthy of me" (Matt 10:37). The transformative healing of the reign of God announced by Jesus is not available through the narrow confines of family-first relationships. Rather, the mother-love care for children and others must extend out into the community, the wider community, the global community.

The reclaiming of sacrifice for a world in need runs the danger long identified by feminist theology of patterns of a patriarchal outlook that demands the sacrifice of women to the detriment of self.[20] Certainly, this remains a live concern. But the mother care to which we are called is not about biology—whether the biology of she or he who is mother or the biology of the one receiving the care. The mother care of Christ expands beyond the bounds of biology to pour forth for a world in need. That is, it is not biological mothers who are called to sacrifice; we are all called to sacrifice. To operate as if the transformation of a world in need will come without cost is to ignore the material realities of an embodied condition in a globalized world. For Christians to be willing to participate in the sacrifice that hurts is to embrace the human condition of our own vulnerability. In the words of Judith Butler:

> We come into the world unknowing and dependent, and, to a certain degree, we remain that way... [I]nfancy constitutes a necessary dependency, one that we never fully leave behind. Bodies still must be apprehended as given over. Part of understanding the oppression of lives is precisely to understand that there is no way to argue away this condition of a primary vulnerability, of being given over to the touch of the other, even if, or precisely when, there is no other there, and no support for our lives. To counter oppression requires that one understand that lives are supported and maintained differentially, that there are radically different ways in which human physical vulnerability is distributed across the globe.[21]

The acceptance of the human condition of vulnerability and the recognition of the differential experience of this vulnerability call forth a response of the Christian mother love across boundaries for a world in need.

CHRISTOLOGY FOR A WORLD IN NEED: INTERRELIGIOUS SOLIDARITIES

In our global age, the mother love of Christians mothered by Christ must extend to the global community and be willing to cross religious borders. A story from a young Muslim woman engaged in interfaith solidarity resonates with the mother care of Jesus and the necessity for envisioning affinities that arise from our human condition, despite cultural and religious differences. This young Muslim was a resident of Jerusalem, and her outlook had been structured by the media's portrayal of Jews in the conflict of the Middle East, which grew to a hatred of Jews and a general distrust of any non-Muslims in her community. Although she lived and worked side-by-side with Jews, Christians, and people of the Druze faith, she described these working relationships as distant and filled with distrust. It was not until she found herself in the maternity ward's common nursery shortly after having given birth to her daughter that her experience of her neighbors of other faiths shifted from seeing them as "the enemy" to recognizing their common humanity. For around the room were new mothers of every religion represented in the region—women whose backgrounds placed them on opposing sides of the conflict, women from families who were enemies divided by their faiths. But as she sat in this nursery, exhausted from the pains of childbirth, holding her daughter in her arms while her daughter nursed at empty breasts, she had an insight.

She had just lived through months of physical transformation and physical sacrifice, through sickness and change in her public persona. After months of anticipation and preparation, and after hours of agony and pushing and pain, somehow she had brought a small new life into the world. This new life was utterly dependent upon her, completely vulnerable. And the young mother was vulnerable too, dependent upon some reality beyond herself as she waited for her milk to come in. Having chosen to breast-feed her newborn, in the first days of the baby's life she was helpless until the milk began to flow. She waited, as her child sometimes wailed, as her daughter lost ounces that felt like pounds. The new mother was exhausted, helpless, and vulnerable, as she could do nothing but wait.

For this young Muslim mother, this experience of her own vulnerable humanity—dependent on a force, a reality greater than herself—provided a foundation for recognizing the humanity of the other. And this young woman had the powerful realization that she shared with every single mother who surrounded her—the Christian, the Jew, the Druze—the desperate experience of waiting for her milk to come in. It was at this moment of profound realization of what connected this group as new mothers, a connection that was physical and embodied, that she recognized the common humanity of her neighbors of other faiths. This experience of connection with other new mothers transcended the boundaries of religion that had so long distanced her from her coworkers and neighbors in the conflict. It was this recognition of shared humanity through the particularity of being vulnerable as a new mother that led her to take part in an interreligious dialogue circle of women concerned for peacemaking in their city.

The subsequent dialogue among this young mother and her neighbors was not focused on "how rationally to convince someone from another tradition that yours is true."[22] Rather, their conversations developed out of a keen sense of the necessity to work together to protect the bodies of their sons and daughters, their husbands and parents. They talked about how each of them was vulnerable and how neighbors of diverse religious backgrounds might share the same physical space in a way that allowed for the fullest human flourishing. In the process, they drew on their religions to envision a way forward, but their primary focus was not to compare and contrast the diverse details of doctrine, but rather to preserve the integrity of vulnerable bodies in a location where human well-being was threatened daily.

In telling her story, the young woman provided a metaphor for the desperate search for a common foundation for peace refracted through the lens of motherhood. She closed her reflection with the following words:

> *We feed them milk, we feed them love,*
> *We feed them hatred,*
> *Whatever we feed them they will eat*
> *And they will become.*

In these words, we are broadened out from the circumscribed experience of women in the nursing ward to a symbolic representation of how each of us feeds the other, with maternal relationality as metaphor for the ongoing actions of women and men as we bring one another into being. We are all waiting for our milk to come in. We are all seeking the resources and the strength to sustain our world, our children, and future generations, in contexts divided by religious differences. Desperation arises from the sense of urgency that the earth and its inhabitants face in our times of limited resources, corporate greed, and national distrust. The metaphor of waiting for our milk to come in derives from one woman's embodied experience and is offered as a powerful metaphor through which women and men might share the experience of desperately wanting to be agents of sustenance and change in our religiously plural world.

If the Christian is fashioned on Christ as breast-feeding mother, s/he too is waiting for her milk to come in. As the twelfth-century vision held, "nothing is better fitted to serve as our mother than charity. These cherish and make us advance, feed us and nourish us, and refresh us with the milk of twofold affection: love, that is, for God and for neighbor."[23] And in our interreligious and globalized world, the neighbor to whom our care extends stands in need across religious boundaries. A Christology sufficient for a globalized world increasingly interconnected with religious difference and increasingly aware of the pervasiveness of injustice is a Christology that must stand on behalf of those in need. I am thinking with a hybridized Christ, a Christ-Christa who, having been nurtured by her mother emerges from out of embodied experiences of sacrifice and relationship to nurture the other. Such a Christ-Christa stands on behalf of a broken world. But standing on behalf of the other must not be a patronizing gesture. Rather, it must be understood in the way that Homi Bhabha envisions, where speaking on behalf means being willing to "half" oneself, to restructure one's interests and privileges in solidarity with the other.[24] As a mother, I act on behalf all the time. And while I first feared that this meant the loss of me, it is an invitation to a dynamic evolvement of myself. In the parallel language of Christian theology, God was not fearful of becoming less in the person of Jesus, but lives in and through Jesus of Nazareth as a way of dynamically involving Godself in the world, because behalfing/halfing does not diminish, but calls something particular into being.

In this age of interreligious awareness, I am also willing to share the divinity of God with other persons, figures, and events that emerge from a wide variety of religious realities. In a sense, I am willing to halve Christ, because God is infinite.

> "The *Divine Mother* exists in everything, animate and inanimate, in the form of power or energy. It is that power that sustains us through our lives and ultimately guides us to our respective destination," quotes Swarupa Ghose, a housewife with a newborn baby in her lap.[25]

As this mother, Swarupa Ghose, reminds us, the visions of God and the experiences of being human illumined in various religions are multiple. But this is also reflected in motherhood. Far from a unitary or universal experience, motherhood is a site of radical multiplicity. The subject-position "mother" is a most hybrid one. First, this is seen in the way that motherhood varies across cultures, historical contexts, and social locations. Motherhood could be the constricting limitations of raising seven children that propels one into advocacy for women's greater social and political freedoms, as was the case with Elizabeth Cady Stanton, who, no doubt, had all kinds of help in the child-rearing duties that enabled her to take on such an active political role.[26] Motherhood could be the surrogate role forced on slave women as mammy to white households in the American South.[27] Egyptian mothers created women's space and women's culture separated from the male-ordered public sphere, fostering essential family networks and becoming the transmitters of a living Islam, as the memoir of Leila Ahmed recounts.[28] The mother role could be identified with the soccer mom who juggles multiple responsibilities in North American comfort, or it could be identified with the immigrant mother who has left her own children behind to care for someone else's family in the affluence of a North American suburb. Mothers have borne their babies on their backs as they work the fields of China; and mothers have borne the symbol of the nation on their bodies as they struggled for independence under the sign of "Mother India."[29] The subject position "mother" is a hybrid one, not only in light of the cultural, geographic, and economic differences that infuse the experiences within "motherhood" as a category, but also in that any particular subject in the position of mother is multiple, as mother is called into a variety of roles, responsibilities, and relationships, none of which quite capture the whole.[30]

In this constructive revisioning of Christ that is in continuity with the creative process of all Christologies down through the ages, the hybridity of motherhood reminds us of the finally unpindownable nature of christological reflection itself. It invites a consideration of Christ through this particular fashioning of motherhood as metaphor and a particular form of motherhood as a lens through which to vision the story of Christian identity amid difference. But it invites the multiplicity of meanings that might come forth in christological reflection from a wide variety of subject-positions—of mothers and others—that will continue to unfold the mystery of Christ meaningfully today.

Notes

1. Kwok Pui-lan, "Engendering Christ: Who Do You Say That I Am?" in *Postcolonial Imagination and Feminist Theology* (Louisville: Westminster John Knox, 2005), 171.

2. This is Roland Robertson's term. See his "Church-State Relations and the World System," in *Church-State Relations: Tensions and Transitions*, ed. Thomas Robbins and Roland Robertson (New Brunswick, NJ: Transaction, 1987), 39–52.

3. Elisabeth Schüssler Fiorenza, *The Book of Revelation: Justice and Judgment*, 2nd ed. (Minneapolis: Fortress Press, 1998), 4.

4. Tina Beattie, *God's Mother, Eve's Advocate: A Marian Narrative of Women's Salvation* (New York: Continuum, 2002), 39.

5. Nancy Julia Chodorow, "Gender, Relation, and Difference in Psycho-analytic Perspective," in *Feminist Social Thought*, ed. Diana Tietjens Meyers (New York and London: Routledge, 1997), 11. Reprinted from *Socialist Review* 9, no. 46 (1979): 51–69.

6. Judith Butler, revisiting Sigmund Freud's theory of separation and mourning in *Gender Trouble: Feminism and the Subversion of Identity*, 2nd ed. (New York: Routledge, 1990), 78.

7. Recent writings on the role of Mary in Christian theology have tended to see her importance as "mother of God" substantively in the form of her accepting impregnation, providing the site for gestation, and birthing a savior into the world. See, for example, *Mary, Mother of God*, ed. Carl E. Braaten and Robert W. Jenson (Grand Rapids: Eerdmans, 2004). Feminist reclaimings of an alternative portrait include the historical-critical work of Elizabeth Johnson, *Truly Our Sister* (New York: Continuum, 2006) and earlier in the work of Rosemary Radford Ruether, *Sexism and God-Talk* (Boston: Beacon, 1983).

8. Judith Butler, "Beside Oneself: On the Limits of Sexual Autonomy," in *Undoing Gender* (New York: Routledge, 2004), 18.

9. Catherine Keller, "Seeking and Sucking: On Relation and Essence in Feminist Theology," in *Horizons in Feminist Theology: Identity, Tradition and Norms*, ed. Rebecca S. Chopp and Sheila Greeve Davaney (Minneapolis: Fortress Press, 1997), 58.

10. Morwenna Griffiths, *Feminisms and the Self: The Web of Identity* (New York: Routledge, 1995), 92.

11. Linell Elizabeth Cady, "Identity, Feminist Theory and Theology," in Chopp and Davaney, *Horizons in Feminist Theology*, 24.

12. Elisabeth Schüssler Fiorenza, *In Memory of Her: A Feminist Theological Reconstruction of Christian Origins* (New York: Crossroad, 1992), 135.

13. Clement of Alexandria, *The Instructor*, 1.6. on Paul's 1 Corinthians 3:2, in *Ante-Nicene Fathers: Translations of the Writings of the Fathers Down to AD 325*, vol. 2, ed. Alexander Roberts and James Donaldson (Grand Rapids: Eerdmans, 1951), 218.

14. Caroline Walker Bynum, *Jesus as Mother: Studies in the Spirituality of the High Middle Ages* (Berkeley: University of California Press, 1982), 114.

15. Ibid., 117, quoting Bernard of Clairvaux, Letter 322, PL 182: col. 527.

16. Ibid., 123, quoting Aelred *De institutione*, chap. 26, *Opera omnia* 1:658; trans. M. P. Mcpherson, in *The Works of Aelred of Rievaulx* 1: *Treatises and Pastoral Prayer* (Spencer, Mass.: Cistercian Fathers, 1971), 73.

17. Margaret R. Miles, *A Complex Delight: The Secularization of the Breast 1350–1750* (Berkeley: University of California Press, 2008), 33–53.

18. According to Gail Paterson Corrington, the earliest Christian use of the image of lactating mother echoes pre-Christian religious traditions in the figure of Isis lactans. Corrington's argument is that the image itself becomes dissociated from real women's experiences as it gets transferred to a God-imaged

male. See Gail Paterson Corrington, "The Milk of Salvation: Redemption by the Mother in Late Antiquity and Early Christianity," *Harvard Theological Review* 82, no. 4 (Oct. 1989): 393–420.

19. I am especially aware of the diversity of reasons why women do and do not breast-feed—ranging from cultural practices to economic need *not* to breast-feed—and women for whom breast-feeding is a source of death for the child, for example, in the lives of women with AIDS. My aim is not to identify breast-feeding as the desired practice, but rather, recognizing that it is a practice for some women, to draw from this experience theological insights.

20. Valerie Saiving Goldstein, "The Human Condition: A Feminine View," *Journal of Religion* 40, no. 2 (April 1960): 100–112.

21. Butler, *Undoing Gender*, 24.

22. This quote is from *The Philosophical Challenge of Religious Diversity,* ed. Philip L. Quinn and Kevin Meeker (New York: Oxford University Press, 2000), 2. It represents how interreligious dialogue is often conceived as a conflictual comparison, rather than the source of theological insight and cooperative solidarities.

23. This comes from Aelred of Rievaulx (d. 1167), quoted in Bynum, 124.

24. Homi Bhabha, keynote address of Conference on *Sex and Religion in Migration,* Yale University, September 15, 2005.

25. Lina Gupta, "Affirmation of Self: A Hindu Woman's Journey," in *Women's Voices in World Religions,* ed. Hille Haker et al. (London: SCM, 2006), 90.

26. See, for example, Elizabeth Cady Stanton, *Eighty Years and More: Reminiscences 1815–1897* (Boston: Northeastern University Press, 1993).

27. Delores S. Williams, "Black Women's Surrogacy Experience and the Christian Notion of Redemption," in *After Patriarchy: Feminist Transformations of the World's Religions,* ed. Paula M. Cooey, William R. Eakin, and Jay B. McDaniel (Maryknoll, NY: Orbis, 1991), 1–14. [Note that the article also appears in this volume as chapter 16, p. 199.]

28. Leila Ahmed, *A Border Passage: From Cairo to America—A Woman's Journey* (New York: Penguin, 2000).

29. Radha Kumar, *The History of Doing: An Illustrated Account of Movements for Women's Rights and Feminism in India 1800–1990* (London: Verso, 1993).

30. It is important to note that these constructions of "mother" may or may not have been created by those who inhabit them, and may or may not be willingly inhabited. Whether or not a particular construction of mother is liberating and life-giving requires closer analysis of the context and the lives impacted by a particular way of framing motherhood.

23

CHRIST AS BRIDE / GROOM: A LUTHERAN FEMINIST RELATIONAL CHRISTOLOGY

Kathryn A. Kleinhans (USA)

Feminist thought has posed several important challenges to Christian theology and praxis. These challenges are perhaps most famously expressed by the following:

> If God is male, then the male is God.
> —*Mary Daly*[1]

> Can a male savior save women?
> —*Rosemary Radford Ruether*[2]

> Is it any wonder that there is so much abuse in modern society when the predominant image or theology of the culture is of "divine child abuse"—God the Father demanding and carrying out the suffering and death of his own son?
> —*Joanne Carlson Brown and Rebecca Parker*[3]

In these passages we see the dynamic interrelationship between Christology and soteriology, two classic theological loci that are distinct but closely intertwined. Christian language about who Jesus is and Christian language about what Jesus did and does are two sides of the same coin. The christological and soteriological debates of the first four ecumenical councils attest to the concern that what Jesus did matters precisely because it was God incarnate who did it.

Hence the problem. As feminist critique has demonstrated, the history of Christianity since Nicaea and Chalcedon is hardly an innocent one. The maleness of Jesus has functioned to support androcentrism and patriarchy in church and society. The image of the suffering servant has been invoked to reinforce both familial and ecclesial patterns of dominance and submission.

Jesus as a Challenge for Feminist Theology

In response to the problems of Jesus' maleness, of Jesus' suffering, and of the ways in which the Christian tradition has used these elements in the suppression of women, some feminist theologians have attempted to decouple Christology and soteriology, redefining understandings of Christ and salvation. These revisionist Christologies take several forms, but their common thread is rejection of the traditional claim that Jesus is a unique manifestation of God's saving presence and action. Feminist theologians Joanne Carlson Brown and Rebecca Parker envision a Christianity in which "Jesus is one manifestation of Immanuel but not uniquely so, whose life exemplified justice, radical love, and liberation."[4] Similarly, Carter Heyward urges a shift in focus from "the Christ" to "that which is christic."[5] Rejecting "christologies that base themselves in Jesus" as inadequate, Rita Nakashima Brock redefines Christology as "the logical explanation of Christian faith claims about divine presence and salvific activity in human life."[6] Given these radical redefinitions, one is hard pressed to understand why it is important for these feminist theologians to name their subject matter in some sense a Christology rather than simply a theology. When the historical Jesus is divorced from Christology, what is the value of the Christ symbol? If the incarnational baby is problematic enough to be thrown out with the patriarchal bathwater, why keep using his name?

In this respect, I appreciate the frankness of post-Christian feminist theologians who reject Christianity precisely because they understand the uniqueness of Jesus as the Christ to be an essential Christian claim. Some Christian feminists have defended revisionist Christologies on the grounds that historical religions change and develop over time. Daphne Hampson, a post-Christian theist, rightly responds that without some affirmation of religious particularity and uniqueness for the Christ event, Christianity ceases to be Christianity and becomes something else instead.[7]

These debates are not only theoretical but personal. I myself am a practicing Christian who regularly recites the Apostles' and Nicene Creeds in worship as an expression of my faith. I am also an ordained Lutheran pastor who has chosen to make promises to preach and teach in accordance with the scriptures and the Lutheran confessions. Given this faith and these commitments, rejecting the centrality, uniqueness, and saving personal work of Jesus Christ[8] is simply not an option for me. To the extent that this is a constraint, it is an informed and freely chosen one. I believe that the Lutheran theological tradition has rich resources with which to respond constructively to the challenges posed by feminist critique.

Much of the critique of the maleness of Jesus as a tool for gender dominance and of the suffering of Jesus as a tool for physical dominance reveals an assumption that the function of Jesus Christ is primarily exemplary. The figure of a crucified male Christ is problematic for many feminists because, seen as an exemplar, it suggests that the appropriate behavior for Christians is to be male (like Jesus is) and to suffer for others (like Jesus did). Thus, upholding the uniqueness of Jesus as the Christ seems to essentialize characteristics that are either impossible or undesirable for women.

But is the uniqueness of Jesus Christ to be rejected because it provides problematic examples for women (indeed, also for men) to follow? Or is there a way to understand the uniqueness that might actually help to free us from the heteronomy of exemplary Christologies and soteriologies? In other words, might a fresh feminist understanding of a uniquely incarnate Jesus Christ call us into the fullness of our *own* redeemed uniqueness rather than requiring our conformity to harmful images and behaviors?

Lutheran feminists are well situated to articulate such a Christology. Historically, Lutherans have been suspicious of exemplary theologies because of the concern that an emphasis on imitating Christ could lead to works righteousness. In "A Brief Instruction on What to Look for and Expect in the Gospels," for example, Martin Luther warns against "changing Christ into a Moses"[9] when we focus more on Christ as an example for us rather than a gift to us.

Despite both feminist criticism of the damage perpetuated by a suffering male role model and Lutheran criticism of the danger of legalism, imitative theologies continue to flourish. Christ is held up as an example not only for individual emulation but for institutional, ecclesial emulation as well (as, for example, with doctrines of ministry that require clergy to be male in order to represent Christ). Thus, the critical agenda shared by feminist and Lutheran theologians remains both relevant and necessary.

But from a perspective suspicious of exemplary theology in general, revisionist feminist Christologies do not solve the fundamental problem. Shifting the focus from Jesus Christ to "the christic" (Heyward) or to "Christa/Community" (Brock) retains the assumption that

Christology's primary function is exemplary; it simply redefines that which is to be imitated. For Lutherans, neither an imitative Christology nor an imitative soteriology will do. The call to live as Jesus lived is no more sufficient than the command to suffer as Jesus suffered.

Is there a constructive alternative to exemplary theologies that takes feminist concerns into account? Lutheran theology has typically relied on forensic language in which the legal verdict of innocence is granted to guilty sinners because of Christ's voluntary sacrifice on their behalf. This classic Lutheran "for you" emphasis counters the imitative "like him" or "like this" model, but it has problems of its own. A theology of "Jesus does it all for us" can reinforce models of passivity, dependence, and submission that are detrimental to women's well-being. Eliminating the call to imitate Christ, however "Christ" is construed, also seems to eliminate the value of human agency. Feminist concerns thus leave Lutherans navigating between Scylla and Charybdis, seemingly faced with the choice either to reject God's saving initiative and action on our behalf or to reject our own agency as created and redeemed women and men.

RELATIONAL CHRISTOLOGY: INSIGHTS FROM FINLAND AND CHALCEDON

In recent years, Finnish Luther scholars have argued that a one-sided emphasis on forensic justification is inadequate to do justice to Luther's theology. They call attention to a neglected theme in Luther: union with Christ, also described as the real presence of Christ in the believer through faith. This Finnish reading of Luther is congruent with language that is present but often ignored in the Lutheran confessions, namely, that forensic justification is also effective justification. The imputation of righteousness effects regeneration in the believer. I find in this recovered insight a useful image not only for talking about Christian faith and life but also for developing a more robust Christology that is both Lutheran and feminist.

Like [theologian] Mary Streufert...I also find resources for feminist Christology in the christological formulations of the early church. The word *homoousios*, "of one substance," was introduced at the Council of Nicaea as a technical christological term. The creedal statement adopted at Nicaea in 325 CE explicitly rejected the Arian understanding that Jesus Christ is *homoiousios*, "of similar substance," with God. A century later, in 451 CE, the Council of Chalcedon adopted a christological definition that developed the point still further, insisting that Christ is *homoousios* with God and *homoousios* with humans.

It is important to note that the Chalcedonian Definition does not simply define Christ as both completely (*teleion*) divine and completely human. It explains each of the two natures relationally: Jesus Christ is *homoousios* "with the Father" and *homoousios* "with us." The christological claim is not that Jesus is "like" God and "like" humans but that Jesus *is* fully, perfectly, both God and human. These relationships of identification are constitutive for Christology. The two natures of Christ are intimately and uniquely joined in an inseparable union, in which, nonetheless, each remains distinct.

What implications does this Christology have for understanding how Christians relate to Christ? Might it suggest that the optimal identity for Christians is not to be "like" Jesus, as imitative Christologies and soteriologies posit, but to be "with" Jesus in an intimate, even constitutive, union? Might a Christology of intimate personal union address the concerns of feminist theologians without sacrificing the Lutheran conviction that salvation is a free gift from God through faith in Christ? I believe that it does.

CHRIST AS BRIDE/GROOM: READING LUTHER CONSTRUCTIVELY

I propose Luther's nuptial description of the union between Christ and the believer as a surprisingly fruitful resource for such a relational Christology. The best-known formulation of this image is in Luther's 1520 treatise "The Freedom of a Christian":

> The third incomparable benefit of faith is that it unites the soul with Christ as a bride is united with her bridegroom. By this mystery, as the Apostle teaches, Christ and the soul become one flesh [Eph 5:31–32]. And if they are one flesh and there is between them a true marriage—indeed the most perfect of all marriages, since human marriages are but poor examples of this one true marriage—it follows that everything they have they hold in common, the good as well as the evil. Accordingly the believing soul can boast of and glory in whatever Christ has as though it were its own, and whatever the soul has Christ claims as his own. Let us compare these and we shall see inestimable benefits. Christ is full of grace, life, and salvation. The soul is full of sins, death, and damnation. Now let faith come between them and sins, death, and damnation will be Christ's, while grace, life, and salvation will be the soul's; for if Christ is a bridegroom, he must take upon himself the things which are

his bride's and bestow upon her the things that are his. If he gives her his body and very self, how shall he not give her all that is his? And if he takes the body of the bride, how shall he not take all that is hers?[10]

This nuptial imagery certainly can be interpreted or heard in ways that are detrimental to women. Some feminists reject the bridegroom-bride metaphor itself as intrinsically hierarchical, on the grounds that it defines the woman as an extension of the man's identity.[11] As Luther's comparison develops, the details become even more problematic for women. In Luther's description of the particular attributes each participant brings to the marriage, the believing soul, personified as female, contributes nothing of value. In fact, what she brings into the marriage has negative value: "sins, death, and damnation." Anything and everything good she possesses she receives from her male partner. Given the gendered language of the contrast between Christ and the believer, Luther's nuptial metaphor can easily serve to reinforce both the subordination and the negative valuation of women.

Yet for a theologian in the Lutheran tradition, the passage is not easily dismissed, as it is the source of one of the central soteriological images of Lutheran theology, the so-called happy exchange. Rather than rejecting the nuptial imagery in Lutheran theology—and indeed in the scriptures from which Luther drew it—as intrinsically patriarchal, I choose to wrestle with the tradition, in order to bring forth a blessing.[12] In particular, I propose that reading Luther's nuptial imagery not only as a soteriological expression but as a christological one can generate more constructive insights. What might neglected aspects of the marriage metaphor tell us about who Christ is and about who we are in Christ—not just about what Christ does?

I certainly am not attempting to argue that Luther was a feminist as we understand the term, nor do I claim to respond comprehensively to all feminist critique of Luther. My more modest goal is to offer a constructive reading of Luther, using and claiming his nuptial imagery in a way that yields new insights. I argue that neglected aspects of Luther's marriage metaphor can be positive resources for a feminist Lutheran Christology.

On the surface, the language of "exchange" emphasizes a forensic understanding of justification. Luther's description is clearly transactional: the groom takes what is the bride's and the bride takes what is the groom's. But this transactional language appears precisely as an illustration of a reality that, for Luther, is fundamentally relational: faith unites the believer with Christ!

Four aspects of Luther's use of the marriage metaphor are worth examining more closely: (1) the difference between Luther's use of nuptial imagery and late medieval use; (2) the transformational nature of the union; (3) the uniqueness of the union; and (4) the mutuality and full sharing resulting from the union.

The Difference Between Luther's Use of Nuptial Imagery and Late Medieval Use
The use of nuptial imagery to describe the relationship between Christ and the Christian is of course first found in the scriptures themselves. By the late middle ages, such language was in fairly common use among mystics, both male and female. The goal of mysticism was an experience of union with the divine, classically described in three stages of mystical ascent: purification, illumination, and union. For some mystics, union with God was experienced as a vision of spiritual marriage to Christ.

Set against this background, Luther's use of nuptial imagery is noteworthy in several respects. First, the union is effected by faith; it is not the culmination of disciplined human effort. Indeed, Luther reversed the direction of the action, describing Christ as a bridegroom who "spontaneously pursues us"[13] as his bride. Second, because sinners are justified through faith alone, it is not necessary to distance oneself from one's sinful state in order to experience union with God. The believer enters into the marriage relationship precisely as he or she is. Purification is the result of union with God in Christ, not its prerequisite. Third, medieval mystics typically emphasized physical union with Christ in his suffering. Luther, on the other hand, describes this marital union as a happy or joyous exchange, union with Christ in his victory over sin, death, and damnation. Clearly, Luther is doing something new with this nuptial imagery of union.

The Transformational Nature of the Union
While Luther's use of nuptial imagery rejects the active striving of the medieval mystics, nonetheless it is not entirely passive. As noted above, an understanding of the marital union in which the bride remains entirely dependent on the groom is as problematic as an understanding which emphasizes the need to struggle and suffer to become like Jesus. In his sermon on "Two Kinds of Righteousness," Luther offers a more general, less transactional use of nuptial imagery, highlighting the importance of individual response. He describes a relationship in which the response of the beloved consummates or completes the marriage:

[T]hrough the first righteousness arises the voice of the bridegroom who says to the soul, "I am yours," but through the

second comes the voice of the bride who answers, "I am
yours." Then the marriage is consummated; it becomes strong
and complete in accordance with the Song of Solomon [2:16]:
"My beloved is mine and I am his."[14]

According to Luther, then, the nuptial union does not negate the individuality of the bride; indeed, it requires it.

Luther emphasizes that the marital union is more than transactional, an exchange of dowries. It is also intimate. Precisely in its intimacy, the union is transformational. Luther describes the way in which
the gift of Christ's "alien righteousness" engenders a "proper righteousness" in the believer that is truly one's own. But does this marriage
union transform only the believer or is Christ also somehow transformed in the relationship?

We recognize that human identity changes as a result of relationships. I am spouse of Alan. I am mother of Chris and Paul. In one
sense, I am genuinely and demonstrably still the person I was born and
baptized as fifty years ago. But, as a result of these relationships, I am
myself differently now than I was before. I am who I am in relationship
with others. My identity is defined and expressed in relationship.

Similarly, when the Word of God takes on flesh, the Word remains
the second person of the Holy Trinity, who was in the beginning with
God and through whom the world was created; but the Word is the
Word differently in and after the incarnation, because of the hypostatic
union of the divine and human natures. When the Chalcedonian Definition asserts that Christ is fully divine and fully human, it explains
these terms not only ontologically but relationally, not only what Christ
is but how Christ is, namely, that Jesus Christ is *homoousios* "with the
Father" and *homoousios* "with us." As is the case with human identity, so
too with the identity of Christ: Christ is who Christ is in relationship.
Christological identity is defined and expressed not only in relationship
with God but also in relationship with humans.

The Uniqueness of the Union

Feminist scholar Mary Daly aptly and memorably criticized the way in
which traditional Christology has functioned to ascribe divine status to
all men. For Luther, however, it is clear that the uniqueness of Jesus
Christ generates a relationship between the Christian and Christ that is
itself unique. Indeed, Luther uses nuptial language specifically to criticize the medieval hierarchy of the church in a way that resonates
strongly with the feminist critique of patriarchy. He explicitly warns
Christians against the danger of "false bridegrooms" and lambastes

church officials who falsely present themselves as bridegrooms, usurping the place of Christ.

This critique is not an isolated instance but a recurring theme: in a variety of his writings—biblical commentaries, theological treatises, and polemical treatises—Luther insists on the uniqueness of Christ the bridegroom over against the claims of the institutional church to be Christ's representatives. Several brief examples suffice: "No one is allowed to be both a husband and a bridegroom except Christ alone, as John 3:29 says."[15] Luther asserts even more pointedly, "In their writings the popes claimed that they were the bridegrooms of the Christian Church and that the bishops were the bridegrooms of their dioceses. In reality, they were panders."[16] As these passages demonstrate, Luther's use of nuptial imagery explicitly rejects androcentric generalization. One might say that, for Luther, because God is uniquely incarnate in Jesus Christ, other males dare not presume to assume a divinized status. This aspect of Luther's theology is worth recovering and applying in church and society as a critique of the hierarchical structures of our day that claim to embody divine authority.

The understanding that the uniqueness of Jesus Christ engenders the uniqueness of the Christian's relationship with Christ can be used as a critical principle not only to challenge androcentrism and patriarchy but also to challenge a glorification of suffering. While there have certainly been pieties of suffering and ascetic self-denial in the history of Christianity, the classic Christian affirmation is not that suffering is intrinsically salutary but, rather, that Christ's suffering is uniquely salutary. When Christians do suffer, it is not to be understood as the fulfillment of a command to suffer like Jesus but as an almost organic consequence of union: when one part of the body suffers, the whole body suffers.

The Mutuality and Full Sharing Resulting from the Union
Feminist reaction against Luther's use of nuptial imagery is, as stated above, related to the way in which the (female) bride is described as having negative worth while the (male) groom is described as having infinite worth which he stoops to share with the female. This critique focuses primarily on the state of the two parties *prior* to the happy exchange. Luther describes the aftermath of the spousal union and the ongoing character of the marriage relationship in ways that are more egalitarian. The bride is not simply the nominal beneficiary of her husband's wealth and status. Rather, she assumes full authority in managing the now joint household.

Luther describes the marriage union between Christ and the believer using the tangible legal image of community property: "For groom and bride have everything in common...She is part of his body, and she bears the keys at her side."[17] Although Luther considered human marriage to be an incomplete reflection of this union, his own marriage provides glimpses into his understanding of the joint authority the believer really shares with Christ. While hardly egalitarian by current standards, the Luthers' marriage was characterized by more mutuality than was typical in the sixteenth century. Luther placed significant trust in his wife's abilities. Katherine ran the Luther household, managing finances, buying and selling property, and generating new income streams. To be sure, Luther's views of human marriage are not without contradiction.[18] On the one hand, Luther shared the common assumption that wives should be obedient to their husbands; yet, on the other hand, Luther could refer to his wife both affectionately and respectfully as his "Lord Katie," and on at least one occasion to himself as her "obedient servant."[19] Luther did not appoint a guardian for Katherine in his will but named her as his sole heir and as guardian for their children. The fact that this decision was not honored by Luther's contemporaries is a testament to how radical Luther's acknowledgment of Katherine as a genuine partner was in his time.

Unfortunately, the mutuality Luther envisions concerning the marriage union between Christ and the believer is sometimes obscured by the patriarchal assumptions of his translators. Consider the following translation:

> Thus the bridegroom also says to the bride: "If you will marry me, behold, then I will give you the keys and all my goods." Now she is no longer merely a woman; she is her husband's helpmate, who possesses her husband's property and body.[20]

The English suggests that the status of being "merely a woman" is negligible while becoming "her husband's helpmate" is something of a promotion. Luther's German[21] is striking on several counts. The German word Luther used to translate the Hebrew of Genesis 2:18, which English translations render as "helpmate," is *Gehilfin*. But the German word Luther uses here is *mennin* (*Maennin*, in standard modern German), a feminine form of the word *Mann* (male person). This is the term Luther used (it may be a neologism) in his translation of Genesis 2:23, reflecting the Hebrew wordplay *ish* and *ishshah* to describe the duality of the first human couple. The use of the deliberately constructed form *mennin* rather than a common word for female or woman suggests a complementary created partnership rather than a diminutive status. According to Luther, the woman is not simply "a female figure" but "a woman" as God created her to be! Moreover, there is no possessive pronoun in Luther's text. She is not "her husband's" helper or "his" woman.

In his commentary on this very passage, Luther further develops a complementary understanding of the union:

> Whatever the husband has, this the wife has and possesses in its entirety. Their partnership involves not only their means but children, food, bed, and dwelling; their purposes, too, are the same. The result is that the husband differs from the wife in no other respect than in sex.[22]

Luther's description of the real relationship between spouses and the full extent of their sharing is much like the classic christological description of the communication of attributes. In Jesus Christ, human and divine natures are fully joined in one person. In the relationship between Christ and the believer, the two are just as fully united, and with just as real consequences, in faith.

QUEERING THE MARRIAGE METAPHOR

Nuptial imagery for the relationship between Christ and the believer, whether in Luther or in the scriptures themselves, can be read as a reflection—and a reinforcement—of the lesser status and value ascribed to women. To lift up Luther's description of the attributes each participant (the divine bridegroom and his sinful bride) brings to the union as a model for gender and status in human marriages would certainly be problematic from a feminist perspective. But there are elements within Luther's use of the marriage metaphor that offer resources for reclaiming this biblical image in a more egalitarian way. The key to a more generative reading of Luther is to focus not on the transactional elements in isolation but on the intimate, transformative nature of the marriage relationship.

Christology is not and should not be an abstract doctrine. The study of who Jesus Christ is needs to encompass considerations of who Jesus Christ is in relationship with God and who Jesus Christ is in relationship with us. Constructive engagement with the marriage metaphor can help us understand what this means and also what it does not mean. The goal of marriage is not that I *become like* my spouse. It's that I *be one with* my spouse. This is precisely the distinction between the creedal *homoousios* ("one" or "the same") and the rejected Arian *homoiousios* ("similar").

In challenging role-model Christologies and soteriologies, a Lutheran feminist theology can respond to concerns regarding the maleness and the suffering of Jesus by emphasizing an intimate personal relationship with Christ and the benefits and new reality that accompany the relationship. True, the sharing of community property results from a gift, but it is a gift that is now truly ours to use with full authority. Despite Luther's gendered use of the marriage metaphor, the benefits of being in relationship with Christ are no less a gift for male Christians than for female.

The growing reality of legally recognized same-sex marriage adds a new dimension to a re-reading of Luther's spousal imagery. When marriage is understood as an exclusively heterosexual estate, then the maleness of Jesus as bridegroom implies the femaleness of the believer. However, when marriage is understood as a gender-neutral estate, then the focus shifts from the gender of the two partners to the intimacy, uniqueness, and full sharing of their spousal relationship.

While Luther uses the gendered imagery of his day, it is plain that gender is not the central concern in Luther's use of nuptial imagery, either in his description of Christians or in his description of Christ himself. In a series of lectures on Isaiah, Luther uses nuptial language in ways that transgress gender expectations for both parties in the relationship, describing the believer also as bridegroom and describing Christ also as bride. Given the maleness of the historical Jesus, the believer, whether male or female, is typically cast in the female role of bride. Commenting on the nuptial images in Isaiah 61:10, Luther not only makes the expected comparison of Christ and the church to bridegroom and bride but also, quite unexpectedly, identifies believers with the typically male role of bridegroom. In the marriage union of faith, believers take upon themselves the identity and role of Christ. Luther concludes, "Thus all of us who believe are by faith bridegrooms and priests, something the world does not see but faith accepts."[23] The believer is now by faith both bride and bridegroom! Luther also describes Christ with this dual nuptial identity. Reflecting on the maternal imagery of Isaiah 66:9, Luther writes:

> He says that He is the author of begetting. "I, however, do not appear to be fertile. On the contrary, I, God, am sterile, yes, dead and crucified. But I keep My method of bearing for Myself. I give others the power to bring forth, and I can bring

forth too. I am both Bridegroom and Bride. I can beget and give birth, and I can give others the power of begetting."[24]

This joining of the typically dichotomized, gendered roles of bridegroom and bride is nothing less than striking.

I am proposing in this chapter the image of Christ as bride/groom as a rich resource for a feminist Lutheran relational Christology. I use the hybrid form bride/groom to emphasize that gender is not the point in Luther's use of the term. The backslash signals not an alternative, bride or groom, but an inclusive rendering in which Christ the bride/groom functions symbolically as both male and female. While the hybridized term bride/groom resists an either/or gender dichotomy, it also resists the tendency to exclude gender as irrelevant by referring to a generic, degendered spouse. Christians relate to Christ in our particularity, trusting that the relationship both encompasses and transcends our gendered existence. Indeed, the scriptural and ecclesial language of the church as the body of Christ seems to confirm this insight. The phrase *body of Christ* refers not only to the historical Jesus of Nazareth but to the church. Christ is both male and female in the world today, in the bodies of Christian believers.

The christological question is: Who is Jesus Christ? A Lutheran feminist response might be: Jesus Christ is the Word of God incarnate. And Jesus Christ is the one who, as fully divine and fully human, is our most intimate life-partner with whom we are united and transformed.

Notes

1. Mary Daly, *Beyond God the Father: Toward a Philosophy of Women's Liberation* (Boston: Beacon, 1973), 19.

2. Rosemary Radford Ruether, *Sexism and God-Talk: Toward a Feminist Theology* (Boston: Beacon, 1983), 116.

3. Joanne Carlson Brown and Rebecca Parker, "For God So Loved the World?" in *Christianity, Patriarchy, and Abuse: A Feminist Critique*, ed. Joanne Carlson Brown and Carole R. Bohn (New York: Pilgrim, 1989), 26.

4. Ibid., 27.

5. Carter Heyward, *Speaking of Christ: A Lesbian Feminist Voice* (New York: Pilgrim, 1989), 18.

6. Rita Nakashima Brock, *Journeys by Heart: A Christology of Erotic Power* (New York: Crossroad, 1988), 51.

7. Daphne Hampson, *After Christianity* (Valley Forge, PA: Trinity Press International, 1996), chaps. 1–2.

8. Because of the interrelationship of Christology and soteriology, I prefer to use the phrase *personal work of Christ* rather than the classic distinction between "the person of Christ" and "the work of Christ."

9. "A Brief Instruction on What to Look for and Expect in the Gospels," LW 35:123.

10. "The Freedom of a Christian, 1520," LW 31:351.

11. Rita Nakashima Brock, "And a Little Child Will Lead Us: Christology and Child Abuse," in *Christianity, Patriarchy, and Abuse*, 51.

12. See Joy Ann McDougall, "Women's Work: Feminist Theology for a New Generation," *The Christian Century* (July 26, 2005): 20–25.

13. "Selected Psalms I: Psalm 45," LW 12:279.

14. "Two Kinds of Righteousness, 1519," LW 31:300.

15. "Lectures on Titus, 1527," LW 29:18.

16. "Sermons on the Gospel of St. John: The Fortieth Sermon," LW 22:440.

17. "Sermons on the Gospel of St. John: The Forty-second Sermon," LW 22:450.

18. See Kristen E. Kvam, "Luther, Eve, and Theological Anthropology: Reassessing the Reformer's Response to the *Frauenfrage*" (PhD diss., Emory University, 1992), on "Luther's waverings between hierarchical and egalitarian understandings" of gender relationships.

19. "To Mrs. Martin Luther, October 4, 1529," LW 49:238.

20. "Sermons on the Gospel of St. John: The Forty-third Sermon," LW 22:460.

21. "*So ist sie dan nicht schlecht ein weibsbildt, sondern eine mennin, die des mannes gutter and leibes mechtig ist*," WA 47:172.

22. "Lectures on Genesis, 1535," LW 1:137.

23. "Lectures on Isaiah, 1528:Chapter 61," LW 17:342.

24. "Lectures on Isaiah, 1528: Chapter 66," LW 17:406.

24

CHRISTMAS

"AND BECAME HU/MAN"

Teresa Berger (Germany/USA)

Every time I recite the creed, but never more urgently than at Christmas, I confess that God became "human." The two letters *h* and *u* usually bring me slightly out of sync with the rhythm of the congregation, which continues to confess simply that God became "man." Such a confession is not an option for me. I cannot bear to render the succinct beauty of the Creed's *et homo factus est* with the English "and became man." The Latin *homo*—as distinct from the Latin term for a male (*vir*)—means human, after all. The same is true for the original Greek in which the Nicene Creed was crafted. The root of the term *enanthrōpēsanta,* "and became human," is the Greek word *anthrōpos,* "human being." Any translation of *enanthrōpēsanta* should capture this truth at the heart of our confession of faith: The Word took human form in the incarnation, rather than maleness only. The maleness of the Incarnate Word seems to be of no interest to the Nicene Creed. Maybe this strikes me as so obvious because in my mother tongue, rendering the creed appropriately never was a problem in the first place. German, my first language, knows two quite different terms—*Mann,* meaning "male," and *Mensch,* meaning "human being." The translation of the creed into the vernacular of my childhood was unequivocal: and *ist Mensch geworden.* God became *human.* The English language, unfortunately, used the same term, "man," to mean both the "male" and "human." Because of this linguistic particularity, our confession of faith in English has been rendered ambiguous. Especially on Christmas Day, the confession of the deepest meaning of what happened at Bethlehem deserves more clarity than the words "and became man" are able to yield.

There is no need to deny, of course, that in Jesus of Nazareth, God became human *and* a male, or, more precisely, God became human in the gendered particularity of maleness. Why, then, do I insist on confessing that God became "human" when all around me people opt for the shorter confession of God becoming "man"? Why might it be important to distinguish the two, after all?

THE INCARNATION: OF REDEMPTION AND OF CHROMOSOMAL PARTICULARITY

The first reason for distinguishing between God becoming human and God becoming male is a theological one. The words of the creed were carefully crafted, and we do well to attend to the creed's choice of words, if only out of reverence for and faithfulness to the inspiring meticulousness of our tradition. But it is not simply a matter of faithfulness to the original words of the creed. These words also safeguard a profound truth of our faith. In insisting that God became human, the creed stresses that what is life-giving for humanity in the incarnation is that God assumed the human, not the male, condition. God redeemed humanity by becoming one of us. The chromosomal particularity of the incarnation is a contingent reality, as was Jesus' height, or the color of his eyes, or the size of his feet.

A second reason for distinguishing between God becoming human and God becoming male is the fact that the gendered particularity of the incarnation is much less clear-cut today than it ever was. Many of us by now accept the fact that "maleness" and "femaleness" largely are socially constructed categories. What, then, does it mean to emphasize the "maleness" of the redeemer? Even if we went with something as seemingly basic as chromosomal identity, biological research tells us that humans exist in more than two chromosomal patterns. There are not only the male XY and the female XX patterns, but there are also XXX, XXY, XYY, XO, and occasional XXXX forms. In fact, almost six million human beings today live with chromosomal patterns other than the two dominant male and female ones.[1] What exactly do we claim, then, when we confess that God became "male"? I am afraid the answer to that question often involves an argument about external genitalia. The much emphasized "natural resemblance,"[2] for example, that supposedly needs to exist between Christ and a priest is never linked to Jesus' height, or the color of his eyes, or the size of his feet. Neither does it seem to have anything to do with beards, or with Jesus being circumcised. What is left as the crux for "natural resemblance," then, is what (mercifully?) is least visible in priestly functions.

The wording of our confession of faith, on the other hand, is very clear: God became human; external genitalia simply are not the point. The particularities of Jesus' earthly life were a necessary part of the incarnation, but they are not what redeem. Karl Rahner puts this well: "Why do we have to accept the mediator [between God and humankind] to be a man and not a woman? Our answer will surely be that the maleness of the mediator is ultimately irrelevant for his universal significance as Savior of us all. Maleness is simply part of the contingent particularity...which the eternal Word of God had to take upon itself."[3]

A third reason for insisting on the distinction between Jesus' humanity and Jesus' maleness lies in the realm of language—more precisely, current North American developments and changes in the English language. It might have been appropriate to confess that God became man when "man" was still in common usage as a generic term for humanity (although even then this terminology was risky, since it occluded the distinction between maleness and humanness). The time is gone, however, when "man" could safely be assumed to refer also to women, at least in North American English. The church, in pretending that the older generic use of "man" can still function in the liturgy, alienates people, especially women who linguistically have entered the twenty-first century. But there is yet a deeper problem. In insisting on the highly ambiguous term "man," the church occludes the truth the creed spoke so clearly for its own time and language, namely, that the salvific importance of the incarnation lies with God assuming humanity, not maleness.

An interesting light is thrown on this whole problem by a closer look at the Christian tradition and its ways of interpreting gender as integral to the incarnation. From among the wealth of possible themes, I wish to highlight but one—female images for christological truths. These images, I suggest, hold an important corrective for those to whom the maleness of the redeemer seems to be of such utmost importance.

THE BREADTH OF THE TRADITION: JESUS AS BREAST MILK, AND OTHER IMPOSSIBILITIES

The holy scriptures and the Christian tradition offer a wide variety of images for God. Among these images are several that are feminine. Jesus himself expressed his love for Jerusalem in maternal images: "Jerusalem, Jerusalem...How often have I desired to gather your children together as a hen gathers her brood under her wings" (Matt 23:37 NRSV). Along similar lines, some of the earliest Christian communities shaped their christological reflections by imaging Jesus as the prophet of Wisdom, a feminine personification of God's presence witnessed to in the Hebrew scriptures.[4] A marked lack of concern about questions of christological gender representation surfaces again and again in the Christian tradition. This lack of concern with the narrow confines of Jesus' maleness leads to a sense of ease with feminine images for the presence of God and to the acknowledgment that women, too, stand *in persona Christi*. Here are some examples of these often overlooked elements within the Christian tradition.

In the late second century, in one of the accounts of martyrdom that came to be collected, persecuted Christians from Lugdunum in Gaul told of seeing a crucified woman as an image of their crucified Savior. The fact that it was a woman who was martyred "cruciformly" for her faith only intensified her Christlikeness, because for the witnesses, the martyrdom of the supposedly weaker sex held special power. Here is what these Christians reported:

> Blandina was hung on a post and exposed as food for the wild beasts let loose in the arena. She looked as if she was hanging in the form of a cross, and through her ardent prayers she stimulated great enthusiasm in those undergoing their ordeal, who in their agony saw with their outward eyes in the person of their sister the One who was crucified for them...[5]

For the other martyrs, the cruciform Blandina rendered visible the crucified Christ, and this not in some metaphorical sense but for "their outward eyes." Blandina's cruciform body imaged Christ's body on the cross. Cruciformity thus was the locus of natural resemblance, not the genitalia or gender of the one hanging on the cross.

The metaphor of the Eucharist as mother's milk and of Christ as the nursing breasts of God takes us in the opposite direction, namely, the representation of christological truths in feminine images. In this particular case, the very celebration of the Eucharist itself encouraged a feminine-maternal image of God or was influenced by such an image. A liturgical pointer to this influence can be found in those early Christian communities that blessed and served a chalice containing milk and honey along with bread and wine to the newly baptized at Easter and Pentecost. The patristic scholar Johannes Betz, who first brought to light the importance of these early eucharistic images and practices, wrote: "The metaphor [of the Eucharist as milk and of Christ as the breasts of the Father] was attractive to Christians whose image of God encompassed maternal aspects."[6] The image of the Eucharist as nursing is not limited to early Christian communities, however. The motif is present also in the visions of the fourteenth-century anchoress Julian of Norwich, for example:

> But our true Mother Jesus . . . must needs nourish us, for the precious love of motherhood has made him our debtor. The mother can give her child to suck of her milk, but our precious Mother Jesus can feed us with himself, and does, most courteously and most tenderly, with the blessed sacrament, which is the precious food of true life.[7]

The "Jesus-our-mother" motif on which Julian meditates is among the best known feminine christological images of our tradition. But Julian is not alone. Three hundred years before Julian, Anselm of Canterbury (ca. 1033–1109) meditated:

> And you, Jesus, are you not also a mother?
> Are you not the mother who, like a hen,
> gathers her chickens under her wings?
> Truly, Lord, you are a mother; . . .
> It is by your death that they have been born,
> for if you had not been in labor,
> you could not have borne death; . . .
> So you, Lord God, are the great mother.[8]

Feminine christological motifs are much more widespread than Anselm's and Julian's writings alone suggest. Female images for Christ are found in medieval devotional literature most noticeably in three areas.[9] First, the sacrificial death of Jesus on the cross is described as a birth, that is to say, the Crucified is seen as a woman in the travail of childbirth. This image of Jesus' death as maternal labor is present, for example, in the meditations of the thirteenth-century Carthusian mystic, Marguerite d'Oingt (d. 1310). She writes:

> Are you not my mother and more than mother? . . . Oh, Sweet Lord Jesus Christ, who ever saw any mother suffer such a birth! But when the hour of the birth came you were placed on the hard bed of the cross where you could not move or turn

around or stretch your limbs as someone who suffers such
great pain should be able to do;...And surely it was no wonder that your veins were broken when you gave birth to the
world all in one day.[10]

The thought of Jesus' death as a form of birthing is not that far-
fetched, I would suggest. Jesus himself evoked the image of a woman in
childbirth on the night before he died: "When a woman is in labor, she
has pain, because her hour has come. But when her child is born, she no
longer remembers the anguish..." (John 16:21). More poignantly, Jesus
died with the psalm on his lips that images God as a midwife. Psalm 22,
which begins with the haunting "My God, my God, why have you forsaken me?" sharpens the sense of betrayal by reminding God of the
midwifery God practiced at the psalmist's birth:

Yet it was you who took me from the womb;
You kept me safe on my mother's breast.
On you I was cast from my birth,
And since my mother bore me you have been my God.
    (Ps 22:9ff.)

Jesus' dying psalm thus links death and birth in concrete ways.
Some of the medieval devotional writers emphasized that link in imaging Jesus' dying as maternal labor.
    A second example of feminine images of Jesus in the devotional lit-
erature of the Middle Ages is provided by the motif of Jesus as mother.
Anselm of Canterbury and Julian of Norwich are two of the best-
known exponents of this motif. Almost three hundred years after
Anselm wrote his moving meditation on "Christ, my mother,"[11] the anchoress and visionary Julian of Norwich (c. 1342–after 1413) meditates:

So Jesus Christ, who opposes good to evil, is our true Mother.
We have our being from him, where the foundation of motherhood begins, with all the sweet protection of love which endlessly follows. As truly as God is our Father, so truly is God
our Mother.[12]

Third, Christ's self-sacrifice in the eucharistic meal is imaged as
breast-feeding; that is to say, Christ is seen as a mother who feeds her
children at her breast. As we have seen, the image of the Eucharist as
God's mother milk is already present in the early church and among

medieval writers, but it also, for example, finds an echo in the writings of the sixteenth-century lay theologian and reformer Katharina Schütz Zell. Meditating on the passion, Zell writes:

> [Christ] gives the analogy of bitter labor and says: "A woman when she bears a child has anguish and sorrow" [John 16:21] and He applies all of this to His suffering, in which He so hard and bitterly bore us, nourished us and made us alive, gave us to drink from His breast and side with water and blood, as a mother nurses her child.[13]

In a contemporary of Zell, the monastic reformer and mystic Teresa of Avila , this image of breast-feeding is applied to the heights of mystical experiences:

> It seems to the soul it is left suspended in those divine arms, leaning on that sacred side and those divine breasts. It doesn't know how to do anything more than rejoice, sustained by the divine milk with which its Spouse is nourishing it … An infant doesn't understand how it grows nor does it know how it gets its milk, for without its sucking or doing anything, often the milk is put into its mouth. Likewise, here, the soul is completely ignorant … It doesn't know what to compare His grace to, unless to the great love a mother has for her child in nourishing and caressing it.[14]

The image of a woman on the cross also resurfaces in the Middle Ages. A Dominican friend of Lukardis of Oberweimar (ca. 1274–1309) had a vision of a crucifixion in which he saw Lukardis hanging on a cross. A voice, self-identifying as the voice of God, indicated that the woman on the cross was Lukardis, who came to be identified with the Crucified Christ because she suffered so much.[15] Lukardis of Oberweimar also was one of the women who received the stigmata and so carried signs of the crucifixion on her very body (the phenomenon to this day is rare among men).

The fluidity in gender representations to which all these examples witness also is present in other areas than that of Christology. Representations of the Virgin Mary and other holy women dressed in liturgical vestments are a case in point. Here too, typical gender stereotypes are reversed, in that women—at least in the religious imaginary—take over functions at the time reserved for men. This is the case, for example, in the visions of Saint Juliana of Cornillon, who appeared as an altar server; in a vision of Blessed Benevenuta, who saw Mary as the celebrant of the Mass; in a vision of Saint Mechthild of Magdeburg, who experienced Mary as choreographing the celebration of the Mass; and in an ecstatic vision of Blessed Ida of Leuwen, who saw herself dressed in liturgical vestments and so received the Eucharist.[16] Mary, above all, was easily coded as "priestly," since she was the one who first gave humanity Jesus' body and blood.

Many other examples of the fluidity in gender representations from within the Christian tradition could be mentioned. The examples make clear what historians and scholars in gender studies frequently stress, namely, that gender representations were surprisingly fluid at least until the dawn of modernity. That is to say, while images might use male or female representations, gender was not necessarily the central focus of the images. That which we today decode as a highly charged gender image might not have had gender as its primary focus at all. Thus, female images could be used in devotion to Christ and in christological reflection, and male images could be used in Marian piety.

CHRISTMAS AS REAL PRESENCE

So much for a look at the tradition of the church, which clearly is richer in gender representations than most people suspect. Given this richness of the Catholic tradition when it comes to gender representations, it becomes ever more problematic to emphasize the *maleness* of the Redeemer in the creed. Not only is such a confession untrue to the original language of the creed, but it also betrays the English language as spoken in the twenty-first century. The confession of Jesus as "man," moreover, occludes the fundamental truth of the incarnation, namely, that God saves humanity by rendering Godself present in human form. Last but not least, the confession that God became "man" leaves little space for the imaginative richness and fluidity of confessions of Jesus as "our mother," as the breast-milk of the Father, and as the One in labor on the cross, birthing new life in death.

On Christmas day, as on no other day of the liturgical year, our faith's answer to life's deepest questions seems to be simply this: *et homo factus est.* When we wonder how on earth God redeems, really redeems concrete human lives, the answer of Christmas is clear. God redeems through rendering Godself present in the midst of concrete human lives. There is nothing peculiarly "male" about this redemption, just as there is nothing spectacular or glamorous about it. There is just presence, real presence. Whatever we know of redemption is either in that kind of real presence, or it simply is not real.

Notes

1. See Christine E. Gudorf, "The Erosion of Sexual Dimorphism: Challenges to Religion and Religious Ethics," *Journal of the American Academy of Religion* 69 (2001): 863–91, here 874ff.

2. Thomas Aquinas speaks of a "natural resemblance" between sacramental signs and that which they signify. In its 1976 Declaration *Inter Insigniores,* the Congregation for the Doctrine of the Faith used Thomas's affirmation of a "natural resemblance" in order to substantiate its own claim that the priest has to be male, since otherwise "it would be difficult to see in the minister the image of Christ" (*Inter Insigniores,* in *The Order of Priesthood: Nine Commentaries on the Vatican Decree "Inter Insigniores"* [Huntington, IN: Our Sunday Visitor, 1978], 1–20, here 12).

3. Karl Rahner, *Schriften zur Theologie* 16 (Zurich: Benziger, 1984), 330–31 (translation mine).

4. See further Elizabeth A. Johnson, "Wisdom Was Made Flesh and Pitched Her Tent Among Us," in *Reconstructing the Christ Symbol: Essays in Feminist Christology,* ed. Maryanne Stevens (New York: Paulist Press, 1993), 95–117: Elisabeth Schüssler Fiorenza, "Jesus: Miriam's Child, Sophia's Prophet," *Critical Issues in Feminist Christology* (New York: Continuum, 1994).

5. Eusebius, *The History of the Church from Christ to Constantine* (London: Penguin Books, 1989), 145.

6. Johannes Betz, "Die Eucharistie als Gottes Milch in frühchristlicher Sicht," *Zeitschrift für Katholische Theologie* 106 (1984): 1–26, 167–85, here 184 (translation mine).

7. Julian of Norwich, *Showings,* trans. Edmund Colledge and James Walsh (New York: Paulist Press, 1978), 298.

8. Anselm of Canterbury, "Prayer to St Paul," in *The Prayers and Meditations of St Anselm with the Proslogion,* trans. Sister Benedicta Ward, Penguin Classics (Harmondsworth: Penguin, 1973), 153ff. Copyright © Benedicta Ward, 1973. Reproduced by permission of Penguin Books Ltd., London.

9. See also Caroline Walker Bynum, "'... And Woman his Humanity': Female Imagery in the Religious Writing of the Later Middle Ages," in *Fragmentation and Redemption: Essays on Gender and the Human Body in Medieval Religion* (New York: Zone Books, 1992), 151–79, here 158.

10. *The Writings of Margaret of Oingt, Medieval Prioress and Mystic,* trans. with an introduction, essay, and notes by Renate Blumenfeld-Kosinski, Focus Library of Medieval Women (Newburyport, MA: Focus Information Group, 1990), 31. For the original Latin text, see *Les Oeuvres de Marguerite d'Oingt,* ed. and trans. Antonin Duraffour et al., *Publications de l'Institut de Linguistique Romane de Lyon* (Paris: Belles Lettres, 1965), 77–79.

11. Anselm of Canterbury, "Prayer to St Paul," 155.

12. Julian of Norwich, *Showings*, 295.

13. Quoted in Elsie Anne McKee, "Katharina Schütz Zell and the 'Our Father,'" in *Oratio: Das Gebet in patristischer and reformatorischer Sicht*, ed. Emidio Campi et al., Forschungen zur Kirchen- and Dogmengeschichte 76 (Göttingen: Vandenhoeck & Ruprecht, 1999), 239–47, here 242f.

14. Teresa of Ávila, "Meditations on the Song of Songs 4:4," in *The Collected Works of St. Teresa of Ávila*, vol. 2, trans. Kieran Kavanaugh and Otilio Rodriguez (Washington, DC: Institute of Carmelite Studies, 1980), 244ff.

15. See further Caroline Walker Bynum, "The Female Body and Religious Practice in the Later Middle Ages," in *Fragmentation and Redemption*, 181–238, here 181.

16. See Peter Dinzelbacher, "Rollenverweigerung, religiöser Aufbruch and mystisches Erleben mittelalterlicher Frauen," in *Religiöse Frauenbewegung and mystische Frömmigkeit im Mittelalter*, ed. Peter Dinzelbacher and D. R. Bauer (Cologne: Bohlau, 1988), 1–58, here 43–44.

25

THE PASSION OF THE WOMB: WOMEN RE-LIVING THE EUCHARIST

Astrid Lobo Gajiwala (India)

Women have given their bodies to be broken and their blood to be spilt in every part of the world, responding to Jesus's call to "Do this in memory of me."
—Mary Lynn Sheetz

THIS IS MY BODY, BROKEN FOR YOU

"This is my body given up for you," she croons. "Take and eat."

Guiding her shrivelled breast to parched lips, she strokes the wisps of sun-bleached hair off her baby's face as it settles itself into the crook of her arm. It is all she has left to offer in her sacrifice of motherhood. The blood and bones have gone before, nurturing the germ of life in the warm waters deep within her. Chronic anaemia and osteoporosis are the signs of this eucharistic ritual that binds all women together across the divides of creed, caste, race and class... dying to ourselves so that another may have life in a process that never ends. Being poured out, almost drained to the last drop, for another.

I was spared the unrelenting nausea but not the breathlessness and the excruciating cramps, nor the acidity and immobilizing backaches. My life was full of rules: don't bend, don't lift heavy objects, don't wear heels, don't travel by bus or rickshaw, don't stand for too long, don't sit for too long, don't go out during the eclipse... constant reminders that there was another heart pulsating inside me, another being who would claim my body for life. No more could I eat to live. In this maternal self-sacrifice the law of survival was turned on its head: precious calories deliberately taken in only to be given away to another.

I never questioned the price, for I had the means. But what of my undernourished sisters? Their bodies protest the repeated pregnancies that demand what they can no longer provide, and yet their spirits refuse to abandon their flesh. Little ones slung across their emaciated torsos, they continue their backbreaking work in the fields or at construction sites. Loads they cannot put down even as they walk miles in search of firewood or water. At home they set a eucharistic meal drawing on their meager reserves, body and blood providing sustenance for hungry mouths. Too often they become a statistic in the high mortality rates for Indian mothers and infants. Death and life for them [are] so intimately intertwined—as [was the case] for the sacrificial Lamb of God.

The birthing, however, also brings with it the wonder of the breath of God moving within the womb, bringing forth human life. It is a re-creation of the mystery of the divine presence in eucharistic flesh—one, yet different. "I remember the way I felt," says Lori Challinor, "after my children were born, holding my sleeping infant after the birth, when everyone else had finally left us alone. Two different people, when an hour before there had been only one, so newly separated that neither of us were sure if the new boundaries were real or imagined."[1] So, too, must the God-Mother hold us close, suckle us tenderly, and whisper a never to be forgotten memory, "This is my body, this is my blood," as She sends us on our way.

In women this eucharistic bonding is crystallized in the ever-present maternal instinct that winds its way through the tears of childhood to the heartaches of adolescence and the insecurities of early adulthood. Caring and sensitive, in a flash it unleashes its power and fury when its charges are threatened, in a replay of divine retribution captured dramatically by *Kali*, the Hindu goddess of destruction. Through the prophet God asks, "Can a woman forget the child of her womb?" (Is 49:15). When the human fails, then comes the Eternal Mother to defend her bodily image as its innocent blood is spilt on the altars of power, greed, and lust. She is there in the mothers of children lost in political purges, who challenge the indifference and injustice of governments; in the war widows all over the world struggling to begin life afresh; in the women in refugee camps eking out an existence for themselves and their families; in the prostitutes and victims of abuse who still find it in their hearts to love. Swooping down, Her cry rends the universe as she gathers up Her broken children to Her ample bosom and gently cradles them, wiping away their tears, breathing back life into their empty eyes.

I catch a glimpse of Her in the women who preside at Life's eucharistic banquet, breaking the bread of their lives to feed the hungry of the world. In unconditional love these humble breadmakers sow the grain, reaping the harvest in hope and faith. In the making of the one bread of Life they allow themselves to be crushed, like the grain of wheat, its identity lost in its transformation. Into the dough they knead the yeast of gentle caresses, constant availability, listening ears, helping hands and a sense of the Absolute in and beyond all. As their hands pummel the dough into it goes the salt of their tears—of hunger, deprivations of education and growth, stunted careers, missed opportunities, frustrations, and sexual humiliations. With the fire of their loving, God-fearing lives as mothers, teachers, and community sustainers, they bake simple bread, making food that is accessible even to the poor, nourishing both bodily and spiritual hunger.

Theirs is a daily re-living of the Last Supper (John 13:33) when Jesus takes the bread, blesses it, breaks it and gives it to his *teknion* ("little ones") to eat.[2] Significantly, by this gesture Jesus not only confirms his self-giving in the sacrifice of his motherhood, but he also places himself among women, the traditional preparers and servers of family food.[3] He is the mother calling to her young children to come and eat after a hard day's work (John 21:9–13). His motherly heart is concerned about the late hour and the need to feed those dependent on him, and as the woman of the house he stretches the family meal to accommodate the *atithi* ("unexpected guest") (Mark 6:34–42).

The table he sets is round—without sides, margins, preferential seating, first or last, beginning or end.[4] The wedding garment he demands is neither a red cap nor a clerical collar, nor even a baptismal robe, but a conversion of heart that is inspired by the Holy Spirit (1 Cor 12:3). It is reminiscent of the messianic end-time banquet,[5] when all will sit together at the table without distinctions of any kind, and God, our Mother, will fill every mouth with food.

The meal itself is so typical of the East. It brings together the human and the Divine in a communitarian dimension that "gathers all space and time into the intense moment of remembrance, thanksgiving and hope."[6] Different generations sit down to eat together, to be strengthened and united in ways that will nourish generations to come. At the center is the woman, cooking the meal, setting the table, ensuring that there is enough for all, even as she spiritualizes the ritual. "My grandmother would always offer food to her ancestors before she sat down to eat. She would place it out for the birds to eat or give it to the cow," explains my Hindu husband. On visits to my Hindu uncle's home, before every meal I have watched my aunt prepare a *thali* (steel plate) of food for the household deities, later to be distributed as *prasad* (blessed offering). Often the woman of the house will give part of the food to the *bhikshu* (monk), in symbolic hospitality to the poor, the orphan, and the outsider. It is a sign that goes beyond charity to an "observance of *dharma* with all its implications for justice and sharing."[7] "Precisely because the grain of rice is deeply spiritual," says theologian K. M. George, "we should be doubly concerned about the lack of it for millions of our humble sisters and brothers."[8] And we should never forget that in the search for food it is women, the poorest of the poor, on whom most responsibility rests.

So concerned are they about their charges that often they forget their own bodies. Who is there to care for women? "I will give you rest and wash your tired feet," says Jesus. "Come and eat, I have prepared a banquet for you," he invites them. Perhaps that is why women have a deep affinity for the eucharistic ritual. It brings them comfort, hope, and renewal.

In a celebration that uses Christ's body and blood to symbolize deep spiritual truths, women also perceive an affirmation of the sacredness of their own bodiliness. No more "unclean" labels that desecrate women's signalling of their readiness to support new life. Gone too the "seductress," making way for the New Woman, comfortable and confident in the beauty of her body, exploring and accepting its rhythms with the passage of time. Children sometimes are catalysts in this body consciousness. "So many nights I didn't touch your hair," my seven-year-old son reproached me on my return after a couple of days away from home. His older sisters lay silently beside me, one with a finger exploring my navel, the other with her hand on my breast. It made me aware of my body in a way I had never been before, awakening me to its *Shakti* ("female energy") into which they seemed to need to plug in to sustain their human spirits.

This joyful acceptance of the body is a reversal of the centuries-old tradition of the church that looked down on women, associating them with the "less spiritual" body. It also ties in with feminist theology's rejection of the dualistic system we have inherited that opposes men and women, spirit and nature, history and nature, soul and body.[9] If feminists today are going back in search of the goddess religions it is precisely in an attempt to recover the intrinsic sacrality of women, evident in their fertility. By doing so they hope to reconnect nature and history, body and spirit.

THIS IS MY BLOOD, POURED OUT FOR YOU

"This is the cup of my blood which shall be shed for you." When I hear these eucharistic words, images of crucified women flash before my eyes. Sr. Rani Maria lying on the side of a jungle road soaked in her own blood; eliminated because she dared to feed and shelter the tribal poor of Udainagar against exploitation and harassment. Bhanwaridevi, a simple village "*sathin*" ("woman helper") of Rajasthan, who was gang raped for courageously opposing the practice of child marriage in the house of the *sarpanch* (village chief). Medha Patkar, whose life is dedicated to saving "expendable" tribals from submersion in the waters of development. Gladys Staines, binding the wounds of leprosy patients in Manoharpur even as she copes with the gaping wounds caused by a husband and children being torn from her side.

"When I hold up the cup I think of women's blood," says Lyn Brakeman, an Episcopal priest and pastoral psychotherapist.[10] Month after month it flows, this river of energy. No wounds or death in this uniquely woman-experience, only a readiness to receive in order to give till death to oneself brings new life. Sometimes a curse, sometimes a blessing, it marks woman's place in the natural cycles of Mother Earth, and through her, man's. Not surprisingly, tribal women bury their placentas after giving birth, returning this flesh and blood to the sacred womb from whence all life emerges.

Many celebrate this rite of passage into womanhood...a crimson cord that binds mother and daughter for life, bringing them together in an intimate sharing of the seasons of their bodies. "Sit down and listen my daughter to the wonders your body has in store for you..." Wide-eyed, she listened, questions bubbling out before I could finish. An age-old ritual forged in blood that slowly opens itself to embrace all women as they narrate their stories of menstruation, childbirth, and menopause, every telling a commemoration of their intuition for life, born of their closeness to the Earth, "the primary sacrament of God's presence."[11] (Can this be why that all the four evangelists present women as the first to witness New Life?[12])

At the consecration Brakeman holds up the bread and celebrates wholesome life-giving connections. Then she breaks the bread and grieves broken connections. "These are the passions behind the Passion."[13] In them I remember passionate human love marked with the shedding of woman's blood. Man and woman offering to each other their bodies, uncovering their imperfections, savoring the sweetness of flesh and blood in unions around and beyond the womb. Tragically there is too the bloody coupling—a tearing of flesh, a letting of blood in a violation that strips a woman naked, like a lamb ready for the slaying. These are the blood ties that remind us that "amid the prettified adornments of the altar meal there lurks the dark reality of innocent slaughter"[14] of the Lamb of God.

Other covenants come to mind. My women friends sharing gospel stories, nurturing, laughing, weeping, protesting... in body and blood relationships, some strong and growing, others faded with time, a few damaged by human failings. Women moving across the boundaries of rich and poor, East and West, one religion and another, transforming their lives in communion, much like the Master did as he gave of himself to Pharisees and scribes, tax-collectors and prostitutes, men, women and children, Jews, Samaritans and Syrophoenicians, refusing to recognize human divisions. My thoughts go too to the women I know, denying themselves marriage and the life that comes with it, to tend to sick and aging parents, or serve the unwashed and unwanted in institutions. I remember consecrated women and men who work with the marginalized and help them regain their dignity. They stand as eucharistic signs, celebrating human connectedness, proclaiming one body and blood.

Do This in Memory of Me

Tragically, in the institutional church, women are reduced to little more than spectators in the eucharistic ritual. They may be the unifiers in families, close and extended, but they are forbidden to preside at the sacrament of unity. They may serve as eucharistic ministers but without any rights of their own, only as substitutes for priests (Canons 910, 911). They cannot be installed as lectors (Canon 230:1), nor be ordained as deacons. And the final ignominy, these servants of the community cannot even have their feet washed in commemoration of Jesus's call to service. And so they sit in the pew, waiting... hoping... sharing.[15]

In a powerful poem that provokes the imagination, Frances Croake Frank brings together the key issues of "God-with-us" and women: the incarnation, women's experience of the Real Presence and gender discrimination in the Church.[16]

Did the woman say,
When she held him for the first time in the dark of a stable,
After the pain and the bleeding and the crying,
"This is my body, this is my blood"?

Did the woman say,
When she held him for the last time in the dark rain on a hilltop,
After the pain and the bleeding and the dying,
"This is my body, this is my blood"?

Well that she said it to him then,
For dry old men,
brocaded robes belying barrenness,
Ordain that she not say it for him now.

Reflecting women's spirituality, there is no distinction here of the sacred and the profane. The life-giving blood of childbirth is intermingled with the life-giving blood of sacrificial death. The words of consecration recall the consummation of the Word made flesh even as they hint at the continuing self-emptying that is women's life. And running through it all is the pain—of the womb, of letting go, of exclusion.

For women this pain is intrinsic to their experience of the Eucharist, making it impossible to explore this reality without mentioning the ban on the ordination of women. This exclusion is a shadowy presence at the Eucharist, setting limits to women's participation in this community meal. For many women it stands as a counter-witness to Jesus's nondiscriminatory table sharing that is without conditions of participation, for it introduces an element of separation—gender. Bad enough that the church has replaced Jesus's welcome mat with a ticket; for women there is now also fine print. Ironically too, in a sacrament that celebrates humanity in all its fullness through the embodiment of the Divine in human flesh, women experience a denial of their humanity, thus making a mockery of the radical union of God and the human.

"Why bother to come?" I sometimes ask myself when the priest holds up the host and I hear the voice of my church: "Male hands alone can make holy this sacrifice." But go I do, like women the world over, sifting through the patriarchal morass to uncover the Christic core in whom there is neither Jew nor gentile, slave nor free, male nor female (Gal 3:28), taking secret comfort in the knowing that:

The Divine became human,
Penetrated a woman's womb.
(Patriarchy had no place!)
Like soft petals enfolding
A crystal dewdrop,
The seed nestled in a female form ...
"You shall touch the Divine!"[17]

Women religious the world over experience the hurt and anger of this exclusion most acutely. They resent having to depend on a stranger for their spiritual nourishment and they are unwilling to be humiliated by priests who use the Eucharist as a weapon of power, withholding it on a whim. They are tired and frustrated by the church's refusal to recognize their priesthood in the breaking of their bread. Increasingly, these women and their lay sisters are creating their own rituals, gathering in Christ's name, sharing bread and wine, using symbols taken out of their knowing and loving. What many of these groups miss, though, is the connection with the universal church.[18]

Feminist theologians offer them an alternative by focusing the spotlight on the faithful. Mary Collins, for instance, suggests that women need not let the Eucharist be co-opted by the clergy as their own as the sacraments belong to the whole church.[19] Vicki Balabanski goes further to remind us that the presence of the community at the Eucharist is not incidental to the action taking place, but of the essence. Every person is involved in this *Zikaron* ("remembrance"), and "Christ's presence is not so much in the elements themselves, the bread and wine, as in the people and in their act of participating in sharing the bread and wine."[20]

Renate Rose points out that the Eucharist in fact, was never "instituted," either by Jesus or by his disciples. Instead *"it was born* in the process of forming a new community ethic of love and reconciliation. It was inspired and conceived out of Jesus's life..." becoming a movement, flowing from the continuity of Jesus's spirit to *metanoia* in those who receive him.[21] Such an understanding places the ecclesial assembly, not the one who presides, at the center of the celebration. As Susan Ross, associate professor of theology, Loyola University, Chicago, elaborates, this makes the Eucharist a lavish gift to be shared, not scarce gold to be parceled out piecemeal only to those who qualify. Like the multiplication of the loaves and fishes, the eucharistic feast ought to be a living symbol of the openness and generosity of the Christian community. That it so often fails to live up to this generosity is a scandal.[22]

It is a measure of women's resilience that instead of staying in the silent background [where] the prohibition of their ordination seeks to thrust them, they have emerged to push the discussion of women and the sacraments to deeper levels. As Ross astutely observes, "because the current official Catholic position on ordination rules out the presence of women in the priesthood, Catholic feminist theologians have the opportunity to take a more creative approach to the sacraments than simple inclusion in the present system."[23] Discarding Thomas Aquinas's definition of sacrament *instrumentally*, in terms of function, feminists have focused on Karl Rahner's *symbolic* expression to reconnect the sacraments with their personal and ecclesial dimensions.[24] It is an extension of the sacramental theology of Edward Schillebeeckx for whom sacraments are more than mere "pipelines" of grace, but rather "places where human beings live out in a symbolic way the life of the gospel."[25]

This rooting of the sacrament in ordinary life is typical of women's approach to spirituality that defies the traditional separation and grading of the "spiritual" versus the "rest."[26] For the most part their quiet moments of meditation are found not in retreats which too often are a luxury they cannot afford, but as they stir the cooking pot, or travel in a bus to work, or pat a child to sleep. Their embrace of their love partners holds a thanksgiving more powerful than any religious ritual, and scrubbing the floor or dirty dishes brings with it an inner cleansing that only God is witness to. In their contemplation of the setting sun as they walk the endless miles to fetch water is a prayer no words can capture and in the words drawn out from my computer is a consciousness of the Divine that I would not exchange for any priestly blessing. As Val Webb, author of *In Defense of Doubt*, points out, "Spirituality (for women) is not a different level of being, but rather feelings, doubts, physical pain, sexuality, all intertwined, sometimes chaotically, into a life."[27] It is not a question of finding God in our selves and our lives, but becoming conscious of the ongoing activity of God and responding with love.

It is this spirituality that animates women's sacramental ministry, taking it beyond the confines of ordained priesthood. Sure, women mind the exclusion—the denial of full imitations of the male bias on the wonderfully free person of Jesus Christ and the clericalization that makes of women second-class citizens in the church. But for the rest they enjoy a priesthood that is infused with women's wisdom—their capacity for relationship that bonds not just person to person, but the human to the Earth and God within us; their spirituality that recognizes no boundaries between the sacred and life but instead leads them to live every ordinary moment in relation to God; their ability to remain connected through systems that encourage "power with" and "power among" and "power for," rather than "power over"; and their closeness to life that makes them so vulnerable to love that they cannot help but be moved to serve.

Ironically, women have come to an awareness of their priesthood because they have been denied the experience of official priestly ministry.[28] Most contemporary feminist theologians, in fact, are no longer interested in an inclusion of women in the existing ministerial set-up of the church. They are beginning to question whether it is at all possible for them to "do this in memory of me" in the existing patriarchal design of the church. Opt out or work for change from within—this is their dilemma.

What is becoming increasingly clear, however, is that the church has much to gain from women's inclusion—a richer understanding of ritual activity and God's presence in human life through women's recovery of the sacredness of the everyday; a holistic approach to being human that refuses to be defined by biological sex differences; a returning of the sacraments to the whole church, and a going back to the priesthood of the gospels where power is put to service.

THE CHALLENGE

It must be said that women's demand for ordination cannot be reduced to a power struggle. Their exclusion addresses a deeper issue—recognition of their full humanity, not only "in Christ" but also in all of society and the church. How is it possible, they ask, to sit together to eat and drink the Passover food of freedom from bondage and yet not see women's chains of oppression? Worse, with what conscience can we receive the blessing of liberation and then join the ranks of the oppressors[29] by preventing those who faithfully set the table from setting the agenda? It is a travesty of the ritual that, Paul warns, has dire consequences: "Whoever therefore eats the bread or drinks the cup of the Lord in an unworthy manner will be answerable for the body and blood of the Lord" (1 Cor. 11:27).

Women's questioning also uncovers the church's narrow interpretation of the *faciendi* ("making") of the Eucharist. Conditioned by a patriarchal society that sees man as the head, the church has reduced this sign to the presiding minister and his maleness. The call to make the Eucharist, however, is not realized only in the one who presides, but in all who give flesh to the Eucharist in life.[30] This understanding, coupled with women's changing roles in society, make it imperative that the church rethink its theology of priesthood, so as to make place not only for women, but for a new kind of priesthood, one at which women excel.

And finally, women's experience of the Eucharist also presents a challenge to the church "to transform the ways in which we live out the Christian belief that Christ lives among us in the flesh and blood of the Church."[31] Their very lives remind the church constantly of the central eucharistic symbols—not bread and wine, but *broken* bread and *poured-out* wine.[32] Through marginalization, exploitation, and starvation women continue to provide. Can the church, with its human and material wealth spread across the globe, claim "communion with Christ" of the *anawim* and do any less? As Monika Hellwig writes in her book, *The Eucharist and the Hunger of the World*, "To accept the bread of the Eucharist is to accept to be bread and sustenance for the poor of the world."[33]

Such an acceptance, however, means more than the charitable distribution of food, important though that is. It must go beyond to a solidarity that recognizes the one Body in the impoverished poor. It must dig deep and unearth the roots of the "feminization of poverty," a phenomenon that is experienced the world over. It must challenge the unchecked growth of globalization that feeds on the poor, robbing them of their lands, exploiting their labor, and driving their women and children to prostitution. It must work for debt relief and a more equitable distribution of the world's resources.

Anything less cannot be an act of remembrance of the one who is the Bread of Life.

Notes

1. Lori Challinor, "The Worth of Women-Created Worship," *Daughters of Sarah* 21, no. 4 (Fall 1995): 31.

2. Subhash Anand, "The Inculturation of the Eucharistic Liturgy," *Vidyajyoti Journal of Theological Reflection* 57, no. 5 (May 1993): 285.

3. Ibid., 280.

4. Christine Grumm, *In Search of a Round Table*, in the book of the same name, ed. Musimbi R. A. Kanyoro (WCC, 1997), 28–39, cited by Yong Ting Jin, "Women Reclaiming Their Place at the Table," In *God's Image* 17, no. 4 (1998): 16.

5. Vicki Balabanski, "Anamnesis: Remembering Through the Lord's Supper," *In God's Image* 13, no. 2 (Summer 1994): 15.

6. K. M. George, "The Sacred Grain," paper presented at the FABC Conference of Asian Theologians II, Bangalore, India, Aug. 1999.

7. Ibid.

8. Ibid.

9. Rosemary Radford Ruether, *New Woman/New Earth: Sexist Ideologies and Human Liberation* (New York: Seabury, 1975).

10. Lyn Brakeman, "Passions Behind the Passion: Body and Blood Remembrances in the Eucharist," *Daughters of Sarah* (Fall 1995): 22.

11. Anand, "The Inculturation of the Eucharistic Liturgy," 286.

12. Ibid.

13. Brakeman, "Passions Behind the Passion," 20.

14. Ibid., 21.

15. Ranjini Rebera, "A Woman's Hands," poem published in *Ecumenical Decade 1988–1998, Churches in Solidarity with Women: Prayers and Poems, Songs and Stories* (Geneva: WCC, 1988).

16. Frances Croake Frank, cited by Susan A. Ross, "God's Embodiment and Women," in *Freeing Theology: The Essentials of Theology in Feminist Perspective*, ed. Catherine Mowry LaCugna (San Francisco: Harper SanFrancisco, 1993), 186.

17. Ranjini Rebera, "A Woman's Hands."

18. Ross, "God's Embodiment and Women," 204.

19. Mary Collins, "Women in Relation to the Institutional Church," lecture given at the Leadership Council of Women Religious, Albuquerque, 1991.

20. Balabanski, "Anamnesis," 14.

21. Renate Rose and Patria Agustin, "The Eucharist Section of BEM Revisited," *In God's Image* 10, no. 1 (Spring 1991): 33.

22. Ross, "God's Embodiment and Women," 204–5.

23. Ibid., 187.

24. Ibid., 188–89.

25. Ibid., 191.

26. Val Webb, "Spirituality: A Perpetuation of Dualism for Women?" *Daughters of Sarah* (Fall 1995): 64.

27. Ibid.

28. Ross, "God's Embodiment and Women," 205.

29. Balabanski, "Anamnesis," 15.

30. Tony Charanghat, ed., *The Examiner*, Mumbai.

31. Ross, "God's Embodiment and Women," 207.

32. Balabanski, "Anamnesis," 13.

33. Monika Hellwig, *The Eucharist and the Hunger of the World* (Lanham, MD: Sheed and Ward, 1992), 72.

LAST WORD

[Jesus said] "Jerusalem, Jerusalem, you that kill the prophets and stone those who are sent to you! How often have I longed to gather your children together, as a hen gathers her brood under her wings, and you refused!" (Luke 13:34)

*Prayer for the Feast of the Epiphany**

Mother Hen,
You watch over your chicks by day
and cover them with your wings by night.
Gather your children to the warmth of your breast,
that your church be strengthened by your care,
and in love reach out to embrace the world;
Mother, Child, and Spirit of Love,
now and everyday. Amen.

---

*Mary Kathleen Speegle Schmitt, *Seasons of the Feminine Divine: Christian Feminist Prayers for the Liturgical Cycle*, 1993.

CONTRIBUTORS

María Pilar Aquino is Professor of Theology and Religious Studies at the University of San Diego in San Diego, California.

Teresa Berger is Professor of Liturgical Studies and Thomas E. Golden Jr. Professor of Catholic Theology at Yale Divinity School and the Yale Institute of Sacred Music in New Haven, Connecticut.

Maria Clara Lucchetti Bingemer is Professor of Theology at Pontifical Catholic University of Rio de Janeiro in Rio de Janeiro, Brazil.

Francine Cardman is Associate Professor of Historical Theology and Church History at the School of Theology and Ministry, Boston College, Massachusetts.

Chung Hyun Kyung is Associate Professor of Ecumenical Theology and Interfaith Engagement at Union Theological Seminary in New York City.

M. Shawn Copeland is Professor of Theology at Boston College, Massachusetts.

Kelly Brown Douglas is Professor of Religion at Goucher College in Baltimore, Maryland.

Virginia Fabella is Lecturer and former Dean at the Institute of Formation and Religious Studies in Quezon City, Philippines.

Jeannine Hill Fletcher is Professor of Theology at Fordham University in New York City.

Astrid Lobo Gajiwala, a scientist, is head of the Tissue Bank at the Tata Memorial Hospital in Mumbai, India, and a long-time consultant to the Catholic bishops of India on gender issues.

Jacquelyn Grant is Callaway Professor of Systematic Theology at the Interdenominational Theological Union in Atlanta, Georgia.

Carter Heyward is Professor (emerita) at Episcopal Divinity School in Cambridge, Massachusetts, where she was Howard Chandler Robbins Professor of Theology.

Teresia M. Hinga is Associate Professor of Theology and Religious Studies at Santa Clara University in Santa Clara, California.

Elizabeth A. Johnson is Distinguished Professor of Theology at Fordham University in New York City.

Kathryn Kleinhans is Professor of Religion and McCoy Family Distinguished Chair in Lutheran Heritage and Mission at Wartburg College in Waverly, Iowa.

Kwok Pui-lan is William F. Cole Professor of Christian Theology and Spirituality at Episcopal Divinity School in Cambridge, Massachusetts.

Ellen Leonard is Professor of Theology (emerita) at the University of Saint Michael's College, University of Toronto in Toronto, Canada.

Loida I. Martell-Otero is Professor of Constructive Theology at Palmer Theological Seminary of Eastern University in King of Prussia, Pennsylvania.

Joy Ann McDougall is Associate Professor of Systematic Theology at Candler School of Theology, Emory University in Atlanta, Georgia.

Mercy Amba Oduyoye is Director of the Institute of African Women in Religion and Culture at Trinity Theological Seminary in Accra, Ghana.

Teresa Okure is Professor of New Testament and Gender Hermeneutics at the Catholic Institute of West Africa in Port Harcourt, Nigeria.

Judith Plaskow is Professor (emerita) of Religious Studies at Manhattan College in New York City.

Sandra Schneiders is Professor (emerita) of New Testament Studies and Christian Spirituality at Jesuit School of Theology of Santa Clara University in Berkeley, California.

Dorothee Soelle (d. 2003) lectured at the University of Cologne and was a professor of Systematic Theology at Union Theological Seminary in New York City.

Lee Miena Skye, a former post-doctoral fellow at Harvard Divinity School, is an active lecturer and writer in theology in Australia.

Judith Vusi is a Lecturer in Theology at Mobile Bible College in Vanuatu.

Elaine Wainwright is Professor of Theology (emerita) at the University of Auckland in New Zealand, and currently working as an independent scholar.

Delores Williams is Professor of Theology and Culture (emerita) at Union Theological Seminary in New York City.

SOURCES

1. Sandra Schneiders, "Encountering and Proclaiming the Risen Jesus," in *Written That You May Believe: Encountering Jesus in the Fourth Gospel*. New York: Crossroad, 1999: 110–13, 192–201. Copyright © 1999 by Sandra S. Schneiders. Reprinted by arrangement with The Crossroad Publishing Company. www. crossroadpublishing.com.

2. Teresa Okure, "The Significance Today of Jesus' Commission to Mary Magdalene," *International Review of Mission* 81, no. 322 (1992): 177–88.

3. Joy Ann McDougall, "Rising with Mary: Re-visioning a Feminist Theology of the Cross and Resurrection," *Theology Today* 69, no. 2 (2012): 166–76.

4. Ellen Leonard, "Women and Christ: Toward Inclusive Christologies," *Toronto Journal of Theology* 6, no. 2 (1990): 266–85; abridged.

5. Elaine Wainwright, "But Who Do You Say That I Am? An Australian Feminist Response," *Pacifica* 10, no. 2 (1997): 156–72.

6. Letty Russell & J. Shannon Clarkson, eds., *Dictionary of Feminist Theologies*. Louisville, KY: Westminster John Knox Press, 1996:
>   Kelly Brown Douglas, "Christ, Jesus," 38–39
>   Carter Heyward, "Christa," 39–40
>   Francine Cardman, "Christology," 40–43.

7. Judith Plaskow, "Feminist Anti-Judaism and the Christian God," *Journal of Feminist Studies in Religion* 7, no. 2 (1991): 99–108; and "Anti-Judaism in Feminist Christian Interpretation," in *Searching the Scriptures, Vol. 1: A Feminist Introduction*, ed. Elisabeth Schüssler Fiorenza with Shelley Matthews. New York: Crossroad, 1993: 124–29; abridged. Copyright © 1993 by Elisabeth Schüssler Fiorenza. Reprinted by arrangement with The Crossroad Publishing Company. www.crossroadpublishing.com.

8. Chung Hyun Kyung, "Who Is Jesus for Asian Women?" in *Asian Faces of Jesus*, ed. R. S. Sugirtharajah. Maryknoll, NY: Orbis, 1993: 223–46; abridged.

9. Virginia Fabella, "Christology from an Asian Woman's Perspective," in *Asian Faces of Jesus*, ed. R. S. Sugirtharajah. Maryknoll, NY: Orbis, 1993: 211–22; abridged.

10. Teresia Hinga, "Jesus Christ and the Liberation of Women in Africa," in *The Will to Arise: Women, Tradition, and the Church in Africa*, ed. Mercy Amba Oduyoye and Musimbi Kanyoro. Maryknoll, NY: Orbis, 1992: 183–94.

11. Mercy Amba Oduyoye, "Jesus Christ," in *The Cambridge Companion of Feminist Theology*, ed. Susan Frank Parsons. Cambridge: Cambridge University Press, 2002: 151–70.

12. Lee Miena Skye, "Australian Aboriginal Women's Christologies," in *Hope Abundant, Third World and Indigenous Women's Theology*, ed. Kwok Pui-lan. Maryknoll, NY: Orbis, 2010: 194–202.

13. Judith Vusi, "Lord of the Insignificant: A Christ for Ni-Vanuatu Women," in *Weavings: Women Doing Theology in Oceania*, ed. Lydia Johnson and Joan Alleluia Filemoni-Tofaeono. Suva: Weavers, South Pacific Association of Theological Schools and Institute of Pacific Studies, University of the South Pacific, 2003: 58–61.

14. Maria Clara Lucchetti Bingemer, "Masculinity, Femininity, and the Christ," in *Jesus as Christ: What Is at Stake in Christology?* (*Concilium* 2008, no. 3), ed. Andres Torres Queiruga, Lisa Sowle Cahill, and Maria Clara Bingemer. Maryknoll, NY: Orbis, 2008: 73–83. Copyright © 2008 by Maria Clara Bingemer and SCM Press. Reproduced in English by permission of SCM Press.

15. María Pilar Aquino, "Jesus Christ: Life and Liberation in a Discipleship of Equals," in her *Our Cry for Life: Feminist Theology from Latin America*. Maryknoll, NY: Orbis, 1993: 138–49.

16. Delores Williams, "Black Women's Surrogacy Experience and the Christian Notion of Redemption," in *After Patriarchy: Feminist Transformations of the World Religions*, ed. Paula Cooey, William Eakin, and Jay McDaniel. Maryknoll, NY: Orbis, 1993: 1–14.

17. Jacqueline Grant, "Subjectification as a Requirement for Christological Construction," in *Lift Every Voice: Constructing Christian Theologies from the Underside*, ed. Susan Brooks Thistlethwaite and Mary Potter Engel. Maryknoll, NY: Orbis, 1998: 207–20.

18. Loida Martell-Otero, "From *Satas* to *Santas—Sobrajas* No More: Salvation in the Spaces of the Everyday," in *Latina Evangélicas: A Theological Survey from the Margins*, by Loida Martell-Otero, Zaida Maldonado Pérez, and Elizabeth Conde-Frazier. Eugene, OR: Cascade Books, 2013: 33–51; abridged.

19. Dorothee Soelle, "Christ, the Man for Others," in *Theology for Skeptics*. Minneapolis: Fortress, 1995: 85–97.

20. Kwok Pui-lan, "Engendering Christ," in *Toward a New Heaven and a New Earth: Essays in Honor of Elisabeth Schüssler Fiorenza*, ed. Fernando Segovia. Maryknoll, NY: Orbis, 2003: 300–13.

21. Shawn Copeland, "Marking the Body of Jesus, the Body of Christ," in her *Enfleshing Freedom: Body, Race, and Being*. Minneapolis: Fortress, 2010: 55–84; abridged.

22. Jeannine Hill Fletcher, "Christology Between Identity and Difference: On Behalf of a World in Need," in *Frontiers in Catholic Feminist Theology: Shoulder to Shoulder*, ed. Susan Abraham and Elena Procario-Foley. Minneapolis: Fortress, 2009: 79–96.

23. Kathryn Kleinhans, "Christ as Bride/Groom: A Lutheran Feminist Relational Christology," in *Transformative Lutheran Theologies*, ed. Mary Streufert. Minneapolis: Fortress, 2010: 123–34.

24. Teresa Berger, "Christmas: And Became Hu/man," in *Fragments of Real Presence: Liturgical Traditions in the Hands of Women*. New York: Crossroad, 2005: 127–34. Copyright © 2005 by Teresa Berger. Reprinted by arrangement with The Crossroad Publishing Company. www.crossroadpublishing.com.

25. Astrid Lobo Gajiwala, "The Passion of the Womb: Women Re-living the Eucharist," in *Body and Sexuality: Theology of Women in Asia*, ed. Agnes Brazal and Andrea Lizares Si. Manila University Press, 2007: 187–200.

INDEX

Aboriginal people: becoming Christian, 163; child rearing by, 163; establishing identity, 165; fundamentalism and, 169; gender structure of, 163; healing methods of, 164–65; interest of, in education, 164; spiritualness of, 162–65; suffering of, 169–71; worldview of, interest in, 162

abuelita theologies, 233

Africa: alienation in, 135; captivity of, threefold, 150; centers of refuge in, 135–36, 147; Christianity in, 27, 134, 136, 146; covenant of blood in, 28; devil's presence in, 135; feminism in, 131; holistic view of life in, 150; identity crisis in, from missionaries, 134–35; images in, for Christ, 134, 136–38; mass conversions in, 147; oral Christology in, 144–45, 147; prophetic leaders in, 138; women in, relationships with, 28; written Christology in, 145–53

African-Americans: affirming their dignity, 218; miseducation of, 218; objectification of, 216–17; prayers of, 226; subjectification of, 217–18, 223; teachings to, about Jesus, 217. *See also* African-American women

African-American women: activism among, 224; as coerced sexual partners for white men, 201–5; coerced surrogacy of, 199–203 (*See also surrogacy listings*); fieldwork by, 203–5; domination of, 199, 212; identifying with Jesus, 226–27; masculinization of, 201–2, 207; among the most oppressed of the oppressed, 215, 228; negative stereotypes of, 207; objectification of, 223–24; redemption and,

210–12; resurrection's significance for, 225; roles for, 215; stereotypes of, 215; subjectification of, 224, 229; triple jeopardy of, 217, 224–25, 228; universality of, 225; voluntary surrogacy of, 199, 200, 203–7; work for, after emancipation, 205. *See also* African-Americans

African Christian theology, 141–42, 146–47, 158

African Christian women: Christology and, 134–36; Holy Spirit and, 156; language of, for Jesus, 141–43, 154–55; spirituality of, source of, 150; theology of, 82, 146, 158

African independent churches, 137, 138

Afua Kuma, 143, 144–45, 147, 149–55

Althaus-Reid, Marcella, 264–65, 267, 272

American Indian culture, Jesus and, 262

androcentrism, distortions of, 38

Anselm of Canterbury, 51, 111, 209, 234, 288, 317

anthropology: integral, 180; patriarchal, 190; 260

anti-Judaism: awareness of, 95, 96–97; Christian, 88, 93–94; by Christian feminists, 95–98; eradication of, 95, 96–98; feminist, 86–91, 94–98; religious difference and, 96

apostle to the apostles, 1, 4, 5, 19, 25

apostleship, commissioning tied to, 19

Aquinas, Thomas, 133, 177, 321n2, 330

Asian women: cherishing the incarnation, 107; Christologies of, 120–29; claiming authority, 106–7; conditions for, 120; confidence of, 108–9; inferior status of, 128; liberation for, 126–27; new images of, for Jesus, 108–18; relating to Jesus' suffering, 103–5; suffering

woman, Christ as, 51–52, 56
womanhood, 149–50, 202
womanist theology, 78–80, 82, 215;
    Australian Indigenous women con-
    tributing to, 165–66; Black Christ and,
    261–62; Christology and, 224–25
womanness, 154
women: affinity of, for the Eucharist,
    326–27; in African independent
    churches, 137; belonging to multiple
    communities, 87; bodies of, and reign
    of God, 192–95; called to wholeness
    and selfhood, 54; as caregivers, 155;
    challenging the church about its op-
    pression, 220–21; Christology used
    against, xi, 177; contributions of, un-
    recognized, 173; dignity of, 193; disci-
    pleship of, 33; in early Christian
    communities, 54; embodiment of, 52,
    56, 326; exclusion of, 180; Filipino re-
    sistance movement, 110; first to re-
    ceive news of the resurrection, 194;
    fulfilling scapegoat role, 132; full
    rights for, 194; gospels' representa-
    tions of, 54–55; humanity of, 332;
    identified with Christ, 182; imitating
    Christ, 132; impurity of, 193; indoctri-
    nation of, 220; in persona Christi, 316;
    interrelatedness of, 53; in Jesus' time,
    97, 178; Jesus' attitude toward, 95, 97,
    122–23, 178–80, 156–57, 190–94,
    221–22; leading the Christian com-
    munity, 150; liberation for, 132–33;
liberation movement for (19th c.),
    220; missionary contributions of,
    29–30; objectification of, 216–17,
    219–20; as oppressed of the op-
    pressed, 45, 192; oppression of, xi,
    36–39, 50, 53, 56, 179–80, 188; ordina-
    tion of, 48, 133, 190, 264, 329, 330–32;
    as other, xi; as paradigms of disciple-
    ship, 54; pluralistic experience of, 49;
    presence of, at birth of the church,
    196; priesthood of, 331–32; represent-
    ing the oppressed, 179–80; role of, in
    early Christianity, 5; roles for, dis-
    torted, 221; sacredness of bodies, 49;
    self-definition of, 220; self-esteem for,
    195; self-sacrifice of, 289–92; service
    of, in the Bible, 174; sharing in disci-
    pleship and Jesus' ministry, 186; as
    spectators at the Eucharist, 328–29;
    spirituality of, 331; subjectification of,
    219–21, 223; suffrage for, 220; testi-
    mony of, 4; witness of, in early
    Christian era, 26, 29
"Women and the Christ Event" (EATWOT
    Asian Women's Consultation), 109
women-church, 53–54
women religious, 330
women's movement, 217; addressing reli-
    gion and theology, 221; black women
    and, 224; church's resistance to, 220
women theologians, numbers of, x
Woodson, Carter G., 204, 205, 218
works righteousness, 301